FOR SUCH A TIME AS THIS?

One Man's Spiritual Journey

Stephen G. Humble

For Such a Time as This?
One Man's Spiritual Journey

Copyright © 2018 by Stephen G. Humble
ISBN: 978-0998101392

Empyrion Publishing
PO Box 784327
Winter Garden, FL
info@EmpyrionPublishing.com

Cover picture by Patricia G. Humble, taken on Logan Lick Road in Clark
County, KY on January 31, 2018

Cover designed by friends at Harris and Ward, 222 E. Short St. #210,
Lexington, KY

Printed in the United States of America

Dedication

To my daughters, Stephanie and Andrea
to my sons-in-law, Daniel Loveland and Daniel Rake
to my 14 grandchildren and any more yet to come

In memory of my son, Elijah (1972—1996),
in the continuing mutual commitment
to serve God's purposes together

Acknowledgments

You give marvelous comrades to me:
the faithful who dwell in your land...[1]

Although this book concerns my own spiritual journey, I would have had no such journey without the influence of the many people who have shared this life with me. It is impossible to name all or even most of them, not even those who have contributed greatly to the journey. Yet, a few must be mentioned.

First, I thank the brothers and sisters with whom I have shared fellowship in the Jesus our Lord within several communities of faith since childhood. You have shared yourselves and your own love for God generously, and in so doing have helped me to progress this far along the way. Some have contributed through the years more than they know by simply asking from time to time, "Have you worked on your book lately?"

I would have had no journey apart from my parents, the late Richard and Virginia (Geiger) Humble, who brought me up in "the fear and admonition of the Lord." Because of them I grew in a God-aware environment. They laid the foundations of love for Jesus, wisdom about living, and abundant knowledge of the Bible in my life from the start.

My children Elijah, Stephanie, and Andrea, my sons-in-law Daniel Loveland and Daniel Rake, and my grandchildren have given me the primary motivation to share my story. As King David sang, "One generation shall commend your works to another, and shall declare your mighty acts." (Psalm 145:4) I am a blessed man!

Patricia, my wife, has lived most of the journey with me. Although she knows full well my many weaknesses, still she gives herself, her love, and her support freely even after nearly 47 years of marriage. She is the crown, "far more precious than jewels," of my life. (Proverbs 12:4; 31:10). Truly, "God … gives grace to the humble" (James 4:6). Thank you, my love, not least for the cover photo!

One great weakness of this book (among many I am sure) is that the huge and vital role my three ladies, Patricia, Stephanie, and Andrea, have played in the journey is still untold. It is not forgotten.

---

[1] Lyrics from John B. Foley, S. J., "For You Are My God" based on Psalm 16:3.

Donna Rees, my editor, turned hard work into a labor of love. Her technical help, her encouragement, and her prayers have made this a far better book than it would have been. My friends Grant Ostrander and Corey Maple made the book's striking cover possible.

Above all, I give thanks and honor to Jesus who called me, gave me a new start, and is working out his redemption in this broken man.

> *Now to him who is able to do far more abundantly than all that we ask or think, according to the power at work within us, to him be glory in the church and in Christ Jesus throughout all generations, forever and ever. Amen.*
>
> — Ephesians 3:20-21

Blessed are those who find strength in you.
Their hearts are on the road that leads to you.
(Psalm 84:5 God's Word)

There's a promised land somewhere beyond the mountains. I was born to look for it …. I was born for the trail, not for the journey's end …. We were born to discover and to build, you and I, for the others who will come after us. They will live in a richer, sweeter land but we will have made the trails.

— Louis L'Amour, *The Man from Broken Hills*

And love is not the easy thing
The only baggage you can bring …
And love is not the easy thing ….
The only baggage you can bring
Is all that you can't leave behind

— U2, "Walk On"

We learn to live and then we forgive
O'er the road we're bound to go
More frailer than the flowers, these precious hours
That keep us so tightly bound
You come to my eyes like a vision from the skies
And I'll be with you when the deal goes down

— Bob Dylan, "When The Deal Goes Down"

It is not our part to master all the tides of the world, but to do what is in us for the succour of those years wherein we are set, uprooting the evil in the fields that we know, so that those who live after may have clean earth to till. What weather they shall have is not ours to rule.

— J. R. R. Tolkien, *The Return of the King*

Thunder on the mountain rolling to the ground
Gonna get up in the morning walk the hard road down
Some sweet day I'll stand beside my king
I wouldn't betray your love or any other thing
— Bob Dylan, "Thunder On The
Mountain"

Table of Contents

****

Introduction

The phone rang about 10:15 p.m. on July 4, 1996. We had left our Winchester-Clark County 4th of July celebration early. Along with a number of people from our church community, we had gone out to Lykins Park to picnic, listen to music, and watch the fireworks that Thursday evening. For some reason, the music seemed like noise, and we decided to head on home about 9:30. Patricia had been in bed a few minutes; I was still watching TV.

I answered the phone.

"Dad," I heard our daughter-in-law, Jenny, say, "you and Mom need to come to Berea Hospital right away. Elijah has had a heart attack."

"Is it serious?" I asked.

"Yes," she said. "Please come as soon as you can."

A few minutes later, Patricia and I left our home to make the 45-minute drive to Berea.

A heart attack? At age 23? On the way to Berea, Patricia and I wondered whether our son might die, as I suppose any parents would, but we could barely even imagine it as a possibility, let alone entertain the thought seriously. We thought the best thing we could do would be to worship. So we did. We sang songs from the Scriptures to the Lord, including "I Exalt Thee" (Psalm 97:9) and "Thou Art Worthy" (Revelation 4:11). We prayed. In our prayers we sought to commit Elijah, ourselves, and our fears to the Lord. We also prayed for strength and help for our Jenny.

When we arrived at the hospital, Tom Watson, one of Elijah's close friends and a fellow student at Berea College, met us at the door into the emergency room.

"How bad is it?" I asked.

"It's bad," Tom responded.

However, when Tom directed us on through the waiting area into a small, private room where Jenny; her mother, Wanda; and also Tom's wife, Susie, were sitting, I

1

knew that Elijah had died. As a pastor I had been with several families when they had been taken to a private room like that in order to receive bad news about a loved one.

As we entered the room, Dr. Bill Greiser, a surgeon and friend from Winchester, entered through a door on the other side of the room. We greeted each other, but I don't remember details other than that he said gently: "I'm sorry. Elijah is gone."

Patricia said, "Gone where?"

Jenny replied, "He died, Mom."

Patricia began to cry, and she, Jenny, Wanda, and I stood for a little while holding onto one another.

Beginning a few days after the funeral, I wrote down some of my memories and thoughts from that terrible time. With very slight editing, following are a few passages from that record:

> The most amazing thing to me, the unsettling thing, was that in those first minutes, I had no tears. It seemed that everyone was crying except me, and maybe Dr. Greiser. Patricia's first cries and tears seemed to be for Jenny, but she soon began to face her own grief.
>
> I was there. I tried to hold Patricia and Jenny. I gave what little strength and encouragement and sympathy I could, but I felt distant and numb. I felt as though there was a big, empty hole in my belly and chest. Emotionally I could not touch this thing.
>
> On the other hand, my spirit was toward the Lord. I believe that this was mostly God's sheer grace given for that moment, but I also think the fact that we had chosen an inner posture of trust and worship on the drive to the hospital had something to do with my inner condition when confronted with the awful facts. I had an almost immediate conviction that God was present, that he had not been taken by surprise, and that somehow he meant this for good.
>
> I don't know how to make a clear distinction between the soul and spirit in words. And certainly, at that time, I was not thinking about theological abstractions nor about the structure of personhood. But I do know that

emotionally I felt distant and numb. Mentally I was trying to believe what I had heard and to make it fit into the picture. And yet at a deeper level, I *knew* Elijah was dead and I *knew* he was also alive with the Lord, and I *knew* that God was working in this for good. I was not thinking these thoughts. It was an inner *knowledge* at a deeper level than my mind that undergirded me and informed the process with which my mind and emotions were dealing.

After a while the first period of weeping subsided. We had a time of prayer together, worshipping and yielding to the will of God …

Very soon after hearing that Elijah was dead, I realized that this was the big test. This was where I had to find out whether everything we had believed and said through the years would hold true.[2] I sensed three things that I had to do in this crisis. I suppose the Lord gave me these three thoughts, but all I really know is that I *knew* that these were vital responses to make.

1. I must not try to understand this event with my mind or ask "Why?"
2. I had to trust God and entrust Elijah to God.
3. I had to worship.

I am oriented to wanting to understand. I am always trying to see the big picture and to see how the events and circumstances of life fit in. Somehow, this time I knew that path would lead to a dead end, at least for a while. This one did not fit any scenario I could have conceived. It was too big for my mind to handle.

Trusting God meant that I had to recognize that he is of good character and he does and allows only what is good and right. I had to choose to believe in him. I had to lean into his goodness and sovereignty. And all of us, including Elijah, were his. He owns us by virtue of the fact that we are his creations. We are his because he redeemed us in Christ. And we are his because, in response to the revelation of his grace, we had chosen to submit our lives to his Lordship. Patricia and I know that he gave us

---

[2] From time to time through the preceding years, the question had passed through my mind as to whether or not I would be able to stay faithful to God if one of our children were to die. Still, I never believed it would really happen. Now that it had happened, however, where was I to turn but to the Lord?

children to love, train, and steward for him. Elijah, and our girls also, are his first, just as we are. Our God has every right to dispose of our lives according to his own will and purposes.

And our only appropriate response, the only one that made any sense at all or could help in any significant way, was to worship our Lord, to bow before him in our broken hearts in this agonizing moment and season, to offer him honor and praise and adoration. To acknowledge his majesty, sovereignty, and goodness. To offer Elijah and ourselves afresh to his will and purposes. To rest in his love, mercy, goodness, righteousness, faithfulness, and omniscience.

We waited there in the emergency room with Jenny until our daughters, Stephanie and Andrea, could be located and brought to the hospital. By the time they arrived, several of our close friends had also come.

At last we began to prepare to leave for home. I think it was 14-year-old Andrea who asked if we could pray together first. We all formed a circle and we prayed and we wept and we worshipped. Andrea, with quavering voice, started to sing Psalm 33:20–22, a passage that Darrin Marlowe, our friend and our church's worship leader, had set to music, a song that Elijah and Jenny had asked Darrin and his wife, Paula, to sing at their wedding.

> *We wait in hope for the Lord; he is our help and our shield.*
> *In him our hearts rejoice, for we trust in his holy name.*
> *May your love, may your unfailing love,*
> *Rest upon us, rest upon us.*
> *May your love, may your unfailing love,*
> *Rest upon us, even as we put our hope in you.*

I don't know how long we worshipped, but we experienced the presence of God. His peace ministered to us in our distress. At some point, I began to pray that the anointing and call and sense of the purpose of God that so many had perceived on Elijah in his youth would somehow—through his death—be multiplied to others of his generation and that they would dedicate their lives to serve God's purposes for their generation, just as King David had in his generation (Acts 13:36). This remains my prayer. It is the greatest thing that I can think of that would give meaning to

Elijah's "premature" death.[3]

Although stunned beyond words and unexpectedly ushered into a long, nearly unbearable season of grief, we would have been completely devastated had it not been for the faithfulness of the Lord and the faithfulness of our family—both natural and spiritual.

****

By God's grace we kept on trusting God and entrusting Elijah to God and taking a posture of worship. It was no one-time thing. Time after time, for a long time—and even to this day every once in a while—the pain of that loss would hit us and we would have to choose that posture "one more time." Our journey through that terrible loss and grief is a story all its own, but not a hopeless one, because "in the valley of the shadow of death" our Shepherd truly was with us.

The desire I had when we prayed at the hospital that night remains. The longing to see many from Elijah's generation come to know and follow Jesus fully has continued and intensified over these past twenty-one years since his death. I began writing this book in honor of his memory a few months after he died, but from the beginning, I was writing for his sisters, Stephanie and Andrea; for his friends; and for those who might have become his friends had he not died so young. In more recent years I have also had my grandchildren and the people of their generation in mind, and as I have written, I have prayed that they will carry the story forward into their own generation.

My primary goal has been to share about several key truths—not mental concepts but fundamental realities—that God began to unveil and to work into my life when I was young, truths that I still long to live out more fully now that I am getting old. It has become my deep conviction that these truths are foundational for life in God and life in this world and that the current generation must be equipped with them in order to live effectively in this extremely challenging time, perhaps even a turning point in history.

In the spring of 2017, some friends recommended several books that I felt compelled to read: Rod Dreher's *The Benedict Option: A Strategy for Christians in a Post-Christian Nation,*[4] Charles J. Chaput's *Strangers in a Strange Land: Living the Catholic*

---

[3] Quoted as written from my personal journal from July, 1996.
[4] Published by Sentinel, 2017.

Faith in a Post-Christian World,[5] and Anthony Esolen's *Out of the Ashes: Rebuilding American Culture.*[6] These books analyze our present culture and society and urge those who follow Jesus to embrace fully our calling to be the people of God, to be his salt and his light, in these days of darkness.

While I was still reading these books, another little book came to my attention. On a whim, as it seemed at the time, I ordered James W. Thompson's *The Church in Exile: God's Counterculture in a Non-Christian World.*[7] In this little book, Thompson shows that the message that the apostle Peter had for the suffering people of God living in the hostile world of the Roman Empire is a message we desperately need to take hold of today.

These books renewed and solidified my conviction that those foundational truths upon which a number of us from my generation had sought to build our lives and our church communities are even more pertinent today than they were forty or fifty years ago when we, like pioneers, began to try to work out those spiritual realities in our everyday world. As I read, I also was convinced that I must finish the account of my personal journey with its struggles and failures and small successes, whether or not anyone would ever want to read it.

Although this book is autobiographical in content, my primary purpose for writing has not been to tell the facts of my life. Rather, I have tried to share my "spiritual journey"—the way in which God took hold of my life and has led me to know him and to offer myself in service to him.

The word *spiritual* is tricky because it can mean very different things, particularly in our contemporary ways of viewing the world. This is far too complicated a matter for me to address in detail, but two of the most common contemporary uses of *spiritual* may help to describe what I mean by *spiritual.*

In recent decades, i.e., the postmodern world, *spiritual* has come to reference any mystical or philosophical ideas that people may have or that they may practice. It is fashionable to be a "spiritual" person with some sort of "spirituality," as long as there is no claim made that said spirituality is actually true and right for everyone. "It's true for me" is the common claim.

---

[5] Published by Henry Holt and Company, 2017.
[6] Published by Regnery Publishing, 2017.
[7] Leafwood Publishers—Abilene Christian University Press, 2010.

For those primarily influenced by "modern" ways of thought—modern, that is, as the predecessor of postmodern—there is a sharp distinction, even a division, between the material world, or the "real" world, and the "spiritual" world, if there even is a spiritual world. The late Dr. Francis Schaeffer described this division as "upper story" separated from "lower story."[8]

The lower story is the material world, the world of nature, the creation, the world that can be experienced by the five physical senses and known by reason. It is the world that science seeks to explore and explain.

The "upper story" has been called the world of grace, of God the Creator, the world of heaven and "heavenly" things, the world that, if it exists at all and can be known at all, can be known only by revelation and faith.

Many Christians who have this mind-set (although usually unaware of it) emphasize the truth that can be known by God's revelation in Scripture, but the tendency is strong for that truth to be relevant to one's inner life or Sunday life or religious life but not something that has much to do with the world of everyday life, except, perhaps, to provide a basis for morality. Some other Christians think the spiritual realm is "known" by a "leap of faith"—by a choice to believe in spite of the fact that the belief is not grounded in rational understanding and not open to the five senses.

In contradistinction to any of these, when I speak about my spiritual journey, I am talking about my actual experience of God the Creator interacting with me and changing me right in the midst of this everyday world, which he created and in which I live.

Yes, God is distinct from his creation. Yes, there is the unseen reality: the reality of God and the heavenlies, and there is the reality that we see: the visible, created world. The apostle Paul distinguished between these two realities, when he wrote: "… We look not to the things that are seen but to the things that are unseen. For the things that are seen are transient, but the things that are unseen are eternal." (2 Corinthians 4:18)

The unseen and the seen are distinct, but they are not divided, according to the Scriptures. God existed before the world, God created the world, and God is actively involved in the world. Yet, the disobedience of man brought about the fall, which has created a blockage between man and God—a separation that man alone is not

[8] See Schaeffer's *The God Who Is There*, first published in 1968 by IVP Press. A brief explanation is in *How Should We Then Live*, first published in 1976.

able to bridge but one that God has already bridged. Far from a spirituality that is mystical or philosophical, I will be sharing about my journey with the God who created and rules the universe, the God who is far greater than his creation and yet joined himself to creation in Jesus the Messiah, the bridge by which fallen and sinful people may be reconciled and brought back into a functioning relationship with God, who created us. By God's grace and mercy, I, like millions of others in history, have been reconciled to God through Jesus, and I am being restored by God's own Holy Spirit, as the whole creation eventually will be.

These days many people are fascinated by TV programs centered on the physical restoration of homes. My story is one example of restoration. It is part of the ultimate restoration story, the restoring of all things (Acts 3:19–21, Colossians 1:19–20, Ephesians 1:9–10). The apostle John foresaw it and heard God's declaration:

> Then I saw a new heaven and a new earth, for the first heaven and the first earth had passed away, and the sea was no more. And I saw the holy city, new Jerusalem, coming down out of heaven from God, prepared as a bride adorned for her husband. And I heard a loud voice from the throne saying, "Behold, the dwelling place of God is with man. He will dwell with them, and they will be his people, and God himself will be with them as their God. He will wipe away every tear from their eyes, and death shall be no more, neither shall there be mourning, nor crying, nor pain anymore, for the former things have passed away.

> And he who was seated on the throne said, **"Behold, I am making all things new."** Also he said, "Write this down, for these words are trustworthy and true." (Revelation 21:1–5, bold print added for emphasis)

Mine is not the story of a great hero or of a spiritual giant or of a holy man. It is the story of a quite average person whom God has graciously called to follow Jesus, not because I was worthy but because, as the apostle Paul said, God uses the foolish, the weak, and the common for his good purposes (1 Corinthians 2:26–31). Concerning his own call, Paul also wrote:

> Not that I have already obtained all this, or have already arrived at my goal, **but I press on to take hold of that for which Christ Jesus took hold of me.** … One thing I do: Forgetting what is behind and straining toward what is ahead, I press on toward the goal to win the prize for which God has called me heavenward in Christ Jesus. (Philippians 3:12–14, NIV,

bold print added for emphasis)

Paul's declaration sums up the way I have desired to live, even though I have failed often. God helping me, it is also the way I desire to finish my life.

A number of years ago, my friend, Joseph Holbrook, mentioned the title of Eugene Peterson's book, *Long Obedience in the Same Direction.*[9] *What a great epitaph that would be,* I have thought many times, if only I could truly live that way—fully obedient and steadily, even doggedly if necessary, pursuing Jesus and trying to lead our family and our small church to do so with me.

In truth, a more fitting epitaph would probably read as follows: "... As we both crawl toward the Lamp,"[10] words that the late musician, Larry Norman, used to describe the spiritual journey that he and his friend, Randy Stonehill, had begun.

---

[9] Eugene H. Peterson, *A Long Obedience in the Same Direction: Discipleship in an Instant Society* (Westmont, IL: IVP Connect, 1980). Peterson attributes the phrase "long obedience in the same direction" to Friedrich Nietzsche in his 1886 book, *Beyond Good and Evil:* "The essential thing 'in heaven and earth' is that there should be a long obedience in the same direction; there thereby results, and has always resulted in the long run, something which has made life worth living."

[10] Larry Norman, "Song for a Small Circle of Friends," *In Another Land*, 1976 album.

1

Beginnings

It seems strange now, but I felt excited and edgy that afternoon in early 1969 when I began to read from a copy of *Good News for Modern Man: The New Testament in Today's English Version*. In light of the many translations available today, those feelings probably seem inexplicable. At that time, however, the King James Version was the only true Bible. I can remember having seen only one other translation before that: the New English Bible, which my dad and our other church leaders saw as heretical.

Good News for Modern Man even looked dangerous, with its gray paperback cover and the line drawings inside. Because of the everyday, simple language, reading it was like reading a newspaper or a popular book. It seemed weird to think of God speaking in such down-to-earth, understandable words. That day, while sitting in my dorm room at Circleville Bible College, I had picked up the copy that had been given to me—by whom I can't remember—and had flipped it open and begun to read. I found myself reading in 1 Corinthians. At first it was simply a curiosity, but then I read:

> In the letter that I wrote you I told you not to associate with immoral people. Now I did not mean pagans who are immoral, or greedy, or lawbreakers, or who worship idols. To avoid them you would have to get out of the world completely! What I meant was that you should not associate with a man who calls himself a brother but is immoral, or greedy, or worships idols, or is a slanderer, or a drunkard, or a lawbreaker. Don't even sit down to eat with such a person.
>
> After all, it is none of my business to judge outsiders. God will judge them. But should you not judge the members of your own fellowship? As the scripture says, "Take the evil man out of your group." (1 Corinthians 5:9–13[11])

"The Bible does not say that!" I exclaimed aloud. Two statements had jumped out at me.

---

[11] *Good News for Modern Man: The New Testament in Today's English* (New York: American Bible Society, 1966).

1. "I told you not to associate with immoral people. Now I did not mean pagans who are immoral, or greedy, or lawbreakers, or who worship idols. To avoid them you would have to get out of the world completely!"

2. "After all, it is none of my business to judge outsiders. God will judge them. But should you not judge the members of your own fellowship? As the scripture says, 'Take the evil man from your group.'"

Immediately, I grabbed up **the Bible**—the King James Version, that is—and looked up the passage. To my amazement, **the Bible did say that after all**. The first statement startled me because the church tradition in which I had grown up emphasized separation from the *world*, which I had understood to include separation from *worldly people.* The second statement was startling also because I realized that, to my knowledge, our churches did not practice this *judging* of one another. The only situations that I could remember that had anything to do with situations similar to these were a few when a pastor had committed adultery and, when found out, seemed to disappear out of our midst. I could not think of a single situation in which this kind of discipline had been practiced in our churches. Besides that, I realized that I did not really know enough about the personal lives of those with whom I worshipped to know whether any might be involved in these types of sin.

Little did I know that this simple experience would prove to be a significant step in a journey toward a new understanding of God's church and of his purposes. I was on the way to a revolution in how I would perceive the church and the world. I had unknowingly come to a fork in the path of my life. Without forethought or understanding, when I began that day to wrestle with what I "saw" in this text, I started down a path that would take me in a very different direction than I ever could have imagined.

I now see, however, that the direction I chose that day was not simply a result of chance but was largely a result of prior choices, forces, and events. Some of these were deliberate choices I had made; the way I had been brought up was a definite factor. The times were influential as well. And, based on information gained years later, I believe that I was also beginning to receive a heritage rooted in the hopes and vision and journeys of my forefathers.

****

I was born on May 19, 1949, in west central Ohio and raised in Circleville, Ohio, a small city 25 miles south of Columbus. My parents were godly people and raised my sisters, my brother, and me to fear God. Mom and Dad had been faithful to teach us God's ways according to their best knowledge and ability. Dad was a minister—a pastor, a Bible college president, a denominational executive and administrator, and a traveling teacher and evangelist—teaching and preaching in numerous churches in quite a few denominations. My mother was his right hand, vitally involved in serving Dad, as well as in serving with him—until the last several years of her life during which she suffered from Alzheimer's disease. Mom, mercifully, went to be with the Lord in November 2008. Dad died five years later in August 2013. I have three younger siblings: Debbie, Marvene, and Wes.

Our family roots are in the Churches of Christ in Christian Union, a small non-Pentecostal, holiness denomination, headquartered in Circleville. My paternal grandfather, Frank Humble, a farmer who loved and served God wholeheartedly (and whom I looked upon as a "saint"), was one of the very early members of the Churches of Christ in Christian Union movement. He was as dedicated to God and to the church as any preacher, so zealous that in 1919 he even moved his family from Pike County in southern Ohio to Champagne County in west central Ohio in order to be part of an all-things-in-common Christian communal farm—a piece of family history that even Dad didn't know until a book about Christian Union's history was published in 1980.[12] Grandpa's first wife, Clara, my grandmother, died when Dad was 15; however, I remember well the stories Dad and my uncles told about the integrity and sense of honor that characterized her.

My maternal grandparents, Irvin and Loretta Geiger, from Mt. Savage, Maryland, were also genuine Christians who attended the Evangelical United Brethren Church (now a part of the United Methodist Church), although they had been raised as members of a Lutheran congregation. One of my treasures is a Bible that I inherited from Mom which had been given to her parents by the evangelist who was preaching a revival at that EUB church when my grandparents and my mom were converted.

A few years ago, I found out that both Grandpa and Grandma were descendants of Jacob Hochstetler, a Swiss Amish man who immigrated to Pennsylvania in 1738 in order to freely practice his faith. He became an Anabaptist hero because he held to his convictions about pacifism, even when Indians attacked his family in 1757 during the French and Indian War. Hochstetler's wife and two of his children, one son and one daughter, were killed, while Jacob and two other sons were carried away as captives. Later he got free, remarried, and produced more children. Eventually, his

---

[12] *A Goodly Heritage: History of the Churches of Christ in Christian Union*, Kenneth Brown & P. Lewis Brevard, Circle Press, Inc., Circleville, Ohio, 1980, p. 135.

sons were set free as well. My maternal grandparents came from two different lines of Hochstetler's descendants.

With a heritage like this, the Holy Spirit has been after me, drawing me toward God, for as long as I can remember. One of my very first memories is the time at age 4 when I responded to an altar call (invitation) and went forward to kneel at the altar (a wooden rail across the front of the church sanctuary, often called the mourners' bench) following Dad's sermon, "Come to the Feast."[13] There, I confessed my sins and asked Jesus to forgive me and save me. Later Dad told me several times that at that young age I could give meaningful explanations of the two key doctrines in our church: the doctrines of salvation (justification) and entire sanctification. I certainly cannot remember a time when I did not have a conscious understanding of these and other teachings. I was fed Biblical teaching and preaching just as regularly as I was fed physical food.

We were in church meetings often. We participated in the weekly Sunday School, Sunday morning worship, the Sunday evening youth meeting at 6:30, and the Sunday evening evangelistic service at 7:30. We participated in the weekly Wednesday night prayer service. We participated in the annual Vacation Bible School. We attended at least two revival meetings a year, normally consisting of church services every night for one or two weeks, sometimes even longer. There was youth camp for a week in the summer and at least one camp meeting per summer, running ten days with three main preaching services each day, as well as daily prayer meetings, testimony meetings, and missionary meetings.

Since Dad was a pastor and a denominational leader, the best preachers in the holiness movement came to our church to preach—and to our home, where they ate my mother's widely praised cooking. I still wonder if they came to our church so eagerly because they wanted to preach or because they esteemed Dad or because they wanted to eat at Mom's table.

The church was our life. We went *into the world* to go to school or to shop or to play Little League baseball and, of course, most dads in our church went there to make a living. But the church was our community. Our entertainment, our recreation, our friends—nearly everything that counted was in the church community.

---

[13] I did not remember the sermon or its title or the exact date. However, after Dad died, my brother discovered it in the record of sermons Dad had kept. Under the notation about the sermon, Dad had written "Stephen came to altar." See Appendix One.

The Bible was the centerpiece of life. One of our denomination's cardinal principles was "The Bible is the only rule for faith and practice." We sought to make the Bible the absolute standard of what we believed and how we lived.

I value that heritage deeply.

At about age 12, I felt the *call*. Following a revival service in which "the walking Bible," Rev. J. Elton Trueblood, had preached, as I walked across East Ohio Street from our church building to the church parsonage, I sensed an inner awareness that God was leading me toward *the ministry*. I interpreted this call according to all I knew at the time: it *obviously* meant that I would be either a pastor (leader of a local church), an evangelist (itinerate preacher going from church to church preaching revival meetings), or a missionary (a Christian worker who served in a foreign nation).

I never forgot that call; however, I did not make any conscious effort to respond to it other than to offer an internal "yes" at that moment. Nor did I begin in any way to prepare myself to fulfill that call. I look back at much of childhood as a series of "salvation" encounters followed by "backsliding" and efforts to be a "normal sinner boy." Maybe, because of the intense pressure that I saw my dad endure while serving as head of our denomination in his thirties while I was a teen, I had no desire for responsibility. In fact, I did not really want the call and therefore sought to avoid it.

I did have an extended period of spiritual fervor in the ninth and tenth grades. At that time, I participated in a small but committed youth group led by Dwight and Claudette Hershey and had a close friendship with Phil Conrad, who was three years older and who influenced me for good. Then, about the time Phil graduated from high school and went on to Bible college, I backslid once again and spent a year being as rebellious as I dared—given the realities that I "feared" my parents and that I really didn't want to hurt my dad's reputation.

I made a "final" commitment to Jesus Christ on April 22, 1966, during my junior year of high school. On March 19, 1967, Dad sent me out to preach for the first time, and I preached a sermon titled "Laborers Together" from 1 Corinthians 3:8–9. After high school I went on to attend Circleville Bible College. During my three years there, I preached on average once a week at a variety of churches.

In September 1967, a classmate nominated me for freshman class president at the college. I declined but let them run my name for vice president and was elected. Later that fall, the class president resigned, and I ended up being president after all.

I was conducting the January 1969 class meeting soon after New Year's Day and three weeks before the end of the first semester. Everything was normal until Helen Lovelace put forth a motion that our class sponsor an early morning prayer meeting at 6 a.m. for the next three weeks, leading up to the week of revival services that were scheduled to kick off the second semester. Who was going to be so unspiritual as to speak against or vote against such a proposal? Certainly not the class president. Motion passed!

As those three weeks began, I, who prior to this had barely made class by eight o'clock, did not crawl out of bed each morning because I desired to pray. I did not go because of any conscious "hunger for God." I did not go because I was a spiritual man. I went only because I did not want anyone *to think* that I was not spiritual.

In spite of the bad motivation and the hypocrisy, however, in looking back I perceive that God was drawing me. Hunger did begin to grow. And even before the week of revival, God began to answer, rather dramatically, specific prayers that we prayed. The hunger increased.

By the time the revival services began, there was some reviving already beginning to manifest. During that week I began to get even hungrier, to the point of feeling some measure of spiritual desperation. In order to describe the nature of the hunger, and in order to put the result of my hungering in context, I must step back again and give some theological background.

****

The holiness churches follow the Wesleyan-Arminian tradition. They are Arminian in that they hold to the views of Jacobus Arminius (1560–1609), a Dutch theologian of the later Reformation period who differed with certain doctrines held by the Calvinists. Arminius, as church historian Philip Schaff points out, regarded Calvin's work highly, saying, "Next to the study of the Scriptures which I earnestly inculcate, I exhort my pupils to peruse Calvin's *Commentaries* ...."[14] Arminius said that Calvin "possessed above most others, or rather above all other men, what may be called an eminent spirit of prophecy .... His *Institutes* ought to be studied ...." Arminius took issue not so much with Calvin's teaching as with "scholastic Calvinism,"[15] the more rigid theological positions of those who followed Calvin's teaching.

---

[14] Philip Schaff, *History of the Christian Church*, Vol. VIII (Grand Rapids, MI: Wm. B. Eerdmans Publishing Company, 1988), p. 280.

[15] Ibid., p. 262.

Whereas John Calvin (1509–1564) emphasized God's sovereignty over human responsibility, Arminius sought to bring back an appropriate emphasis on the importance of God's love for mankind and of man's response to God. Schaff wrote: "The Calvinistic system is popularly … identified with the Augustinian system, and shares its merit as a profound exposition of the Pauline doctrines of sin and grace, but also its fundamental defect of confining the saving grace of God and the atoning work of Christ to a small circle of the elect, and ignoring the general love of God to all mankind (John 3:16). It is a theology of Divine Sovereignty rather than of Divine love …."[16]

Calvin died four years after Arminius's birth. Ten years after Arminius's death, reacting to his influence, Calvinists at the Synod of Dort officially adopted the five points that came to be known as TULIP: (1) total depravity, (2) unconditional election (or predestination), (3) limited atonement, (4) irresistible grace, and (5) the perseverance of the saints. The followers of Arminius's teaching stood against these doctrines either wholly or in part.

To quote Schaff again: "Calvinism emphasizes divine sovereignty and free grace; Arminianism emphasizes human responsibility. The one restricts the saving grace to the elect; the other extends it to all men on the condition of faith. Both are right in what they assert; both are wrong in what they deny. If one important truth is pressed to the exclusion of another truth of equal importance, it becomes an error, and loses its hold upon the conscience."[17]

It may seem strange to look back four hundred years to a theological conflict in order discuss a spiritual conflict in the life of a 20-year-old college student, especially in a postmodern world where truth is widely held to be nonexistent or simply a personal viewpoint. However, this theological conflict was a major factor in the spiritual climate in which I was raised. The battle between Arminianism and Calvinism was very real to the preachers and teachers who influenced me. I had the distinct impression that Calvinists either bordered on, or had crossed over into, heresy, and that their doctrines—especially that of perseverance of the saints (commonly called eternal security)—were tools the devil was using to deceive many people.

The theological conflict was played out very graphically in my life in the up-and-down, in-and-out nature of my walk with God. I perceived salvation to be a work of God that I must receive through an act of my faith and *keep* through acts of my obedience, thus the cycle of "getting saved" and "backsliding" spoken of earlier.

---

[16] Ibid., p. 261.
[17] Ibid., p. 815.

Though my theology didn't change, my faith and experience changed on that 22nd day of April, 1966. After a year or so of inner rebellion (expressed outwardly in relatively mild forms, considering the times), as a high school junior I attended a weekend conference sponsored by Circleville Bible College. On one level it was a weekend of recruiting new students. On another it was an evangelistic outreach. I participated for neither of those reasons but rather because I knew that there would be girls in attendance. While driving to the conference on Thursday evening, April 21, my neighbor and close friend, Don Benner, and I made a mutual commitment not to "get saved."

However, late the next morning while we were watching a choir "rehearsal," all *heaven* broke loose. God's presence was tangibly felt in the room. As was not uncommon in the holiness heritage, some young people began to cry and others to shout for joy, and a sense of conviction of sin and of lostness and a hunger for God came upon others of us. Many began to "go to the altar" to repent and be born again.

From past experiences, I could remember the joy that others were manifesting, and I experienced a strong desire to "come home" to God and to be forgiven and feel clean and accepted again. However, I held back for what seemed like a long time, holding onto the back of the pew in front of me with white knuckles. At some point, John Maxwell, who is now a widely known Christian leader, came to me and challenged me to go forward, and at last I did.

I knelt at the altar for what must have been 45 minutes, alternately or even simultaneously praying and crying and wishing and hoping and despairing. I had no real doubt that God would accept me, but I was very sure that I could not live the life afterward and thus would have only a short-lived experience. I wanted it to be "for real" this time.

After a time, tall, lanky Don Crooks, a college student, knelt down in front of me on the other side of the mourners' bench and "got in my face." Don prayed with me and talked with me. He perceived the issue. Taking up a Bible, he opened it to 1 John 1:9 and directed me to read aloud: "If we confess our sins, he [God] is faithful and just to forgive us our sins, and to cleanse us from all unrighteousness" (KJV). Well, I knew that verse, by memory even; I had memorized it as a member of a Bible quiz team.

Don went further. He challenged me to read it again, but this time to substitute my name for the pronouns *we* and *us:* "If *Steve Humble* confesses *Steve Humble's* sins, he [God] is faithful and just to forgive *Steve Humble's* sins, and to cleanse *Steve Humble* from all unrighteousness."

Then Don pointed his long, bony index finger right at me and said: "Steve, I dare you to take God at his word. I dare you to take hold of this promise and make it your own and hold onto it and to live by it, even to the point, if necessary, of standing before God in the final judgment and reminding him that you are holding him to his word."

At that moment, my knowledge of the verse moved from my memory to the deepest core of my being. *I saw it! I believed it! I knew it!* My forgiveness from God and my acceptance by God did not depend on me and on my ability to obey. Rather, my forgiveness and my acceptance were founded on what God had promised and on what he had provided through the death of his Son, Jesus, who had died on the cross in my place.

From that moment to this very day, more than fifty years later, I have never doubted God's forgiveness and acceptance. Have I always been a man of faith and obedience since that day? By no means! I have failed often. I take no pleasure in my sins and shortcomings; however, I continue to rejoice in the fact that God has saved me according to his word. I do not have to save myself.

The debate about Calvinistic and Arminian theology continues with some. Even in my own mind, I cannot fully reconcile or defend either position, nor can I reject or refute either one. But this *I do know:* once I was unsettled and insecure about my relationship to God; now I am grounded and secure in the reality that God has forgiven me and accepted me and that he will keep me to the end!

I am not absolutely certain that there is no possibility that I could renounce or reject that relationship if I wanted to do so. However, *I do know* that I don't want to and that I have no intention even to try. *I do know* that 1 John 1:9 is just as certain a promise to me today as it was on April 22, 1966. Simply writing this account brings back some of the wonder and the joy of that reconciliation and coming home. Thanks be to God!

Even so, there is yet another theological matter that was a significant factor in my spiritual desperation during the week of the second-semester revival in January 1969.

****

Our church tradition was not only Arminian; it was also, and even primarily, Wesleyan.

John Wesley (1703–1791) was an Arminian, and he took a strong stand against certain Calvinistic teachings. Even so, Wesley esteemed some Calvinists and for many years worked closely with fellow Methodist George Whitefield, the great evangelist, who held to Calvinist theology.

Wesley preached at Whitefield's funeral, saying: "Have we read or heard of any person since the apostles, who testified the gospel of the grace of God through so widely extended a space, through so large a part of the habitable world? Have we read or heard of any person, who called so many thousands, so many myriads of sinners to repentance? Above all, have we read or heard of any, who has been a blessed instrument in his hand of bringing so many sinners from darkness to light, and from the power of Satan unto God?"[18]

I include this quotation because Wesley, though an adamant opponent of some Calvinistic doctrine, was not an opponent of those who held that doctrine, something that cannot be said of all who follow in the Wesleyan tradition.

In my own life, however, it was not Wesley's Arminianism that was a factor in my spiritual crisis in early 1969. Rather, it was Wesley's doctrine of entire sanctification, or Christian perfection, that was the issue for me at that time. Wesley's reading of the early Church Fathers, especially those from the Eastern churches, and his reading of William Law, author of *Christian Perfection* and *Serious Call*, influenced him in the development of this teaching.

It is beyond the scope of this book to examine and to evaluate Wesley's thought in detail. What matters here is the understanding that I received two centuries later in the Wesleyan holiness movement and the impact of that understanding on my own spiritual journey.

I was taught that entire sanctification (sometimes called the "baptism in the Spirit" in holiness circles) is a "second, definite, instantaneous work of grace subsequent to the new birth (regeneration and justification)." Sanctification, in this view, is the act of God in response to the human faith in which, after full surrender and consecration of one's life, the believer's heart is cleansed from inbred sin. According to this doctrine, in this experience the old man (the carnal nature, the flesh [Greek: *sarx*]) is crucified and eradicated so that the believer no longer has the tendency or bent toward sin and is free to obey God. This Christian perfection is not understood to preclude the possibility of the person making mistakes because of the human

---

[18] Ibid., p. 566.

weakness of his emotions and understanding, but it is understood to set him free so that he does not have to commit willful sins. It is seen as a perfecting in motive, a perfecting of the heart, and a perfecting in love, rather than as an absolute perfection of behavior, or a sinless perfection.

It is important in understanding this teaching to take into account the Wesleyan definition of *sin:* "Sin is a willful transgression of a known law of God." This definition is based on James 4:17, which says, "… to him who knoweth to do good and doeth it not, to him it is sin" (KJV), a statement understood to be a further clarification of the broader definition of *sin* given in 1 John 3:4: "… Sin is the transgression of the law" (KJV). This more limited understanding of what constitutes a sin helps explain how such a high standard can be taught.

However, what was taught and the experience that I was looking for were not one and the same. While I could quote these theological tenets and thought that I understood them, two days after coming to faith in regard to God's forgiving and justifying me, I went forward to the altar again and began to seek entire sanctification.

This search continued quite often from that point in April 1966 through 1968. I would pray for sanctification, sometimes in public meetings and sometimes in private prayer, until I found relief from the internal struggle and felt able to claim the experience. However, within a few days after the prayer, I would find myself struggling with the same temptations and falling into sin yet again. I did not question God's forgiveness when I repented, but I could not continue to profess sanctification when I saw no evidence that the tendency or bent toward sinning had been eradicated.

Over the course of those months of seeking, there were periods when I just went on living, enjoying the forgiveness of God. However, there were also periods of heaviness and condemnation because I could not live up to the standard of Christian perfection that I expected of myself. During January 1969, after the early morning prayer meetings began, this search became a kind of spiritual desperation.

On Wednesday morning of the week of the school revival, during a free hour before chapel I went to the men's prayer room in the old block dorm there at the Ohio Street campus of Circleville Bible College (now Ohio Christian University) and got down to the bottom line with God. I cried out to the Lord for help, admitting to him that I could not live the life. I found myself saying to the Lord that I was going to quit testifying to some experience of sanctification. I committed to the Lord that from that time forward I would give him the glory for any successes in my life and that I would be honest about my failures and struggles. I told the Lord of my desperation for help from him. At some point during that hour, I came to peace with God and knew that something significant had transpired. I wasn't sure what had changed, but I left that room with awareness that my relationship with God had changed in some way. I had confidence that I would see changes in my life in the days ahead.

Looking back from the vantage point of time and further experience, I believe that there in that prayer room I received what is commonly called the baptism in, or the infilling of, the Holy Spirit. I believe that the Holy Spirit awakened my spirit and came to dwell in me when I was born again. However, following this subsequent experience of the Holy Spirit in 1969, I experienced significant change in two areas of my life. First, a hunger for and insight into the Scriptures began to grow. I have already related one of the first and more dramatic times of insight—when I saw 1 Corinthians 5 in a new way. The parameters of my understanding and some of my assumptions began to change.

Second, my preaching changed. For two to three years following this prayer room encounter with God, no matter how diligently I prepared for my preaching engagements (and I did prepare), I consistently was moved by the Spirit to preach extemporaneously a different message. From that time on I preached with a different urgency and, as far as I can tell, with more effectiveness.

Although I began to have new insight into the nature of the church, which was to bring major change to my journey, I did not yet perceive the reality of the church being the "body of Christ" and the importance of the gifts of the Holy Spirit. The journey had begun, but the discovery of those realities was yet to come.

****

I must mention one person who came into my life briefly at this point. Alan Barnes entered our Bible College the very week of that revival and was assigned to be my roommate. Alan was a member of the United Methodist Church. The Methodist churches are the historical outworking of the Holy Club of which Oxford University students John Wesley, Charles Wesley, and George Whitefield were members; members of this group were so disciplined in their pursuit of God that they were derisively dubbed "Methodists" by fellow students. To be sure, there are many godly, Bible-believing Methodists these days. However, we also knew that many Methodists did not emphasize the holiness doctrines the same way we did, and clearly there were many liberal Methodists, who, in our view, had departed from the faith.

Thus, I did not expect much from Alan. He was quiet and studious and not very vocal. The first thing about Alan that got my attention was his struggle with the way prayer was practiced in our church services. Our customary way of praying, at least once during each service, was to call upon one person to lead out in a time of prayer. That person would speak out a few words, and then the room would erupt with virtually everyone praying aloud, simultaneously, for a period of time. Normally the person appointed to lead out would continue praying aloud until everyone else had quit, and then he or she would close the prayer time with the obligatory "in Jesus' name, we pray. Amen." We called this united prayer, and I grew up thinking this was the way all spiritually alive Christians prayed.

The fact that our way of praying bothered Alan was a sure sign to me that he was from one of the cold, formal liberal churches. Alan, however, was concerned about whether or not united prayer violated the instruction regarding church meetings found in 1 Corinthians 14:40: "Let all things be done decently and in order" (KJV); however, he came to peace about our way of praying when he found Acts 4:24, which seemed like it might indicate this type of united prayer: "And when they heard that, they lifted up their voice to God with one accord …." (KJV) I had to take a closer look at Alan when I realized how serious he was about following the Bible. I had never even thought to measure our church customs according to the Scripture.

Then I began to notice that Alan was studying the Bible—studying it a lot! In questioning him, I discovered that he was studying the Scriptures personally, often for two to three hours a day, in addition to class assignments. I had never known anyone like this, but Alan's example whetted my own appetite for Scripture in those days.

Alan usually went home for the weekend, and one Monday several weeks into the semester, I was politely asking him about his weekend. He told me that he had spent much of the weekend participating in a conference. Curious, I began to draw out of him the nature of this conference. At some point, he used the word *charismatic* to describe the conference. To my recollection, it was the first time I had heard this word used in any similar context, and I asked him to explain what he meant by it. In that explanation, Alan spoke about the gifts of the Spirit and about speaking in tongues.

To be sure, I vaguely remembered hearing strange stories about an Episcopal priest, Dennis Bennett, who had begun to speak in tongues back in the 1950s. Mostly I associated speaking in tongues with Pentecostals. Everything that I had heard about tongues up to that point was that it was either extreme emotionalism (an odd concern for us since in our churches shouting, jumping, and running in the aisles to praise God were not uncommon actions) or else it was a work of the devil, deceiving people.

I knew, of course, that the members of the first church in Jerusalem had spoken in tongues on the Day of Pentecost, but I had been taught that this was a miraculous ability to speak in a foreign language for evangelistic purposes, very different from the "carnal behavior" that Paul had to correct in 1 Corinthians 14.

This was different, though. Alan was certainly not an extremist. He did not display much emotion at all. He had even been concerned about whether or not united prayer violated Scriptural instruction, yet here he was telling me that he quite often prayed in tongues in his personal prayer life.

Frankly, I had no framework with which to process this information. However, I could not deny the presence of God in Alan's life. His hunger for God and the Scriptures was far greater than my own hunger for these things. In that semester, I never saw anything in his life that was inconsistent with the Christian message or with his testimony.

Alan left school after one semester and, though I heard about him occasionally in years to come, I have never seen him again; however, his life left an indelible impression for good, and the discovery that Alan spoke in tongues was a "seed" that he unknowingly planted in me. That "seed" would produce a harvest that I never could have foreseen.

2

Growing Up

Not everything about my life dealt with theological issues and spiritual encounters. In fact, there were (and still are) long periods when life just seemed to go on without any dramatic events. It has been enlightening to me to realize that Abraham, the spiritual father of all who believe God, lived 175 years. None of us knows how many encounters Abraham had with God; what we do know is that the Bible records approximately a dozen times when Abraham had personal encounters and interventions of a more dramatic nature with God, and we know that these took place over the span of about seventy-five years.

In other words, much of life is simply "living." However, one who knows God knows that God is present and at work in all of one's life and that there is opportunity to commune with God even in the most mundane moments and seasons. I, however, am all too often dull and not alert. Often I am not cultivating my consciousness of God, and thus I do not avail myself of all the opportunities to commune with him and to be a co-worker with him.

This book focuses on my spiritual journey rather than on the whole story of my life. Yet, that spiritual journey was not disconnected from the times in which I grew up or from the circumstances of my life. These elements must be considered as well.

Although I have already mentioned my family background and my church background, it is important to share a few more details about my childhood in order to establish a context for the events that took place later.

Our lives were built around my parents' commitment to God and around my dad's call to the ministry. It would be hard to overestimate the quality of the parents through whom God brought me into existence. Mom was a godly woman. I have many memories of her going to her bedroom and shutting the door and crying out to God in prayer. Mom was the hardest working person I have known; even in her later years when she was severely afflicted with Alzheimer's and had lost her sight because of a stroke, she still talked about the work she was planning to do. Mom was tops in teaching children and in running Sunday School and Vacation Bible School. She wrote adult Sunday School material for publication, at first as a "ghost writer" for Dad and then in her own name. Mom is summed up best by my wife's claim that her mother-in-law was the original model for the Proverbs 31 woman.

If, in this writing, I do not seem to speak much about Mom, it is because my relationship with Dad seems to have had more influence on the particulars of my spiritual journey. However, Mom's influence on my character, on my knowledge of the Bible, and on my desire to know and to serve God was huge. Most of all, I am confident that Mom's prayers to God for me have released unmeasurable grace in my life. Like all humans, save one, Mom had her faults, but you had to look pretty hard to find them.

When I was a baby, Dad was working on a bachelor's degree at Cedarville College, then a Presbyterian liberal arts college in southwestern Ohio. He was also pastoring a small church near there.

During part of the first two years of my life, we lived in a 13-foot by 8-foot house trailer, the size of a small camper by today's standards, located on someone's farm. I don't remember that time, of course, but there are three things that have been told and retold about it so that they are like memories. First, the big snow of 1951 occurred while we were living there. Dad often said that the snow had drifted to the roof of the trailer, but there was just enough room between the snow bank and the trailer for him to squeeze out of the door and begin to clear a path to the outhouse. Second, I have a photograph of me outside the trailer playing with our cocker spaniel.

Third, and the most significant thing, while we lived there, my mother contracted the worst form of polio. Polio was a highly dreaded disease in those days before the Salk oral vaccine had been developed. Mom had Bulbar polio, the most severe type, and the doctor told Dad that she would most likely die, and that, if she lived, she would not be able to walk. She lived and she walked, thanks to God and to the prayers of his people! The only aftereffect was that Mom could not swallow on one side of her throat. I stayed with another family while she spent six weeks in the hospital because of the polio. I don't know how traumatic that was for me, but Mom often told about coming home from the hospital and being brokenhearted when she discovered that I didn't recognize her.

We moved to Circleville when I was 2 so that Dad could pastor one of the largest churches in our denomination—and one of the most significant churches, since it was in the denomination's headquarters town. A few months into that pastorate, he also became president of the four-year-old Circleville Bible College, in part because he was one of the few pastors in the denomination with a college degree at that time. After a few months, he resigned from the church to lead the Bible College full-time. After about three years, Dad resigned from the College and went back to pastoring the church, which he continued for several years until he became the general superintendent of the denomination at age 31.

Dad's ministry changes had several implications for me. On the positive side, unlike most children of pastors in our churches, from the age of 2 I grew up in one city, although we lived in numerous houses. This meant that I had stability in relationships through those years. It also meant, for better or for worse, that I was always somewhat in the limelight in our circles because of who my Dad was. On the negative side, Dad carried responsibility beyond his years and experience, even though it wasn't beyond his gifts. This responsibility created internal and external pressure on him that made an impact on our family life and on my relationship with him.

One of my favorite childhood activities was to "go calling" with Dad. When we went to visit older folks, I often got a cookie or some other sweet treat. When we did hospital calls, I sat in the car or in the waiting room. Quite often we went to Columbus to the hospitals, and once in a while we'd stop at White Castle for 8-cent hamburgers. Yum! I still crave a White Castle hamburger from time to time.

Our family hardly ever ate out during my younger years. Even on trips, Mom usually packed food for us to eat along the way. Given the way she cooked, we did not miss anything by not eating out. I do remember that sometime in the late fifties or early sixties, the first McDonald's that I ever knew of opened at the Great Southern Shopping Center on the south side of Columbus, and we did stop there to eat once in a while. In those days, you could buy a hamburger for 15 cents, fries for another 15 cents, and a milkshake—chocolate, of course—for 20 cents: a 50-cent meal! A few years after McDonald's opened, Ponderosa Steakhouse opened next door to it. A few times, we feasted on a rib-eye steak, a salad, and a baked potato or fries for $1.99 at the Ponderosa.

As a younger child I remember playing pitch and catch with Dad. He had been a catcher on his high school baseball team, and he trained me in catching while I was in elementary school. Then, as often as possible, he came and watched my Little League games when I played first for the Circleville Oil team and later for the Circleville Herald team. In warm weather Dad and I would go outside to do our practicing. In the winter, we'd play in our small basement. As a child I didn't think about it, but in looking back I realize that we couldn't have been more than 20 feet apart in that basement. Dad couldn't throw overhand because the ceiling was too low, so he'd throw sidearm—hard. It was catch the ball or else since there was no escape at that distance, and I especially had to stop any bad pitches that bounced in front of me or I could have gotten hurt.

When I caught behind a batter, Dad always insisted that I wear a mask, even in pickup games, which I did, if he was present. I found out why he insisted on the mask at one of our annual July 4th Sunday School picnics in Logan Elm Park. After lunch the men and older boys would form two teams for softball. (I had developed enough skill as a catcher that I got to play with them when I was still in grade school.)

Once, probably the summer after the sixth grade, when I was catching at the picnic, Dad was up to bat for the other team. As he had trained me, I squatted, bouncing on my toes, as close behind the plate as I dared to position myself. The pitch came in, and like Casey in the poem, Dad swung the bat mightily, only he connected with the ball and it went sailing away. Dad had swung so hard that he came all the way around with the bat and cracked it up alongside of my head. I saw stars at 3 o' clock in the afternoon. The mask may well have saved my life. The blow left a huge, painful bump on my head above and behind the ear, but the mask had protected my temple, and I received no permanent injury. Dad, however, forgot to run the bases.

Our baseball playing stopped during Christmas vacation of my seventh-grade year. We had gone to Maryland to visit my maternal grandmother and Aunt Esther. It had snowed but thawed while we were there. Aunt Esther, who worked in the office of the Frostburg High School about 7 miles away, had had snow chains put on her rear tires in order to drive safely on the mountain roads.

After the thaw, I followed Dad to the garage when he went out to remove the chains from the tires for her. Because melting snow had formed ice on the chains, he was unable to break the chain loose on the driver's side rear tire. He took the bumper jack from the trunk and jacked up the rear end. Then he lay down on his right side and slid under the rear fender just behind the tire so that he could peck at the ice with a tool. As he was pecking, the car must have rocked, because the jack moved and the car fell, crushing his shoulders and chest under the fender. The spring brought the car back up enough that Dad could breathe, and he told me to run to the house, about 25 yards away, to get Mom. I ran!

By the time Mom could come out of the house, followed by Grandma Geiger and Aunt Esther, we met Dad walking painfully toward the house, holding his left arm and shoulder. He said that he had wiggled out from under the car, gotten to his feet, and started to the house because he was concerned that Mom might panic or something.

We took him to the hospital in Cumberland, where X-rays revealed that his collarbone had broken in an unusual way, almost in a diagonal, with one small, three-cornered piece actually broken off and sticking up so that it pushed up the skin, making a bump just left of center at the base of his neck. They could not set the bone. They simply wrapped him up and let it heal that way. Thus, our baseball days came to an early end, because even after the bone had healed, the small, sharp bone sticking up caused pain if he threw the ball very hard.

Late in the summer of the year when I started tenth grade, we moved 2 miles out of town to the new general superintendent's house on Bolender Pontius Road, across the road from the home of my close friend, Don Benner. Our house was built on the far corner of a farm that we called the church farm. This farm had been bought by the denomination during the Depression with money that was raised largely by people saving pennies in cans on their kitchen tables. The vision had been to build an orphanage there, but that had never come to pass. Building the general superintendent's house was an early step toward moving the Bible College and the headquarters, and more recently the Circleville Camp Meeting, from the old Mount of Praise Campgrounds on Ohio Street.

At the time we moved there, however, the farm had been rented out and was still being farmed. Behind our house, there was a small field used only for a hog lot, and the renters allowed us to fence off a small triangle, perhaps 40 yards wide by 70 yards long, bordered by a creek bank on one side and the property line fence on the other. There we built a shed with wood from an old dormitory that had been torn down at the Campgrounds so that a new dormitory could be built for Circleville Bible College. The shed had two parts: a stall on the left and a storage area on the right, divided by a manger.

Then we bought a horse. Dandy, we named him. For the next three years, Dandy was important to my life. He meant fun and regular chores for me. He provided a healthy pleasure and distraction from pressure for Dad. Dad not only rode Dandy but also broke him to pull a small plow and to drive a buggy and a sleigh. And even though Dad and I did not communicate deeply, we did relate often around the horse, so Dandy helped keep a connection of sorts between Dad and me, even when our relationship was suffering.

****

Those were tough years in some ways—for Dad, for me, and for our family. It was the mid-sixties. Rebellion was in the air. As a generation, many baby boomers had been spoiled by Dr. Spock's crackpot teaching and by materialism. Although I didn't understand it at the time, in the 1960s the fruit of our culture's shift into secularism began to manifest. My parents did not follow Spock, and they did not raise us in materialism or secularism; even so, the spirit of the times influenced me more than I recognized then.

It is difficult to describe clearly what it was like to grow up in that complicated time. My grandparents had lived through two world wars. My parents had been born just before the Great Depression, and many of their generation had fought and even died in World War II. They saw others die in Korea for a war that ended in a stalemate rather than in victory. During the outwardly peaceful and prosperous fifties, in which most of us baby boomers grew up, the Cold War was in full force and there was pervasive fear of an imminent atomic war. Virtually every community drew up civil defense plans. Many communities and even some individuals built bomb shelters. Public schools had contingency plans in case of disaster.

I now realize something of the significance of John F. Kennedy's election as President in 1960. At the time, the adults in our church circles seemed most concerned that the election of a Catholic to the presidency would open the door to the Papacy having undue influence, and maybe even control, in the United States. Many expected that some future pope would prove to be the Antichrist who was to control the world for a season in the last days before Jesus's Second Coming. One of the seven cardinal principles for our denomination was that politics were not to be dealt with from the pulpit, a principle derived in reaction to painful divisions in churches located in both the North and the South during the Civil War. In spite of that principle, I remember Dad bringing up in a sermon, before the 1960 election, his concerns about what would happen if a Catholic were to be elected. Apparently his religious concerns outweighed the ban against preaching about political issues.

I had no idea then of the hopes and dreams that President Kennedy represented for many Americans—those humanistic and politically liberal hopes, later characterized idealistically as Camelot. However, for many, those dreams died with Kennedy's assassination on November 22, 1963.

Even in our family, the assassination had our full attention. We did not own a television because my parents were concerned, rightly so as it turns out, that television would have a negative impact on people; they foresaw that television would bring the values and ways of the contemporary culture right into the home, and that over time God's people would tend to become desensitized to sin and "worldliness." On the day of the assassination, however, Dad borrowed a television from a friend in the used furniture business and for several days we spent most our time watching the coverage.

I remember coming home from church on Sunday morning and turning on that television just in time to see Lee Harvey Oswald, the accused assassin, being led from the Dallas police headquarters on his way to the county jail. We actually were watching TV when Jack Ruby pushed through the policemen who were leading Oswald out through a tunnel. I saw Ruby point his pistol and heard the gun go off when he shot Oswald.

We grieved with the nation over the assassination of the President, even though President Kennedy had not been my parents' choice for president. I had no idea that Kennedy's death had ideological implications that would impact the whole culture.

Francis Schaeffer, in his book *How Should We Then Live?* states that the two primary values of our parents' generation had become personal peace and affluence. By "personal peace" Schaeffer essentially meant "give me space to do what pleases me, and don't rock my boat." By "affluence" he meant, essentially, "I'll do whatever it takes to avoid the suffering and insecurity of the Depression and the World War II years and to have the resources to do what I want." Although the basic morality of Christian teaching was still prevalent in the social order, most Americans lived on the memory of Judeo-Christian values but lacked personal faith in God and in his revelation in Scripture. Therefore, there was no sufficient foundation to sustain that morality. It had been undermined in the popular culture, in the public education system, in universities, and even in many churches and Christian colleges and seminaries.

Intuitively, for the most part, the baby boomers recognized this lack of a foundation and the emptiness of these two values of personal peace and affluence. After Kennedy was assassinated, many young adults, especially college students, lost all trust in the older generation. Cultural rebellion against the status quo, against groundless traditions, and against authorities who represented and upheld that tradition began to grow. The Christian churches were assumed to be part of the established order (and all too often they were); thus, in their search for truth and for worthy values, most younger people did not consider the Christian faith to be an option.

The cultural rebellion among the youth had begun to surface in the free speech movement at Berkeley in the early 1960s. A large number of professors in universities and colleges, enamored with humanism, had bought into the utopian goals of socialism. More than a few had gone so far as to embrace Marxism, believing in the promises and ignoring the actual reality of life in Marxist nations. Often, social studies, literature, political science, and philosophy classes were used to destroy what was left of the students' sentimental attachment to Judeo-Christian values and to inculcate in them radical agendas. Throughout the sixties, students in the United States, and in other countries as well, rejected social rules, values, and expectations and began to work to overthrow the establishment structures that propagated and sustained them.

Rebellion alone probably would not have been enough to create a worldwide resistance to the establishment and the calls for change; in the long run people will tend to fight *for* something longer than they will fight *against* something. However, there were two movements that provided many young people with positive causes for which to fight.

The civil rights movement that had begun in the 1950s was a cause worth fighting for. Martin Luther King and the other civil rights leaders had learned how to use television news to expose a major cultural sin in this nation for all to see—racism—and in the South, the system of segregation that fostered and upheld it. This sin was all too often sustained, defended, and even propagated not only by the secular culture but also by those professing belief in God and the Bible. To fight for civil rights was to fight for justice as well as to fight against social hypocrisy.

Opposing the war in Vietnam became another cause to which many baby boomers gave themselves. The United States had become increasingly embroiled in an undeclared war in Southeast Asia, a war to contain the spread of Communist socialism but not a war to defend the United States. Many in the educational establishment resisted the war because of their commitment to socialism. As it became clear that young American men were dying "meaninglessly" in a political war, resistance to the war spread beyond those committed to socialism. To fight against the war was to fight for peace and love—another reason to rebel against the status quo, against the established order, and against the empty values of materialism.

Having learned from the civil rights movement, the antiwar movement started out by engaging in peaceful forms of protest; however, resistance to change by the establishment, along with incitement from the radical left, led many of the more zealous youth to more violent forms of protest and resistance in the second half of the decade. Often dubbed the New Left, the more radical movements sought to tear down the establishment, but most of those involved lacked a clear vision of what a just order would be and even less of how to build it.

Before long, many of the young people became convinced that they would never change the system through protest; therefore, they decided to bail out of "the system" altogether in order to live in their own reality. Many adopted a hedonistic lifestyle following in the steps of author Ken Kesey and his friends in the Beat Generation and turned to the use of hallucinogenic drugs as a means to find truth and meaning, as Harvard Professor Timothy Leary had been advocating. They became known as hippies, and they sought to live a lifestyle of "love," most often expressed in free sexual expression, rejection of personal property, and communalism. For a brief time, especially during the summer of '67 in San Francisco's Haight-Ashbury district, the hippie lifestyle seemed to offer peace, joy, and love, which seemed like wonderful values for their lives.

Ironically, by the time the hippie lifestyle had begun to spread across the nation, many of those who started the movement and propagated it had already discovered that drugs and free sex did not produce utopia. Free sex turned out not to be so "free." Sexually transmitted diseases began to proliferate. Children were conceived who often were not wanted, greatly increasing the demand for more effective birth control methods and readily available, safer abortions. Drugs provided no lasting enlightenment, and drug use also led to many problems. LSD, the drug of choice for enlightenment seekers, could produce "bad trips" and "flashbacks" as easily as it produced supposed enlightenment. Some young people actually committed suicide because of bad trips and flashbacks. Some users went on to harder drugs in search of highs, and many became addicts. Others settled into a lifestyle of marijuana use, able to function in day-to-day life but rarely able to think clearly enough to make the kinds of decisions that would produce a life with purpose.

Eventually, numbers of our generation moved from searching for enlightenment through drug use into searching for it by embracing Eastern religions and practicing meditation. Not a few began to delve into the occult in their hunger to find some escape from the physical, material machine that was presumed to have developed because of the impersonal laws of evolution.

Of course, there were those who simply followed the trends and enjoyed the party life—for a season—but many were genuine seekers, and the search is not to be despised. These rebellious seekers were not apathetic. They were not willing to settle for comfortable but meaningless lives. They wanted to truly live and to live truly. Although they looked in futile and sometimes harmful directions, at least they looked! They did not ignore the inner, God-given desire for truth, for love, for peace, and for joy, even though they looked in the wrong directions.

****

It would be hard to overestimate the influence of music as a force in the youth culture at that time. Jerry Rubin, for instance, who was one of the loudest and most extreme advocates of the rebellion, according to his book *Do It*, saw Elvis Presley as a door opener to rebellion in the popular culture. He wrote that in the 1950s Elvis began to break down the restraints against sexual expression, in white culture at least, by the sensual body movements that he made while singing to rock-and-roll rhythms. (Ironically, there is also evidence that Elvis learned his "sensual movements" by imitating and exaggerating the motion of Southern gospel singers, whose music he loved.) The more parents and those of the older generation condemned Elvis, the more he became a hero for the young. It's hard to believe that Elvis soon became a symbol of American culture in the "good ol' days."

Folk music became identified with the sixties protest movement because of the work of musicians such as Bob Dylan, Joan Baez, and Barry McGuire. Of course, the roots of the relationship between folk music and protest go back further, at least to songs of the labor movement in earlier decades of the 1900s, to the songs of Woody Guthrie, for example. Dylan especially was seen as something of a "prophet" to youth culture. In the mid-sixties, Dylan united the protest emphasis of folk music with the electric and rhythmic sounds of rock music, thus helping to open the door to rock music becoming the voice of the culture of rebellion.

About that time, along came the Beatles with their mop-top haircuts. Their early music seems innocuous enough in content, much of it consisting of catchy sounds but rather silly and childish lyrics about romantic love; however, the Beatles quickly became symbols of the rebellion, and their music helped spread, first, the message of enlightenment through drugs and later the message of enlightenment through Eastern religion and transcendental meditation.

Other musicians, such as the Rolling Stones and Janis Joplin, seemed to give themselves over completely to rebellion and sensuality. They became living symbols and examples of hedonism, living without restraint, doing whatever they pleased in their pursuit of meaning through pleasure.

The protests at the 1968 Democratic Convention in Chicago and the three-day party at Woodstock music festival in 1969 were climactic moments of the cultural rebellion. The 1968 protests brought elements from the spectrum of the rebellion together in political action. This is seen most clearly in the much-publicized trial of the "Chicago Seven."

Actually, eight major leaders of the youthful rebellion were arrested in Chicago. Seven were tried together, hence the title. Tom Hayden, who would later become the husband of Jane Fonda and become a U.S. Congressional Representative from California, and Rennie Davis were co-founders of the radical and sometimes violent group Students for a Democratic Society. David Dellinger was a pacifist and the editor of *Liberation* magazine. Abbie Hoffman and Jerry Rubin were essentially anarchists who united the hippie lifestyle with political activism and were popularly called yippies. Lee Wiener and John Froines were young "community organizers"—the job description that would years later identify President Barack Obama. Bobby Seale was chairman of the violent Black Panther Party. (Seale, in the end, was not tried with the others.) These men represent the conjoining of separate facets of the youth rebellion in one attempt to change "the establishment."

The lyrics from Graham Nash's song "Chicago" echoed the agenda of the protestors at the 1968 convention and also expressed support for the Chicago Seven and especially for Bobby Seale:

> Won't you please come to Chicago
> For the help we can bring
> We can change the world
> Rearrange the world
> It's dying—to get better
> Politicians sit yourselves down, there's nothing for you here
>
> We can change the world
> Rearrange the world
> It's dying—if you believe in justice
> It's dying—and if you believe in freedom
> It's dying—let a man live his own life
> It's dying—rules and regulations, who needs them
>
> Open up the door
> We can change the world ...[19]

The Woodstock Festival and Concert, held on a farm in upstate New York, was idealized as an example of the utopia of which many of that generation dreamed— the dream for a world of freedom and peace and innocence, a world in which every person was significant according to his or her own definition of himself or herself.

---

[19] "Chicago" was first released on Nash's 1971 solo album, *Songs of Beginners*, and later was sung and recorded by Crosby, Stills, Nash, and Young.

These days that dream, or nightmare, of self-definition is widespread and perhaps even more desired.

Joni Mitchell elucidated the dream in her song "Woodstock" (1970), mixing together references to the Biblical Garden of Eden with the New Age ideal of people as "divinity" (golden stardust) who can work out their own salvation:

> I came upon a child of God
> He was walking along the road
> When I asked him, "where are you going?"
> This he told me
> I'm going down to Yasgur's farm
> Gonna join a rock and roll band
> I'm going to camp out on the land
> And try and get my soul free
>
> Then can I walk beside you
> I have come here to lose the smog
> I feel just like a cog
> In something turning
> Well maybe it's the time of year
> Or maybe it's the time of man
> I don't know who I am
> But life is for learning
>
> We are stardust
> We are golden
> And we've got to get ourselves back to the garden [20]

Reality set in. The dream died for most of that generation as the seventies unfolded. The dream of rebuilding the world through political activism seemed to die for many others after the Ohio National Guard shot into a crowd of antiwar protestors at Kent State in May of 1970, killing four students. Riots erupted for a while after that tragedy, but not many really wanted to die in order to change the world. Even a rousing anthem such as Neil Young's "Ohio" could not stir up enough outrage to motivate people to much action.

---

[20] Mitchell's recorded version of "Woodstock" was first released in 1970 on her album *Ladies of the Canyon*, although she began singing it in concerts soon after the Festival. A more well-known version was Crosby, Stills, Nash & Young's rock version on their album *Déjà Vu* (1970). Another CSN&Y version closed out the 1970 documentary film *Woodstock.*

> Tin soldiers and Nixon's bombing
> We're finally on our own
> This summer I hear the drumming
> Four dead in Ohio
>
> Gotta get down to it
> Soldiers are gunning us down
> Should have been done long ago
> What if you knew her and
> Found her dead on the ground
> How can you run when you know
>
> Four dead in Ohio ...[21]

Most young people left the outward rebellion behind after they left college and went out to get jobs and make a living. Some did go on living in communes, and there were some efforts to "get back to the land" and live a simpler, less technological and less materialistic life. The biggest lasting changes included the major shift in sexual mores and the political activism for various causes, such as feminism and the homosexual rights movement. The reality is that Eastern religions and the occult got a solid foothold in the culture for the first time in the history of the United States.

It seems to me that Kris Kristofferson captured the emptiness of dreams lost in the lyrics to "Me and Bobby McGee" (1969), especially as sung by Janis Joplin on the last album that she recorded just before her death by drug overdose on October 4, 1970.

> Freedom's just another word for nothin' left to lose
> Nothin' don't mean nothin' hon' if it ain't free, no no
> Yeah feeling good was easy, Lord, when he sang the blues
> You know feeling good was good enough for me
> Good enough for me and my Bobby McGee ...[22]

****

The tension of the sixties is summed up in my own experience in an incident that took place a couple of days after the Kent State shootings. A few brothers and I, all

---

[21] "Ohio" was recorded by Crosby, Stills, Nash & Young and released in June 1970 in response to the Kent State shootings.

[22] Lyrics given here as sung by Janis Joplin in the first chorus of the song on her LP album *Pearl*.

students at Circleville Bible College, had conducted a weekly Bible study for a group of teens living in a halfway-house-type situation on the premises of the Ohio State Fairgrounds. Having heard that a student demonstration to protest the shootings was going to take place at the Oval, a park-like area on the Ohio State University campus, when the Bible study ended we naively decided to drive over and get a hamburger at the McDonald's across High Street from the Oval. We hoped to be able to see what a demonstration was like.

As we neared High Street driving west on 15th Avenue in John Meadows' red and white Chevrolet, we began to see thousands of young people on the streets, and we saw several fire trucks and emergency vehicles in that area of frat houses and student rentals. We also saw a lot of fog (I assumed it was fog because I didn't smell smoke) a few blocks ahead of us. We expected to see one of the many fraternity houses on fire. We were wondering aloud why our eyes had begun to burn. I was aware of an increasing feeling of tension, anger even, in me without any rational reason for it.

Suddenly, as we drew near the fog, we heard booms and saw something like cans coming through the air toward our car. It was only when a bunch of people wearing helmets and gas masks came toward us through the fog that we realized the fog was actually tear gas. No wonder our eyes were burning! John Meadows whipped the car up an alley on our right. About 40 yards later he had to turn right, only to come to a dead end. He was able to back up and turn around by someone's garage, and we headed back out, turned east onto 15th Avenue, and headed away from the area. Then we tuned into a local station on the car radio and discovered that the demonstrations had turned into riots and that we were driving in an area under curfew.

Our actions were foolish. However, in looking back and remembering the irrational anger that I experienced as we drove up toward the riot area, I can only think that there was strong demonic activity at work in the midst of the human anger and fear and frustration.

A significant part of the dreams and ideals of the sixties, I think, is recorded on film in the documentary *Woodstock: 3 Days of Peace and Music*. The first song in the film's introduction, David Crosby's "Long Time Gone" (1969), decries the world's long, dark night of madness and yet holds out the hope that a new day is about to dawn:

> It's been a long time comin'
> It's been a long time gone.
> But you know, the darkest hour,

> Is always just before the dawn.
> And it appears to be a long time,
> Such a long, long, long time before the dawn.

The film documents the partying, the drug use, the wild music, and the rainstorm; however, to me the most fascinating segments are the sound bites in which young people describe their experience at this event, obviously seeing it as the pinnacle of their lives up to that point and as a model, if not the beginning, of a new world order. The idealism of that time is captured powerfully.

The most striking image of all for me is the image that ends the documentary. The party is over. The music has stopped. The crowd is gone. What, in the beginning of the film, had been a beautiful grassy field has become a garbage-covered mass of mud. A few people are wandering around picking up trash. A few others are looking for lost items. The scene is desolate and ugly. What a parable!

Then, a few months later, while the Rolling Stones were performing at the Altamont Speedway Free Festival, the Hells Angels, who had been hired to provide security, stabbed and beat to death 18-year-old Meredith Hunter, who may have pulled out a gun. There were also three accidental deaths during the festival. The idealism was shattered.

God was not caught off guard by the sixties, nor was he in any way perplexed by them. Christians had for the most part reacted against the rebellious youth rather than to have looked through the rebellion and weirdness to see a generation hungry for purpose and meaning, but God was preparing to apprehend many baby boomers for his kingdom. By the end of the decade a number of young people in the sixties counterculture began to encounter Jesus. Conversions increased until even *Newsweek* magazine recognized this "Jesus Movement" in the fall of 1971.

The fact that I was raised in a conservative Christian subculture, had made a youthful commitment to follow Jesus, and had taken my college studies first in a Bible college and then in a Christian liberal arts college did not fully shield me. I was influenced strongly by the times, by the cultural upheaval, and by the spirit of rebellion. Looking back, I regret the sinful attitudes, the wrong-headed ideas, and the unrighteous behavior that I developed during those years. However, I know that God also has worked for good in spite of, and even through, the bad effects in order to move my life in the direction of his choice for me.

Growing Up

The spiritual journey chronicled in the preceding chapters and the influences of the times led to a sovereign encounter with God in May 1970. I entered into a commitment at that time that, far beyond any knowledge of my own, was to set the course for my life.

****

> For you formed my inward parts;
> you knitted me in my mother's womb.
> I will praise you, for I am fearfully and wonderfully made;
> Marvelous are your works,
> And my soul knows it very well.
> My frame was not hidden from you,
> When I was being made in secret;
> intricately woven in the depths of the earth.
> Your eyes saw my unformed substance;
> in your book were written, every one of them,
> the days that were formed for me,
> when as yet there was none of them. (Psalm 139:13–16)

> For we are his workmanship, created in Christ Jesus for good works, which God prepared beforehand that we should walk in them. (Ephesians 2:10)

> … He [God the Father] chose us in him [Jesus Christ] before the foundation of the world, that we should be holy and blameless before him. In love, he predestined us for adoption to himself as sons through Jesus Christ, according to the purpose of his will, to the praise of his glorious grace, with which he has blessed us in the Beloved. (Ephesians 1:4–6)

> You did not choose me, but I chose you and appointed you that you should go and bear fruit, and that your fruit should abide …. (John 15:16)

> The mind of man plans his way,
> But the LORD directs his steps. (Proverbs 16:9, NASB)

Even if I were able, this would not be the place to try to explain the mystery and paradox of the sovereignty of God and the responsibility of man. Suffice it to say that

I have no doubt that God has had his hand on me and has drawn me to himself from my earliest childhood. I need only to reflect on the heritage that I received from my ancestors in blood and in faith. I need only consider the parents who brought me into the world and trained me. I need only think about the church environment in which I grew up. I need only remember the desire to know God and to please him that has pulled me from within since earliest memory. There is no doubt that God has chosen and called me.

Even so, I am also aware of the conflicting inner pull to follow my own desires and passions and to walk in the ways of the world around me. Could I have gone a different way? Could I yet? All I know is that God has called and I have heard the call and have chosen to surrender to his will and purpose. I made the choice to follow the Lord Jesus as a youth. I have faltered; I have stumbled; I have often taken undesirable detours. But the call remains. And the choice is made as well.

That call and that choice brought me to Circleville Bible College (CBC) in fall of 1967. The call and the choice brought me to faith in the fact that I have been justified before God in Jesus Christ. The call and the choice got me involved in that early morning prayer meeting. The call and the choice led me to that prayer room in the old block dorm where I surrendered myself and offered up my future successes and/or failures to the glory of God. The call and the choice led me into an ongoing and growing walk with God that is sustained by following the leadership of the Holy Spirit.

The morning prayer meeting at CBC continued not just for three weeks but throughout the last three semesters that I was in school. About a dozen students became regulars. As an informal gathering, there was no designated leader for the gathering. In the absence of formally recognized leadership, however, leaders do emerge, whether formally or informally. Thus, over time, John Meadows and I became the "non-leaders" of the prayer meeting. We even developed our own traditions, including closing our time by singing the "Doxology," followed by shouting out a cheer:

V-I-C-T-O-R-Y, Victory is our battle cry!

John and I became close friends as we prayed together, although we had not always been friends. In fact, in our younger years we knew of one another, had formed opinions about each other, and had no desire to become friends.

John's mother, Dorothy Meadows, was a well-known evangelistic preacher in the Churches of Christ in Christian Union, and she held a number of leadership positions.

She and my parents knew one another well. Over the years, she had preached several times in the church Dad pastored. Her ministry in youth revivals and youth camps was a positive influence in my life.

John's father was a member of a different denomination, so he was seldom seen in our circles. Therefore, I knew of John only through his mother, and in spite of my high regard for her, I developed the opinion that John was something of a mama's boy, maybe even a sissy. On the other hand, John had come to the opinion that I was something of a tough guy or hoodlum. I'm sure that my rebellious attitude must have been the basis for that opinion.

The truth is that both John's opinion and mine were wrong! My opinion had begun to be challenged when we entered CBC and John became a member of the Ambassadors Quartet (a group of gospel singers and preachers who were sent out to represent the college in churches) along with some of my good friends. I remember a conversation soon after I had begun college as a freshman when I said to Phil Conrad, who was in the quartet and, in my eyes, had been something of a tough guy himself before surrendering to Jesus, "It must be tough having to travel around with that John Meadows."

Phil replied, "Actually, John's a pretty good guy when you get to know him." That left me wondering.

Then, a few weeks later, I was walking across campus one evening and saw that some guys had set up a bench press on the lawn. As I drew nearer, I realized that the guy lifting at the moment was John. To my great surprise, I discovered that John was pressing 160 pounds—certainly more than I could bench-press. So much for the sissy thing!

A new men's dorm was completed by Christmas, and when we moved in, John and I were assigned rooms next to each other. Gradually we became friends as we began to have more contact with each other. Then, as prayer partners, we began to respect one another more and more.

Late one evening in May 1970, just before John graduated from CBC and went on to Ohio State University in preparation for medical missions, and just before I transferred to Marion College (now Indiana Wesleyan University), we were together in the dormitory lounge. I have no idea now why we were both there, but a conversation began about something or another—most likely having to do with our future plans. About midnight we decided to pray together.

I don't remember at all what we set out to pray about. However, I do remember that out of that prayer we *found ourselves* making a commitment to one another. It was very simple. As I recall, **we agreed to stay in touch no matter where our lives took us and to encourage each other to stay in the middle of whatever God was doing**. As far as I know, the phrase "to stay in the middle of whatever God was doing" was a new concept to me. I have no idea what either of us thought that meant at the time.

I do know that I felt something of the weight of the times. I know that I had become curious about the trends among youth outside the church. I know I had been moved by reports of the revival among college students which had begun earlier that year at Asbury College in Wilmore, Kentucky. However, I do not remember thinking about God doing much of anything beyond what we knew in our small Christian subculture.

Several years later I discovered that in October of that same year, four Bible teachers had made a commitment to one another in a hotel room in Fort Lauderdale, Florida. Although these teachers were from very different backgrounds, each had been baptized in the Holy Spirit according to the charismatic/pentecostal experience. They had been called to intervene in a crisis when the primary leader of a ministry called the Holy Spirit Teaching Mission was exposed in serious sin. Derek Prince, Bob Mumford, Don Basham, and Charles Simpson were on the advisory board of that ministry and had published teaching material in its magazine, *New Wine*. Because of that crisis, they realized that their own lives and independent ministries were unprotected by any functional accountability. In the fear of God, they were moved to submit themselves and their ministries to one another. These teachers had no inkling at that point that what they had done would become a great blessing to many and a scandal to others.

At CBC in 1970, I knew nothing of these men, much less of the commitment they would soon make in that hotel room. Nor did I know that my commitment with John would lead me into relationship with these teachers and to the message that God was entrusting to them to proclaim. I had no idea that I had entered into what the Bible calls a covenant relationship with my friend John. I knew nothing then of Biblical covenants and their import.

Once again the call had come and the choice had been made. It would not be entirely wrong to see my spiritual journey in two parts: first, the path that led to that midnight prayer in a dormitory lounge in May 1970, and second, the path leading from that prayer, the path that is still unfolding even now as I write.

3

Finding a Wife

He who finds a wife finds a good thing and obtains favor from the Lord.
(Proverbs 18:22)

House and wealth are inherited from fathers, but a prudent wife is from the Lord.
(Proverbs 19:14)

It wasn't my own wisdom or a proven method of courtship that brought Patricia McKelvey and me together. Nothing in my life speaks more clearly of the favor of God toward me than does the wife that he provided for me. I wouldn't recommend the process by which our lives were joined, but I applaud and thank God for the result.

This is not the time to share all the details of our romance, but a summary is appropriate. I first remember meeting Pat at the Mount of Praise Camp Meeting in August 1963 when I was 14 years old. (In 1985, the Lord led Pat to accept her full name, Patricia, which means "noble one." Although it was difficult for her to accept that name as an appropriate description of who she is, I can no longer think of her as otherwise than "noble"—Patricia.) That year we worked together in the snack bar and became friends, even though Patricia was a few years older than me. I was in the throes of adolescence at the time, and she was a fun-loving, friendly, freckle-faced young woman. It was remarkable to me that Patricia even paid attention to me at all, given the difference in our ages. We enjoyed seeing each other again the following year at the camp. We began to develop a genuine friendship, even though not all my motives were pure.

The next year, 1965, after making a personal commitment to the Lord, Patricia enrolled as a student at Circleville Bible College in the same town where I was a junior in high school. At first, in September and into October, I would drive into the college specifically to see her, but our relationship was developing in a way that we both knew was going to damage her walk with God. I determined to break off the relationship because I did not want to be responsible before God for hurting her, even though at the time I was not pursuing the Lord myself. She had come to the same decision at that same time; thus, we agreed to stop relating to one another in any sort of romantic way.

Our friendship continued but did not grow much over the next couple of years since we did not get together except when we saw one another in some legitimate context. In 1967, after I entered CBC, we saw one another more because the college was small, we had a few classes together, and Patricia worked in the college library, where I often had to study. For the next two school years we continued relating as friends. During that time Patricia became engaged to another student. I was working on my studies, working part-time at Warden Skinner's Cardinal Market, and preaching somewhere an average of once a week. With that schedule, I did not do much dating.

The friendship began to grow again during my sophomore year. Patricia sprained her ankle and had to walk with crutches for several weeks. Because we had a class together just before lunch, I began to carry her lunch tray to her table and would sit at the same table with her and others. That might seem unusual, but at CBC dating couples were allowed to be together only at specified times and for specific lengths of time; thus, Patricia's fiancé was not permitted to serve her or even to sit at the same table with her. During the middle of the spring semester of 1969, Patricia broke her engagement; however, the breakup was not because of our friendship.

It was in January 1969 that the early morning prayer meeting had begun. Patricia became one of the regulars who met to pray every weekday morning. It was in this way that a spiritual bond was begun between us—in the context of the larger prayer group. Looking back now, it seems significant that Patricia and I had begun to connect this way so soon following my encounter with the Lord in the prayer room on that January morning and in the prayer meeting that was to prove so foundational to my own journey.

Our relationship took on a different dimension on Memorial Day weekend 1969. Following the Sunday night service at Campus Church, I gave Patricia a ride in my car back to her dormitory. Suffice it to say the romance began again, intensely.

By July, it was obvious to me that I had to make a choice. I did not want to hurt Patricia, especially so soon after her broken engagement. I was strongly attracted to her, an attraction that was obviously mutual. I came to the realization that I needed to decide whether or not I was willing for this relationship to be a serious one. Therefore, in July before Patricia went to Maine for a vacation with her family, we agreed to take the two weeks that she was to be gone as a time to search out before the Lord how serious we were willing to be if our relationship were to continue.

At the end of that time, I was certain that I liked Patricia very much and that I was also deeply attracted to her as a woman. However, it was only as I saw her enter the

Port Columbus Airport terminal, her face seemingly aglow after her flight back from Maine, that I *knew* that I was willing to marry this woman if the relationship developed that way. Ironically, it was not seeing me that had put such joy on her face, but rather the fact that the pilot had noticed her looking with fascination into the plane's cockpit at the instruments and had kindly invited her to come in and take a closer look.

By August we had agreed, jokingly to be sure, yet seriously at the same time, to marry. In early September I gave Patricia my high school class ring as a sign of our commitment to marry. For twenty years that class ring was as close as she got to having an engagement ring.

A few days later, our commitment was tested in a way that became a foundation stone in our relationship. My dad, who taught at CBC a couple of days each week, came to me after classes on Tuesday. He knew nothing about the "engagement" into which Patricia and I had entered. How sad is that! I must acknowledge that I was so independent and so foolish as to make this kind of commitment without ever even discussing it with my parents—let alone seeking their guidance and blessing. What a testimony to God's grace and favor that he has blessed the relationship in spite of my foolishness.

Thankfully, Dad came to me. Having heard that Patricia and I were dating, he felt that he had to share some concerns that he and my mom had about our relationship. He presented them to me clearly and, as I look back now, graciously. My initial response was to defend the relationship rather than to hear his heart. My big "defense" was to say, "But, Dad, I can't help it; I love her."

Dad replied, "Boy, you **decide** who you will love." This truth is so simple. Yet, it is also profound in a culture in which romantic love is usually perceived to be the basis and primary reason for relationships between men and women. In my foolishness, I couldn't begin to comprehend the reality and wisdom of these words at that time. However, over the next several days I did find myself wrestling with the concerns that Dad had brought up.

This wrestling led me to offer my desire for Patricia up to the Lord, similar in some respects to the way Abraham offered up Isaac. The following Saturday, while on our weekly date, I told Patricia that I needed to break off the relationship, that I couldn't marry her. I did not handle it in a graceful or even in a manly manner, but I did it. And as far as I knew, it was final.

Afterward, I drove her back to her dorm and let her out of the car and set off for Ward's Market, the grocery where I worked. I had hardly driven out of sight when the Lord spoke to me absolutely clearly, though inaudibly: "It's okay. You can marry Pat if you want," he said.

That was a long, painful afternoon and evening, for both of us, I'm sure. However, by the grace of God and the grace of Patricia, by 10:00 p.m. that Saturday evening we were once again engaged.

What about the concerns of my parents? They had brought up real issues that could have been potential problems for us in the years to come. However, because Dad brought them up, even in the face of my resistance, Patricia and I made decisions then about these matters, which provided the basis for us to deal with them later with minimal struggle. Thank God that Dad came to me. I am still grateful for my parents' love and concern.

Sadly, it was more than ten years later before I actually shared with Dad the impact of his coming to me and how important it had been to our marriage.

Patricia and I were married on July 10, 1971. Little did she know what she had entered into when our lives were joined together and our spiritual journeys began to merge.

****

Patricia had believed for some time that God was calling her to serve as a missionary. I had sensed a call to "ministry" since about age 12. Because there were only three options of which I knew—pastor, evangelist, or missionary, and since I was not aware of a specific call to one of these, soon after our engagement I decided to prepare for missionary work as well. Although even then that seemed an unusual way to make such a choice, I found an inner peace and a growing sense that this was the right direction as we began to plan for the future.

Patricia was to graduate from Circleville Bible College the following spring, in 1970. I would be finishing my junior year. CBC offered only a few degrees at the time: a two-year Christian workers certificate, a four-year bachelor of sacred literature degree, and a five-year bachelor of theology degree. I was in the five-year program but was not really interested in a typical career as a preacher.

My motivation at the time included elements of rebellion against the established thinking and reaction to the status quo of church life. Even so, I also had a deep and genuine conviction that there was a double standard in the church, the expectation of one kind of commitment from so-called "clergy" and another from the "laity." I was, and still am, convinced that all believers are called to commit 100% of their lives and energies to the service of the Lord—whether that service is "in the church," in the home, in the marketplace, or wherever.

Therefore, I did not want to be a pastor or an evangelist or a typical missionary. I decided to prepare to be a self-supporting missionary. Patricia supported me in this. We planned for me to finish that third year at CBC and then transfer into a teacher's college to get a degree. The goal was to go to another nation as a teacher so that I could earn a living while we reached out to people, held Bible studies in our home, and participated in a church in that locality if one existed.

Teach what? I knew I could teach Bible, but that would be "typical missionary work" and not likely to provide an income anyway. My favorite "secular" subject was history, but that did not seem like it would be that much help in getting a job in another nation. In school, I had always been gifted to understand grammar; therefore, I decided to major in English and get certified to teach in secondary schools. Soon after this, I began to plan to go on and get a graduate degree in teaching English as a second language.

Next question: What college? CBC was not accredited at the time, so the choices were rather slim when it came to finding a school that would accept my CBC credits. However, there were a few, and after inquiries and research and some prayer, I applied to Marion College (now Indiana Wesleyan University) in Marion, Indiana, and was accepted for the fall of 1970. Marion accepted two years of my CBC work, so that meant I could get a degree and certification after two years of hard work in Marion.

What do all these details have to do with a spiritual journey? That's an important question. Although I did not consciously recognize it at the time, I was beginning to find out some of the ways that God works to unfold and to accomplish his purposes in a person's life.

Sometimes God speaks. I have never heard him speak audibly; however, there have been several times over the past forty-two years when God has spoken so directly and clearly to me that I simply knew in the very depths of my spirit and mind that it was his voice. Sometimes what God has spoken have been words of insight about some matter. Sometimes he has given words of direction. Of the latter, a few times he has spoken in a way that made a choice clear and possible—such as when he said: "It's okay. You can marry Pat if you want." A few times, he has spoken words that I needed to obey. At least once God told me something that would happen, but there was nothing that I could do to make it happen.

Many times when God has spoken to me it has not been so direct and clear. Sometimes there has been simply an inner conviction or an unexpected insight that I have received as a thought or an inner sense. However, over time as I have continued to "think about the thought," I have realized that this thought or sense was foreign to me. It was not a way of thinking or an insight that was typical of my "way of thinking," and at times I would realize that it was actually beyond my "frame of reference" to think that way. Usually I find myself mentally wrestling with these kinds of words from God over a period of time. As I wrestle I will find confirmation in the Scripture if they are from the Lord (sometimes by searching for it, but more often by stumbling onto it). I also will often hear someone else say something or I will read something in a source other than the Bible that will also provide a measure of confirmation.

Frankly, many times only in hindsight do I recognize that God has spoken. A thought comes to my mind or passes through it, and later after acting on it, or after something comes to pass, I realize that the thought was not my own.

Later in my journey, I was to receive insight about God speaking in these ways when I learned about the tripartite nature of man—spirit, soul, and body. I am sure that God has spoken many more times than I am aware of. Sometimes, because of various distractions, I probably have not heard God when he has spoken, especially in these indirect ways (the still, small voice?). At times I am sure that his words have landed in my busy, trafficked mind and have been lost, like the seeds picked up from the roadway by the birds in the parable Jesus told.

God has often directed my life by words that he has spoken. God is sovereign, omniscient, and omnipotent. God knows me completely. He has worked through my own motivations, my own desires, and my own choices—even my bad motivations, desires, and choices—to move me in the direction that he had chosen. Make no mistake about it: God has not approved of or rewarded my bad motivations, desires, and choices; there are negative consequences that will result from these. But even in my failings I "know that **for those who love God all things work together for good,** for those who are called according to his purpose." (Romans 8.28, bold print added for emphasis)

God has worked providentially through circumstances and situations to press me into the path that he has prepared for me. Sometimes I have been conscious of—and sometimes oblivious to—God's providential directions, but he has been at work, nonetheless. The further I get down the path of my life, the more I can look back and discern a straight path through what had appeared to be twists and turns during the journey.

The primary place where God's direction for life is revealed is in the Scriptures, of course, as the Holy Spirit opens my understanding and applies them to life. Much of what it means to follow God and to accomplish his purpose is simply to know and obey what he has revealed in the Bible. Nothing takes the place of trusting in the Lord Jesus, of depending on the Holy Spirit and obeying the Scriptures.

The point is, however, that no matter how unspiritual the method by which I made the decisions necessary to prepare for missions may seem, the reality is that God was moving me in a direction that I had no ability to foresee. Had Patricia and I understood where the path of our life was actually heading at that time, I am pretty sure that we never would have set out on it. I probably would have chosen a "safer life"—one that I was familiar with and with which I would feel more comfortable. Thank God! I did not know, and so I did not refuse.

4

Setting a Course

In the fall of 1970 I entered Marion College as a junior. The studies were intense, mostly because I had to take so many courses in order to fulfill the requirements of the English education program in time to do my student teaching in the spring of 1972. In looking back, however, it was not the things I studied that were the keys to where God was taking my life. Rather, it was people and ideas and incidents that made the most impact.

At Marion, I became friends with the linguistics professor, Russ Cooper. Russ, after graduating from Marion College a few years earlier, had gone on to study linguistics so that he could be a Bible translator. He had had contact with Wycliffe Bible Translators and with their educational organization, the Summer Institute of Linguistics. He had done his graduate work at the University of Hawaii and had spent time in Papua New Guinea gathering material to use in the dissertation required by his Ph.D. program. In 1970, Russ returned to Marion to teach for a few years; his goal was to stir up others to respond to the need for Bible translators before he and his family returned to Papua New Guinea as members of Wycliffe.

I took several linguistics classes that Russ taught. Although I enjoyed the classes, it was the man himself who was more influential in my life. Russ was, and probably still is, a nonconformist in the highest sense of the word. I found him to be a man of great intelligence with an uncompromising dedication to God; he also refused to conform unthinkingly to the status quo, whether to social or religious expectations.

The Lord used Russ to sow in me the seed about Bible translation. Of particular impact was the fact that Russ was influential in bringing former Wycliffe translator Dr. John Crawford, at the time a professor in English and linguistics at the University of North Dakota, into Marion to make several presentations at a missions conference. Little did I know that meeting Dr. Crawford then would open a door for me several years later.

Russ Cooper was among the most excellent teachers of my school experience. But the Lord also used him to challenge the narrow boxes of my thinking—a more important contribution by far.

Those "boxes" had already begun to be challenged, of course. The ministry of the Holy Spirit in opening up the Scripture to me had begun to open a new way of thinking in me. The very climate, the thoughts and trends of the sixties, had influenced me to begin to see the world through different eyes than those with which I'd grown up. Rev. David Van Hoose's Psychology class at CBC had also contributed to this development because Rev. Van Hoose (who also is my first cousin) confronted us with ways of thinking and ways of explaining the human predicament that were new to me.

I am chagrined when I think about how some of these ideas had influenced me in a negative way, one that was incompatible with the Bible. Yet, had I not been exposed to them, I am not at all sure that I would have been able later to approach the Bible looking for real answers. It was important to my journey for me to ask the hard questions, even if for a time I was influenced by the wrong answers. Otherwise, I probably would have remained in the box of the evangelical/fundamentalist/holiness worldview that I had grown up thinking was the absolute truth. Thank God, much in that framework was and is true, and it has been foundational to my life. However, as long as I held it to be *truth* in an absolute and final sense, I could not progress on the journey toward the ultimate Truth.

Ultimate Truth is absolute and final. Ultimate Truth is the revelation of God in His Son, the "Logos," and is unveiled to us by the Holy Spirit in the Scriptures.[23] At best,

---

[23] Although my understanding of God's people and of the church was only budding at this point in my journey, there is an essential reality that should be considered in the matter of seeking Ultimate Truth.

Many Protestants tend to forget that the Scriptures were written by Spirit-inspired men of God (2 Peter 1:20–21) for "the people of God." Certainly, individual study is essential, but Scripture is not to be "privately interpreted." We are to seek the understanding of Scripture in the context of the people of God, past and present. One of the great disasters of the division among God's people and the churches is that we are more deficient in understanding and applying Scripture accurately than we ought to be. If only God's people would take Jesus's prayer in John 17:17–23 seriously; if only we would heed the apostle Paul's exhortation: "I therefore, a prisoner for the Lord, urge you to walk in a manner worthy of the calling to which you have been called, with all humility and gentleness, with patience, bearing with one another in love, eager to maintain the unity of the Spirit in the bond of peace. There is one body and one Spirit—just as you were called to the one hope that belongs to your call—one Lord, one faith, one baptism, one God and Father of all, who is over all and through all and in all. But grace was given to each one of us according to the measure of Christ's gift.... And he gave the apostles, the prophets, the evangelists, the shepherds and teachers, to equip the saints for the work of ministry, for building up the body of Christ, until we all attain to the unity of the faith and of the knowledge of the Son of God, to mature manhood, to the measure of the stature of the fullness of Christ, so that we may no longer be children, tossed to and fro by the waves and carried about by every

we finite human beings, as the apostle Paul wrote, "... know in part.... For now we see in a mirror dimly ...." (1 Corinthians 13:9, 12) In Christ Jesus we know the Truth, who is first and foremost a person: "I am the Way, and the Truth, and the Life ...." (John 14:6) And, though we know him, we also are enabled by his Spirit to increase in the knowledge of God (i.e., Colossians 1:10). Living things are growing things. If we are not growing in the Truth, then we must consider the real possibility that we are dead to Truth.[24]

A significant aspect of the journey is that God brings people, ideas, and circumstances into our lives in order to cause us to ask questions. God makes us face things that expose the limitations of our present knowledge so that we will seek him for more knowledge. However, it is altogether too easy for us to rest on our unconscious assumptions and even religious-sounding clichés, rather than to face head-on the discomfort of actively trusting in Jesus the Truth, even when we are past the ability to understand.

Bible translator J. B. Phillips wrote a little book titled *Your God Is Too Small.* I have had a copy of the book for years, although I have never gotten around to reading it. I keep it around because, every time I see it, the title reminds me that I need to keep growing in knowing God and his ways rather than to measure God according to the limits of my present understanding.

Thank God for those whom he has used to crack open the boxes in which I would have sought to confine him. Thank God that he has held onto me and led me even when I started to stray onto some dead-end path, either in ideas or in behavior. Truly he is Lord of the journey!

****

---

wind of doctrine, by human cunning, by craftiness in deceitful schemes. Rather, speaking the truth in love, we are to grow up in every way into him who is the head, into Christ, from whom the whole body, joined and held together by every joint with which it is equipped, when each part is working properly, makes the body grow so that it builds itself up in love." (Ephesians 4:1–7, 11–16)

[24] "Christianity is not a series of truths in the plural, but rather truth 'spelled' with a capital 'T.' Truth about total reality, not just about religious things. Biblical Christianity is Truth concerning total reality—and the intellectual holding of that total Truth and then living in the light of that Truth."— Francis Schaeffer, *Address at the University of Notre Dame*, April 1981, as quoted by Nancy Pearcey in the epigraph of *Total Truth: Liberating Christianity from Its Cultural Captivity* (Wheaton, IL: Crossway Books, 2004).

In addition to using people and subjects in my academic experience, God also was using the broader culture of the times to move me along. As horrible and as untenable as it may sound to many Christians, rock-and-roll music has proven to be part of the journey too.

Listening to rock-and-roll music was one of many no-no's in my family and church training—for that matter most things in popular culture were no-no's. It seemed sometimes that our view of the Christian life was defined more by what we were *not* allowed to do than by the things that we could do. I realize now that there was an underlying wisdom behind many of those no-no's. However, at the time, the rules of the Christian life seemed to me more like moralisms than like wisdom for living. Part of this may have had to do with the way they were presented, but I am sure a significant part also had to do with the way I "heard" them.

In my childhood and teen years, one of the indicators of whether or not I was "on" or "off" regarding spiritual things was whether or not I listened to rock music. We didn't believe that any form of dancing was moral. It was not only that rock music was dance music but also that rock musicians, starting with Elvis Presley (in the white community at least), made sexually suggestive movements while performing. Rock music was also a symbol of teen rebellion. Besides that, the rock beat, derived largely from Afro-American music, was associated with the pagan music of Africa—music that in many cases was religiously oriented but toward pagan gods and spirits.

Therefore, when I was "saved" I didn't listen to rock and roll. And when I was "backslidden" I did listen. For instance, I was in a "saved" period when the Beatles came onto the scene; therefore, I never identified with Beetle-mania. When I made that final commitment of my life to the Lord in April 1966, rock music went out of my life.

At this point, let me say that there were and there are good reasons to evaluate the morality and the social impact of dancing, of sexually suggestive movements, and of the music of pagan worship. There are most certainly valid and understandable reasons for objections. However, there will be problems when we simply ban cultural expressions like these as sins without training people to understand the Biblical principles and wisdom that they violate. In addition, we open the door to confusion when we teach people that something like dancing, for instance, is a sin without qualifying it in any way. When a thinking person who has been taught to reject all dancing as sin discovers that the Bible refers to some dancing in a positive way, even as an expression of worship, that person is almost sure to wonder about the credibility of the whole teaching. In overreaction, that person may well accept all dancing without using any discernment at all.

I did listen to contemporary folk music in the mid-sixties—even within the hearing of my parents. It was not unusual for me to sit at the kitchen table on a school night, doing my high school homework, eating a triple-decker peanut butter, mayonnaise, and strawberry jam sandwich (or two), while listening to the folk music program on WBNS out of Columbus, Ohio. Ironically, the lyrics of folk music and the often radical ideas of musicians such as Joan Baez, Bob Dylan, Barry McGuire, and Peter, Paul, and Mary were to prove just as influential, if not more so, on the thinking of the sixties generation than the often inane lyrics of the fifties and early sixties rock-and-roll tunes would.

However, I never questioned the sinfulness of rock music until after I had been in Bible College for a year or two when our Academic Dean, Rev. George Blackstone, returned from a conference at which he had heard a presentation about the evil of rock music. The presentation had so shocked and concerned him that he played a tape recording of it for our chapel service. The speaker, Bob Larson, had been in the rock scene to some degree and then had become a Christian. He, too, rejected all rock music at that time and had written a book against it titled *Hippies, Hindus, and Rock and Roll*. As I remember it, Larson dealt with two matters: (1) the sexual effect of rock and roll's syncopated beat and (2) the messages about drugs and Eastern religions conveyed by the lyrics of many rock songs during that period. Larson played sections of numerous songs to illustrate his point. (Interestingly enough, within a short time, Bob Larson himself began to make a distinction between the problem of bad content versus the rock music form.)

The message, however, had an unintended effect on me. I was preaching an average of once a week at that time, most often to young people. I began to think that I should listen to these songs also if this was the music the young people were listening to; then, I thought, I would be able to address and counter the messages of their music more effectively. Thus, I began to listen to rock music on the radio. When I moved into a dorm at Marion College, one of the guys in the room next door had a large collection of record albums and 8-track tapes. With his permission, I began to listen often to his recordings; these exposed me to rock recordings that never would have made the then-popular "top forty" format on AM radio.

Because of Bob Larson's presentation, I cultivated the habit of listening first to the lyrics, an activity that became easier when many artists began to add song lyrics to the album package, something that had not been done in the earlier rock and roll in which the lyrics, for the most part, were secondary to the music. However, as I listened I developed a taste for the rock sound itself. In a sense, I entered into my generation in a fuller way, whether for good or for ill.

It was in '70 or '71 that I first heard a broadcast of *The Scott Ross Show*. Scott's radio broadcast was a syndicated program originating in Freeville, New York; WCOL, a Columbus rock station, had begun to air the show in our area. Scott Ross had been a New York City disc jockey and had been instrumental in introducing the music of the Rolling Stones to the USA. He had married a member of the Ronettes—one of the major girl groups of the mid-sixties. Scott and his wife, Nedra, had become Christians, but he did not lose his interest in contemporary music.

By 1969 a group of believers had begun to come together with Scott and Nedra to form Love Inn, which, in effect, was a Christian commune.[25] Scott developed a rock music program, playing rock songs that he discussed from a Christian point of view. It was also not unusual for him to "preach" a little and to pray over the air for needs of listeners. From this program, I began to discover that there were a few Christians who were recording Christian lyrics in a folk and rock format. I had no idea when I came across *The Scott Ross Show* that I was coming into contact with influences that would begin to shape the direction of my spiritual growth and of my life.

****

In 1967 the hippie phenomenon in the Haight-Ashbury district of San Francisco hit its peak in terms of publicity and maybe even in influence during the Summer of Love. That summer the media publicized the public "orgies" of free sex and hallucinogenic drug use commonly called love-ins. Thousands of young people went to San Francisco, and the behaviors common to that movement, and to some degree the attitudes and philosophies behind it, spread across the nation.

In the midst of this counterculture movement, however, Jesus began to reveal himself, sometimes dramatically, to a few of the young participants in this counterculture. Most of these had begun to see the hippie lifestyle for the dead-end that it was and were continuing their search for meaning and truth in other directions. Gradually the number of "freaks" (as the counterculture youth called themselves) who turned to Jesus began to grow. Most of them, however, did not, and probably could not, identify with traditional Christianity. Rather, they simply

---

[25] The story of Scott's early life and the story of Love Inn's early years can be found in the book *Scott Free* written by Scott with John and Elizabeth Sherrill (Old Tappen, NJ: Chosen Books, 1976).

continued life as "freaks"; however, they began to worship Jesus, to study the Scriptures, and to seek to live the life of disciples that they saw recorded in the New Testament. In so doing, they began to lay aside the lifestyle of drug use and sexual promiscuity, howbeit some more gradually than others.[26]

However, my first-remembered inkling that God was doing something new in our generation, other than what I had picked up from *The Scott Ross Show*, came from a more religious source. In February 1970 word spread to Circleville Bible College that an unusual moving of the Holy Spirit had begun in a chapel service at Asbury College in Wilmore, Kentucky. That service lasted without dismissal for several days. It was characterized by public confession of sin, repentance, and surrender to the Lord Jesus Christ. Even while the meeting continued, students began to fan out to other Christian colleges and "the revival" began to spread.

At CBC we did not experience dramatic results from this moving of the Spirit; however, I believe it played a big part in motivating John Meadows and me to make that commitment to one another the following May.

To the best of my memory it was not until the fall of 1971, after Patricia and I had married, that I began to be aware of the stirring among youth involved in the counterculture. Then several things happened about the same time, though I cannot remember the exact order of occurrence. *Time* magazine ran a cover article on the Jesus Movement that included reports of huge ocean baptismal services and a new form of music. John Meadows told me about some encounters with long-haired hippie types, openly and boldly committed to Jesus, at Ohio State University, where he had gone to school. I found an ad in *Campus Life* magazine offering a selection of twenty or twenty-five long-play record albums of "Jesus Music." I ordered five of them at the special price of $17, which included postage.

Since our Christmas in 1971 promised to be short on gifts, Patricia talked me into saving the records—before listening to them—in order to wrap them up as a gift for Christmas morning. I had a musical feast that morning as I listened to album after album—most of the time lying on the floor with my head between the two small speakers of our cheap Webcor phonograph. For the most part, the music was not profound musically and not technically well produced. However, it was "alive" with a simple love for Jesus and the sounds of my generation.

---

[26] A number of books and Internet websites document and describe the Jesus Movement; however, one of the best researched and documented accounts is from Jerry Eskridge, *God's Forever Family: The Jesus Movement in America* (New York: Oxford University Press, 2013; also available in digital and audible formats).

Later that week Patricia and I drove to Indianapolis to a concert held in the basement of a big, old, red-brick Baptist church building north of downtown. It featured a band simply called "e." According to the ads I'd seen, e band had previously opened for big-name rock bands, but the members had begun to follow Jesus and were now singing for him. An odd assortment of probably 150 to 200 people gathered in that basement. Some looked like they had stepped out of a conservative Baptist or even a Pentecostal church. Others looked like college students. A few might have been professionals. And quite a number seemed like they might have floated in from the Haight-Ashbury or might still be trying to find their way home from the Woodstock Festival.

It was the atmosphere of warm fellowship, of simple but obvious dedication to Jesus, and of enthusiasm to see others know him that moved me deeply. It spoke to the hunger in me for something more than I had known, something that had the taste of the gospels and the book of Acts.

In addition, e was excellent. Most of their set that night consisted of rearranged Christmas carols—old songs sung in a new musical way with a fresh attitude. I'll never forget the end of that concert—a moving rendition of, incredibly enough, "Carol of the Bells." Obviously, the power wasn't in the lyrics of that song, nor was it actually in the arrangement. Rather, it was the anointing of the Holy Spirit upon these long-haired freaks as they simply used what they knew to give glory to their Lord and Savior. When the last note of the song ended, silence reigned! After what seemed like a long time, the bass player reached back and flipped the switch on his amp. The room was so still that, even where we were sitting cross-legged on a blanket in the back of the room, I clearly heard the snap of that switch. Then the room exploded in spontaneous praise—not for the band, but for the Lord Jesus.

The music on the recordings and in e's concert and the experience of God's presence in that basement spoke to the deepest part of my being. A hunger to *know* the reality of a living and present God more fully began to surface in me.

Not too long after this concert, evangelist Leighton Ford held a crusade in Marion. He brought in a musician named John Fischer to work with youth. Fischer had attended Wheaton College and was not from the youth counterculture, although he had obviously had contact with it. There was something new, fresh, even a bit radical about his message and music. Fischer communicated a deep desire for reality in relationship to God and to all of life. He fed the growing hunger in me. His lyrics and spoken words also challenged status quo Christianity—both in church activity and in personal life.

A month or so later, John and Vicki Meadows came out to Marion to visit Patricia and me. Before too long, John and I left the ladies visiting in the living room. We placed the stereo on the floor in the furniture-less spare room where Patricia and I stored unpacked boxes, and we lay down between the speakers. As we listened to the Jesus music records, we started catching up on things.

John told me about a Saturday evening Bible study that he had started for the Sunday School class he was leading at the North Columbus Church of Christ in Christian Union. A few Sunday School class members had continued after the first couple of weeks—but the Bible study had taken a turn. John had run into a long-haired fellow named Dick Pope who was wearing a badge that spoke about Jesus. During their conversation, John had sensed that, in spite of the hair and hippie-looking clothes, Dick was genuinely a brother in the Lord and had invited him to the Bible study. He had come—and had kept on coming and had begun to bring some other Jesus freaks with him. John had found these young Christians deeply enthused about Jesus. They also not only read the Bible—they read it hungrily and simply believed it and began to practice what they read. John shared how this was stirring up his hunger for God.

Then he told me that after several weeks he had heard one of these brothers making strange sounds quietly during a prayer time. At some point, John realized the man must have been praying in tongues. In spite of the fact that John had been raised believing that the modern-day expression of tongues was not Biblical, he was not willing to write this off. He had seen the fruit of this man's walk in the Lord and had himself been stirred toward the Lord in his fellowship with these brothers. At this point, I grew cautious and warned John to be careful that he not get caught up in error.

I had no interest in speaking in tongues. However, over the next few months I began to hear that several of my fellow students, well known for participating in off-campus parties that included drinking, drug use, and sexual immorality, had surrendered to Jesus. I heard that they had begun to attend a nearby Pentecostal church and were speaking in tongues.

In addition, several times during this period, Patricia and I went to Anderson, Indiana, to worship with a group of Jesus People in the basement of a house. The obvious presence and activity of God among these brothers and sisters made a significant impact on us both. Only after several visits did we find out that many of these people also believed in speaking in tongues. I began to read and re-read the passages that mention tongues in the book of Acts and in 1 Corinthians 12–14. I began to wonder about the place of the gifts of the Holy Spirit in the life of the church.

In the early months of 1972, I read three books that added to my awakened hunger and thirst for God, for the Body of Christ, and for spiritual power. First, at the Leighton Ford crusade I bought Ray C. Stedman's book *Body Life: The Church Comes Alive.*[27] For the first time, I had found someone who was speaking with insight and wisdom to my desire for the reality of the church as the Body of Christ. Here was a pastor and teacher who took seriously what the Scripture teaches about relationships in the church and about the working of the Holy Spirit through the church—and he even had taken definite steps to make room for the working of the Spirit in his church.

Second, somehow I got hold of Chuck Smith's book *The Reproducers: New Life for Thousands.*[28] I could not lay down this simple little book, which documented the work of the Holy Spirit in bringing thousands of young people to Jesus through the ministry of what had been a small church in Costa Mesa, California, a church called Calvary Chapel. Who would have guessed that this movement would give birth to hundreds of churches around the world and that the folk-rock music of its young converts would become the standard for large segments of the church over the next couple of decades? I surely didn't, but I did know that I wanted the reality of church life that the book described.

Third, I read Hal Lindsey's book *Satan Is Alive and Well on Planet Earth.*[29] To my chagrin now, I must say that this book had some credibility with me only because I had read and believed Lindsey's previous book on Biblical prophecy, *The Late Great Planet Earth*—a view of eschatology that I have come to believe more harmful than helpful. *Satan Is Alive and Well on Planet Earth*, however, described a realm of evil spiritual activity of which I knew little or nothing. So ignorant was I of the realm of the occult, of witchcraft, and of the demonic that only three years or so before that time I had thought it probable that when the gospels speak of Jesus casting out demons that it really meant that he was healing mentally ill people. I had begun to be aware by 1972, however, that many from the youth culture who had not turned to Jesus were exploring the occult.

That same spring when I was student teaching at Marion High School, one of my students wrote a paper describing her belief in and practice of "white witchcraft."

---

[27] Published by G/L Regal Books, Glendale, CA, 1972, Stedman was pastor of the Peninsula Bible Church in Palo Alto, California. John Fischer was a member of this church and had recommended the book.

[28] Chuck Smith with Hugh Steven, (Glendale, CA: G/L Regal Books, 1972).

[29] Hal Lindsey with C. C. Carlson, originally published by Zondervan, Grand Rapids, MI, 1970.

Only with some difficulty did I come to the realization that she was serious. Lindsay's book helped me realize that the Bible was really true when it spoke of these matters. It was also influential in that I began to be aware that there are realms that I cannot "know" by means of my mind or my physical senses only.

As a student teacher, I taught four classes—three of "regular" senior English and one of senior honors students. In a way beyond any previous personal experience, through my contact with my students I began to see the lostness and hopelessness of some and the searching through drugs and intellectual and spiritual ideas of others. I became aware that the church as I had known it was essentially irrelevant and powerless to deal with the problems of that generation.

In June of 1972, John Meadows and I joined nearly 100,000 young people who descended on Dallas, Texas, for Explo '72. This event, sponsored by Campus Crusade, was set up to train young people in Crusade's method of evangelism. Frankly, I didn't get all that much from the training. However, at that event I met and worshipped with Christian young people from every conceivable background and form of church. About 80,000 of us met in the Cotton Bowl for the evening celebrations. On Saturday, an estimated 160,000 of us attended an all-day Jesus music festival.

During that week in Dallas a transformation that had begun several years before was accomplished. No longer would I be only Steve Humble, Christian and child of the holiness movement. From that time on, I would primarily be Steve Humble, disciple of Jesus and member of my own generation. I had irrevocably identified with what I saw God doing in my day.

5

Moved by the Spirit

As it turned out, key steps in working out my identification as a follower of Jesus in my own generation were to be taken while working alongside Franklin Hauser, a man of my parents' generation, in the context of a holiness church, the Waite Park Wesleyan Church in northeast Minneapolis.

It's amazing how seemingly insignificant and unrelated events can open the door to a major step in the path of one's life. After Patricia and I had moved to Marion, Indiana, for my last year in college, we began to look for a church. Although I had been in Marion the year before and had visited several churches, I had not connected with any. It was important to Patricia, especially, that we have a church home in Marion.

The second Sunday after we had moved into our apartment, we attended the evening service at the South Marion Friends Church—why, I don't really know. Perhaps it was because one of our favorite professors at Circleville Bible College, Dr. Amos Henry, was a Quaker. South Marion Friends Church was evangelical and held to the holiness message with which we had grown up. That first Sunday night, we saw the Brookshires, a couple whom we had met briefly a month and a half earlier.

We had driven out to Marion for a couple of days in July in order to find a place to live. Following up on a lead about a trailer near the campus that might be for rent, we drove to the place and found that there were two trailers on a small lot. No one was home at the supposedly available trailer, so I walked next door to see if someone there could tell us how to contact the owner. I knocked on the door—a normal knock on a wooden house door, but a bang on the metal trailer door. I heard a man yell brusquely, "Come on in, and don't knock the door down."

I opened the door and stepped inside gingerly. There I saw an elderly man sitting on the couch and an elderly woman standing in the kitchen area. He was as surprised to see a stranger as I had been to be invited in. It turned out that he had seen us pull up and thought that we were the couple who had lived next door the previous school year. The man invited me in for coffee. I called Patricia in, and we had our first visit with Lucius and Minnie Brookshire, and our first cups of Luzianne coffee—instant coffee with chicory. After running into the Brookshires again at South Marion Friends Church, we shared many visits over the next nine months. Almost every

Sunday night after church, we went to the Brookshires' trailer to enjoy Luzianne coffee and day-old, or older, doughnuts.

Our first year of marriage was rich in experience and lean in finance. I had been able to get a job, through the college, working twenty hours a week at the South Marion Boys Club. My check came through the college business office; I would stop by the office, sign the check, and leave the money to cover tuition costs. Patricia had saved a few hundred dollars the year before while working at General Electric in Circleville. After moving to Marion, she found a job soliciting telephone catalog sales for the local Sears store. She brought home $41 a week.

We made it through Christmas by living very carefully on Patricia's pay and the money she had saved. We shared our Christmas dinner on the evening of Christmas Day with Lucius and Minnie, who came over to eat soup beans and corn bread with us. We found a grocery that sold baloney for 39 cents a pound—and we ate a lot of it. Later we were told that this grocery had once been shut down a while for selling horse meat as hamburger. Who knows what may have been in the baloney we ate.

Soon after Christmas, the transmission in our 1965 Comet broke down. There were no replacements available for that type transmission in any junkyard within 200 miles. We had to junk the car for $20, receiving that much only because the tires were good. Our elderly friend, Lucius, helped us find a 1963 Ford for $299.

Then we were broke—down to $41 a week—but we were always able to pay our bills, and most of the time we had some food. Patricia got pregnant in February. She went to a doctor once to confirm the pregnancy; there were no home tests available in those days. We had no money for prenatal care.

One week we had no money and just a few cans of hominy, some crackers, and some sauerkraut for food. The sauerkraut was important; Patricia ate it cold every morning to settle her stomach during the period of morning sickness, and then she took crackers to work for her lunch. (According to her, that's about all she could eat during the day because of the battle with morning sickness.) As far as I can remember we told no one about our lack of money and food; however, every night that particular week, people from South Marion Friends Church invited us to their homes to eat dinner. The pastor and his wife had us come to Sunday dinner. Then, on Sunday evening after church, we arrived home to find two bags of groceries and $20 by the door to our apartment.

Another time when we were flat broke I opened my mailbox in the college student center and found a blank envelope containing four $5 bills. Some way or another God always provided enough for us to get by.

Patricia and I got involved in the bus ministry at South Marion Friends Church. Along with another couple, we rode a Sunday School bus each Sunday morning in order to make friends with the children and to help keep order on the bus. As we got off the bus one Sunday in early January 1972, Neal Hauser, a fellow Marion College student, met us and asked if I would fill in as teacher in the College and Career Sunday School class. I agreed to do so. To my surprise and relief, the lesson that Sunday covered Mark 8:34–38, a passage from which I had preached many times.

Neal was impressed by the lesson I presented, apparently thinking that I had presented it completely extemporaneously. After the Sunday evening service, Neal came to me and asked if I had ever considered being a youth pastor. I told him about our plans to be self-supporting missionaries.

A few days later, Neal approached me in the college student center. He told me that his dad, a pastor in Minneapolis, was looking for a youth pastor. Neal had told his dad about me, and his dad had requested that I write to him and tell him about myself. I offhandedly said that I would consider it but actually gave it no serious thought at the time since I "knew" where we were headed.

A month or so later I realized that I had neither written to Neal's dad nor had I even given the request consideration. Yet I had not been able to forget about the request either. Therefore, I wrote a letter describing the facts of my life and informed Pastor Hauser that I was not interested in being a youth pastor.

Not long after that, Neal approached me again to say that his father was coming to Marion College to visit Neal and his siblings. Neal said that Pastor Hauser wanted to meet Patricia and me at that time. Seeking to be polite, I invited him, through Neal, to come to dinner at our apartment while he was in town. He accepted.

On the appointed evening, when the doorbell rang I went down the stairs and opened the door. I came face to face with a sandy-haired teddy bear of a man, probably 6 feet 2 inches and 230 pounds. By the time we had exchanged greetings and started up the stairs I had already begun to connect with Pastor Hauser. Before the evening was over, a desire to be with him had begun to grow in me. This was confusing since I "knew" that we were headed for the mission field.

Over the next few weeks the desire to work with Pastor Hauser continued to increase. Therefore, in early April when he contacted us and invited us to fly up to visit the Waite Park Wesleyan Church in order to be interviewed by the church board and to meet the people, we agreed. At the time we still "knew" that we were to go to graduate school and then to the mission field, but we also had a strong pull to be with Pastor Hauser again.

On Friday, April 30, Patricia and I flew to Minneapolis to spend a weekend there. Wes and Jan Long met us at the airport and took us to dinner at The Steak House in Columbia Heights. Even though Wes and Jan were my parents' ages, we found ourselves very comfortable with them.

After the meal we went to meet the church board members and their spouses in the Fireside Room at the Waite Park Wesleyan Church building. I don't remember much about the interview except for one unforgettable moment: We were sitting in a large circle. A sixtyish-looking man, sitting almost directly across the room from me, looked me straight in the eye and asked in a soft-spoken yet authoritative-sounding voice, "If we make you our youth pastor, what will be your program?"

Realizing that my answer would most likely disqualify me, I replied with virtually no hesitation: "Sir, I've been using my energy to get through college. I've been planning to go on to graduate school. My wife and I have been planning to go into foreign missions. I don't have a program. The only thing I'd know to do would be to look for any young people who are ready to begin a serious Bible study and see what God would do."

There was no response to this answer. The interview simply went on for some time after that and then ended with a time of sharing refreshments and informal conversation. During this fellowship time, however, board member Herb Pearson said to me: "If you are offered a position as youth pastor here, it will be because of the way you answered the question that George [Walquist] asked about your program. Our youth have had one program after another, and there has been little to show for it."

Patricia and I were indeed offered the position, and after a few days of prayer and thought we came to the assurance that it was God's will for us take the offer. Thus, in early July 1972, shortly after I participated in the Explo '72 conference in Dallas, we packed up a U-Haul trailer, hitched it to the back of our baby-blue '63 Ford, and headed for Minneapolis.

****

In only nineteen months in Waite Park Wesleyan Church, we were adopted into that church family so fully that even now, forty-five years later, we still think of the people of that church as "ours." Much of the vision of Christ's church and of the kingdom of God that we are still wrestling to work out and to live, I received in "seed" form during those months.

We lived in an apartment in the church building. In addition to being youth pastors, we also did the janitorial work. This living situation put us right at the heart of the church community, making us easily accessible to everyone and allowing us to quickly get a sense of the pulse of the church's life.

We inherited two youth functions. We became responsible for three Sunday School classes—the junior high class, the high school class, and the college/career (young adults). We also led a Wednesday night youth meeting for all three age groups, held at the same time that adults and younger children in the church also had their own programs.

When we arrived that July, the youth functions were virtually "dead." Most of the young people who participated seemed to be there because it was expected, or mandated, by their parents.

There was one bright spot. The church had held a missions conference in the spring. The main speaker had been Paul Decker, who had been a missionary in Africa. (I had heard Decker speak during the January 1972 Spiritual Emphasis week at Marion College.) Decker had had experiences in Africa that had moved him to think and act outside the box of the typical Wesleyan, holiness perspective. While at Waite Park, Decker had ministered to Laura, a troubled teen and an intelligent young lady with cerebral palsy. During the ministry session, Decker had discerned the influence of evil spirits working in the girl and had identified and cast out fifteen or sixteen specific demons. The change in Laura had been dramatic. Her deliverance had made quite a stir in the church, especially among the adults, a number of whom gained a sense of expectation and faith for the youth.

That summer, on Sunday mornings Pastor Hauser was teaching on the gifts of the Holy Spirit—certainly a radical topic in those circles, and a timely one for me given the contacts that I'd had with Jesus People over the previous months. In addition, Pastor Hauser was inviting different guest speakers to minister during the Sunday night services. Most, if not all, of these speakers were either Pentecostal or Charismatic.

One Sunday evening soon after we arrived, instead of a speaker, Pastor Hauser had invited the TV Choir from Soul's Harbor, a large Independent Assembly of God church in downtown Minneapolis. I don't remember anything about the group's singing. However, during the last song of their presentation, several members of the choir began to circulate among the congregation. One young man came to me and began to pray quietly over me. Part of his prayer was in tongues—the first time I had actually ever heard anyone pray in tongues. I had no strong reaction to this other than to be aware that it seemed appropriate and that God's presence seemed quite near while this young man prayed for me. (One of the young women also prayed with Patricia. She responded to that young lady's prayer in tongues quite differently than I had responded to the prayer in tongues for me.)

This incident fed my growing hunger to have more of the Lord in my life. The next morning I went downstairs to the church sanctuary to pray. I remember saying fervently to the Lord, "If you want me to have the gift of tongues, I would like to have it." I was thinking of 1 Corinthians 12:11, which says that the Holy Spirit apportions the spiritual gifts to individuals according to his will. I did not expect an immediate answer, but I believe that I clearly heard the Lord speaking in my spirit, "You will, but not now." Immediately a peace came over me, a confidence that God was at work and that I would indeed have the gift of tongues at the right time.

Within a couple of weeks of our arrival at Waite Park, I announced to the church that we would be beginning a Bible study for youth in our apartment on Tuesday nights. I specifically asked the parents not to force their teens to come, because it seemed right to have an activity for those who were personally motivated toward God. The first Tuesday five teens showed up. The second Tuesday, three came. These three teens became the first to show real commitment, but gradually over the next month or so a few more began to come to the Bible study. Fifteen to twenty youth from that Bible study became the core group for all that happened over the next year and a half.

On one of the first Sundays after our move, I saw a young man of about 19 or 20 who had fairly long hair. Outside of the church his hair would have hardly been noticeable in those days, but the young people at Waite Park church were "straight," just normal, middle-class church kids. (Back then, *straight* meant the opposite of *hippie* or counterculture freaks, not the opposite of *homosexual* as it means now.) I introduced myself to the young man; he told me that his name was Ron Odell, and we began to talk. I discovered two things in that conversation: (1) his parents were one of the couples who in their youth had helped start Waite Park, and (2) he played the guitar. I asked him to play guitar for our youth gathering in the Fireside Room, which we had announced would follow that evening's service. He said he would and then volunteered to do a special number in the church service that evening as well, having heard us announce that the youth were to be responsible for that gathering. I readily agreed, even though I did not know whether Ron even had a relationship with the Lord.

As it turned out, whatever relationship Ron may have had with God was at least dormant at that time. Ron was not very good on the guitar either. In the adult service, he attempted to play and sing "What a Friend We Have in Jesus." He sang the standard familiar tune, but he was playing the music from a book of "folk-style hymns." Same lyrics, completely different tune. It was really bad!

Was Ron embarrassed? Not that anyone could tell. When he had finished the "special," Ron said with a smile, "I'll be featured in Fireside Room following this service." Later on, I would discover that he was humble and unassuming, yet self-confident. Little did I know that this atypical young man would become a vital part of the work and one of my best friends.

The next time I saw Ron was on a Sunday afternoon a couple of weeks later. He showed up at our door to let me know that he and a buddy were leaving shortly for a three-week motorcycle trip to the Canadian Rockies and the northwestern United States. He had come by to ask me to pray for him. I did. Still not at all clear about Ron's relationship with the Lord, among other things I prayed that God would reveal himself to Ron in a completely new way on that trip. That incident became the first of many times when Ron would drop by for "some prayer," as naturally and casually as other people drop by for a cup of coffee.

In late August we took the youth group away for a weekend retreat. A turning point in our work at Waite Park, an unrecognized turning point in the moment, occurred on Saturday night. We were gathered around a fireplace in an unlit room—in the chilly central Minnesota climate it passed for a campfire service. During that service we invited the young people to make a new or a fresh commitment to the Lord by writing down their commitment on a piece of paper and then offering it to him by placing the paper in the fire. We invited them to share their commitment with the group if they desired to do so.

It was a fairly typical meeting of that sort except for one commitment. Ron spoke out, quite casually: "Lord, it's about time you and I got it together. I give my life to you." Ron's words stood out, not because they were dramatic or even seemed important. Rather, they were memorable because they were so "unspiritual." Most of us did not think this was any way to talk to God, and it certainly did not seem like the way to "get saved." Where were the tears and the emotions and the fervent prayers that we associated with repentance? Where was "the sinner's prayer"? Where were the joy and the testimony of feeling forgiven and accepted by God? Needless to say I left without much thought of significant change having taken place—until the following Monday evening.

It was about 5:15 p.m. on Monday when Patricia and I heard a knock on our apartment door. It was Ron, and he was virtually glowing. With excitement he told us of how he had been witnessing about the Lord to his co-workers at the dry cleaner where he worked as a truck driver. He told us how he had talked about Jesus through the opened passenger-side door to people on the sidewalk whenever he had to stop for stoplights. Ron was on fire with love for the Lord. Sharing the good news was as natural for him as eating—and apparently more fun.

I was stunned. I had not even put much stock in his commitment. Here he was doing the work of an evangelist already, joyfully and naturally. Talking about Jesus, that is, witnessing or evangelizing, outside of church meetings was "the big challenge." Nothing about the responsibility of a Christian intimidated me more. Nothing made me feel guiltier about my failure than my fear of witnessing. Here was a newly committed Christian to whom witnessing was as normal as breathing.

With Ron, witnessing was not a temporary activity; rather, it became a way of life. Obviously, God had gifted him as an evangelist. Over the next months, I also experienced more freedom in sharing the good news as Ron and I began to hang out. We passed out "Jesus Papers" (newspapers produced by various groups of Jesus People). We walked the streets of Hennepin Avenue and the Nicollet Street Mall in downtown Minneapolis, looking for people with whom we could talk about Jesus. We led the youth in setting up a table in the Apache Plaza Shopping Mall to "campaign for Jesus" during the 1972 presidential election campaigns. We drove around looking for hitchhikers whom we would pick up; then we would take them wherever they were going in the Twin Cities area as long as they would talk about Jesus and "spiritual things" with us. The Lord had put Ron and me together to begin to work as a team before I even realized that one of God's normal ways of working is to join people into corporate units to do the work of ministry.

****

Apart from any planning on man's part, God brought another member to the team that he was building. A few weeks after Patricia and I had moved to Minneapolis, Pastor Hauser informed me of the church board's decision to hire Jay Swisher part-time (with the huge salary of $25 per week) to lead the church in the area of music, with the specific goal of building a choir. Pastor Hauser informed me that Jay was a single man about my age whose family had at one time been in Waite Park Church, and that he was moving back to Minneapolis. Pastor Hauser encouraged me to reach out to Jay and befriend him. He suggested that Jay might be able to help us with music in our youth work. Therefore, Patricia and I asked Jay to stay for lunch after church on his first Sunday with us.

Jay and I, and Patricia too, connected almost immediately. I knew he was "all right" when I played my new *Love Song* record album for him—he really liked it. Like me, Jay was motivated to teach. Although our backgrounds were different, we quickly found ourselves sharing camaraderie in the Spirit, centered in a hunger to know God and to know the Scriptures. Jay's joyful attitude and his sensitivity toward other people especially endeared him to Patricia.

Jay recruited and worked with a choir for a few weeks, and they presented one song on a Sunday, and then no more, ever. It wasn't that it was a bad choir or a bad idea—it simply became apparent that it was not God's idea. The Lord was working in the church at that time in such a way that we had little interest in doing things only because that's what churches do; rather, we were hungry to find what God was doing and to do it with him.

Jay began to participate in the youth activities right away. The addition of his musical skill was an obvious benefit to the work. However, Jay's biggest contribution, by far, was the example of his life: his sincere, fully dedicated devotion to Christ, his walk of obedience to the Holy Spirit, his love for the Scripture, and his commitment to the brotherhood.

Jay will be our friend forever. His friendship is one of those special ones. We worked together smoothly. We spent large amounts of time together with little or no conflict. After the Waite Park years, we have often not even had contact for years at a time—but when we do, by phone, by letter, by visit, or now by email, we just pick up where we are at present, catching up on some details from the years between as we go, delighting in the discovery that we still share the same camaraderie in the Spirit and have continued to grow similarly in the life of God's kingdom. Jay began to develop a relationship with Rosalie, whom he later married, in our Tuesday night Bible study. He has been an elder in a Plymouth Brethren church for many years.

I had been hired to pastor the Waite Park youth. The Lord made us part of a team. Patricia was not an insignificant member of the team. She provided an important and effective example of Christian womanhood as a person, a wife and, before long, a mother. She was an effective teacher in the Sunday School classes that we offered. She opened her home freely as a place where young people were invited to drop in and hang out.

With loving flexibility and no prior notice, she would set out one or two or more extra plates at mealtime—providing meals on a tiny grocery budget and sometimes literally asking God to multiply the food, as Jesus had multiplied the loaves and fishes. One particular evening, I invited Jay and Ron to eat with us, not realizing that Patricia was working with less than half a pound of hamburger. Knowing she did not have enough for everyone, she prayed for the hamburger to be multiplied as she made it into meatloaf. Then one of the teenage girls came by, so Patricia invited her to stay as well. The five of us ate all the meatloaf we wanted and had some left over.

Patricia is far more personable than I am; therefore, her role in connecting relationally with the young people was vital. She was able to relate to those "on the edge" of the group much better than I could. The fact that she is a few years older than me was a blessing to our work because she was able to be something of a second mom to the young people as well as to be a big sister, especially to the girls.

I marvel, even today as I write, at God's sovereignty and meticulous work in forming such a team. In no way would I have foreseen his plan. And even the godly, experienced people who made up the Waite Park Church board, nor Pastor Hauser himself, would have seen the need for this team, let alone been able to pull it together. Thank God! My faith is encouraged even now as I remember it.

****

Soon I discovered that God had provided another significant friendship for us as well. About the same time that we came to Waite Park, Dr. Dan Hadlock and his wife Lynn began to attend the church. We had met them, but they really came to the forefront of our attention in August when the transmission went out of our blue Ford. The word got out about the problem, and Dan and Lynn, who had only just begun to visit the church, contributed the money to have the transmission rebuilt.

The Hadlocks had young children and were never directly involved in the youth work, but we soon became friends. Before long, Dan began to meet with Jay, Ron, and me in a weekly "Bible study." Supposedly we were studying the book of Romans; however, in nearly a year and a half of getting together, we never did finish the book. We would start to read a few verses; then we would cross-reference all over the Bible. Before long we would move from Biblical themes to personal sharing and prayer. Without my ever having heard of the concept, the Lord had provided me with an accountability group with whom I felt free to share anything. We gave one another full acceptance and support without hesitating to call one another to live up to God's call and standard. Later the Lord added Doug Millage and, later still, his brother Mark to the group after each of them had begun to follow the Lord. It is impossible to overemphasize the important contribution made in my life by this group; it became both a vital and foundational aid to my growth at that time and also a piece of my long-term desire to see men grow together in the Lord.

The work in the youth group began to develop, and our team's influence among the teens steadily grew during the fall. Pastor Hauser rarely told us what to do in the youth work, but in August 1972 he did give one assignment to us. One of his elementary-age daughters had come home from school one day the previous spring with some information presented in her classroom as sex education; this information was diametrically opposed to Pastor Hauser's convictions—and even more important, to Biblical principles. He asked that we use the Sunday School classes to give a Biblical perspective on sexuality, dating, and marriage.

We knew of no models for dealing with such a topic in a Sunday School. Chicken-heart that I was, I asked Patricia to take that class. Therefore, in the fall quarter, she started "sex education" with the junior high age group. She was about seven months pregnant when the class started; she had our first child, Elijah, on November 6, 1972, while that class was still going on. The class was great. She was a living object lesson. She handled things with honesty and wisdom. The young people received teaching from her without becoming silly or embarrassed. Parents were amazed and grateful.

In the winter quarter, Patricia took on the senior high people. There were some dicey moments, but she handled a few inappropriate remarks with humor and ease. The emphasis with this group was on dating relationships and sexual purity.

The spring quarter with the "college and career" group was tougher for her. It focused more on marriage and family issues. At that time, we did not know enough to separate the men and women. She was not comfortable talking to a group—including men about her own age—on these topics. Also, several of the women were quite unlikely to ever marry at all. Wisely Patricia refused to teach this session.

Unfortunately, in those days we had not been challenged to even consider that our American culture might be off base in its approach to boy/girl relationships. We had not yet seen that recreational dating in and of itself was a serious part of the problem, setting up young people for sexual temptation and, in effect, "encouraging" them to hurt one another rather than to edify one another. We had not yet been exposed to the truth that dating as a part of courtship is appropriate when one is actually ready to enter a marriage relationship but is a foolish way to socialize.

We also had not seen that from a Scriptural perspective God has given parents the primary responsibility to educate and train their children—and that no area of training is more important than imparting basic values and life skills. Having us, or rather Patricia, deal with this material on sex and men/women relationships was far better than leaving it to public schools. Would that we had known, however, that it would have been better yet to work with the parents so that they could train their own children. Even so, Pastor Hauser and we were doing the best we could. God honored Patricia's willingness and used her to strengthen some basic convictions that many of those young people bought into and lived by.

The foundations in relationship and truth were being laid that fall. The next significant "event" in our work with the youth was to have John and Vicki Meadows come up from Ohio to lead a "youth revival" between Christmas and New Year's Day.

****

God met us powerfully in the days that we shared together with the Meadows that week. Our gatherings were more like the "Jesus People" meetings that Patricia and I had visited than what we had known previously as "youth revival meetings."

John and I had kept our "covenant" from May 1970. On occasion we had talked by phone, but since neither of us had much money, we started mailing cassette tapes to one another. It wasn't too long until we were exchanging 90-minute tapes once a month or so.

Looking back at it now, I am blessed to consider the trust placed in us by the Waite Park Church board. The members of the church board authorized me to invite John and Vicki to come share with the youth, based solely on our recommendation, since they knew nothing about the Meadows. The church board also purchased the airline tickets and provided an honorarium.

The events of that week did not happen in a vacuum, of course. For one thing, many adults in the church had been praying for some time, specifically, that God would move upon their youth. Also, most of the young people had parents who had sown the things of God faithfully into their children over the years. The dynamic working of the Holy Spirit that had been received and fostered in the church by the leadership provided an atmosphere of freedom. Not insignificantly, Pastor Hauser's teaching on the gifts of the Holy Spirit in prior months had opened the door to expectation for something more than the typical youth revival meetings that one might have expected in the churches with which we were familiar.

We had experienced God's grace in our efforts during the preceding months. We could see that several of the young people were growing in their spiritual hunger to know and serve God. The youth Bible study had grown slowly and steadily, as had the Wednesday night meeting. Jay had helped us learn to sing many of the "Scripture songs" that were beginning to be sung in those years. There was vibrancy in our singing time, and there was a growing hunger for God's Word among us. In addition, the example of Ron's changed life was making an impact on the younger teens.

John and Vicki flew into Minneapolis on the afternoon of Christmas Eve. (I wonder now what John and Vicki's parents thought about them spending that Christmas with us rather than with their families.) Patricia and I went to the airport to pick them up. There, we discovered, as John and Vicki came from the plane into the terminal, that Jack and Rosie Hickman were also waiting to greet them. It turned out that the Hickmans were members of a Jesus People house church that met near the Ohio State campus. The Meadows had become involved with this house church. Jack and Rosie had moved to the Twin Cities so that Jack could study at a Bible college sponsored by Compassion Christian Center located in a suburb north of us. Compassion was a formerly Lutheran church that had become Charismatic.

We arrived at the church building (and our apartment) just as Waite Park's traditional Christmas Eve candlelight service was ending. As the people were moving from the sanctuary into the hall to go out to their cars, in we came bringing John, with his "afro-like" hair, and Jack and Rosie, looking just like hippies whom we could have picked up hitchhiking on I-35W. It must have stretched the middle-class people of Waite Park, and especially the parents of the teens who were entrusting their young people to us. However, we were all greeted warmly with genuine, godly love.

On Christmas Day, Jay, Ron, John, and I listened to a tape of Calvary Chapel's pastor, Chuck Smith, teaching on the baptism of the Holy Spirit. To this day, that message by Chuck Smith is one of my favorites on the subject; his simple teaching and anecdotes made us all hungry to know Jesus more intimately.

As the tape ended, John headed for the restroom. Quite a while later when he came out it was evident that something unusual had taken place. He was "fairly glowing" with joy as he came back into the room and announced quietly that he had begun to speak in tongues while in the restroom. We all rejoiced with him, none more than Jay, who had begun to pray in tongues a few weeks earlier during his own personal prayer time.

The rest of the day was spent in rich fellowship!

The youth gatherings started on the evening of December 26. I do not remember enough to describe these meetings in detail. I can only say that the overall impact of that week made an indelible impression on my life—simply because God's presence was so rich among us.

I do remember one evening when the conviction of the Holy Spirit moved among the young people in a particularly powerful way. For example, one young high school senior, Mark Millage, had seemed totally uninterested in following the Lord. He appeared to have come to the meeting only because his parents had pressured him to do so. However, the Holy Spirit confronted Mark so strongly that he literally fell out of his chair and lay face-down on the floor weeping and repenting. He changed dramatically that night and lived differently from that time on, soon becoming the fifth member of our men's Bible study.

I also remember that word began to get out that God was up to something among us. A few times during the fall I had visited a Christian coffeehouse held on weekend evenings at a Christian-owned smorgasbord restaurant. Several adults from the coffeehouse showed up on the last couple of nights, including one who was supposedly a prophet. He was the first person whom I had ever met who was described as a prophet, a designation given him in the house church circles where he fellowshipped.

Suffice it to say, I was suspicious of him. I had come to believe that the spiritual gifts listed in 1 Corinthians 12 are just as valid today as in New Testament times. Nevertheless, that did not mean that I believed the ministry gifts (offices, some would say) listed in Ephesians 4 were still operating in the church, not those of apostles and prophets, anyway. Fortunately, the brother did not say much. He would not have been warmly received.

The work that God had begun to do that fall began to be evident after those meetings with the Meadows. The work among the youth began to grow. Attendance also began to grow. It wasn't too long until more than twenty were attending the weekly Bible study. We would typically have between thirty and forty present on Wednesday night and also on Sunday morning. A core group of fifteen to twenty young people participated in all three groups.

During the summer of 1973, we offered the youth a discipleship school. Although we were overly ambitious in the amount of work we assigned, overemphasizing information instead of imparting the Lord's way of life to the teens, the Lord blessed our efforts abundantly and most of the core group are still following Jesus today.

****

One morning in late January or early February 1973, I visited the Bible school conducted by Compassion Christian Center. Jack Hickman had been studying there. Since we had met the Hickmans at Christmas, Ersel and Patrice Shrider had also moved from the Columbus fellowship so that Ersel could enter the Bible school. The Hickmans and Shriders were becoming friends with Patricia and me. Jack and Ersel had been wanting me to visit the Bible school.

I attended the class on the book of Acts with Jack. Even now, all these years later, I can remember the professor, John Matthews, teaching from the seventeenth chapter. He talked about the powerful gospel demonstrated and preached by Paul and his team—good news so powerful that the Jewish opponents cried out against them, "These who have turned the world upside down have come here too" (17:6). The teaching fed my growing desire to discover the power of the gospel again!

Then we went to chapel. The speaker was Lutheran missionary-evangelist Herb Mjorud, but I didn't pay much attention to his name that day and quickly forgot it, having no idea that a few months later I would have reason to remember it again.

Mr. Mjorud had made several trips to the Philippines to preach and was getting ready to leave shortly on another trip there. After he had finished speaking, we were invited to gather around him in order to pray for him and the mission trip. As I was quietly praying, it was as though visible syllables in some language other than English were inscribed across my brain. I clearly sensed the Lord saying to me, "You can speak in tongues now if you want." Therefore, I began to "read" all the syllables that I saw, and then I continued praying quietly using sounds that I did not recognize. I was mildly excited that I had received this gift of the Holy Spirit, but it was not some spectacular spiritual or emotional experience.

About that time, I sensed the Lord was giving me a word of encouragement for Mr. Mjorud concerning the effectiveness of his ministry in the coming trip; I spoke out the words that I felt God was giving.

I prayed in tongues most of the way back to our apartment and often over the next day or two. Within a few days, however, I began to be skeptical. Was I just making up these strange sounds by my own initiative? A battle raged within me. Had I received the true gift of tongues, or was I only fooling myself? *Besides*, I kept thinking, *even if this was the real thing, what value did it have?* For the next few weeks I felt silly making inane sounds. I would go for days at a time and not "pray in tongues."

However, after nearly a month of this battle, I took another hard look at the Scriptures in Acts and Corinthians that mention tongues, and I began to hold the issue seriously before the Lord. I came to three conclusions: (1) the gift of tongues is scriptural, (2) the Holy Spirit had actually offered this gift to me, and (3) I needed to exercise the gift whether it ever seemed real or made any sense to my mind. At that point I made a decision to pray in tongues consistently and to trust the Holy Spirit concerning the value and reality of the gift.

A few days later, as I was reading in 2 Corinthians 10, verses 3–5 "jumped out" at me:

> For while we spend our life in a body of flesh, we do not war with carnal weapons. For the weapons of our warfare are not physical, but they are powerful with God's help for the tearing down of fortresses, inasmuch as we tear down reasonings and every proud barrier that is raised up against the knowledge of God and lead every thought into subjection to Christ…. (2 Corinthians 10:3–5, MLB)

It struck me that tongues was one of these weapons, not a physical weapon but a spiritual one. I saw that it was as though my mind were imprisoned within a fortress. I knew, according to Isaiah 55, that God had declared that my thoughts were not his thoughts and that his thoughts were much higher than mine. Previously I had thought that I could learn God's thoughts only by studying. However, now I could see that ways of thinking (reasonings or speculations and proud barriers or lofty

76

thoughts) were the walls that kept me from perceiving God's thoughts—not simply lack of study. My mind-set had been captured at a deep level by the thought systems of this world.

I perceived that by praying and singing with the Spirit (or with my spirit)—that is, "in tongues," according to 1 Corinthians 14:14–15—it was as though I were shooting cannon balls into the walls around my mind. I perceived that as my spirit agreed with the Spirit of God—agreed on things that my worldly mind-set could not grasp, let alone agree with—the fortress would begin to be torn down. As the mental walls came down, I could begin to bring my thoughts into subjection to Christ; that is, I could align my thinking with his!

I had come to the place where I was committed to use the gift of tongues as a step of obedience. With this insight from Scripture, I began to pray in the Spirit with even more faith and conviction.

Three significant events occurred in the following months, the significance of which I did not see at all until the third event revealed their connection. Only in hindsight did I begin to connect them with praying in tongues.

The first event occurred early in March. Pastor Hauser called me into his office and told me to set aside the first week of April. He said that he had registered us to attend the Basic Youth Conflicts Seminar to be held in St. Paul. I remember that Pastor Hauser showed me a brochure about the seminar, but he did not mention any speaker nor did I notice mention of one in the brochure. He did say that the seminar was coming to the Twin Cities for the first time and that it had been highly recommended to him by friends. I remember him saying that the seminar was being advertised only by word of mouth.

The second event occurred one morning later in March while I was getting ready to leave the house in order to drive my friend Dan Hadlock to the airport. The "prophet" from the house groups who had come to our youth meetings in December showed up at our apartment. I was more than a little skeptical about his "ministry"; for some unknown reason I didn't even like this fellow and did not want him around.

He asked to speak with me for a few minutes. I reluctantly invited him in. He began to read some Scriptures in Proverbs and Jeremiah. The only thing I remember about the readings was that they included the words *wisdom* and *understanding*. After reading, he looked me in the eyes and said, "The Lord is saying to you, 'Get wisdom and get understanding.' "

I replied, a bit sarcastically as I recall, "Wisdom and understanding about what?"

He said: "I don't know. The Lord just says, 'Get wisdom and get understanding.'" And very shortly thereafter he left.

After I had picked up Dan, I laughingly told him about the "nut" who had come by with a word for me. I did not think much more about it.

These two incidents became connected when, on the first Monday evening in April, Pastor Hauser and I drove to the St. Paul Civic Center. I was amazed so many people had gathered there—about 9,000. There was no singing, no introductions, and no fanfare. At 7 p.m. a rather small, unassuming man walked out onto the stage set up on the floor of the arena below us. Without a word he turned on an overhead projector and wrote down the words *Wisdom* and *Understanding.* His starting point was to define these words. Needless to say, he had my attention.

Although I don't remember actually hearing the man's name until Wednesday evening, the presentation on Tuesday was life-changing for me. On that night, Mr. Bill Gothard talked about spiritual authority, about the God-established chain of command. I was struck with conviction, conviction that increased throughout the week. Through Mr. Gothard, the Holy Spirit revealed to me that I was a rebel—not just a bit rebellious, but a rebel in spirit and nature. Along with conviction came the grace to repent.

By the end of the week I knew that I had to call my dad and ask his forgiveness for my rebellious attitude and words and actions toward him. I did call him. I had no idea how deeply I had hurt Dad until I heard his response: "Well, son, we'll see if you change." Obviously I had violated trust to the point where he could not just accept my words but would need to see the fruit of my repentance.

Because of the revelation of my sin that God had given, I was not offended by Dad's response. Even though I was grieved, I understood. And his response, I believe, helped to solidify my conviction to change.

I have not always been perfect in submitting to authority or in using authority since that time, but I have consistently sought to recognize and to walk under those whom God has delegated to carry spiritual authority in my life. My ways of thinking and my ways of behaving have been changed permanently in this regard, even as I have continued to grow in my understanding of spiritual authority and in the wisdom with which I receive it as well as exercise it.

Although I cannot prove it, I have become fully convinced that it was by praying in the Spirit—in tongues—that my mind was released from captivity to the rebellious spirit that characterizes fallen man and very specifically characterized my generation. Because the fortress had been knocked down, I was able to "hear" in my spirit what the Holy Spirit was saying through Mr. Gothard; I could see that I had been a rebel in heart. I had the power in God to subject my mind to the mind of Christ in this area.

6

Hungry for More

Coffeehouses were popular in those days. These were nothing upscale like the present-day coffee shops where people go to buy exotic blends and expensive coffee paraphernalia; there were no comfortable seating areas and fancy desserts—at least not in any I ever visited. These coffeehouses were usually located near universities or in areas of town where young people hung out. I never knew of one that offered any coffee other than the old regular brands such as Maxwell House or Folgers. In those days I knew nothing about flavored coffees, let alone espressos, lattes, mochas, and cappuccinos. Some did offer a few types of tea and maybe some "exotic" fruit juices, such as papaya juice or guava juice.

Large spools around which the lines used by the electric or telephone company had been rolled often served as tables. Folding chairs were pretty much standard seating. Usually there were candles on the table and low lights. The walls were often decorated with posters—content determined by the interests of those who ran the particular coffeehouse. It wasn't unusual for there to be a rack that held newspapers or magazines. In a coffeehouse run by Christians, posters consisted of Scripture or some religious theme, and the written material was most often evangelistic in tone. Secular coffeehouses would feature material representing various other counterculture lifestyles.

At one end of the room there would usually be a small stage from which some poet might read, or a musician, maybe even a band, might play and sing. Much of the time, patrons talked quietly at the tables as much as they listened to the performers. Some would drop in for a short time; others might stay the whole evening.

I enjoyed visiting a number of the Christian coffeehouses around the city. Frankly, there was something about the counterculture that appealed to me. On one level I am sure that at first the draw was connected to the rebellious spirit at work in me. However, there was also something in me that was, in a good way, resisting the status quo and wanting to connect with what God was doing in my generation.

One coffeehouse was a bit different. On Friday and Saturday nights the Kings Inn, a smorgasbord restaurant owned by believers, became a "coffeehouse" in an effort to evangelize teens. It was not unusual to have 100 to 150 teens there at any given time on those nights.

It was at the Kings Inn that I first ran into "house church" people. These particular people often mentioned the author Watchman Nee. Most of them were quite negative toward organized churches and several had serious reservations about the legitimacy of my "call" to work in a denominational church. I was hungry enough for reality in Christ and for the early expressions of the faith I was seeing in the New Testament that I kept coming around in spite of feeling that some considered me unenlightened or even somewhat suspect.

Because of the sectarian attitude of some of those who "professed" to be nonsectarian, New Testament Christians, I had no desire to read anything by Nee. Before long, however, Wes Long, the lay leader at Waite Park Wesleyan, mentioned Watchman Nee's work to me, especially recommending his book *The Normal Christian Life*. I read the book and began to look for others by Nee. Not long after the Gothard seminar, Pastor Hauser recommended Nee's *Spiritual Authority*, which I found and devoured.

Ironically, a couple years later I finally found a copy of Nee's book *The Normal Christian Church Life*, the book that these "sectarian nonsectarians" had often referred to, seemingly holding it up pretty close to Scripture in terms of truth. I started reading with the preface, in which Nee revealed his great reluctance to produce an English edition of the book. In the book he presented the Biblical insights and principles behind the way that Nee and his co-workers had founded churches in China. He was obviously concerned that the book not be misunderstood and misapplied. He ended the preface with these words:

> One of the prayers I have offered in connection with this book is that
> the Lord should keep it from those who oppose and would use it as a
> chart for attack and also from those who agree and would use it as a
> manual for service. I dread the latter far more than the former.[30]

Thankfully, in spite of the fact that some of the people who spoke to me about Watchman Nee were among those attempting to use his book as "a manual," there were others such as Wes Long and Pastor Hauser who helped me overcome my negative reaction.

I can hardly overemphasize the way in which the Lord used Nee's books in my life over the next several years. Through Nee I came to see in a fresh way the place of the cross in my life. I began to desire to live life directed by the Holy Spirit working

---

[30] Watchman Nee, *The Normal Christian Church Life* (Colorado Springs, CO: International Students Press, 1969).

through my spirit rather than to live by the power of my will or of my mind or of my emotions or of my bodily passions. I wanted to be broken from dependence on my human strength and gifts and knowledge so that I could live in dependence on the power of God. Through Nee I began to see more clearly God's ways of dealing with a person and His ways of preparing the human vessel to give God's life to others. Nee added to my hunger to see the church today be like the church I read about in the Bible.

As yet I have never been part of an actual house church movement, but even today I am convinced that there is something in the basic principles and patterns that are essential to the life and effective ministry of the present-day church.

While at Waite Park I not only began to see that God was at work in house churches, but I also became convinced that he was doing a significant work in some of the mainline denominations through the Charismatic Renewal.

Although I have never personally identified with the Charismatic movement as such, I was deeply influenced and eventually became a part of two of the works that grew from it. But that was future. While at Waite Park my knowledge of the Charismatic Renewal was for the most part gained from written reports and testimonies. There were several in the Waite Park Church who identified themselves as Charismatics. I respected most of them, but a few of them disturbed me because they periodically missed our gatherings in order to go to some Pentecostal or Charismatic church—claiming that they needed to get "recharged" from time to time. A number of the summer Sunday night speakers that Pastor Hauser brought in were Charismatic, including a Lutheran evangelist and an Episcopalian psychiatrist.

One of those speakers was a Catholic priest. If anyone had tried to tell me then that only a few years later I would be working alongside Tim Nolan in a Christian community that was born in the context of the Catholic Charismatic Renewal, I would never have believed it. We certainly had no inkling of that future when Pastor Hauser invited Patricia and me to go with him, his wife, and the Longs to attend a Catholic Charismatic prayer meeting held in the gymnasium of Regina High School in South Minneapolis.

We attended a couple of prayer meetings at Regina during those years. At first, I was simply curious about the phenomenon of Catholics claiming to be filled with the Holy Spirit. I certainly did not go expecting to see several hundred people enthusiastically singing, worshipping, praying, prophesying, testifying, and listening to simple gospel messages, but that's what I saw.

The metal folding chairs were arranged in circles around an area about 15 feet in diameter. The speakers and the musicians used microphones that stood in the center area. The songs were mostly choruses and folk-style songs. The most memorable times were when spontaneously, all around the room, people would begin to sing, usually very quietly, in tongues. Each one sang in his or her own prayer language to his or her own "tune." The individual voices were so subdued that a listener could hardly be sure that they were using tongues, but the voices rose up together in a haunting harmonious sound that brought to mind what it must have been like to hear some medieval choir in some great cathedral.

At one of the meetings, a young man went up to the microphone to share a testimony. At first there was nothing wrong with his words, per se, but something about his sharing seemed discordant with the spirit of the gathering. The discord was subtle, however, until he declared, "I have seen the Messiah and his name is Maharaj Ji …" (a 14-year-old guru from India who was popular at the time). Almost before the speaker had the name out, Patricia jumped to her feet, hands raised high in the air, and began to sing, "Jesus is Lord." Soon the whole group was declaring the Lordship of Jesus in song along with her. Meanwhile two brothers "escorted" the young man from the room. Patricia's action at that time was unplanned and to a degree astonishing since she was very skeptical about the charismatic dimension.

The prayer meeting was sponsored by a group called The Servants of the Light. In our wildest thoughts we would not have guessed that this very group would become the community of which we would later become members!

Another seemingly insignificant occurrence that turned out to be vitally important was that Dr. Dan Hadlock's sister and her friend came to visit. When we invited the two ladies over for dinner at our home in order to get acquainted, they told us about their involvement in a Washington, D.C., Christian community. That group was associated with L'Abri Fellowship, the ministry that Dr. Francis Schaeffer and his wife, Edith, had begun. I don't believe that I had even heard of Dr. Schaeffer prior to that time.

The women gave me a copy of his book *The God Who Is There*. It may have been the most difficult book I had read up to that time. I certainly did not understand some parts of it, but I read it, as quickly as I could, mostly to be able to tell the women that I had done so and in order to try to converse with them. Little did I know that these ladies had introduced me to a way of thinking and of seeing the world that I would be digesting, using, and then propagating for the rest of my life.

In November 1973 at my invitation, John Meadows returned to Minneapolis in order to attend the Basic Youth Conflicts Seminar with Patricia and me. Again, word spread by word of mouth only, and the second time that the seminar was held in the Twin Cities there were 16,000 who attended.

Repeating the seminar was certainly worthwhile; however, it was not the most significant thing of the week for me. John had brought three tapes that he thought I should hear—copies of copies of copies, barely audible on my small cassette player.

Here we were attending a seminar with teaching from 7 to 10 p.m. Monday through Thursday, 9 a.m. to 10 p.m. on Friday, and 9 a.m. to 8 p.m. on Saturday. I should have had my fill of teaching, but I started the first tape and I could not stop listening to them until I had been through them all. On lunch and dinner breaks on Friday and Saturday I would be in my seat, tape player pressed up to my ear, devouring these messages.

I introduced John to Bill Gothard's message that week. In turn, John introduced me to the teaching of Bob Mumford, Charles Simpson, and Derek Prince. I heard something fresh in these tapes. The messages gripped my heart, both confirming things I'd been seeing and hearing and also opening my eyes to new things in the Word of God. Yet, once again I had no idea of the future, no idea that the messages of these teachers were opening a significant part of my destiny.

Bob's message, "Shadow or Substance," had to do with the fact that the Body of Christ is not something mystical but rather that it consists of real relationships with real people, relationships ordained by God and lived out in obedience to God's Word. Relationships that work through conflict; relationships based on acceptance of one another, warts and all; relationships in which we grow toward maturity in Christ together to the end that our relationships become a true reflection of the life of the Triune God.

Charles talked about "The Church in the Home." He challenged me to see that the family was a microcosm of the larger church. He began to make me aware that if there is not integrity in the relationship between husbands and wives and between parents and children, then there cannot be integrity in the household of faith, the church, either.

These two messages touched that hunger in me for true Biblical reality. They helped me begin to see far more clearly that church is not something "religious" or "spiritual" in some weird way. Rather, I became more clearly aware that God wanted the qualities of the "other world" to be worked out in the everyday relationships and situations in this world.

I had begun to be aware of the reality of the occult realm and the influence of demonic activity in this present world. However, Derek's message, "God's Atomic Weapon: The Power of the Blood," brought more clarity to the nature of spiritual warfare and direct demonic influence. He introduced me to the practice of confessing the truth according to the Scripture as a weapon against the devil. Within a couple of years, I would need this truth, not as a concept, but as a weapon in the struggle to overcome during my own time of trial.

I believe it was John who signed me up to receive *New Wine* magazine, the monthly publication of Christian Growth Ministries, of which these three men along with another teacher, Don Basham, had become the overseers. I received my first issue about that time. I had never seen a magazine packed full of Biblical teaching so relevant and "alive" as were the articles in *New Wine*.[31] That teaching, along with tapes from Christian Growth Ministries and the individual teachers, soon became a hugely significant part of the foundation for my life, vision, and ministry.

I was not growing and changing only because of outside influences such as Nee, Gothard, and Christian Growth Ministries. The work of the Spirit in the church, the influence and example of Pastor Hauser, the sharing around the Scriptures with the small men's group, and the dynamics of our youth work were significant. Along with that, the Scriptures themselves were more "living and active" to me than at any previous time (and possibly any later time) in my life. What I was hearing from others rang true with what I was seeing in God's Word.

****

While at Waite Park I began to read the Scriptures more avidly than ever before. As I've already written, a significant change had begun when I first read *Good News for Modern Man* back in Bible college. The number of translations that were readily available in those days was quite limited. However, while in Minneapolis I purchased my first copies of the New American Standard Bible and of the Modern Language

---

[31] I still have most of the issues of *New Wine* stored away. However, thanks to Charles Simpson's ministry, all issues are now available online: https://csmpublishing.org/publications/new-wine-magazine.

Bible (Berkley Version). I also picked up a small volume consisting of a paraphrase of the New Testament epistles titled *Letters to Street Christians* by "two brothers from Berkeley" who were members of the Christian World Liberation Front, a ministry based on the UCLA Berkeley campus.

I found that changing translations from time to time stirred up my initiative to read and gave me a fresh perspective on what I read—and still does. I also learned that comparing translations to one another often added to my understanding of passages.

During that time I also started a pattern of reading that I kept up as much as possible for most of the 1970s. I think I may have first heard of the method in a booklet on discipleship published by David Wilkerson's ministry. Each day I tried to read five chapters in the Old Testament, five chapters in the New Testament, five chapters in Psalms, and one chapter in Proverbs. If I had been able to read this way every single day, I would have read Psalms and Proverbs every month, the New Testament in a bit less than two months, and the Old Testament in seven or eight months.

I was quite consistent with the readings in Psalms and Proverbs—and continued that pattern much of the time for fifteen to twenty years. It usually took me three or four months to read the New Testament and about a year to read the Old Testament. I had never read the Bible through until I started this discipline. By the late 1970s I had read through the entire Bible several times.

One of the great benefits that I derived from this method of reading was that I began to see the unity of the Scripture. Often, I found myself reading the same theme on the same day from more than one section of the Scripture. It was not unusual on a given day to come across a passage in Psalms that was clearly related to the very material I was reading elsewhere in the Old Testament that day. The New Testament reading often referred to, or even quoted, something that I had read the same day in the Old Testament and/or in Psalms.

Another benefit gained by reading this way was that I became far more familiar with where to find specific Scripture passages. This benefit was in line with a goal I had set for myself in the summer of 1970, the summer before I left Circleville to study at Marion College.

The previous semester a few brothers, including John Meadows and me, had formed a team that led a Thursday night Bible Study for some teenage boys who were being held in a kind of "halfway house" on the Ohio State Fairgrounds. Most of these guys had been in the Boys Industrial School as juvenile offenders. Most were being held at the Fairgrounds as a "halfway" stop between full incarceration at the Boys Industrial School and full release.

One evening after the Bible study ended at about 9 p.m., we escorted the guys back to their dorm. One of the counselors (i.e., a guard without a gun) had come by and listened in on our study that evening. After the boys had gone into the dorm, this man began to challenge what we had been doing. A philosophy major at Ohio State University, he was deeply concerned that our approach, rather than helping, would be harmful to the guys. In his opinion the boys had gotten into trouble in the first place mostly because they were hopeless; he said that they had been told all of their lives that they were "no good" and did not have a good sense of self-worth. He believed, therefore, that for us to come in and tell them that they were sinners who needed saving would only deepen their hopelessness and low self-esteem—thus, their problems could only increase.

We engaged the man in conversation for well over an hour that evening. He obviously started out fully convinced that he needed to get through to us; he must have become at least somewhat interested in what we had to say, because we all agreed to return the next evening in order to take up the conversation again.

During our conversation the second evening, one of the brothers quoted a verse of Scripture. He said something like "Somewhere in the Bible, Jesus said, 'You must be born again.' " It struck me immediately that the quotation would probably have been far more effective if the brother had been able to look up the quotation and show it to the man. The context of Jesus's statement was his encounter with Nicodemus in John 3, the very discussion in which we find John 3:16, probably the most familiar verse in the Bible. Here was a senior in Bible college who did not know where to find such a key passage and did not know the context of John 3:16.

Although I had known that particular reference, as I reflected on the evening I became deeply convicted that I must learn to know the Bible thoroughly and be able to use it at a moment's notice in any situation. Reading the Bible in the manner I have described above was a huge help in making this conviction become closer to reality. Reading larger sections of Scripture helped me to get the "flow" of the content in the individual books. I began to make a specific effort to remember the essential theme of each chapter as it fit into the development of each book. After a time, I noticed that quite often upon hearing a Bible phrase or verse I could match it mentally with the book and the chapter because of the way it fit into the themes that I had learned. It got so that some brothers jokingly called me a "walking concordance." It was not unusual for people to look to me for help if they wanted to know where to find a passage.

Since the early 1980s I have not practiced this discipline consistently. However, even today I find that I can still remember where many passages are in the Bible, and quite often I can locate rather easily even those that I don't recall immediately.

The biggest benefit of all is that I began to recognize the major themes in the Bible. Besides reading the Bible this way during those years, my favorite way of studying the Bible has been to use a good concordance like Young's or Strong's and a good cross-reference system, found in better editions of the Bible. (It is even easier to study this way now, of course, because of all the online tools.) These tools helped me discover themes and to see how they are developed throughout the Scriptures. In this way, I came to the realization that there were important subjects about which I knew little or nothing.

While at Waite Park, I began to discover that the gospel is the "gospel of the kingdom." Of course, I had read and heard that phrase previously, but I had never given it much thought. I do remember one discussion in my Gospels class at CBC in which we talked about whether or not the "kingdom of God" and the "kingdom of heaven" meant the same thing. I don't remember that we came to any firm conclusion.

If asked, I would have said that the gospel is the good news that Jesus died for our sins so that we can be forgiven and saved from hell, which later I came to see was only one part—in one sense, a benefit—of the gospel. As I was reading Acts 28 one day, I noticed that Paul, imprisoned in Rome, talked with Jews who came to him about the kingdom of God. A few verses later I saw that when Gentiles came to Paul, he also spoke with them about the kingdom of God. I had grown up in an environment where the assumptions of premillennial dispensationalism were givens. (I'll discuss this more later. At the time, I hardly knew the term myself.) According to those assumptions, the kingdom of God was something that had to do with the future—either with the Jews in the millennium or with the eternal kingdom in the age to come. So, I began to wonder, why was Paul talking about the kingdom instead of primarily proclaiming the need for these Jews and Gentiles to accept the Savior who would forgive their sins?

For the first time, I took real note that both John the Baptist and Jesus called people to repent because the kingdom of God was at hand. I remembered that Jesus's parables most often opened with these words: "the kingdom of God (or heaven) is like ...."

Jesus had even stated that if it was by the Spirit of God that he cast out demons, then the kingdom "has come upon you." (Matthew 12:28) I saw that Jesus, in the forty days between his resurrection and ascension, spoke about the things pertaining to the kingdom of God. It was about that time that John Matthews, in the class at Compassion's Bible school (the morning that I had begun to pray in tongues), had pointed out in Acts 17 that the message that had "turned the world upside down" was that the apostles were undermining Caesar by declaring "there is another King—Jesus."

Then I looked more carefully at Peter's message on the Day of Pentecost. Peter had explained the outpouring of the Holy Spirit and tongues as signs that "the last days" had now begun. He declared that, although his hearers had crucified Jesus in spite of God's testimony concerning him through miracles, wonders, and signs, God had raised Jesus from the dead and had exalted him to the throne, where the Father said, "Sit and rule." Everything in Peter's sermon built up to this one statement: "Therefore, let all the house of Israel know assuredly that God has made this Jesus, whom you crucified, both Lord and Christ" (Acts 2:36)—and Peter ended his message with that declaration. The gospel message I began to comprehend is that Jesus is *now* the Messianic King.

Many of Peter's hearers were deeply convicted by this message that Jesus is the Lord of heaven and earth. They cried out, "What shall we do?" Only then did Peter tell them to repent and to be baptized; he told them that their sins would be forgiven and that they would receive the promised gift of the Holy Spirit.[32]

I had long before learned the Great Commission in this way: "Go therefore and make disciples of all the nations, baptizing them in the name of the Father and of the Son and of the Holy Spirit." But now I took notice of the verses that preceded and followed this statement.

---

[32] Although my understanding of this passage changed greatly at that time, I still did not comprehend Peter's final declaration fully. Like most English readers, I took the word *Lord* to mean that Jesus was in charge (the king), and I thought of the word *Christ* as a title referring to his divinity—to the degree that I thought about it at all. Much later, I realized that the word *Christ* is a transliteration of the Greek word *christos*, which means "anointed one," and that *christos* is the Greek word that is used to translate the Hebrew word for *messiah*. Thus, Peter is declaring that **Jesus is the long-awaited king, the son of David** who, God had promised, would sit on King David's throne and fulfill God's promises to David and to Israel. On the other hand, since Peter was a Jew preaching to Jews, it is the word *Lord* that more likely speaks of Jesus's divinity, since Jews use the word *Lord* in place of *Yahweh*, the covenant name of God, rather than to take a chance on taking "Yahweh's" name in vain.

Jesus came near and said to them, "All authority has been given to me in heaven and on earth. Go, therefore, and make disciples of all nations, baptizing them in the name of the Father and of the Son and of the Holy Spirit, teaching them to observe everything I have commanded you. And remember, I am with you always, to the end of the age." (Matthew 28:18– 20)

Jesus based the commission on these words: "All authority has been given to me in heaven and on earth." The commission was not based on a future kingdom but rather on authority that Jesus had already received.

And the Commission, as I had learned it, was incomplete. Jesus not only said to go, to make disciples, and to baptize, but he also said to "teach them (i.e., those baptized) to *obey*[33] everything that I have commanded you" (italics added for emphasis). This was the King's commission to his representatives, his ambassadors.

With the commission, the King made a promise: "Remember, I am with you always, even to the end of the age." It is not just that at the end of the age he would come back—which, of course, he will—but that now, in this age, he already has all the authority in heaven and on earth and promises to be with those he commissioned while they call all people and all nations to submit to his rule as long as this age lasts.

Then, in John 3 I discovered that the point of being born again was to "see" and to "enter" the kingdom of God. My attention was first drawn to this by Bob Mumford's teaching. As I meditated on Jesus's words to Nicodemus, I first began to get inklings that the way we had emphasized the new birth as the qualifier for getting us into "heaven" after we die was hindering us from seeing clearly what it means to live in Jesus's kingdom in this life.

These insights were powerful. I knew I had to understand the gospel and proclaim it differently. However, I did not realize that God was making foundational changes in my basic assumptions about the world and the purposes of God. I had no idea that it would take years for me even to begin to get my mind around these changes and their implications; it was a journey that I am on to this day. At that time I did set my heart and mind to "seek first *the kingdom of God* and his righteousness ...." (Matthew 6:33, italics added for emphasis)

---

[33] The Greek word translated *obey* is also often translated *observe*.

Even while I was seeing that the central message of the gospel is the kingdom of God, I was also discovering that Jesus was not looking for converts but disciples—those who would follow him, patterning their life after his. I saw that it was from among the larger group of disciples that Jesus chose twelve whom he called apostles, "those sent on a mission."

Upon further study of the Great Commission, given to the eleven apostles after Judas's death, I found that there was one primary command and three participial phrases that elucidated that command. Jesus actually said, "As you are *going*, **make disciples** …, *baptizing* them …, *teaching* them …."

I discovered in Acts that believers were those who became disciples and that the name "Christian" came later, probably a derisive label coined by opponents (Acts 11:19–26). It seemed important to reemphasize that we believers are to be those who actually follow Jesus, learning to think like him and to act like him.

After I received the insight into the passage about the gift of tongues in 2 Corinthians, the understanding that my thinking had to change grew. I began to see fresh implications in Romans 12:1–2. In this passage Paul exhorts us that the only reasonable response to God's grace in Christ is to offer our "bodies as a living sacrifice" of worship. This means that our behavior is to be transformed, not aligned with the world system but aligned with God's will. This alignment will come about through the renewing of our minds.

I gave a teaching several times in those days that I titled "See! A New View!"[34] Little did I know that I was beginning to wrestle with issues that I would later come to know and teach as Biblical worldview, even before the words *world* and *view* had been combined into a single compound word.

At Waite Park I also first began to become acquainted with the idea of Christian community and developed an interest to know more. I read about Jesus people "communes" in California. I became interested in the Love Inn Community, the community in Freeville, New York, where *The Scott Ross Show* was produced. The history of that community, which I heard on cassette tape, had a big impact on me. I heard about Reba Place Fellowship in Chicago and also about the group that came to be called Sojourners, as well as others.

---

[34] See Appendix Two.

The fact is that the seeds of most of the kingdom realities that I have spent my life trying to understand and live were sown and/or germinated in that year and a half in Waite Park Wesleyan Church. Although Waite Park moved back toward its comfortable traditions not long after we moved away, we were blessed to be there at a unique time when the atmosphere was alive with godly love, spiritual hunger, and Biblical revelation. Under Pastor Hauser's leadership, God brought together a number of people who were seeking the Lord with all their hearts. It was the most seminal period in my life.

****

Wycliffe missionary Wayne Huff and his wife, Alice, came to speak at Waite Park's annual missions conference in May 1973. Wayne and his wife had worked in Guatemala for several years; however, because one of their children had a serious learning disability, the Huffs were working in the States as recruiters for Wycliffe. I was impressed with Wayne's sincere love for the Lord and his open heart toward the work of the Holy Spirit. Meeting the Huffs made me think again about missions and about the mission of Wycliffe Bible Translators. I had not thought much about Wycliffe since leaving Marion, where I'd studied under Russ Cooper and met Dr. John Crawford.

In October 1973 Patricia and I, along with our baby, Elijah, went back to Ohio to see our parents. My dad helped us pay for the trip by offering me the chance to help him work on a house that he and Mom were remodeling.

During that week, as I worked with Dad, I think he became convinced that positive changes in me—starting with my repentance from rebellion—were genuinely taking place, and we had good fellowship with one another. I did not tell him about the moving of the Spirit at Waite Park because I knew that he strongly opposed the "tongues movement," believing it to be a deception. I returned to Minneapolis rejoicing that healing had begun in my relationship with Dad.

Everywhere I turned those days, God seemed to feed the hunger in me to seek his kingdom and to be part of what he was doing in the earth in my generation. Between Christmas and the New Year holiday, Jay Swisher and I took a number of the Waite Park youth to Urbana '73, InterVarsity's mission conference at the campus of the University of Illinois. This conference was held every three years. That year approximately 16,000 young people gathered.

The speakers included Paul E. Little, John R. W. Stott, Edmund P. Clowney, Samuel Escobar, and Elisabeth Elliot. The message of David Howard, brother of Elisabeth Elliot, spoke to me most. Howard had been working as a missionary in Costa Rica and Columbia and was the director of Urbana '73. He told about how his eyes had been opened to the work of the Holy Spirit and to building communities of faith through the work of God in Columbia. Gregorio Landero, a leader of the church in Columbia, accompanied Howard; Landero's testimony concerning God's work among his people made a deep impact on me.

I was also stirred by hearing Scott Ross speak at a workshop. His assigned topic was media, but his message fed my hunger to know God and to find his kingdom and community.

After a cold, cold drive (about -20º outside) in an uninsulated van with only a front-end heater, we arrived back home about midnight on New Year's Eve just as the New Year's Eve service was ending. Soon after greeting me, Patricia told me that Joe Johnson would be calling me about 12:30 a.m.

7

An Unexpected Path

The late Rev. Joe Johnson, whom we usually called Brother Joe, was a man several years older than my dad and one whom I deeply respected. Brother Joe's wife had deserted the Lord and her husband many years before this phone call, and he had remained single. He had been an effective pastor—loved deeply, not only by his own church but also by many in Madison County, Ohio, where he had driven a school bus and served many of the poor in his community. He had given freely of himself and his time to lead youth camps in the Churches of Christ in Christian Union (CCCU). He had worked tirelessly at any kind of manual job or administrative job necessary to make possible the youth camps and camp meetings of the denomination.

More than all this, Brother Joe's spirit and demeanor communicated love and acceptance—especially to young people. He loved to talk like he was gruff and grouchy, but it was clearly a front. After "retiring," he started an inner-city mission in Columbus, Ohio. Even until his death in 2013 at age 96, he still was deeply involved in the ministry of that mission. If the Churches of Christ in Christian Union canonized saints, Brother Joe should be one of the first to be recognized!

Brother Joe was serving as a district superintendent in Christian Union and I was working in a Wesleyan Church; therefore, I could not imagine why he was calling me in Minneapolis—or what could be so urgent that he would call at 12:30 in the morning, but I soon found out.

The promised call came, and we greeted one another. Brother Joe, as usual, got right down to business. There was a group of people in Richland Center, Wisconsin, who wanted to start a church that would be a part of CCCU. The nearest CCCU churches were in Indiana, and no pastor was readily available. He requested that Patricia and I meet him in Richland Center the second weekend of January. He wanted me to preach there, and he wanted to discuss our moving there to pastor.

I had no desire at all to leave Waite Park. Patricia and I had found a home among the people of our church and were ready to put our roots down deep. But out of respect for Brother Joe, I said that I would consider coming and would let him know within a few days.

After the holiday, I met with Pastor Hauser and told him about the call and the request. I was stunned when he encouraged me to meet with Brother Joe and to be open to what the Lord might be directing for us. I felt no rejection or anything of the sort; it was only that I had come to think that the Lord had brought together a team that would be together over the long haul right there in Northeast Minneapolis. I was not looking for openings.

Back in the spring of 1973, Waite Park had purchased a van for us to use in the youth work. We were also told that we could use the van for personal use. One morning in May 1973 I had dropped in unannounced on the Hickmans at their apartment. I discovered them and the Shriders sitting in a circle on the floor of the apartment, their pooled finances—less than $100—on the floor in the middle. They were praying for money for their move back to Ohio. One of their cars was not powerful enough to pull a trailer, and the other had a rusted-out place in the frame so that it was unsafe to use it. As I joined them in prayer I began to think, *What should I do?* I had no extra money, but Patricia and I did have access to the van, and our old '63 Ford was not being used. I said, "I'm not sure my car will make the trip, but you are welcome to have it if you want to try." They jumped at the offer.

On the day the Hickmans and Shriders were to leave for Ohio, pulling the trailer with the Ford, I received a call saying that they had made it only to the east side of St. Paul when the transmission light had come on. They had stopped at a service station, where they discovered that the transmission fluid was 2 quarts low. They asked me to have people pray. We did.

Later, after they had arrived safely in Lancaster, Ohio, they reported that the transmission had lost a quart of fluid every 50 miles until they reached Eau Claire, Wisconsin. After that it went down a quart every 100 miles until they reached Chicago. Then they had no more problems. Several years later when Patricia and I were visiting the Meadows in Lancaster, the Shriders came to visit us—driving that Ford!

Thus, we did not own a car, and it did not seem right to use the church van to look into another job. Therefore, on the second Friday of January, Patricia and I with our toddler, Elijah, boarded a Greyhound bus for the ride to Richland Center, Wisconsin.

****

In January, darkness falls in Minneapolis by 4:30 p.m. We boarded the bus in mid-afternoon, so we did not see much on the ride to Richland Center. I know we drove down alongside the Mississippi River and crossed over into La Crosse, Wisconsin, on U.S. Highway 14. About 75 miles later we came into Richland Center, and the bus dropped us off at the hotel near downtown. We called a cab and rode in it to the Lamplighter Motel on U.S. 14, east of town, where Brother Joe was waiting for us.

Once we had taken our luggage into our room, we went to Brother Joe's room to talk with him. After catching up a bit, we began to discuss the situation there in Richland Center. I blurted out: "Brother Joe, you do not want me to pastor here. I speak in tongues."

I had thought that this declaration would be the end of his request, but not so. In response to his questions I told some of my story. I also told him that while I clearly believed in the continuing validity of the gifts of the Spirit and the gift of tongues in particular, I did not hold any one gift to be the evidence of the baptism in the Holy Spirit. I told him that, as I understood it, the gifts are distributed by the Holy Spirit according to his will, and that one gift is not universal to all men.[35]

Brother Joe reached into his briefcase and pulled out a small booklet titled *What We Teach*, which CCCU had published previously. I did not remember having seen the booklet before. To my surprise, it included a statement about the gifts of the Holy Spirit. There were two parts to the statement. The first essentially said, "We believe in all the gifts of the Holy Spirit, but we do not believe that any one gift is the evidence of the baptism in the Holy Spirit." The second part stated CCCU's strong belief in divine healing.

The position I had shared with Brother Joe was essentially the same—if one took the words in the booklet literally. He said that he knew people whom he respected as brothers and sisters in Christ who spoke in tongues. He went on to say that he saw no reason that my experience and belief should keep me from coming to pastor this new church as long as I did not try to promote speaking in tongues. My response was that this should be no problem as long as I was free to share my experience if anyone asked me, since it was the Holy Spirit's business to give the gifts.

I must say, however, that I knew Brother Joe's position on this matter was not typical of CCCU leaders, including the view of Dad, a former general superintendent. I have no way of knowing what was in Brother Joe's thinking at that point. I have wondered if he questioned the viability of this "church" plant anyway. Since it was a few hundred miles to the nearest CCCU church, I also have thought that maybe he did not believe my experience could have much impact in the denomination anyway.

---

[35] I took this understanding from 1 Corinthians 12:11 without fully considering other relevant passages that may point to a different conclusion.

As I understood it, however, I had done my part—I had been honest and open with the one who represented the authority of God and of CCCU in that situation. Therefore, instead of being released from making a decision, Patricia and I had to seriously begin to seek God to learn whether or not he was calling us to Richland Center.

The more I learned about the situation in Richland Center, the less appealing it was to think about helping to start a church in that town. The people wanting a church had split from the local Church of the Nazarene in support of the former Nazarene pastor, who had been disciplined by the Nazarene denomination.

The local church had begun a building addition, and the pastor, without authorization from the church board, had authorized the contractors to spend about $30,000 more than the original contract. Apparently, this was the third time he had done something like this in a Nazarene church; therefore, the denominational leaders had stripped him of his ordination credentials.

This pastor had then approached a leader in CCCU asking to become a CCCU pastor. I do not know whether that leader failed to check out his background or not, but he had been received into CCCU and was looking for an opportunity to pastor a church.

Several families who had retained their loyalty to him left the Nazarene church to begin a new church, and the former pastor had encouraged them to contact CCCU. Since Wisconsin was closest to the churches over which Brother Joe had oversight, he had become responsible for this proposed church plant.

As far as cities go, Minneapolis is about as good as they get. There are seven lakes around the west and south sides, all joined by parks with walking tracks and bike paths, plus numerous other parks in the city. The next morning as we left the motel and were able to see our surroundings in the daylight, we found ourselves in a rural wonderland. From the motel door we looked over snow-covered farmland to the southwest. A few miles farther away, tree-covered hills rose up sharply like mini-mountains with rock bluffs standing out like sentinels among the leafless trees on the points of the hills.

As we drove toward town on U.S. 14 we could see that a similar hill rose steeply a few hundred feet high on the edge of town. Starting on the southeast edge of town, the hill wrapped around the east side and curved back in on the northeast. As we came into town we could see that several of the side streets to the east ended at the base of the hill. We discovered more hills northwest of town and directly west of town. The Pine River flowing in from the north split the hills and then flowed on south just to the west of town.

We discovered that Richland Center lay in the valley of the Pine, nestled between hills on three sides. Most of the hills, we would discover, had ridges on top that extended into miles of rolling land. Whole farms sat atop the hills up on the ridges. Other farms lay in creek valleys between these ridges. In a word, it was a beautiful place, even in mid-winter.

We met the people who wanted to start a church that weekend, and I preached at a Sunday morning gathering of about thirty-five people. They seemed to be nice enough people, but I was not very impressed with the situation. I had no desire at all to get involved with a splinter group from another church.

On Sunday afternoon, we returned to Minneapolis. Although I was not inclined to move to Richland Center, I did go back home prayerfully seeking to know God's will.

****

To my surprise, I gradually began to become convinced that it might be right to move to Wisconsin. As I continued to talk about it with Pastor Hauser and the brothers in the Bible study group, everyone seemed to confirm that I should go.

Brother Joe had asked me to return to Richland Center two weeks after the first visit in order to conduct services for the new church. Thus, Patricia and I went again. This time we stayed with one of the families in the church. That weekend Patricia and agreed that it was right for us to move to Richland Center to try to start this church, in spite of the fact that in principle I was against the division that had resulted in the formation of this church.

We returned to Minneapolis, where I announced that I would be resigning as youth pastor in order to pastor in Richland Center. I was so convinced that this was God's will that I simply made the commitment without even considering the fact that in CCCU the local church had to elect a pastor. Brother Joe could strongly recommend us, but according to CCCU polity, the people of the church had to call a pastor.

The following weekend I flew to Madison, Wisconsin, where Brother Joe met me and we drove on to Richland Center together. He had scheduled the church vote that Sunday. We arrived on Saturday and, to our surprise, discovered that the former Nazarene pastor had also shown up. He was planning on the church having a choice as to whether to call him or me, and most of these people had already demonstrated their loyalty to him by leaving the Nazarene church.

It was an uncomfortable situation; however, Brother Joe made it absolutely clear to the church board and to this former pastor that, while the church did not have to choose me, under no circumstances would this pastor be allowed to start a church in Richland Center under the auspices of CCCU.

Brother Joe preached that Sunday morning. At the end of the service, the church voted to call me as pastor. Following the service, we had a meal together with the church and then returned to our motel. In mid-afternoon, the former pastor showed up at the motel wanting to talk with us.

The man had an aggressive personality. He came in with a notebook and began to lay out all sorts of ideas and programs that he believed were necessary to build a church. One of his "principles" has remained in my memory all these years because I believed it wrong and also because it seemed to shed light on his failings. He said: "What you need to do is get the church into debt by starting a building project. That way they will have a common project to work on and a commitment that will keep them together." (Later the man did pastor two different CCCU churches—neither under Brother Joe's oversight—predictably, he caused serious problems in each church.)

After what seemed a long and insufferable time, the man left the room and apparently left town. No sooner had he gone than Brother Joe sighed and said, "I couldn't ask you and Patricia to come here."

Immediately, I responded, "That's good, because I don't want to come here anyway."

These statements, obviously emotionally based responses, completely ignored the fact that I had come to the conviction that God had called me to Richland Center. That evening, I announced that I was not going to accept the call after all. I went on to preach on unity; in that sermon I exhorted the people to humble themselves, to repent of their divisive actions, and to return to the Nazarene church.

****

I returned to Minneapolis with, as Chuck Berry sang, "no particular place to go." I had resigned from Waite Park. My resignation had been accepted. Although there was no dissatisfaction with Patricia's and my service, it had been confirmed that our time there was complete. Now I had refused to take the church in Richland Center. Needless to say, I was in a predicament.

Less than a month ago, I had not had the slightest inclination to leave Waite Park or Minneapolis. Now I had committed to leave the church. Over the course of the next couple of weeks, not one, but eleven different opportunities and possibilities came up for consideration—none of my own initiation; these ranged from taking a Wesleyan church in Iowa to beginning training with Wycliffe Bible Translators.

I was terribly confused. How was I to decide? In desperation, I started a fast on a Monday morning, determined not to eat again until I knew what God wanted of me.

Early Wednesday morning I arose from bed and left our second-floor apartment in the Waite Park building and went down to the Fireside Room, where I often read and prayed. I laid my Bible on a counter and, as was my custom in the winter, knelt to start a fire in the fireplace. As the wood began to burn I cried aloud, "O God, what do you want me to do?"

Although I did not expect an immediate answer, words came to my mind, an answer from God that could not have been clearer if he had spoken aloud: "I already told you. And you said you would not do it."

I began to weep and repent before the Lord. I decided to call Brother Joe as soon as appropriate that morning so that I could apologize and see if the opportunity in Richland Center was still available.

Arising from my knees, I walked over to my Bible, which I had unwittingly left open on the counter. Following my Bible reading pattern, I had come to the book of Jeremiah early in January, about the same time that I had first visited Richland Center. However, all month I had kept bogging down after a few chapters; thus, I had started over at the beginning of the book several times. It may have been because I had been to those pages so often recently, but the Bible had fallen open to Jeremiah that morning. As I reached out to pick up the book, my eyes went immediately to a specific place on the page—Jeremiah 3:18–19. The words I saw immediately confirmed—in an indisputable way to my mind at that time—the encounter that I had just had with the Lord.

> … "They will come together from the land of the north to the land which I gave your fathers as an inheritance.

"Then I said,
>   'How I would set you among My sons
>   And give you a pleasant land,
>   The most beautiful inheritance of the nations!'
>   And I said, 'You shall call Me, My Father,
>   And not turn away from following Me.' " (NASB)

Looking at the passage now, the memory of how powerfully God spoke to me through these words at that time remains clear in my mind. Over the years I have looked at the passage a number of times and I am always surprised to see that the passage itself does not mention "rich land." Somehow, the mention of a "pleasant land" and a "beautiful inheritance" translated into my mind as "rich land."

The passage did refer to "coming from the north," which would be true of our move from Minneapolis to Richland Center. Geographically speaking, Richland County and Richland Center were as beautiful a place as I had ever seen. And these words, "and not turn away from following Me," seemed to speak directly to my refusal to accept the call, the act of which I had just repented.

I had no way of knowing then that the words "You shall call Me, My Father, and not turn away from following Me" were soon to take on new and profound personal significance.

I never questioned from that time forward that God had called me to this new work. The land was a blessing. After we once again had a car to drive, Patricia and I often went for long rides through the hills. We never tired of the scenery in Richland County and southwestern Wisconsin.

The people of the church rented a little house for us right on U.S. 14, the next-to-last house on the south end of town. Often I crossed the highway, walked a few yards to the south, climbed a fence, crossed a small pasture and climbed up to a rock bluff on the point of the hill. From that rock I could see most of Richland Center and a vast area of the river valley. It became a favorite place to pray.

Before long we found that we needed the promise of Jeremiah 3 and the gift of this natural beauty. While we have a number of good memories of the time in Richland Center, it also proved to be a spiritual wilderness—a place of testing. It became a time in which we had to keep making the choice not to turn back from following our Father.

8

A Painful Breach

We moved to Richland Center in mid-February 1974. One of the young men of the church brought his pickup and trailer up to the Twin Cities. With help from Waite Park friends, we loaded up our belongings and moved out.

I had preached a farewell sermon on our last Sunday night there. Actually, for the first time in my life, I read my sermon. As I began to prepare, I was moved, by the Lord, I believed, to write out in essay form a sermon on unity and diversity in the church. I was so convinced that the Lord had given me the message that I did not feel free to add to it—so I read it to the people. I do not know what impact it had with the people. I also had no idea that this message would become the first piece of my writing to be published. I had no idea that I would be developing this theme for years to come; the concept of unity and diversity, I would later come to understand, is one of the building blocks of a Biblical worldview.

After arriving in town, we located the house at 1330 Sextonville Road (which is also U.S. 14). Several of the church people were waiting to greet us, excited to show us the house and to help us unload our belongings. The house was small, white with red trim, badly in need of fresh paint, sitting about 12 feet off the highway. An enclosed porch with several windows sagged off the front of the house. Once we opened the front door and stepped into the kitchen we could see and smell why they were so excited. They had obviously worked hard to clean the house as well as possible and to put fresh paint on all the inner walls.

The house itself had four small rooms—a kitchen, a living room, and two bedrooms separated by doorways but no doors. There was also a tiny bathroom and a rickety set of stairs going down into the cellar, which was dry but had an unpleasant odor that we discovered came from a small leak in the waste line from the toilet.

To be honest, after living in apartments in Circleville, in Marion, and in Minneapolis, it was a bit exciting to have "our own home." So what if the basement was fragrant and the porch looked like it might fall off? So what if you could stand in the doorway between the kitchen and living room on a winter morning and feel cold air coming through leaky windows from all directions? So what? It was our home.

As I had done in moving to Waite Park, I was so intent on finding and doing God's will that I had not even asked about wages. Once we had moved to Richland Center, the members of the church board informed us that they were committed to pay us $50 each week for salary; plus, they would rent the house and pay the utilities. Adding the rent and house costs together our income was $78.21 per week.

We still had no car, and we could not afford one, so for the first two months we walked, bummed rides, or occasionally took a taxi. While this limited our mobility, it did save us money so that we actually set aside $100 in those two months.

Then Brother Joe brought us a car that CCCU had purchased for us to use, a 1968 two-tone brown Dodge Monaco station wagon purchased for $800. We were thrilled. We also were glad that gas at the time was less than 50 cents a gallon since that car did drink up the gas.

Once we had a car, we were able to get around. I could actually start calling on church members who lived beyond walking distance. However, we could no longer save money; now we needed more.

By late April I was able to get a job driving a school bus for Earl Conley, a private contractor who owned four buses and had a contract to drive for the Richland County schools. Earl paid me $11 per day to drive my scenic 45-mile route morning and evening.

It would be difficult to find a more beautiful drive. I would discover the next winter that it had its challenges, however. The scenic gravel roads up the hills were treacherous on snow. Twice I could not make it up a freshly snow-covered hill. With nowhere to turn around, I had to try to back up a quarter-mile or more—using only my outside mirrors since the bus windows were too steamed up to see through. I made it back safely the first time on a straight road.

The second time I got stuck going up a wooded hill on a curvy, tree-lined road. I was able to back up, negotiating the curves, as long as the trees marked the sides of the road. At the bottom I came to open fields, where snow had drifted across the road and had filled in ditches along the sides. I got safely past an old barn and an empty house, but when I came to a straight section through the field, I steered a bit too far to the right; the right rear wheels dropped into the ditch. I was stranded along with thirty or so students.

One of the older high school boys walked to the nearest house, where he phoned for help. An hour or so later, Earl came backing up the road behind me with his bus. He hooked up a log chain to my bus and was able to pull it out. Then he, driving forward, pulled us safely back to the highway. Someone had contacted parents along the bad roads, and they came out to meet us at safe stops—usually in four-wheel-drive vehicles. We all got home late but safe.

By February and March, the gravel roads, narrow in the best times, were barely the width of one lane because of the banks of plowed snow on the sides. The snow was piled so high that even in the high bus seat I could not see over the banks. When I met a car on those roads, the car would back up to the nearest turnoff and let the bus pass.

In addition to the daily route, occasionally I would be asked to drive students on a field trip or to take a team to an athletic event. On these trips I could make $2.50 per hour and I would be paid for the whole time—not just driving time. As a driver I could usually get into the events free if I so chose. And, if we stopped at McDonald's or a few other fast-food places, as a driver I could receive a free meal. Usually I did not participate in the events but rather took books with me and used the non-driving time for study.

On the whole, driving a school bus was a pleasant job—though there were challenges as well as the occasional need to deal with the orneriness of a few older boys. I did not make much money, but it was enough.

I drove only for the last month that school year. During the time of confusion after I had rejected the call to Richland Center, Patricia and I had once again begun to consider our desire to be involved in foreign missions. Even after repenting and then moving, we continued to feel pulled to pursue work in foreign missions.

In April 1974 we decided that we should apply to attend the Summer Institute of Linguistics (the scientific and training arm of Wycliffe Bible Translators) at the University of North Dakota. We sent in the application and were accepted—on condition that we would immediately send in the $90 registration fee and that we commit to pay nearly $1,000 before the Summer Institute ended in mid-August. We took $90 from the $100 that we had saved when we had no car and sent it in. And we began to pray for financial aid.

From previous contacts we had learned that Wycliffe's policy for members was that they not solicit funds. They could, and should, talk freely about their work in Wycliffe but should talk about their financial need only when specifically asked about it. It seemed to us that we should make this policy our own as well, trusting the Lord to supply our needs.

A few days after we sent in the registration fee, we received $100 in the mail—from whom and for what reason I do not remember now. I had been reading through Proverbs monthly for some time. When we received this money, about one-tenth of our projected summer expenses, the words of Proverbs 3:9–10 came to mind and I could not get rid of them.

> Honor the Lord from your wealth,
> And from the first of all your produce;
> So your barns will be filled with plenty,
> And your vats will overflow with new wine. (NASB)

I began to feel that we ought to give this $100 away since it represented the firstfruits of our prayers. Eventually, I tentatively shared the Scripture with Patricia; she rose to the challenge, telling me to do what I believed was right with her full support. So it was that we sent $25 each to four different ministries.

The day after we put this money in the mail, the mailman delivered to us a cashier's check for $200 drawn on the St. Anthony National Bank—a small bank near Waite Park church. Although we have some suspicions, we never did find out which human actually sent that money. We had no doubt that ultimately the Lord had provided it, at just the right time to confirm our decision to study with SIL.

****

We had consulted with Brother Joe as we had been making the decision to study at SIL. Once the decision was made, we talked with the church about it. Brother Joe found a young couple from Circleville Bible College who were willing to come to Richland Center to serve the church during our absence. That couple was to be paid the salary that we had been receiving. We had no source of income for the summer.

A few days into the month of June, we left Richland Center and drove to Circleville in order to attend CCCU's annual Ministerial Convention. We planned to stay with my parents in Waverly, Ohio, during the convention on Tuesday and Wednesday, and then we planned to visit Patricia's parents in Portsmouth before we headed back north at the end of the week.

At the convention, on Tuesday I had lunch with John Meadows, who was an assistant pastor at the Lancaster CCCU, where John Maxwell, now well known for his seminars and books on leadership, was the senior pastor. Throughout the meal we talked about the events of the past months, as well as what we had been reading and hearing. As usual we stimulated one another to keep pressing to recognize the present-day work of the Lord and to be in it.

The following events are difficult to share because they have to do with Dad as well as with me. I do not want to write about them because I do not want to cast Dad in a bad light. Such is not the case. I was foolish and wrong in many ways in the troubles that follow. Whether Dad made mistakes or not is between the Lord and him. I know that he was doing the best he knew according to his deepest convictions. What Dad did, he did because he loved me and wanted the best for me. Ironically, I also loved him and desperately—too desperately—wanted his approval, I later came to see. We both were fully committed to serve the same Lord, but because of differing convictions and human weakness we hurt each other badly in the process. Thankfully, the end of the matter is better than the beginning.

Toward the end of the meal I had begun to share with John the ways in which my relationship with my dad had been continuing to improve. I was rejoicing because of the positive growth in that relationship. I continued sharing on this subject as we walked out of the dining hall and headed back to the chapel for the afternoon sessions. Just as we reached the door to leave the dining hall, I was saying to John, "There is only one thing I still can't talk with Dad about," referring to having received the gift of tongues. As these words left my mouth, I glanced to the left and saw Dad using the pay phone in the corner. I knew immediately that he had heard those words; his face showed obvious grief and pain.

Sorrow and fear gripped me in an instant. I sent John on while I waited for Dad to get off the phone. Dad and I went upstairs into one of the classrooms. I kept trying to explain the context of the statement while Dad was pressing me to tell him what I couldn't talk to him about. Desperately, I tried hard to explain myself without talking about tongues, but there was no way. Eventually I said it: "I pray in tongues."

Dad responded immediately by praying fervently for me to be free of this spiritual deception—so fervently that I ended up on the floor with him standing over me praying for demons to come out of me. I knew his response was genuine, based on his convictions and on his love for his son.

Part of the approval I sought was for Dad to "understand" me. Looking back from my present vantage point, I now am confident that he understood me far better than I could recognize at the time. By violating trust and having been a rebellious son, I had not established a foundation for communication around this significant difference in our doctrinal understanding and spiritual experience.

I think it must have brought up in his mind incidents from my teen years when I had unwisely sought counsel from other adults about my relationship with dad. My cry to them had been that Dad did not understand me. These people had gone to Dad, probably trying to help, but had come across to him as critical and condemning. He had felt betrayed by me then—not without reason, as I see it now.

Given our past relationship, Dad understandably saw tongue-speaking as one more rebellion. No explanation I could give would change that perception. However, not only did I pray in tongues, but I also had had a deep revelation of spiritual authority. Although as an adult I was not under my dad's authority in the same way I should have been as a child, I knew that I needed to be open to hearing the Lord through him as an adult—he still was my father after all.

After a long, painful effort to communicate, we had made no progress. Then Dad asked, "Does John Meadows also speak in tongues?" I tried to avoid answering for John, but my inability to deny that John also prayed in tongues left the clear impression that he did.

At last we left the classroom in an impasse—an impasse that continued during the rest of our stay with Dad and Mom.

As soon as I could get to John, I told him what had happened. As quickly as possible he told John Maxwell about it. Incredibly, John Maxwell's response was: "I do not speak in tongues and do not know why you think you need to do so. However, I know you and trust you and I will stand by you." Neither John Meadows nor I expected such a response from John any more than I had expected Brother Joe's response a few months earlier.

I came to understand that a similar response was not an option for Dad. In addition to the doctrinal issue, my past rebellion had undermined trust too far, and the repentance that I had made was too recent, making it difficult to rebuild a bridge of trust between us. The fact that we were geographically separated by hundreds of miles, making face-to-face communication infrequent, added to the difficulty in working out our relationship.

Dad's convictions against the modern-day "tongues movement" were deep, and they were shared by most leaders in CCCU. In fact, during the very time that I had been in Richland Center, the CCCU General Board, which included my dad, Brother Joe, and also John Meadow's mother, had been working on clarifying an official denominational position on tongues. The bottom line of their position was that the gift of tongues recorded in Scripture was the gift of speaking supernaturally in a known language for the purpose of evangelism. The "tongues" mentioned in 1 Corinthians 14, according to this position, were not the gift of tongues but were natural languages. Paul, they believed, was addressing the problem of people in the same local church insisting on speaking in their own native languages even though others in the church could not understand them. According to this position, modern tongues as used by Pentecostals and Charismatics is either an expression of uncontrolled emotionalism or a sign of demonic activity.

Although, until this encounter, I did not know that this had been taken as an official position by CCCU, it was no surprise to me since it was consistent with what I had heard preached as a child. Although it was a deeply painful time, even then I could see that Dad had no option other than to stand against what he believed to be false doctrine and heretical practice. Therefore, I had no resentment toward him because of it.

I certainly did not understand then that God was going to use this broken relationship with my earthly father as a means to draw me into far greater fellowship with and dependence on my heavenly Father. That realization came to me gradually over the next fifteen years or more. However, it would be more than forty years before I understood that God had spoken to me already about what he was going to accomplish: "And I said, 'You shall call Me, My Father, and not turn away from following Me,'" the Lord had said through Jeremiah 3:19, the passage God had used to confirm my call to Richland Center.

When Patricia and I left my parents' home on Thursday morning, we were still at an impasse except that, out of concern to deal with the authority issue, I had promised Dad that I would refrain from praying in tongues while we tried to resolve the issue. I also knew that Dad had already brought the matter before the denomination's General Board.

It had not been a pleasant visit for any of us.

9

Separation

With deep sadness, Patricia and I left for Portsmouth in order to visit her parents for a couple of days.

On one of the evenings there, Patricia's father and I drove into New Boston on an errand. As we traveled, I told him about the controversy that was stirring because of the issue of tongues. I did not want him to hear rumors or secondhand accounts, and he needed to know because of the effect all this would have on his daughter.

His response both surprised and helped me. He said: "I do not speak in tongues. But I know that it is in the Bible. And, if I believed God wanted me to speak in tongues, I would do so." He went on to express his support for me as I sought to follow the Lord.

On Saturday, we returned to Wisconsin. After preaching on Sunday, we left to go on to Grand Forks, North Dakota, to begin training to be Bible translators. We left the key to our house so that the young couple who would care for the church could live there over the summer.

Wycliffe Bible Translators (WBT) is a missionary organization in the sense that the purpose is to aid in spreading the gospel by providing the Bible in all the languages of the world. WBT has focused on reaching tribal groups who have no written language. The Wycliffe missionary is not primarily a church planter or teacher. Rather, he or she is a trained linguist who goes out to live among a tribal people in order to learn their language and their culture.

Cameron Townsend, who came to be known as Uncle Cam, founded Wycliffe Bible Translators after translating the New Testament into a Guatemalan Indian (Native American) language in the 1920s. Uncle Cam had no prior translation experience. He had gone to Guatemala to sell Spanish Bibles in 1917, only to discover that most of people in the Native American tribes used Spanish only as a second language. Many of them could not read Spanish. Most of their native languages did not have a written form, so the Bible was not accessible to them.

Uncle Cam felt compelled to make the Scriptures available to these people in their own language so that they could read the good news about Jesus for themselves.

Although he had no prior linguistic training, he learned the language of one tribe, produced an alphabet, and translated the New Testament.

As he worked, Uncle Cam had a growing desire and drive to see the New Testament made available in every language in the world. Therefore, in 1934 he began a summer program, which he called the Summer Institute of Linguistics, in order to train linguists so that they could translate the Scriptures for other tribes. SIL officially became a scholarly and humanitarian organization that began to serve internationally. In 1942 Uncle Cam formed Wycliffe Bible Translators as a vehicle to connect with churches in order to recruit Bible translators and to raise support for the work.

Guatemala and other nations in Central and South America were officially Catholic nations, and Protestant missionaries were not allowed to work there. Therefore, Uncle Cam diplomatically formed contracts with the governing authorities for SIL to develop written languages for tribal peoples, to teach literacy, and to translate materials concerning health and agriculture and works of "high moral value" in order to promote their general welfare. "Works of high moral value" was understood unofficially to mean the Bible, but that was not made official in order not to conflict with the Catholic Church authorities.

As the years passed, Uncle Cam used this strategy of contracting for SIL to work with civil governments by doing linguistic and humanitarian work to open the doors for Bible translation teams to work in several Communist nations where missionary work was prohibited.

This approach meant that the Wycliffe missionary could not come in and seek to plant a church or do "Christian" work in a direct manner. However, through building relationships with the native speakers, and especially through working with native speakers in translating the Scripture, the gospel was communicated. Often the native translator came to believe in the Lord Jesus and to follow him; in these cases, the Wycliffe missionary was often able to disciple the native translator. Sometimes native churches began to grow out of this relationship. In other places, Wycliffe missionaries were able to serve workers from other missions in the area who were spreading the gospel but lacked the training to translate the Bible.

The distinction between going out as a linguist instead of a missionary was important to my journey. On the one hand, it fit well with my desire to break down the big distinction in the level of commitment expected of the "clergy" in contrast to the "laity." On the other hand, my motivation was to spread the good news about Jesus, resulting in the formation of communities of disciples. It seemed to me that WBT/SIL's methodology fit well with both these desires.

In 1974, when Patricia and I first participated in one of the summer schools, SIL was a two-summer program requiring most students to do a semester's worth of graduate-level training in linguistics in each ten-week summer session. There were special forums presented during the summer schools to introduce students to principles of anthropology and sociology, which Wycliffe missionaries had found to be important to their work. Depending on academic background, some students took the first-year material for undergraduate credit. Some spouses, including Patricia, took the courses on a pass/fail basis, not trying to get college credit. It was an intense ten weeks!

As it turned out, Patricia and I have not yet used our linguistic training in a direct way. However, the three summers that we spent in SIL proved to be important in unexpected ways.

First, I was deeply moved by the dedication of the WBT/SIL workers. These were people who had offered years of their lives to do this work, many times in primitive conditions. Many of them had worked for advanced academic degrees, not only to get more training but also to become more credible to the governments where they worked and to be qualified to teach in these university settings. They were so committed to the call to translate the Scriptures that, rather than work only in their own language assignments, they would give up two or three months, at their own financial expense, in order to train new workers.

Second, I found at SIL that Baptists, Methodists, Presbyterians, Lutherans, Pentecostals, and others could love and respect one another and could work together in unity to accomplish a common task. In my background, I had developed suspicion and judgment toward Christians who did not believe and worship like our group. My attitudes had begun to change through contact with the Jesus Movement and the Charismatic Renewal; however, actually living in a dorm complex, eating meals, studying, and recreating together for ten weeks with dedicated believers from other backgrounds opened me to a new respect and love for the larger Body of Christ. What's more, I came to realize that many of these people knew God in ways I did not yet know him and that some had proved more dedication to him than I had.

Third, a few of the SIL staff and students were charismatic. Several of these staff members and a few students met to pray early each morning. That small prayer group became a source of spiritual encouragement for me. On Thursday evenings several from the prayer group would attend a charismatic prayer meeting, sponsored by the

Body of Christ Community and held in the basement of St. Michael's Catholic Church. Each summer in Grand Forks a few of these SIL people participated in the Thursday evening prayer meeting, as well as some of the other activities of the Body of Christ Community. One Thursday night Patricia and I went along. Had we been told, we would never have believed that attending this meeting would eventually become hugely significant in our journey.

I enjoyed the meeting. Patricia had still not bought into the charismatic gifts and expression, and worshipping with Catholics was not her preference. I was not too sure about the Catholic part, but I appreciated the worship and the sharing in the meeting.

After the meeting, true to my nature, I headed for the book table. I saw a number of books with which I was familiar, as well as several that I did not recognize. One small book, however, captured my attention. Co-written by a priest and Larry Alberts, who had led the meeting that night, the book was titled *Mary Is a Pentecostal*. I glanced through it and, curiosity aroused, I shelled out the $0.75 price and took it back to our room.

I read it through that night before going to sleep. The title, of course, came from the fact that Mary, Jesus's mother, had been in the upper room on the Day of Pentecost. Because of the Catholic emphasis on the role of Mary, I could see that this would be a way to validate Charismatic spirituality among Catholics.

The book also related several incidents when Mary supposedly had made appearances to Charismatics—not only to Catholics, but also to Protestants, whom she was calling to return to the Roman Catholic Church. The book named some of Larry's friends in the Body of Christ Community who had converted to Catholicism. The primary message I took from the book was that the Charismatic Renewal was a primary hope for restoring "the departed brethren" (in other words, Protestants) to the Roman church.

In a word, I took offense, deep offense. I made an inner vow to never go back to one of those meetings. Not only was I more than skeptical about these supposed visitations, but I also abhorred the idea of Protestants returning to the "whore of Babylon," a term often applied to the Roman Church by several of the preachers whom I had heard as a child. I fully intended to keep that vow!

However, there was not much time to think about such matters that summer. I had to focus on the classwork, and there was still the school bill to pay. I do not remember how it happened, but over the course of that summer the money gradually came in to pay off the school bill. Our personal expenses were small, since our meals and rooms were provided. But there were some personal expenses, including laundry, and we did have a year-and-a-half-old son.

In those days I don't believe disposable diapers existed yet. If they had, we could not have afforded to use them. I remember one time that we had $0.26 and had to wash the diapers. Patricia took that last quarter and put the diapers in the washer. We hung them all over our two dorm rooms to dry.

A week before the summer session ended, I went in and checked the balance on our school bill. We still owed about $150 dollars. No money came in that week. We had five dollars; yet, we had to leave and were scheduled to drive about 1,100 miles to Richland Center and on to Circleville.

On the final day, after we had packed our car I went back to the finance office. I had no choice but to apologize. We had not kept our commitment to pay off the bill before school ended. However, when the staff member looked up my account it had been paid off and there was $50 left over.

I left that room, nearly floating, with $55 in my wallet. As I walked toward the car, one of the missionaries stopped me. He informed me that the Lord had led him and his wife to give Patricia and me $20 for our trip home.

God had certainly met us financially! He had provided all our needs at that point. With $75 in our possession and thanksgiving flowing from our lips, we headed out.

****

Soon after arriving at the University of North Dakota in Grand Forks, I had written a letter to my dad. Later, I wished that I had kept a copy of the letter so that I could verify that what I had written was actually what I meant to say. It had been my intention to reaffirm my commitment to *refrain* from speaking in tongues. As I remember it, I had committed myself to restudy the matter of the gifts, particularly the matter of tongues, in the Bible in an effort to see if I had gone astray. I also recall writing that if God had not given me the gift of praying in tongues, then I would have to start over. By this, I meant that, if it were not God who had led me into this, then I was not sure that I knew God at all.

Whatever I wrote in that letter must have been ambiguous, but I did not realize that until several months later.

I had no time for a serious Bible study during the summer institute. But I did keep my word and refrained from using the gift of tongues in personal prayer and at the early morning prayer meeting as well.

In mid-August the summer school ended. We drove back to Richland Center and spent a night or two at home. To our surprise, the Bible College student who had substituted for me was still in town. He and his wife had moved across the street from our house to stay with a family from the church. Soon after we came home, the young student came over to our house in order to inform us that the people of the church had asked him to stay and pastor the church rather than for us to return.

In that conversation he also told me that he had been reading some of my books concerning the gifts of the Spirit and had begun to pray in tongues. These days he is still involved with a Charismatic church; also his dad, a CCCU preacher, later left the denomination to pastor a traditional Pentecostal church, and his younger brother pastors a Charismatic church in the Dayton, Ohio, area. The Holy Spirit certainly used my books to make an impact on that family.

I did not argue with the young man. I did not consult with the church members. I remembered that shortly before leaving for SIL I had offended a few ladies with one of my decisions. I also knew that at least one husband, a member of the church board, had taken up his wife's offense. I thought maybe this situation had developed as a result of that offense.

However, we had already planned to go right on to Ohio for the CCCU's General Council and annual camp meeting at Circleville. Rather than start a fight over the matter, Patricia and I left for Circleville without even staying for Sunday services.

Having seen so recently how God had provided financially, it was easy to believe that he would provide for us now in this situation as well.

Soon after arriving at the campground, I found Brother Joe and told him about the situation in Richland Center. He said that I was not to worry about it. He said that he would take care of the matter and that we should plan to go right on back to Richland Center once the camp meeting had ended. Within a few days, the young man and his wife were back in Ohio.

During the Council, Rev. Willard Cozad, whose term as general superintendent was about to end, called me into his office to discuss the matter of praying in tongues. Although he did not actually encourage me to pray in tongues, I found him to be personally supportive of me and interested in my journey. I gave him a copy of the sermon on unity and diversity that I had preached as my farewell message to the Waite Park church. To my surprise, he had the message published in the September issue of CCCU's denominational paper, *The Advocate*.[36]

After receiving my sermon from Rev. Cozad, the editor of *The Advocate*, P. Lewis Brevard, approached me later during the camp meeting and asked me to send him more articles.

We stayed with my parents most of the time during the Council and the camp because they lived nearby. As far as I can recall we did not talk about the tongues issue. Of course, we also spent some of the time in Portsmouth with Patricia's family. Then we headed home to Wisconsin.

We arrived safely and began to unload the car. As we had approached Richland Center, we had assessed our financial condition. We knew that we would need groceries right away. We also knew there would be no paycheck for a week.

A little more than two weeks before, we had left Grand Forks with $75. We had traveled nearly 2,000 miles. We had had no choice but to buy our meals along the way. It had helped, of course, that we stayed with our parents while in Ohio, but there were other expenditures as well. I do not recall now when or from whom we received money along the way, but we must have received some because we arrived home with $33.

Shortly after our arrival, we began to open mail. The first piece I opened was a bill for auto insurance, due that day. The amount of the bill: $33. *Thank God we can pay that bill,* I thought, *but now we are truly broke.*

The second piece of mail I opened was a card from my sister and brother-in-law. In the card I found a check for $30. What do you know? We were able buy some groceries after all. Does God know how to provide, or what?

****

---

[36] See Appendix Three.

The time in Richland Center, though not easy, was productive in some ways. Before we left Minneapolis God had begun to open my eyes to the need for unity among the churches in a geographic area.

I recall one incident from our Waite Park days that may help reveal the vision that was developing in me. Scott Ross and another brother from the Love Inn Community in Freeville, New York, had come to the Twin Cities to meet with some leaders about working together in a citywide outreach. Scott's radio show had been drawing a large audience in the area, and it seemed like his coming in person as the speaker would be an excellent way to draw in youth to hear the gospel. However, after several hours of discussion Scott had informed us that he and his team could not come at that time. He said that according to their discernment there was not enough substantial unity between the leaders and the ministries involved to do effective follow-up after the outreach.

New Wine magazine, which I had begun to read avidly each month, also presented the vision of the believers and leaders in a city working together in unity.

Not long after I had arrived in Richland Center, I was glad to discover a few area pastors who had a similar vision for unity in the church. Meredith Twining, a Free Methodist pastor, introduced me to Arvid Moen, the pastor of a United Methodist circuit in the county, and also to the Assembly of God pastor. The four of us began to meet together weekly for prayer and fellowship.

Arvid soon moved away to take a different church but not before I discovered that he had actually been to conferences sponsored by the *New Wine* teachers in Fort Lauderdale, Florida. Although we did not know one another well, or for very long, Arvid was used by the Lord to confirm the work the Lord had begun in me. Also, before he moved, Arvid told us about his brother-in-law, who was pastoring a Free Methodist church in Grand Forks.

I grew in my understanding during that time. A primary factor in that growth continued to be the Scripture reading regimen that I had begun in Minneapolis. *New Wine* magazine and several tape series offered in that magazine were lifelines of teaching. I subscribed to Bob Mumford's Lifechangers Recommended Tapes, a monthly ministry that introduced me to the messages of numerous Bible teachers whom the Lord used to open my eyes to the wealth of truth in the broader Body of Christ. I also continued to read books by Watchman Nee, especially after discovering that a Christian bookstore in our neighboring town, Viroqua, carried many of his books—more than I had known existed.

During that period, the Lord especially used Nee's writing to help me understand God's way of working in a man to help him have victory over sin and to become the sort of person through whom God's life could flow out and touch others. In the fall of 1974, I wrote an article recommending Nee's book *The Normal Christian Life*, and I also wrote a testimonial of the way I had been learning to practice Nee's teaching in my own life. I sent the articles in to Mr. Brevard. He published them in the November and December 1974 issues of *The Advocate*.

Living in Richland Center was something of a lonely period for Patricia and me. We had left great friendships in Minneapolis. Many of the young people there had become family to us. However, we were not able to form close friendships in our Richland Center church. There were only a few in the church whom we could actually trust and, if we had become close to that few, others would have been jealous and stirred up problems.

Our next-door neighbors, the Greens, were agnostics. Ironically, they became better friends with us than most of our church members.

During that time, a serious flaw in Patricia's and my relationship came fully to light. We loved one another deeply and we were as committed to one another as ever. However, I had "run ahead" in terms of my understanding of Scripture and some theological matters, changing dramatically in my understanding and experience. I had grown—but not *with* my wife. I had grown along with the brothers in my accountability group. I continued to grow through my relationship with John Meadows, with whom I was exchanging long cassette tape updates. I grew because of the books I was reading and the tapes that I was devouring, but I had failed to lead my wife well and to adjust my pace to her need.

Patricia is not inclined to take interest in things that she perceives to be theological and academic. She is much more practically minded. She did not seem to mind me reading and listening, but she was fearful of the changes she saw happening in me. She recognized that I could not continue to change in my beliefs without that bringing change in the direction of our lives.

We came to see that communication was a serious weakness in our relationship. We were friends and we were lovers, but we had a difficult time talking about the spiritual changes that were taking place in my mind and in the practice of my faith.

Then and now we really need each other. Her practical strengths lie in my weak areas. I should have learned how to support, encourage, and help her grow in her understanding and experience of God. Unfortunately, I pushed and pulled rather than coming alongside her. I meant well, most of the time, but too often I came across like a "cattle drover," not like a friend and shepherd.

While at Waite Park, we had begun to hear teaching on the Christian family emphasized by teachers in the Body of Christ. One of the first books that I read on this subject, Larry Christenson's *The Christian Family*, strongly challenged me and has proved to be foundational. While we lived in Richland Center, we kept hearing more and more teaching on this subject. After a time, we "knew" the principles. Living them was a different matter, especially for me.

We lived in Richland Center a little less than a year and a half. When it came time to leave, we had not yet learned to communicate and to operate as one, particularly when it came to issues of the Spirit. We had come face-to-face with our need, which was necessary.

In the spring of 1974, Brother Joe had brought two Korean church leaders to visit the church. The CCCU leadership wanted Patricia and me to consider moving to Korea in order to help start a Bible college. I exchanged several letters with the General Missionary Superintendent exploring this possibility.

In the fall of 1974, Brother Joe and the new CCCU general superintendent, Rev. Donovan Humble, my dad's first cousin, came to visit the church. It was a good visit. One conversation stands out in my memory. We were walking down the sidewalk on a cold fall evening, going to a meeting with the church in the basement of City Hall, where we were holding our services. We were discussing the history of the church there in Richland Center. I had observed that even though I had wanted to help these people reconcile with the Nazarene church, in addition to the relational rifts, most of the people in this church were socioeconomically like Christian Union people, one or two steps lower than Nazarenes. The other men laughed a bit, and one of them remarked that my observation was insightful for one so young.

Then Brother Donovan said: "Denominations are not Biblical anyway. They are man's attempt to help God." There was no time to follow up on the statement, but it stunned me. I had come to the conclusion that denominations were a serious problem—institutionalizing the divisions in the church. I do not think Brother Donovan meant anything pejorative by his remark. I think he was simply speaking factually. But it strengthened my growing discomfort with working in a denomination.

The business of the gift of tongues had not been settled. I was still refraining from praying in tongues as I had promised. I had done all the research and study again. I had tried hard to pray about the matter. I knew it could not be sanctioned by the authorities in CCCU. I also knew that it would deeply wound my parents if I began again to pray in tongues. However, I could not continue to deny either what I had come to believe Scripture taught or what I had experienced.

We drove back to Ohio to celebrate Christmas with our families. I was heavyhearted because I knew I was going to have to talk with Dad about my convictions concerning the gift of tongues.

Dad really reached out to me during that visit. It was as though the "tongues thing" had never been an issue between us. He spent quite a bit of time with me. He bought me a pair of Florsheim shoes—the most expensive brand that I knew of back then. And for Christmas he gave me his favorite 12-gauge shotgun, a five-shot, pump-action Ithaca. I am confident that Dad was not trying to buy me off or anything, but it was obvious that he was pleased with me.

I could not figure out why he was so free with me. And I failed. I did not break the mood by talking about what was on my heart.

As Patricia and I headed back to Richland Center, I knew that by putting off the conversation I had only made things harder.

For three weeks, I wrestled with what to do. Then I spent five hours writing a five-page letter to Dad detailing my struggle over the previous months and laying out my understanding of the Scriptural teaching concerning the gifts of the Spirit. I wrote that I had to be faithful to God and that I could no longer in good conscience continue to refrain from praying in tongues. With sad resolve I posted the letter. Then I fasted for several days—until I knew the letter had had time to reach my parents in Ohio.

I heard nothing from them for two or three weeks. Then Mom called. With an obviously broken heart she told me how badly she and Dad were wounded. She also told me that Dad had had no choice but to inform the general superintendent about the situation and thus to begin the process of separating us from Churches of Christ in Christian Union.

To my dismay, I learned later from John Meadows that there had been a serious misunderstanding or miscommunication between Dad and me. In my understanding, I had made a commitment in the letter of the previous June to refrain from praying in tongues while I prayed and studied through the matter again. Apparently, Dad had read that commitment as a commitment to renounce tongues altogether.

It turned out that the matter of John and me speaking in tongues had been discussed in CCCU's General Board meeting in the summer of 1974. John's mother was on the board, along with my dad. John's mother had reported to him that, during that discussion, Dad had said that I had renounced speaking in tongues. How awful it must have been for Dad. His firstborn son had gone off track into deception and the prodigal had returned, he thought. But then, his son had gone wrong again. He had to take back his own words to his fellow leaders.

Several weeks later Dad and I spoke to one another on the phone, although awkwardly. By early summer we had begun to correspond again. Thankfully we kept trying to relate with each other even though we often ended the contacts painfully.

I had no idea at that time that my efforts to make things better would only make them more difficult. I kept trying to get Dad to understand me. Therefore, our conversations became arguments. My letters caused more pain. The tapes and books that I sent to Dad, thinking that maybe he could at least come to understand, seemed to him to be efforts to convert him.

Both of us wanted to see the relationship restored; yet, we were at an impasse. Dad truly believed I needed to renounce the gift of tongues and return to the way he believed. I fully believed that I would be denying God to do so.

Jesus, in prayer to the Father, had said, "And this is eternal life, that they know you, the only true God, and Jesus Christ whom you have sent" (John 17:3). I did not understand then that this painful rift with Dad was an early step in a "journey" that would lead me to know my heavenly Father in a far greater way than I had known him before.

That spring CCCU sent two pastors, one of whom was my cousin, out to Wisconsin in order to try to bring me back to their way of thinking. Then in May, Brother Joe came out to Richland Center to officially release me from the denomination. When I handed him my Council ministerial license certificate, he wept.

In the months ahead, I often thought about something Jesus had said:

> Do not think that I have come to bring peace to the earth. I have not come to bring peace, but a sword. For I have come to set a man against his father, and a daughter against her mother, and a daughter-in-law

against her mother-in-law. And a person's enemies will be those of his own household. Whoever loves father or mother more than me is not worthy of me, and whoever loves son or daughter more than me is not worthy of me. And whoever does not take his cross and follow me is not worthy of me. Whoever finds his life will lose it, and whoever loses his life for my sake will find it. (Matthew 10:34–39)

Make no mistake about it; I do not blame Jesus for my rebellious attitude, which had been such a significant factor in the division that came between my parents and me. I do not blame him for my other weaknesses and failures that contributed to the problem. I have come to believe, however, that God did use this division as a way to free me to follow a path that he had planned for me—one that I have serious doubt I would have taken without this temporary division with my parents and the resulting separation from the familial ties that I had with CCCU.

As I came to see later, the nature of the kingdom of God is such that any "treasure"— whether a person, a thing, or a desire—that would keep one from absolutely surrendering himself or herself to the will of the King, is something that God in his love and mercy will expose, and he will call for the person to die to that thing.

The "treasure" onto which I was holding, I now believe, was a misplaced hope or expectation or demand that my parents, and especially my dad, accept and approve of me on my terms. Of course, there is a proper sort of acceptance that parents should give their children, but that acceptance does not include unqualified approval of any and every choice or action their children may make.

We left Richland Center in June. During our last couple of months there, I had helped the church purchase the Jehovah's Witness Kingdom Hall. Our last Sunday in Richland Center was the church's first Sunday in their new building. We returned to Grand Forks for our second summer at SIL.

Community with Whom?

Before leaving Richland Center, upon the recommendation of my friend Meredith Twining, I was offered the opportunity to pastor a Free Methodist church in Illinois after we had been released by CCCU. I considered it, but not for long. I had no desire to get connected to another denomination. I have often said: "I got kicked out of CCCU because of speaking in tongues. If they had known my convictions about the church, they would have had a lot more reason to get rid of me." My desire was to see unity in a visible community of believers who truly lived in Christ's love for one another and to see unity among the "households of faith" in a specific locality. All too often loyalty to denominations separates Christians and hinders them from living the gospel as the visible testimony Jesus wants his followers to be, as he made so clear in John 13:34–35 and John 17:16–23.

Relationally, the separation from our heritage was incredibly painful. Even so, there was another sense in which it was freeing to me to be able to seek a church expression more in line with my growing Scriptural convictions.

We had not had to do much soul searching about where to go after Richland Center, though. We were convinced that we had been called to missions, and we believed that joining Wycliffe Bible Translators was the next step for us. That spring we made application for membership, including submitting long doctrinal statements on key points of the Christian faith.

Therefore, in June 1975 we returned to SIL for our second year, hoping that we would be accepted to serve with WBT as translators in Papua New Guinea. I planned to stay in Grand Forks for a year in order to complete all the classroom work for a master's degree in linguistics. Then, according to our plan, I would write my thesis paper on information gathered about the language of the people to which we would be assigned.

This time we sold much of what we owned, loaded up everything else in a U-Haul trailer, and headed north for the summer school. The previous summer we had met Arvid Moen's brother-in-law Bob Buck, the pastor of the Free Methodist Church in Grand Forks. I contacted Bob and he was kind enough to allow us to store our things in an attic area in their church building for the summer. We actually did not take much. Since we planned to go on to the mission field, we had sold most of our furniture. Besides taking our beds, we mostly took pots and pans, dishes, clothing, and books—things that we could pack up in boxes to be stored.

We had a few hundred dollars and some faith—along with a good dose of naivety. We figured we would need about $2,000 that summer for tuition, living expenses, and moving expenses, including whatever it took to get into housing for the next school year.

Yet again, God met all of our needs, although not always in the time frame that we expected. One particular incident stands out. Having been accepted into the graduate school, I sought to apply at the university housing office for a place in married student housing for the fall semester. I discovered that we needed a $50 deposit even to get onto the waiting list—a list that already had about 150 couples waiting for housing. We did not have $50, and a week or so later we still did not have it.

Patricia and I were so concerned that one Thursday, in desperation, we skipped a morning class in order to pray for help. After a significant time of prayer, both Patricia and I felt absolutely convinced that God had given us assurance that he would provide the money we needed. We experienced a deep peace.

At lunch the couple who always ate at our table in the cafeteria asked why we had not come to class, and we told them. The next Thursday, the husband asked if we had ever received the money. Jokingly, I replied, "No, I guess God's not going to take care of us this time."

As soon as the words came out, I was struck with the realization that my words had revealed a core of unbelief and mistrust in spite of the inner assurance we had received the week before. Patricia immediately looked at me, and I could see that she knew also that I had unwittingly made an accusation against God that revealed my heart attitude. I was repentant, but the words were out.

Later that afternoon, Patricia met me in the hall near our mailbox. Tears were in her eyes as she handed me an envelope. Someone had put $50 cash inside the envelope. That person had put a postage stamp on the envelope and had carefully tried to make it look like it had been postmarked, but we saw that it was not actually postmarked. We were quite sure that our table mates had given us the money. One of us remarked: "Just wait. Tomorrow we will receive God's provision."

We had the $50, but it was bittersweet. We put in our deposit and became #157 on the housing request list.

The next day, sure enough, in the mail we received a letter and also a $50 check from John Meadows. His letter revealed that on the previous Thursday, the day we had prayed so desperately, John had felt prompted by the Lord to send us $50. John had been separated from CCCU just as we had, and he had no job at the time of this prompting. Still, he had gone to the bank almost immediately and had withdrawn $50 from and his and Vicki's savings account. In the letter, John apologized because he had then forgotten to send the money for a few days.

We are convinced that John forgot to mail the money because God wanted me to see my unbelief and mistrust. Now we had received $100, all of which we needed, but twice as much as we had asked God for. What a mixture of joy and sorrow I experienced that day!

About that time, Dr. John Crawford, a former WBT translator who at this time was a professor at the university, suggested that I apply for a graduate teaching assistant position in the English Department for the fall and spring semesters. I did apply, and I was accepted. To our surprise and delight, because of the teaching position, we were bumped up from #157 to #6 on the housing list. Thus, the door was opened to a very adequate two-bedroom apartment at 415 Northwestern Drive.

Much about that summer of 1975 is vague to me. My wife was convinced that I was depressed—although she talked to the Lord about it, rather than to me. More than I realized, I was torn apart because of the way I had hurt my parents and the separation between us.

I participated in the early morning prayer meeting as I had the previous summer. I was free to pray in the Spirit and did. Consistent with the inner vow I had made the year before, we did not return to the Catholic prayer meeting.

At the end of the summer, we were accepted into Wycliffe Bible Translators as missionaries in training and were assigned to the Papua New Guinea branch. We planned for me to finish my classwork in the spring of 1975 and then later that year to go on to Papua New Guinea for jungle camp training and tribal assignment.

On the night of the celebration in which we and others were received into Wycliffe, two friends, Steve Marlett and Cathy Moser, were also accepted. Cathy's parents, Ed and Becky, Wycliffe missionaries to the Seri Indians in Mexico, had been working at the SIL in North Dakota for many summers. The same evening that the Mosers celebrated their daughter's acceptance into Wycliffe, Cathy and Steve were engaged to be married. What a joyous night it was for their family. About midnight Ed lay down on his bed and Becky walked down the hall to the bathroom. When she returned after taking a shower, she found Ed dead; he had had a heart attack.

124

All of us were stunned when we heard the news the next morning, of course; however, everyone was also grateful that Ed had been able to live long enough to see Cathy engaged to a good man and to see her and her fiancé commit themselves to Bible translation.

Ed's funeral was something new for us. It was truly a *celebration* of his going to be with the Lord and of the hope of resurrection. To symbolize this joy and hope, Becky and Cathy wore white dresses to the funeral. And together with them we worshipped in the presence of the Lord that day!

****

As the summer session ended and we moved into our new apartment, I became aware of how much I needed help from the Lord. I remembered the title of the first Derek Prince tape that John Meadows had given me, "God's Atomic Weapon: The Power of the Blood." I listened to it again. At the climax of the message, Derek listed a number of Scriptures concerning the benefits provided by Jesus's blood. Referring to Revelation 12:10–11, Derek led his listeners to declare to the devil what the Word of God says the blood of Jesus accomplishes for believers. In my need, I began to declare these passages daily and often several times a day.[37]

I was aware that the teachers who produced *New Wine* magazine, along with a number of Catholic Charismatic Renewal leaders, were going to hold a Men's Shepherds Conference in Kansas City in September 1975. I wanted to go in the worst way, but with my new teaching job and classes there was no way that I could. However, I was able to give some money to John Meadows and to Bob Buck, the Free Methodist pastor, to help make it possible for them to go.

As the time approached for the conference, I began to consider the fact that the *New Wine* teachers were working with Catholic leaders. The thought began to grow that I should go back and visit the local Catholic Charismatic prayer meeting. It is my belief that my confession of the provision made by Jesus's shed blood had begun to work in me and helped me be open to the thought.

At any rate, I acted on this thought during the week of the Men's Shepherds Conference. When Patricia and I went to the prayer meeting, to my surprise I found out that the leaders of the prayer meeting were in Kansas City at the conference. Over the next week, I began to think, *If these leaders are open to the influence of the*

[37] See Appendix Four.

125

New Wine *teachers and to the Catholic leaders with whom the teachers work, then there might be hope for this group yet.*

So it was that again the following Thursday, Patricia and I attended the prayer meeting. A brother named Michael Callaghan was leading the meeting. Ironically, it was Larry Alberts, the man who had co-written the book on Mary, who gave a report on the conference.

One thing Larry discussed struck me deeply. He told about a vision that a woman in a Lutheran church had received, a vision that her pastor, Larry Christenson, had shared with the leaders at the conference. The woman had seen a massive logjam in a river. All sorts of logs were jammed up and none was getting through to the sawmill. No efforts of the loggers could break up this jam. Then the water began to rise. As the water rose higher and higher, more and more logs broke free and floated down to the sawmill, where the bark was cut off, the logs were cut into boards, and the boards were stacked in an orderly fashion according to their kind—oak with oak, cherry with cherry, and so forth.

The interpretation given of this vision was that it was a picture of the members of Christ's church—all jammed up and banging one another and stuck. The rising water represented the outpouring of the Holy Spirit. As the Spirit set God's people free, God would take them through the sawmill, which represented his dealings to cleanse and purify his people, and set them in order for the building of his spiritual temple, the church. (See Ephesians 2:19–22 and 1 Peter 2:4–5.)

As Larry Alberts talked about the vision, I was deeply convicted because of the way I had judged him and the Catholic brothers and sisters after reading his book. I had had no room in my perspective for God to work with them, to clean them up, to bring them into order, and to use them. I knew God was working on me and changing me, but at some deep level I did not believe that he would work with Catholics too.

By the time Larry finished, I knew that I had to confess my sin and ask forgiveness. As Larry sat down, I stood up to talk. Michael Callaghan, however, did not know me or what I wanted to share. Concerned, I'm sure, that I would bring a crosscurrent into the meeting, Michael asked me to sit down and wait until the end of the meeting, when there would be time for testimonies.

I sat down, amazed and rejoicing. Michael, in my view, had exercised spiritual authority, and I was looking to be rightly related to God's earthly authorities. Patricia did not react the same way. She was offended on my behalf because I was so "rudely" told to sit down.

Later in the meeting I did have an opportunity to confess and ask forgiveness. This whole incident worked something good in me. I felt more free than I had in a long time.

For several weeks, Patricia and I went back to the prayer meeting. However, it was threatening to her. After all, we were dealing with "Pentecostals" who were Catholics—both groups outside the boundaries of acceptable Christianity, according to our background. She was fearful that I was leading her into error. We would go to the prayer meeting and then come home and fight until the wee hours of the morning. After a time I decided it wasn't worth it to have all these fights over the prayer meeting, so we quit going.

We settled into our responsibilities and our life as a family. I focused on my studies and my teaching assignment—two sections of freshman English. Patricia had begun to teach at a nursery school. This was a good job in that it provided some money for us and she was able to take Elijah, who turned 3 that fall, with her. He was in a different classroom, but it was not at all like leaving him with a sitter and going off to work somewhere else.

We continued to attend the Free Methodist Church. We also met some folks at the university who had a Sunday evening meal and Bible study in their homes. There were several couples and a few single people in the group. Of these couples, Rich and Sarah Foss, Ed and Esther Johnson, and at least one single brother lived together communally as a Christian household, sharing their lives and their income. We became good friends with the people in the Bible study, especially with the Fosses and the Johnsons, and we began to meet with them regularly.

****

A few months later in February or March, Ron Odell, our friend and co-worker from Waite Park Wesleyan, came for a visit. One morning during the visit Ron began to question me about our connection to the church.

We were still attending the Free Methodist Church and had made some friends there, but it was not a place where we could make a commitment or even much of a contribution. Essentially, as far as our placement in the Body of Christ was concerned, we were biding our time. We knew that we needed to be committed somewhere, primarily because we knew that living in Christ, in part, means being rightly joined to the Body of Christ. Moreover, Wycliffe required its members to be members in a local church before going to the field.

I knew that we had no real option but to connect with a church that placed a high value on community relationships, that was open to the gifts and ministry of the Holy Spirit, and that operated with true spiritual authority. We thought about connecting to the newly begun covenant community in Lancaster, Ohio, where our friends the Meadows were involved.

We gave some consideration to our connection with the Bible study group, particularly to the extended household that the Fosses and Johnsons had formed. However, they were seeking for their own connection with the larger Body of Christ—either a community to whom they could look for counsel and oversight or one that they could join. If we were to enter into a committed relationship with these folks, then we would still be looking for our connection.

We also considered, as a more distant possibility, connecting with Campus Church in Minneapolis. We had never had any tangible connection to Campus Church, which was led by an Irishman, Ernest O'Neil; however, I had had enough contact there to know of the high value they placed on both community and missions. Some of the people connected with that church actually had businesses that had grown out of their life together and were used not only to support families but, ideally at least, to help support the church and its missions involvement.

Ron shared with me what amounted to a word from the Lord. He said that I needed to connect to the Body of Christ Community in Grand Forks, the community that sponsored the prayer meeting we had attended, since that was obviously where I knew God to be working in the city. Ron warned me that I was in danger of slowly dying spiritually because I did not have functional connection to the Body of Christ. I knew that he was correct. I had appreciation and affection for the Bucks and others at the Free Methodist Church, but that was not a source from which Patricia and I were being sustained and helped to grow.

Therefore, in the spring of 1976, Patricia and I again began to attend the prayer meetings held in the basement of St. Michael's Catholic Church.

In the months during which we had not been attending, one brother in particular, Mike Hynous, had reached out to us persistently. Through Mike and his wife, Janetta, we had learned a bit more about the community. Although about 70% of the members were Roman Catholic, we had discovered that the other members were either of various Protestant denominations or were nondenominational. The Body of Christ was an "ecumenical" community.

In our background, the word *ecumenical* was not a good word. We associated this word only with the ecumenical movement represented by the National and the World Council of Churches, which we considered an effort by "liberal denominations" to bring the various denominations together around the lowest common denominator. In other words, we saw the ecumenical movement as a compromise of the truth and a denial of Biblical authority. For the most part, I think this was a pretty fair evaluation of a good deal of that movement.

However, in the Body of Christ Community and other similar communities, the word did not connote compromise. Rather, *ecumenical* in this context meant coming together in committed relationships of personal covenant love in recognition of brotherhood in Christ while respecting and supporting each person's heritage and connection to the various denominations.

The members of the Body of Christ Community did not consider the community to be a church. Rather it was an intentional Christian covenant community. My friend Jordan Bajis offers this explanation of intentional Christian community:

> Intentional Christian Community is made up of believers who have made conscious, deliberate, and practical choices to commit their lives to God and one another in ways that direct their lives and set the pitch for their lifestyles. This kind of "community" is distinct and different from the natural, or incidental, community that exists within neighborhoods or in the work place that "just happens," by coincidence or circumstances outside one's control.[38]

We had much to learn about what this meant in practice, but the first step was to overcome our fear and abhorrence of the word *ecumenical*. Over the several next years, some of us who were involved began to use the word *interdenominational* instead of *ecumenical* because the former had a less negative connotation for many conservative Christians. However, even *interdenominational* had to be defined clearly so as to make clear that this type of community was an effort to live in unity without compromising fundamental convictions about the faith.

---

[38] See http://www.rebuildjournal.org/default.html?= for this quotation and more about intentional Christian community.

As we began to regularly attend the prayer meetings, we began to get acquainted with the people in the Body of Christ Community. We were invited by some members to visit them in their homes. I remember having a meal with Joe and Cindy Stokes. The Stokes had at least one small child at that time and they also had several single adults living with them. Joe had been raised in the Church of Christ but had strayed from the Lord. He had come into a relationship with Jesus through the Jesus Movement and become something of a street preacher; then he met Larry Alberts and some of those who formed the Body of Christ Community. In his enthusiasm for what God was doing with these people, Joe had become a Roman Catholic. Cindy, who had come to the university in Grand Forks, had also become a member of the community. They were one of the first couples to marry as members of that community.

We had already begun to gather the items we would need in jungle camp in Papua New Guinea once I had completed the classwork in the linguistics program, but we still did not have a church home when the school year ended. About that time, Dr. John Daly, who led the SIL at the University of North Dakota, contacted us and asked if I would be willing to come back to the summer school and serve as a teaching assistant. Although there would be only a small monetary compensation, at least the opportunity provided us with a place to live and covered most of our expenses for the summer. It also meant that we could keep getting acquainted with the Body of Christ. Therefore, I accepted the opportunity to serve.

When it was time to move out of our student housing apartment and back into the dorm with the SIL people, Mike Hynous offered to bring some friends over to help us clean out the apartment and move our things to storage for the summer. On the designated Saturday morning, both we and also our neighbors were stunned when twenty-five or thirty people showed up at 8 a.m. with ladders and all the cleaning supplies.

After a song and a short prayer, they went to work. Someone must have organized them into teams. Some climbed the ladders and, beginning from the highest point of the cathedral ceilings, they cleaned right down the ceiling, on down the walls, and then across the floor to the doors. Every window, every nook, and every cranny—including the furnace room—were cleaned, spic and span.

I left as the work was starting in order to buy donuts for the crew. Before I got back, most of them had finished and headed home. My neighbor was still standing in front of our apartment. As I came up the walk carrying several boxes of donuts, he exclaimed, "Where do you get friends like these?"

I could not help but think of Jesus's words in John 13:35: "By this all people will know that you are my disciples, if you have love for one another." Here was a tangible testimony observable by all of how God's people take care of one another. People outside the church cannot observe for themselves our love for one another when we are gathered in churches and Bible studies, but they can see it on display in a practical expression of love such as we had seen that day.

****

That spring, I also met with Michael Callaghan, who was leading the Body of Christ Community while Larry Alberts was living temporarily in a similar but larger community, The Word of God Community in Ann Arbor, Michigan, in order to receive some training. Michael told me that if we were to seriously consider joining the community we would need to participate in the Life in the Spirit Seminar. The next one was scheduled for that summer; therefore, on Thursday nights during June and July, we attended the seminar sessions before the prayer meeting.

The Life in Spirit Seminar is an "evangelistic" tool that progressively leads the participant into a personal relationship with Jesus and the Holy Spirit. The material itself covered mostly things that Patricia and I already knew. However, I have come to see how wise it was of the leaders to direct us to start at the beginning. For one thing, if we were to decide to join the community, then we would have come in like anyone else: we would have demonstrated our willingness to submit to leadership and to be taught. There would be no special favors. Also, it would help us discover whether we could agree with the "foundations" for life in the community and build our lives together with the other members.

I discovered the seminar to be doctrinally sound and experientially balanced. It is an excellent tool—especially for reaching people with a Christian background who may never have had a personal relationship with Jesus or who have strayed from the church.

In addition to attending the prayer meeting, which was evangelistic in nature, that summer we were invited to the Body of Christ's community meetings for the membership. Several Sundays these meetings were held in a city park. I quickly discovered that I was a coward about my faith. I felt awkward, conspicuous, and even ashamed to pray and sing in a public place. I was chagrined that these Catholics were so bold in their worship of the Lord, while I, an evangelical Protestant, a Bible-based believer, supposedly sold out to Christ, a missionary-in-training, wanted to hide behind a tree and deny being part of the group while my new friends were freely and enthusiastically worshipping in public.

As the summer school drew toward its close, we still had not made a commitment to the community and still had no local church home. After consulting with our Wycliffe advisor, we decided to stay in Grand Forks another year in order to pursue membership in the community. We also consulted with the community leaders, who expressed their openness to our moving toward membership with the understanding that our intention was to go out from the community to serve with Wycliffe in Papua New Guinea.

Unexpectedly, the opportunity arose for me to be an instructor in the university's English Department for the next school year. I was to teach two classes each semester and receive $750 for each class, which meant that we would have an income of $3,000 for about nine months.

We learned that Jim and Cindy Lily, members of the Body of Christ Community, owned a house with three apartments. They offered us the opportunity to rent one of those apartments starting September 1.

SIL ended in mid-August. The apartment would not open for two weeks, but Mike and Janetta Hynous opened their home to us while they were away in Arizona on vacation. Little did I know that I would encounter the Lord in a powerful and unique way while in the Hynouses' home. The Lord revealed something of his heart and his ways to me—on the evening news, of all things!

Patricia and I had never owned a television, but Mike and Janetta had one. While I was casually watching the news one evening, a story was shown concerning civil war in Lebanon. This was nothing special in itself since, in the 1970s, it seemed that civil war in Lebanon or battles between Lebanon and Israel were constantly in the news.

This time the footage from Beirut grabbed my attention. It was a street scene showing city buildings and rubble where buildings had been. In the distance I could hear blasts of mortar fire, the rat-a-tat-tat of machine guns, and the rumble of tanks. Then, an Arab shepherd leading a few dozen sheep came into view, walking up the street between a tall building on one side and rubble on the other. The shepherd was in the front at the point of a triangle of sheep, packed tightly to one another, the whole flock following as close to the shepherd as possible.

Tears squirted from my eyes as I watched; the mental lights went on. I understood more fully what Jesus meant when he said,

> ... He who enters by the door is the shepherd of the sheep. To him the gatekeeper opens. The sheep hear his voice, and he calls his own sheep by name and leads them out. When he has brought out all his own, he goes before them, and the sheep follow him, for they know his voice....
>
> I am the good shepherd. The good shepherd lays down his life for the sheep. He who is a hired hand and not a shepherd, who does not own the sheep, sees the wolf coming and leaves the sheep and flees, and the wolf snatches them and scatters them. He flees because he is a hired hand and cares nothing for the sheep. I am the good shepherd. I know my own and my own know me, just as the Father knows me and I know the Father; and I lay down my life for the sheep. (John 10:2–4, 11–15)

Through this news footage I perceived in a new way the relationship of the shepherd with the sheep—not only of Jesus, the Good Shepherd, with his sheep, but also the relationship of a true under-shepherd (pastor) with the part of Jesus's flock entrusted to the under-shepherd's care. A shepherd or a pastor is one who walks with the sheep, leading them through the war zone of life, in an intimate relationship of mutual love and trust.

God spoke to me through the evening news to give me a deeper understanding into how he was calling me to live my life.

****

Moving day. On the first Saturday in September, it was time to move into our apartment on University Avenue. As it turned out, there were several moves scheduled among community members that day. The whole community was mobilized and organized for the task.

Moving day began with several dozen community members gathering for prayer in the backyard of Gary and Joanne Altendorf's house—loud prayer, everyone praying at the same time, at 7:30 on a warm Saturday morning on a street with houses built close together, bedroom windows open with "normal people" trying to get a little extra sleep. Of course, I wasn't nervous or anything.

When the prayer time had ended, people took off in well-organized groups. Before dinnertime that Saturday, five households, including ours, had been moved. In one case, the Altendorf family exchanged houses with the Givan family. Crews of ladies went into those two houses and packed up the things in kitchens, bathrooms, and such. While the men moved furniture and boxes, the empty rooms were cleaned. Then, as the furniture and boxes were brought into the new house, things were unpacked and put into place.

The Lopez family moved into a new house, and two single ladies moved into the apartment above ours.

By dinner everyone was virtually settled into a new residence. Never before or since have I seen anything like that.

Thus, our life in the Body of Christ Community began. Over the next few months we had opportunity to get better acquainted with the people in the community and with the lives of love and service that they had chosen to live together. We lived on the first floor of our house. The two single ladies in the community shared the second-floor apartment. Another young family lived in the basement apartment—the wife was very interested in community, the husband cautious about committing himself deeply.

After a time we began to participate in David and Deanna White's "extended household." The Whites lived a few blocks away in a larger house that they shared with several single adults. Another couple, Dan and Mary Kaye Gleason, who had gone through the Life in the Spirit Seminar with us, also were connected with the Whites, as well as a few single men who shared a house together. Sometimes we would all have a meal together. Regularly the ladies would meet in a small group, usually in the daytime. Likewise, the men got together in a group, mostly on an evening because of work schedules.

Soon after Labor Day we were invited to participate in a special weekend—a community weekend it was called. Larry Alberts returned from Michigan for this weekend of teaching and fellowship in which we were introduced to the community's values and basic commitment.

For twelve weeks following the community weekend, Patricia and I participated in the twelve-lesson foundations course—weekly classes in which we were given further practical teaching on matters such as prayer, Bible reading, spiritual authority, working out relational difficulties, and reordering priorities to live a community lifestyle. This course led up to the opportunity to make an "underway commitment" to the community. Perhaps it was the need to make a decision about commitment that made me face up to an increasing dilemma.

It was still our full intention to go on to Papua New Guinea. However, I began to wrestle with whether or not the Body of Christ Community would be our home "church." The Body of Christ, of course, made no claim to be a church; in fact, the community refused to see itself that way. But for me, the community was more like a New Testament church than any "church" I had seen.

However, later in the fall I began to have reservations—not about the community, but about our readiness to go to the mission field. I had grave doubts about my ability as a linguist. Even though my professors had always encouraged me that I was doing well, I never felt that I really had a handle on this field of study. In part, I have since come to the realization that my insecurity had to do with the reality that in linguistics I was being introduced to a new paradigm—a new way of thinking about language. In addition, in training, of necessity we had to deal with small collections of data that illustrated various learning points and gave us opportunity to practice. What we could not do in the training period was to see enough data from any language to begin to see how what we were learning fit into a whole. As a "big picture" person I felt overwhelmed by the mass of details.

I also had found that I did not have a love for the subject matter. I could do the assignments, but reading and studying linguistics material on my own was drudgery—whereas for some of my closest SIL fellow students, linguistics was something they loved. It was a calling to them.

This bothered me enough that on January 21, 1977, I wrote to our Wycliffe advisor, John O'Rorke, and opened up to him my concerns. For some reason he turned our situation over to another Wycliffe advisor to missionaries-in-training, Wayne Huff, whom we had met and had appreciated so deeply while we were at Waite Park Wesleyan.

Wayne responded to my questions and doubts with reassurances, reassurance that Wycliffe's esteem for me was not shaken, reassurances that most missionaries-in-training went through doubts of various kinds. He made clear that Wycliffe still wanted us to serve—but even more wanted us to be confident in the Lord as to what direction to take. The decision, he said, was ours to make.

I had also taken counsel with our community leaders and they, too, were expressing support for me personally while telling me the decision to go or stay was one that I would need to make.

As I pondered Wayne's letter, I had to admit to another, even more important, internal struggle. I wrote back to Wayne about my concern that my motivation for going out under Wycliffe might not be pure. Certainly, I valued greatly Wycliffe's mission to make the Scriptures available in every language group (and I still do), but Bible translation was not my primary motivation. Rather, it was my first desire to see churches planted in every tribe and language group. I had begun to wonder if translation was not a means to an end for me, rather than my primary vision.

Of course, I am sure every Wycliffe translator longs to see a church raised up among the people he or she serves. However, Wycliffe missionaries go into other nations first as SIL linguists, often under contract with the national government to do linguistic work. In many countries they are not allowed to work directly to see churches planted, and certainly that would not be their primary task. I did not know the arrangement Wycliffe had with Papua New Guinea, but I began to sense that I might at the very least find myself in an internal conflict of interest.

Just as important, I told Wayne about my concern over my youth and my relative spiritual immaturity. How was I to be, along with my wife, the primary, if not the only "re-presentation" of Christ that some tribal group would see? I had seen in Scripture that God often spent decades dealing with men to prepare them to fulfill his call on their lives. How could I honestly at that point say, like the apostle Paul, "imitate me," or "follow me as I follow Christ"?

Although I did not write to Wayne about it, I was also concerned because there were several issues in our marriage that Patricia and I had not worked out. I began to think about the fact that if we were to go live with a tribal group that had not been exposed to the gospel, then our marriage would be the primary "picture" that this people would have of Christ and the church. (See Ephesians 5:22–33.) I was uneasy because I did not believe that our relationship was enough of a mirror image of Christ and his bride. It was not that I wanted to hide this concern from Wayne; rather, I did not want to share something that might represent Patricia in any negative light.

Of course, I talked about all these things with Patricia, and she was aware of my struggle and saw the letters that I wrote. She obviously knew that we had plenty to work on, but she was not concerned enough that she really wanted to reevaluate our plans to go out as missionaries—and she was certainly not wanting to stay in a community that practiced the pentecostal gifts of the Spirit, let alone a "Catholic" community. This alone, I think, demonstrates the lack of unity in vision and Christian experience between the two of us at that time.

Over the course of a few months it became increasingly clear to me that whether or not we made a commitment to the community, I could not in good conscience go with Wycliffe at that time. Finally, I told Patricia exactly where I stood. One, I simply could not go to the mission field because of the concerns stated above. Two, I absolutely would not make a commitment to the Body of Christ Community unless she, of her own volition, would make the commitment with me. I told her that I was releasing her into God's hands to make a decision about the community, that I would not pressure her further.

This put Patricia in a tough place, of course. She wanted to please God. She also wanted to stand with me. However, my decision was forcing her to die to what she had felt was her call—to be a missionary. In addition, she was having to battle with fear—fear of new things, things that she had not experienced for herself and things that she was not fully convinced were valid, fear that joining community would cause further separation between us and my parents, fear of Catholicism, and fear of Pentecostalism.

As she says, she finally came to the place where she cried out to God: "I know that I must submit to my husband as unto you. I will do so even if he leads me to the very gates of hell. If he does, you will have to rescue me." This surrender did not resolve all her fears, but it did allow her, in good conscience, to commit to the community with me.

On March 24, 1977, I wrote the following in a letter to Wayne Huff:

> I came to WBT seeking God's will and the door was not closed. I came to
> the Body of Christ Community in obedience to God's will and he has not
> said for me to leave. Thus, although it's hard on my pride and though I
> don't know what to say to those who have been generously sending in
> support for several months, I believe that I must ask WBT to release me
> to serve God through this community.

Wayne wrote a gracious letter back on behalf of Wycliffe. He expressed their willingness to honor our decision, if it was final, even though they wished we had decided differently. The letter was warm but official until the closing. There Wayne listed several specific passages from Psalms, about which he said: "I am praying that these verses will bring guidance and edification to both of you as you wait before the Lord and make your decision. God bless you real good."

Although Wayne listed only references, here are the actual passages as translated in the New American Standard Version, which I was using most of the time in 1977:

> Vindicate me, O Lord, for I have walked in my integrity,
> And I have trusted in the Lord without wavering.
> Examine me, O Lord, and try me;
> Test my mind and my heart.
> For Thy lovingkindness is before my eyes,
> And I have walked in Thy truth. (Psalm 26:1–3)

> My foot stands on a level place;
> In the great congregations I shall bless the Lord. (Psalm 26:12)

> The Lord is my light and my salvation;
> Whom shall I fear?
> The Lord is the defense of my life;
> Whom shall I dread? (Psalm 27:1)

> One thing have I asked from the Lord, that I shall seek:
> That I may dwell in the house of the Lord all the days of my life,
> To behold the beauty of the Lord and to meditate in His temple.
> (Psalm 27:4)

> And now my head will be lifted up above my enemies around me;
> And I will offer in His tent sacrifices with shouts of joy;
> I will sing, yes I will sing praises to the Lord. (Psalm 27:6)

> For my father and my mother have forsaken me,
> But the Lord will take me up.
> Teach me Thy way, O Lord,
> And lead me on a level path,
> Because of my foes. (Psalm 27:10–11)

> Wait for the Lord;
> Be strong, and let your heart take courage;
> Yes, wait for the Lord! (Psalm 27:14)

Thou art my hiding place; Thou dost preserve me from trouble;
Thou dost surround me with songs of deliverance. Selah
I will instruct you and teach you in the way you should go;
I will counsel you with My eye upon you.
Do not be as the horse or the mule, which have no understanding,
Whose trappings include bit and bridle to hold them in check,
Otherwise they will not come near to you.
Many are the sorrows of the wicked;
But he who trusts in the LORD, lovingkindness shall surround him.
Be glad in the Lord, and rejoice, O you righteous,
And shout for joy, all you who are upright in heart. (Psalm 32:7–11)

As I read these verses, I sensed that the Lord had used Wayne to confirm the decision that we needed to make. As I meditated on them I became even more convinced of their applicability to our decision.

1. In the final analysis, it was God's vindication, not man's, that we needed.

2. The reference to the parents forsaking the psalmist was, of course, striking in light of the breach between me and my parents.

3. The psalmist wrote that we are to walk according to God's lovingkindness. The Hebrew word translated *lovingkindness* is *hesed,* which can rightly be translated *covenant love.* And here we were, ready to make a commitment to a covenant community.

4. The passages emphasizing worshipping with shouts of joy and singing songs of praise and deliverance brought to mind defining characteristics of "charismatic" worship.

5. In New Testament thinking, the house of the Lord and the temple refer to God's people, to his community, the church—where we were choosing to commit our lives.

6. Although the passage refers to a level path in a spiritual sense, anyone who has been in Grand Forks can relate literally to a level place as well—the land is as flat as a tabletop there in the Red River Valley.

7. It was certainly my desire to walk willingly by the counsel of God's eye and not require Him to "force" me into His will.

On April 24 we sent our formal letter of resignation. We received formal letters of release from Wycliffe Bible Translators and from the Summer Institute of Linguistics. We also received a wonderful letter of support from Wayne Huff.

Just before we had sent in the formal resignation, however, Michael Callahan and another leader came to us with information they thought we must have before we cut our ties with Wycliffe. The leadership team of the community had come to the conclusion that the community was to move to the Minneapolis-St. Paul area in order to merge with the larger Servants of the Light Community, the same community that had sponsored the Catholic Charismatic prayer meetings that we had visited while at Waite Park. At that time the leaders were still working this through with the people who were fully covenanted with the community. We had not yet formally made the underway commitment, but it was important to the brothers that we not make this major direction change without the knowledge that we would likely need to move.

To us this was not bad news. After our time at Waite Park, thinking about moving to Minneapolis was like thinking about moving home. Interestingly enough, our 4-year-old, Elijah, had been telling us for several weeks that we were going to live in Minneapolis—a place from which we had moved when he was less than 15 months old.

That spring Patricia and I made our underway commitment to the Body of Christ Community, a commitment by which we were saying that we believed the Lord was calling us to join our lives to the brothers and sisters in the community, that we wanted to learn to live according to the community's values, and that we were willing to follow the direction set by the community's leaders. It was an "underway" commitment because it brought us into time of "trying it out." We would live the community life as fully as we could, while both we and the community mutually sought to discover whether it was God's call for us to be joined to one another in a formal and lifelong covenant relationship.

11

Back to Minneapolis

In the fall of 1976 after moving into our apartment, we had found out that Patricia was pregnant again. We were excited even though it was a challenge for us at a time when we were still thinking we would be going to Papua New Guinea before too long. We still had no medical insurance, but after a few months Patricia made an arrangement to pay an obstetrician $60 a month for six months for prenatal care, for the delivery (if routine), and for postnatal care.

In October, Patricia's parents, Arthur and Ida Belle McKelvey, flew out from Ohio to visit us. Patricia's dad had lived in the hills of southern Ohio his whole life. He had made a few trips to Maine to see his oldest daughter, Betty. He probably had visited his daughter Freda in Tennessee at one time or another. But he had not been away from the Ohio River Valley very many times—and certainly not to anywhere like Grand Forks, North Dakota.

We picked up Mother and Dad McKelvey at the airport 15 miles or so west of Grand Forks. It's as though I can still hear Patricia's dad marveling as he looked out across the flat farm land: "I have never seen so much nothing in all my life."

One day during their visit we drove 135 miles north along the Red River Valley to Winnipeg, Canada, on I-29, which became Route 75 after we crossed the Canadian border, so that Elijah, then almost 4 years old, could visit the zoo with his grandparents. We ate a picnic lunch in a city park in which a retired steam locomotive had been parked—particularly special to my father-in-law, who loved trains and had worked in the rail yard at a steel mill.

In order to see more of the landscape, on the way back to Grand Forks we drove south on a road about 30 miles west of I-29 by which we had come north. That whole day we had been driving through flat land where the vistas were broken only by occasional farmhouses and buildings and the groves of trees that had been planted as windbreaks after the dust bowl. Several times on the drive Arthur had looked around and said, "It's so flat you can see the curve on the horizon." Then a few miles south of the Canadian border we unexpectedly drove into the Pembina Gorge near Walhalla, North Dakota. The Gorge was a stunning and spectacular change after the nearly empty landscape we had been driving through.

Those days with Mother and Dad McKelvey became even more special the following March when we learned that Patricia's dad had been diagnosed with cancer in his pancreas.

A highlight that winter, however, was the day 4-year-old Elijah came to his mother and asked her to pray with him; he wanted to give his life to Jesus. We were amazed at the changes that we saw in him in the weeks following that prayer.

As the time for our baby to be born drew nearer, we wondered how we would pay the hospital expenses. Then, a month or so before the birth, the doctor discovered that the baby, although head down as it should have been, had its arm across the top of the head so that it could not descend into the birth canal. The doctor was concerned that the baby might be too far down to move the arm. It looked like Patricia would need to have a Caesarean section.

We called on the community and the Bible study group to pray for the baby to change position so that the birth could be normal. Three weeks later another test showed that the arm had indeed moved and the baby was moving into the birth canal in the normal way.

During those three weeks before we knew the baby's arm was out of the way, the Fosses and Johnsons, who by then were selling their house so that they could move to the Plow Creek Community in western Illinois, informed us that they believed the Lord wanted them to pay the hospital expense up to $1,000. Then Mel and Mary Ann Frank, also selling a home in order to move with the Body of Christ to Minneapolis, told us they wanted to cover any hospital expense over $1,000.

Stephanie was born on May 12, 1977. Holding my son for the first time after his birth had been an incredible experience. I was surprised that holding a daughter was a different thing altogether, not better, but very different. It felt as though I was holding a delicate piece of art—one that might break in my clumsy hands.

My parents came to see us right after Stephanie was born. They drove up to Deer River, Minnesota, where Dad stopped a few days to visit his oldest brother, Roy. Mom took a Greyhound bus across U.S. Highway 2 to Grand Forks so that she could help with the meals and the baby. After a few days, Dad came on over too.

A few days after Mom and Dad left, some close friends from Bible College, Gary and Rosie Gurwell, arrived with their children, Danny and Heidi. They pulled up in an old Checker cab limo, the "Blue Goose," loaded down with virtually everything they owned. The Gurwells had come to Grand Forks to study at SIL, and they stayed with us for the three weeks until the summer school opened. Although it was good to have them with us, cramming two families of four (including a brand-new baby) in a five-room, two-bedroom house tested us all.

Five weeks after Stephanie's birth we moved to Minneapolis. Ron and Patty Landman, who had moved into the apartment below us a few months earlier, were also moving. Ron had gotten an engineering job with Control Data. The company was going to pay his moving expenses. Rather than hire a moving company, Ron rented a U-Haul truck and invited us to put our things in with theirs. Thanks to Control Data and the Landmans, we moved free of charge.

It was a good thing too! My job at the university had ended in mid-May. I had no job. Twice after school ended I had traveled to Minneapolis with other men from the community in order to look for work. On the first trip I was invited for an interview with Comtech, a computer software company. I had applied for a job as a technical writer, an effort to use my experience of teaching technical writing at the university as my primary qualification. If I had been hired, I would have been writing user manuals. I did not get the job because I had no knowledge at all of computers or software; the fact is I did not even know what software was. I had never even seen a computer at the time.

On the first job-seeking visit, several of us men had stayed with the Bob Cunningham family. I remember arriving close to midnight. Bob met us and took us on a tour of the house—even though his family and several single adults who lived in their household were already in bed. A short time later, Hal Langevin, a coordinator (the title given to "elders" in the Catholic ecumenical communities) showed up to welcome us. On the second visit, I stayed in Richard and Connie Jirak's household. At the time none of us had any idea that relationships with both Hal and the Jiraks would prove to be important relationships for our family.

****

In mid-June we loaded the U-Haul, our stuff first and the Landmans' to the rear, and headed out on the 315-mile trip to Minneapolis. The Landmans had purchased a house. With no job and little money, we could not even rent one.

However, Larry Alberts had already moved from Ann Arbor to Minneapolis to become a part of the leadership team of the Servants of the Light Community. He and several brothers had formed a Brotherhood, a community of single men committed to live single for the Lord (i.e., to remain celibate for the sake of ministry). The Brotherhood had purchased a large, old house near the campus of the University of Minnesota; the property included a more modern three-story apartment building, which sat behind the house. In addition to serving the community, the brothers planned to start an outreach on the campus.

Larry, thinking that I would make a good addition to the campus outreach team, had sent word to me, through the Grand Forks leaders, that Patricia and I were to live in the two-bedroom basement apartment. Therefore, after arriving in Minneapolis, when we had unloaded the Landmans' furniture, I drove the truck over to the Brotherhood's house so that we could unload our furniture into our apartment. Patricia and the children followed in our station wagon.

We drove up Twelfth Avenue to the house and parked the truck across the street. Patricia and I took the children from the car and went to find Larry. He was not at home, but one of the brothers took us back to the apartment building so that we could see where we would live.

We walked down the stairs and into the basement apartment. There were indeed two bedrooms and also a large room with a small kitchen area at the east end. Every wall was covered with faded beige paint. The carpet in the living room area still had some beige in spots, but much of it was black with dirt and grime. The brother showing us around told us, apologetically, that previous tenants had brought their motorcycles into the apartment, using the living room for parking and for repair work. The past owners had not cleaned it up, and the Brotherhood men had not yet had time to do so.

After seeing the apartment, the brother invited us to sit in the Brotherhood's house to wait for Larry; however, Patricia let me know that she wanted to talk. We walked back across the street to the car.

In no uncertain terms, Patricia informed me, "There is absolutely no way I will move my children into that filthy place." For the next 40 minutes we fought about that. I was so desperate that I even tried playing the "wives, submit to your husbands as to the Lord" card. It didn't work.

It wasn't that I had any more desire to live in that dirty apartment than Patricia, but I thought there was no choice. After all, Larry represented spiritual authority over our lives and he had "decreed" it. Besides that, how would I house my family anywhere else with no money and no job? I nearly panicked.

144

Then Larry arrived. Nervously, I approached him. After all, I was barely acquainted with him. He was to be my spiritual leader. And my wife was refusing both his leadership and mine concerning the house.

We greeted one another, but before I could say anything, Larry said: "That apartment is not suitable for your family. I have arranged for you to stay with Dan and Joyce Driessen for a few days."

What a relief!

What chagrin! Why had I not been wise enough or man enough to assure my wife that she was right and that we would have to find some other option?

That encounter was a lesson to me. I had begun to discover that although God does give us leaders with spiritual authority, earthly authorities—no matter how spiritual they are—do not have absolute authority.

Ever since God had confronted me with my rebelliousness, I had sought for spiritual authority to which I could submit—and it was right for me to do so. However, that day I started to understand that obedience to earthly spiritual authorities is conditional. There are times to ask questions. There are times when one must work through issues and come to common agreement with God-appointed leaders. And one may not violate his conscience when obeying earthly spiritual authorities. This last matter is tricky: one needs to be sure that his conscience is properly trained—that it is sensitive to the right things—and one must not use it as an excuse in order to get his own way.

Larry had arranged for us to store our furniture and household items in the basement of St. Joseph Catholic School in South Minneapolis. The Servants of the Light were at the time holding many of their meetings in the St. Joe's gym. They had been given permission to use the basement for storage and it was needed badly in that season.

Not only was the Body of Christ Community moving into the Servants, but several other groups and individuals were as well. There were at least three small communities moving in from the state of Washington. A small community was moving down from northern Michigan. There were people moving from prayer groups in Iowa, Nebraska, and Wyoming. In fact, in about a year and a half the Servants would grow from about 600 adult members to more than 1,100 plus 900 children. Much of this growth was because of people moving into the Twin Cities in order to be part of the community.

So it was that we lived for a week with Dan and Joyce Driessen, their daughter, their household and, in effect, with three other community families who lived in the same fourplex in St. Paul. As it turned out, we would soon have opportunity to get much better acquainted with the Driessens.

At the end of that week we headed for Ohio to see Patricia's father, who was by then close to death because of the cancer in his pancreas.

We stayed with Patricia's parents in Ohio for about two weeks. Even though Arthur was so sick, his doctor and his family had not talked about death with him—they had not even told him he had cancer. Patricia's brother Joe, the oldest McKelvey sibling and the only brother, had given orders to all that his dad was not to be told of the cancer or impending death.

The McKelvey home had five small rooms—a living room, a kitchen, two bedrooms, and a tiny bath. Joe and his family lived about a mile away. Patricia has five sisters, all but one married at that time, most with children. Not all the spouses and grandchildren were there at once, but it was crowded—even with the two houses. We were among the first to arrive, so we stayed with Mother and Dad McKelvey.

We did have a few days with them before it got really crowded, and during that time, although I honored the decision not to speak with Arthur about his impending death, I did have opportunities to lead devotions with him and Ida Belle. Believing that I was led by the Holy Spirit, I read each day from 2 Corinthians. In that book Paul writes much about suffering. In chapter four he wrote about carrying death in one's body while giving life to others. It seemed to Patricia and me that while we were there Arthur came to terms with his death and that we were privileged to play a small part in helping him come to peace about it.

While in Ohio, I drove up U.S. 23 to Chillicothe, about an hour north of Patricia's parents' home, in order to help Mom and Dad move from Waverly into the small town of Kingston, Ohio. Other than those two days of moving, we stayed right there with Mother and Dad McKelvey.

Stephanie was only 6 weeks old when we started the trip to Ohio. After two weeks it became evident to us that for Stephanie's sake, and for Arthur's as well, we had to get her away from there. There was simply too much activity. We became convinced that even as a baby she was sensitive to the atmosphere of grief. She was crying almost constantly, and the family understandably wanted her to be quiet. Not only were they concerned about Arthur's well-being, but the crying child was adding to the rest of the family's stress.

Finally, we made the decision to go back to Minneapolis, having agreed that for Stephanie's sake we would not be able to return for the funeral. Shortly after we left, Arthur was taken to the hospital for his final days on earth.

We arrived back in Minneapolis on July 5 and discovered that the Landmans had offered to have us stay with them until an apartment opened up. Dan and Joyce Driessen had made a deal to buy a fourplex in South Minneapolis only four blocks from the Landmans' house. We were one of three couples who were invited to live there, along with the Driessens and their household, once the building was in their possession.

Two days after our arrival at the Landmans' home, we got the call—Patricia's father had died. I got the word while visiting with Larry at the community's main office on Grand Avenue.

As I was leaving to return to the Landmans' house to be with Patricia, Larry asked about our plans for the funeral. I told him that we had already decided that we could not take Stephanie back to Ohio. Larry said that if money was an issue (we had almost nothing, of course), he would see that we had money to fly to Ohio. I thanked him but told him the decision we had made was final. Even though he seemed concerned about the wisdom of the decision, he accepted it.

Obviously, Patricia would have chosen to go home to be with her family for the funeral if it were possible. We were, however, I believed, in full agreement that it simply was not right for us to do so because of the baby. Therefore, on July 10, our tenth wedding anniversary, we were in Minneapolis while Arthur McKelvey was being buried in Ohio.

I do not know how we would have done otherwise at the time; however, the decision to miss the funeral has proved to have had some lasting effects for Patricia. It would be a year before I finally got her to listen to the tape recording of her dad's funeral. Up until then she dreamed virtually every night about missing the funeral. I think missing that funeral was a significant factor in Patricia's battle with fear of serious illness and death over the following years.

In addition, inexplicably to me, it added fuel to the battle Patricia had with trusting community leaders. Somehow, I had shared with her about my conversation with

Larry in a way that left her with the impression that Larry had counseled us not to go back when, in fact, he had offered to pay our way.

The bottom line is that we did not attend the funeral. Two weeks later our apartment opened and we moved into 4248 Pillsbury Avenue, Apartment 2.

****

Like many Twin Cities apartments, those in our building were one room wide, with the rooms laid out front to back. This was not a familiar layout to us, except for the week we had spent with the Driessens in St. Paul. In our building, the front entry led to a foyer with two doors, one to the right and one to the left, and a stairway to the second floor. Apartment 1 was on the right with Apartment 3 above it. We moved into Apartment 2 on the left under Apartment 4.

We entered our apartment through the door into the living and dining room—a long but narrow room. At the rear of the room a doorway led into a reasonably sized kitchen area. Straight across the kitchen from the doorway, we walked down a hallway with a door to the rear—into a rear foyer with another stairway as well as a door to the outside. Just before the exit door, the hall opened on the left to a small area with three doors—one straight ahead to the bathroom, the others to the left and right into the two bedrooms. Each bedroom had built-in closets with large drawers below and cupboards above.

By late August all four apartments would be filled with members of our community. Dan and Mary Kay Gleason, friends from the Body of Christ, moved into one of the upstairs apartments, along with their dog, Wendy. Frank and Nancy Williams and their son, Stephan, just one year older than Elijah, moved into the apartment directly above us. The Driessens and their two small daughters lived in the other downstairs apartment. The Driessens also built two bedrooms in the basement of the building in order to house three single men and three single women who were part of their household.

By the time we were getting settled into the apartment, our new baby, Stephanie, was crying almost constantly. Soon Patricia took Stephanie to our new doctor for her two-month examination. Patricia told Dr. Struve about the constant crying. He asked Patricia questions, drawing out the story of the previous two months.

She told him about my parents' visit and about the family who had stayed with us for a few weeks in the Grand Forks apartment. She told him about the move and about the housing changes. She told him about the trip to Ohio and the death of her father.

The doctor said: "This child needs security and stability. She has been through too many changes. Take her home and change as little as possible in her environment. Don't even change the sheets on her bed unless it is absolutely necessary." That seemed to be an obvious and accurate diagnosis once we heard it.

Gradually Stephanie did begin to get more peaceful. However, she was 11 months old before she finally stopped crying out pitifully in her sleep at night, sometimes awakening herself.

I never thought to consider how the same changes may also have added stress to our lives. Sadly, having never lost a close family member, I simply had no understanding of the grief process my wife was walking through; therefore, I could not really have empathy for her. I was too shortsighted to realize that she would need me to be there for her more than I had needed to be before. I was ready to jump into life in community with both feet.

When the opportunity arose shortly after we moved into our apartment to go with other members of the Servants of the Light to serve at a conference in Kansas City, I jumped at the chance. Looking back, I wonder, "What was I thinking?" It may have been right for me to go, but I was naive at best not to even consider the wisdom of leaving my family for a week while we were making all these changes and had not even gotten settled into our new home. Off I went.

****

The Conference on the Charismatic Renewal in the Christian Churches was sponsored and planned by Charismatic leaders and teachers from a broad spectrum of churches. Approximately 50,000 people came from the U.S. and from other nations to worship together and to be taught. The full contingent gathered in Arrowhead Stadium for evening meetings. In the daytime, meetings were held in different downtown venues for participants according to their church affiliation. About 20,000 Catholics met in one building. Nearly 10,000 nondenominational people met in another venue with the five teachers from *New Wine* magazine. A second large group of nondenominational leaders and people met in a third location. A Lutheran group, an Episcopal group, a Presbyterian group, and other groups also held their own meetings in different gatherings.

Like many from our community and other communities, I went to serve behind the scenes, to play a small part in making the conference possible. I left home on Sunday and was placed on a service team on Monday morning. Our job was to be available where needed. I was asked to do a few things that week, but mostly, with others on the team, I waited in a room, available if called upon. It did not seem like much then, but later on I would realize that being available, ready to act when called upon, is a vital characteristic of a kingdom servant.

In the room that week, I had great fellowship with some fellows from the Love Inn Community in New York and some guys from the Agape Community in Kansas City. The Kansas City brothers invited me to go with them to a concert in the State Theatre on Tuesday night, the night before the conference actually began. The Phil Keaggy Band from Love Inn was featured that night, with Paul Clark from the Agape Community opening the program. What a treat! Phil and Paul had been two of my favorite Jesus Music artists since the early 1970s. A highlight of the evening for me was when Phil introduced Bob Mumford, who was sitting in the balcony, and dedicated the song "Take a Look Around," a song about the kingdom and community, to him.

I was free to attend the evening meetings when all 50,000 of us gathered in Arrowhead Stadium to celebrate in worship and to hear the messages of some top-notch speakers. Two unforgettable moments occurred in those sessions. One was the moment when Bob Mumford flipped to the back of his Bible and declared, "I took a look in the back of the book and WE WIN!" The Holy Spirit fell upon us and we danced and shouted and praised the Lord for nearly half an hour.

The other moment was a sober one. Bruce Yocum from the Word of God Community in Ann Arbor gave a prophetic word. He said again and again in numerous ways, "Weep and mourn for my body is broken." This was obviously a call to repent and intercede because of the divisions in the church as a whole. However, years later I would discover that there were also serious divisions behind the scenes among the leaders of that very conference. In reflection it seems clear that, yes, we were to pray for the divisions in the larger church to be healed but also that we should have been repenting and interceding that "our own house" be brought into order.

I returned home the following Sunday and went back to job hunting.

12

What Does a Servant Do?

You are going to be Hal Langevin's servant. The thought came to me strongly and clearly as if the speaker were sitting next to me. I was reading the Bible and praying early on Monday morning, August 8. Actually, "praying" is too weak a description; I had been crying out of the depths of my heart in desperation.

We had had no income since May. We had moved, traveled to Ohio, and then set up housekeeping. The bills kept coming in. Even though we had received a monetary gift or two, we were broke and I had no job prospects.

Before moving, I had made the two trips job-hunting with other brothers from Grand Forks, with only the one interview coming out of that. Soon after we moved, Bill Bagby, a member of the Servants, recommended that I visit a friend of his who was an employment counselor. The man, at Bill's request, was willing to give me advice about my résumé for no charge. It was not an encouraging experience. My résumé listed a few personal facts, my education history, and my job history from paperboy to farmhand to gas station attendant to pastor to college instructor. The job counselor struck Xs through everything having to do with pastoring and teaching, saying that these would be minuses to most employers. That did not leave much; it looked like I had not worked at all for five years.

Each Sunday I picked up a newspaper, the edition with the most classified ads for jobs. I made many calls. I sent in résumés. I filled out applications. I did not even get one more interview. Desperate for any income, I had applied for a job as a pizza delivery man. I called to follow up on the application. The manager simply said that I was overqualified; I had too much education. It was not the only time I had heard that response.

I was even tempted to question whether we had missed God's leading when we had resigned from Wycliffe and cast our lot with the community, even though at the deepest level I knew better. I was battling with anxiety and fear. On August 5, after expressing my desperation, I began a time of fasting and sought to surrender myself and our situation into the Lord's hands. It was on the beginning of the fourth day of the fast that the thought came: *You are going to be Hal Langevin's servant.*

I was immediately convinced that I had heard from the Lord, although I was perplexed by the content of the statement. Hal was one of the primary leaders in this large community. I had met him only one time at midnight in the home of the

Cunninghams when Hal came to greet the men who had come in that first group to seek jobs. I had no reason to think that Hal even remembered my name. What's more, his servant? No one I knew had servants. Why would Hal have one? What would his servant do?

And yet, in spite of it making no sense, I still believed I had heard the Lord say this to me. Therefore, that morning when I headed out to fill out some more job applications, I first stopped at the Servants' secondary office site on 54th Street just east of Lyndale Avenue. The main office, where the primary leaders, Jack Brombach and Hal, had their offices was on Grand Avenue near 48th Street. The 54th Street office space had been rented for some administrative functions, many related to all the people moving into the Twin Cities in order to join the community.

Mike Callaghan had an office there. His primary job was to assist with moving logistics. Since David White had not yet moved, I was looking to Mike for pastoral care during the transition. He was in the office that morning.

After exchanging greetings, I plunged right in and submitted the word for his discernment: "I believe the Lord spoke to me this morning saying that I am to be Hal Langevin's servant. What's a servant?"

"That's interesting," he responded. "The coordinators have decided that the coordinators (elders) need to have men who help them with their administrative work. Biblically, you could call these helpers deacons, but in the community they will be called servants. But I don't think that this is the Lord speaking to you."

I left at peace. Sure, I still wondered what that had all been about; however, Michael represented spiritual authority in my life at that time. I had submitted the word. He had offered his opinion about it. It was no longer my concern.

We had been invited to have dinner with Bill and Nan Bagby on Tuesday evening at their home on Lyndale Avenue. Dan and Faye Smithwick, who had also moved from Grand Forks, were living with the Bagbys at the time because they had made a deal to buy the Bagbys' home but the Bagbys' new home was not yet available. At about seven o'clock the phone rang. To my surprise, Nan called me to the phone.

"Hello," I said.

"This is Jack Brombach," I heard. "I'm sorry to interrupt your visit, but Mike Callaghan told me where you were and I needed to talk to you as soon as possible.

We have been working to select servants for the coordinators. We want Mike to be my servant and we would like you to be Hal's servant. Could you meet us for breakfast at St. Cyr's Restaurant tomorrow morning so we can talk about it?"

"Yes, sir" I replied calmly—on the outside. "What time should I be there?"

Later, Mike told me that soon after I had left his office, Larry Alberts had walked in. As Larry was leaving, he had said offhandedly: "Pray for us today. We are trying to discern who should be servants to Jack and Hal."

Mike replied: "That's interesting. Steve Humble came in a while ago. He told me that he thought the Lord had told him that he was to be Hal's servant."

I do not remember anything about the rest of that night, but early the next morning I walked the mile and a half from our house to St. Cyr's. Thoughts tumbled through my mind as I walked. Nearing the restaurant, I was crossing the bridge over Minnehaha Creek (known because of the poem *Hiawatha*) when I said aloud, not expecting an answer, of course, "Lord, what does a servant do?"

Immediately, in my spirit I heard God's voice clearly, "Whatever he is told."

The breakfast was anticlimactic in one sense. At that point it was just a matter of detail. There was no question that I would accept the opportunity.

However, to my surprise I discovered that I was being offered employment. I was to make $800 a month. In our five years of marriage we had never made $5,000 in any single year. Now we were to make $9,600 a year.

The next morning, August 11, 1977, I showed up at the Grand Avenue office to start serving Hal.

****

I met Hal at the office that Thursday morning. He introduced me to his secretary, Suzanne Perras, and to Jack Brombach's secretary, Carol Quest, whose desks were in the front room, which previously had been the living room of a house. Jack's office, once a bedroom, was also in the front of the building, to the left of the secretaries' office. Michael Callaghan was moving into his new office in the room behind Jack's. Hal's office, previously the kitchen, was behind the secretaries' office.

We walked down the stairs to the basement. Straight ahead at the bottom of the stairs a door led into a conference room furnished with couches and overstuffed chairs. The door to the right at the bottom of the stairs led into my new office, which contained a desk, two chairs, a bookcase, and a file cabinet.

After looking over the building, Hal and I went back upstairs to his office in order to discuss my new job in more detail. As we talked, I began to get a clearer view of what would be expected of me.

Several coordinators led the Servants of the Light. Among these, Jack was the overall coordinator—which would be comparable to senior pastor, presiding elder, or bishop in church terminology. Hal and Jack worked together as the head coordinators, although Larry Alberts would shortly be added to them; their duties included overseeing the work of the district coordinators, planning the agendas for coordinator meetings, and representing the Servants in the Light in outside connections.

At that time, Hal was leading a geographical district of the community in South Minneapolis consisting of about 125 people, and he was giving pastoral oversight to a few district coordinators and to several leaders of smaller communities in other cities. Hal was also responsible to see that those moving from other communities to be members of the Servants of the Light had the housing they needed. Sometimes it was temporary housing for families, such as we had had with the Driessens and the Landmans; other times it was placement of single adults into various households and into apartments with other singles around the Twin Cities.

My job, simply put, was to assist Hal as called upon. I was to keep track of his schedule. Each morning I was to meet with him to plan the day, which often included running some errands and setting up appointments. He would also assign me research projects as needed. Sometimes he would want to talk through some matter with me to help him clarify his thinking; then, he usually would ask me to organize and write up the conclusions.

The first priority was that I get to know Hal and his way of thinking. I also needed to get familiar with the people in the community. As a practical means to that end, Hal asked me to begin to work with him in placing people in the various living situations.

This meant getting acquainted with the available living situations, learning where they were geographically, who lived in them, and the strengths and weaknesses deriving from the relationships of those living there, from Hal's perspective; plus I would need to become familiar with the specific concerns of those needing housing.

I have never been strong on remembering names and details about people. One of the signs of God's grace and his call for me to serve Hal was that over the next several weeks and months, I found myself able to learn and remember many facts about people—things like where they lived, where they worked, who they lived with, and where they came from. I seemed to become a repository for these sorts of facts, to the point that after a short time, when I would meet someone in the community for the first time face-to-face, often I would already know many things about the person. (Sadly, this grace lifted as soon as my work with Hal was completed, and now I'm as weak as ever in remembering names and details about people.)

One thing I began to learn quickly was that, in order to develop community life, it matters where people live. *To actually live in community means, first of all, living life together.* It is not a matter of meetings and special activities. Regular meetings are necessary, mostly in order to keep the vision clear and to develop and keep oriented around a common commitment. Special events and activities have their place in building a common identity and common experience. However, *truly living in community means sharing life together in very practical ways.*

I began to understand more fully that the new commandment, which Jesus gave to his apostles during the Passover meal, just before his arrest and crucifixion, was not a call to some emotion with a religious or mystical meaning; rather it is a call to a down-to-earth, practical way of living.

> A new commandment I give to you, that you love one another: just as
> I have loved you, you also are to love one another. By this all people
> will know that you are my disciples, if you have love for one another.
> (John 13:34–35)

People will not recognize us as Jesus's disciples because we have deep feelings for one another. People will not recognize us as Jesus's disciples because we "fellowship the back of one another's heads" in church meetings, as Bob Mumford used to say. People will not recognize us as Jesus's disciples because we get together for Bible studies and small group fellowship. Rather, if people are to recognize that we are Jesus's disciples, they need to see our love for one another in action, to see our love for one another demonstrated.

I came to understand that the simplest way to allow people to see our interactions is to live near one another so that we can be involved with one another in real life—borrowing a cup of sugar or a tool, working on a car together, mowing each other's lawns, or caring for each other's children. Of course, we pray together, sing together, worship together, and study together. Why? Because these activities also are part of what it means to live life together as the people of God!

We members of the Servants of the Light made a serious commitment to live life together. To facilitate this commitment, our leaders, like those in a number of other Christian communities, were at that time developing a strategy for building "neighborhood clusters." Our leaders prayerfully and thoughtfully identified neighborhoods scattered throughout the Minneapolis-St. Paul area and designated them to be places where we were encouraged to live near one another. Sometimes there would be someone already living in an area where others could move. The optimum situation would include a variety of housing situations—variety in terms of price, but also variety in type: single-family homes, multiple-family dwellings, and apartment buildings.

The Servants' leaders encouraged new members moving into the Twin Cities to make their homes in these designated areas. Quite a few established members of the community also sold homes and moved into one of the clusters.

Once I began to get settled into my new life as a servant, Patricia and I were able to start focusing on our own new life in the community. Living in the fourplex with other community families enhanced our ability to integrate into community life. The pattern of our life together began to develop in late August after the Driessens had moved into their apartment.

****

Since the community was growing in number quickly, new geographical districts were being identified and new district coordinators appointed. Dan had been appointed coordinator of the newly formed Central District, which encompassed a good deal of the southern sector of Minneapolis. Dan was also the pastoral head of our building and of our men's group. Initially there were four men in our group, four married men (Dan Gleason, Frank Williams, Dan Driessen, and me). Before long, Al Lopez and his family moved into a house across the street and Al was added to our men's group. Sometimes we also met with Dan Kalina, Jay Rosengren, and Ron Lamers, single men who lived with the Driessens. Dan's wife, Joyce, led the women's group, consisting of our wives and sometimes the single women who were members of the Driessens' household.

In the Servants of the Light, which was renamed the Servants of the Lord that fall, the word *head* was used to designate men with pastoral authority. It is another example of avoiding "churchy" words in the community. Not only did this practice help minimize confusion both for members of the community and for the various denominational churches to which the members belonged, but it also allowed us to define the meanings of the words we used, rather than to be boxed in by the religious connotations many "churchy" words carry.[39]

Recognizing and submitting to spiritual authority was an important value to us because we saw that, according to Scripture, God delegates authority to human leaders in the various spheres of life, i.e., husbands are leaders of their wives, parents of their children, civil authorities of citizens, and elders of churches. We recognized that the New Testament method for training new believers and also new leaders is person-to-person discipling in personal relationships. Jesus commissioned the first apostles to go and make disciples whom they were to baptize and teach to obey the Lord's commands. Paul used the same principle in his work, and he described it in his instructions to Timothy: "… And what you have heard from me in the presence of many witnesses entrust to faithful men who will be able to teach others also." (2 Timothy 2.2)

In our community, the body of coordinators was responsible to lead, oversee, and care for the whole body. Each district coordinator worked with a group of men called district heads to oversee and lead a geographical district. The district heads, and sometimes a few others, gave leadership, oversight, and care to the men of the community who were organized into men's groups.[40] The men's group structure provided a means for personal training and discipleship.

We commonly used the word *head* in the community to speak of leaders. The term *head* and the structure itself were derived from the model of Israel's leadership structure in the wilderness. Following the counsel of his father-in-law, Jethro, Moses had the people recommend rulers or heads over thousands, hundreds, fifties, and tens. (Exodus 18:13–26 and Deuteronomy 1:9–15[41]) Later, God would direct Moses to select seventy from among these leaders, upon whom the Spirit of God came; thus, the seventy were divinely ordained and equipped to serve with Moses as elders of the whole nation of Israel. (Numbers 11:21–30)

---

[39] A study of the contemporary usages of the word *church* itself contrasted with the Biblical meaning and usage clearly illustrate the problem we were seeking to avoid.

[40] Although the titles were different, this leadership structure has a lot in common with the societies, classes, and bands that John Wesley used to organize the eighteenth-century Methodist movement.

[41] The KJV, the ESV, and some others translations use the word *head* in Deuteronomy 1:13–15, while other translations use words such as *leader* or *ruler*.

In our building, other than the Driessens, the families were all quite new to living in community. To facilitate our growth, Dan established some guidelines by which we all agreed to live. One agreement was that we put locks on the outside doors of the apartment building; then we kept the doors to our apartments open, except for times when we specifically wanted private family time. This meant our homes were open to others in the building. The freedom to enter one another's homes in this way helped us build a sense of family with one another. In addition, we had a common meal together every Tuesday evening, and all whose church service schedule allowed had Sunday brunch together.

Having made the decision to be in community, I jumped in wholeheartedly—or maybe I should say heedlessly—for the most part. Patricia, on the other hand, had a more difficult transition. It seemed as if she had to overcome resistance with every step into community life. She herself has described her experience as "leaving skid marks from dragging her heels."

Only much later did I come to understand that the difficulty she experienced was not rebellion, nor was it simply due to fear. I did not take into account at all the impact on her that the changes we had made would have. Because of me, she had been thrust out of her church heritage, virtually cut off from my parents, and torn from her sense of call to foreign missions. In addition, she had just had a new baby, had made a major geographical move, had lost her dad, had missed his funeral, had been "homeless" for a few weeks, and had been almost without financial resources for over three months. Then she was put into a situation with virtually no privacy. I went to work five days a week. She was there in the apartment all day with three ladies whom she barely knew. Even so, she continued to choose to follow my lead, and she did gradually adjust to our new life.

From time to time we had household meetings that included all the adults in the building; in these meetings we talked about our life together. We identified things that needed to change. We celebrated together. We worked together maintaining the building. Community life was extremely down-to-earth in such a situation.

Every other week we joined with the others in our district for worship and teaching. The other weeks the whole community gathered for a huge worship celebration and to receive teaching concerning our life together from the head coordinators. Most of us also participated in the weekly outreach prayer meeting.

Patricia and I began to go through training courses designed to help us more fully understand and embrace our shared life. These courses consisted of the Foundations

II course (which had one track for married couples and another for single adults), Christian Personal Relationships, Living in Christian Community, The Christian and His Emotions, The Fruit of the Spirit, and Christians in Mission.

In late winter 1978, the leaders set aside two Saturdays to present a set of teachings on the roles of men and women. Steve Clark from the Word of God Community in Ann Arbor, Michigan, had developed the teaching along with several community members who had helped especially with the research.[42] The material was timely in view of the radical changes developing in American culture with the rising influence of radical feminism and the homosexual rights movement. In this course we received a thorough exegesis of the relevant Scriptural material along with direction for wisely applying the teaching.

The point of the course was to be faithful to the wisdom of God in Scripture without trying to make absolutes where the Bible did not make them. Since we were seeking to develop a common way of life, however, we had to define the ways in which we would apply the Scriptural wisdom in our homes and community. Steve used studies from the social sciences to demonstrate typical roles of men and women in a wide variety of cultures. While there are variations in cultures, we saw that the variations are usually not as extreme as promoted by some who have rejected tradition and are trying to make their own opinions and desires acceptable and, what is more, to establish their own choices as the norm for all of us. Much of the teaching reinforced the values practiced, even if not specifically taught, in my home as I was growing up.

The teaching showed that a division of labor between women and men has been the norm in cultures throughout history. The specifics of the assigned tasks vary, but the fact that there has been a division of labor can hardly be disputed. This should be no surprise to Christians since Scripture as well as the church's creeds reveal that there is a division of labor in the one God. Father, Son, and Holy Spirit coexist in perfect union—equal in every way—yet they are distinct persons who do different "tasks" in perfect cooperation. Likewise, Scripture reveals that human beings, both individuals and the human race, are created in the image of God, an image that is reflected in male and female persons. (Genesis 1:26–28; 2:18, 21–24)

Although the applications taught in the course were mostly practical, it also addressed the matter of teaching authority in the Christian community. The denomination in

---

[42] This material was published in Stephen B. Clark, *Man and Woman in Christ: An Examination of the Roles of Men and Women in Light of Scripture and the Social Sciences* (Ann Arbor, MI: Servant Books, 1980). In my opinion, this book is a definitive treatment of the subject.

which I grew up, like many others that began after the nineteenth-century women's movement, had no restrictions on the role of women in the church. There were several women in our denomination who served as pastors and as evangelists. I had never heard the practice questioned on the basis of Scripture in our churches.

I do remember that while in high school I visited a church in Wapakoneta, Ohio, with Dad, who was general superintendent at the time. A woman pastored that church, and as we left, Dad commented offhandedly, "You almost never see a church pastored by a woman that does not have a lot of problems." While his comment did not seem related to Scripture in his thinking, several years later, when I had begun to study the New Testament more thoroughly, I had begun to question that practice.

I had come to the conviction that the people of God must wrestle with the Biblical teaching found in passages such as 1 Corinthians 11:1–16, 1 Corinthians 14:33–38, and 1 Timothy 2:8–14, even though the passages are challenging to interpret. The application made in the teaching we received from Steve Clark was that in Scripture God has assigned the government and the teaching authority of the church to men. At the same time, it recognized the Christian community's dire need for women who, working in coordination with and in submission to their husbands and community leaders, can lead and teach the women in the community.

In contradistinction to most contemporary discussion, the issue is not equality and worth, nor is it whether or not women can be ministers. We are all equally valuable as God's children, and we are all called to be ministers (i.e., to serve). The fundamental issues are that the distinction of gender is necessary for us because we were created to image God, and the division of labor helps us to fulfill God's purpose for us within the order of his creation.

The Scriptures began to take on even greater meaning as I began to read them from within a community of believers who were intentionally seeking to live out full lives according to the wisdom and instruction of our Lord.

Certainly, the Scriptures can and should be read by each individual, and the Holy Spirit does work in each of us to apply the Scripture to each life. The Scripture should also be studied "theologically" as we seek to understand better the unfolding of the themes and topics that God has revealed, which we commonly call "doctrines" in English.

I began to take note, however, that in the Scriptures where the English word *doctrine* is used in the KJV (and in several other Bible translations), to translate the Greek word, *didaskalia*, the teaching referred to most often is *instruction about how God's people are to live together*,[43] not the "theological" material most Christians call doctrine. The teaching that we received in community was good doctrine in the sense that it was practical instruction and wisdom concerning how to live faithfully as the people of God in the midst of an increasingly corrupt society.[44]

---

[43] A great example of this use of the word *didaskalia* is in Titus 1:9; 2:1–10 (specifically in 2:1, 7, 10).

[44] Scripture calls us to live in such a way as a community in many passages. Romans 13:11–14, Philippians 2:14–16, Ephesians 5:6–15, and 1 Peter 2:9–12 are good examples.

13

Changes

After we had lived in the fourplex a few months, Dan Driessen made an appointment to meet with me in a sitting area we had made in our basement. First, Dan complimented me on my knowledge of the Bible. Then, he informed me that I was making it difficult for others in the household to relate to me by inserting my knowledge of the Bible into most of my conversations. He pointed out that often when I referred to the Bible or quoted from it I would preface my statements with the words "My Bible says ... " Dan told me that this practice virtually stopped others from talking. "After all," he said, "how are they to argue with 'your Bible'?"

While Dan was speaking, tears came to my eyes. He asked me why I had tears; I had no answer. He suggested that the tears might indicate defensiveness because I was reluctant to be corrected. Later I realized that he was partly right; I was defensive about being corrected. In time, though, I also came to understand that at a deeper level I believed that I had to be perfect if I was to be accepted by others. Rather than experience Dan's correction as an expression of his love and commitment to serve me, I feared that he and others would reject me.

Dan did not stop with pointing out my problem; he also set up a way to help me change. He expressly forbad me to quote the Bible at our common meals and in our household activities. Because of my commitment to submit to spiritual authority, I agreed—although not without hurt and fear. After all, I had deliberately cultivated knowledge of the Bible. I had trained myself to "speak the Word" as often as possible. I had never considered the possibility that my brothers and sisters would be put off by it and see me as weird—I had not considered it, in spite of the fact that I had many times shut down conversations with my wife because she felt like I was using the Bible as a weapon against her.

Over the next couple months, I often had to squeeze my knee to keep from quoting the Bible in our gatherings. Quite often I felt I had nothing to say. And Dan was not "nice" about it either; at our common meals I distinctly remember him starting conversations on such topics as creation versus evolution and faith versus works.

I saw this matter only as an exercise in obedience on my part. I was happily stunned when, a few months later, I realized that God had used Dan's prohibition to set me free from a religious affectation that not only put off other people but one that had hindered me from relaxing in my humanity, from enjoying a measure of simple human life, and from deeply connecting with others. One day I simply realized that

I had been freed from an unperceived weight. I found myself rejoicing in being a human being, in my life as a man on earth. I found that I could quit trying so hard to be "spiritual." For a long time afterwards I often spontaneously exclaimed, "It's a good life!"

Ironically, about a year later, the Driessens moved into a home a few blocks away. He and I had both begun to relate to Larry Alberts for further training. Dan called me aside one evening during a gathering at his home. Larry had been pointing out that Dan was deficient in his knowledge of Scripture. Larry had told Dan that he needed to eat Scripture, to sleep Scripture, and to speak Scripture. Dan told me that he had been convicted of his need to change. Then he began to apologize to me for having forbidden me to quote the Bible.

I stopped him. "Dan," I said, "I can't tell you how grateful to God I am that you were not under Larry's care last year when you were working directly with me. I am so much freer as a man since God used you to deal with the way I had been misusing Scripture." How amazing that God would love me enough to leave my brother weak in an area of his life long enough that he could help me in an area of my life in which I was too "strong"! Only then did God begin to strengthen my brother in his area of weakness.

****

In late October, Hal took me to lunch at Curran's Restaurant on 42nd Street and Nicolette Avenue.

The lunch was okay, but the conversation was something else again. For about 20 minutes, Hal told me specific ways in which I was doing a terrific job as his servant. I listened gratefully—and very uncomfortably as well because my parents had made it a policy not to brag on their children lest we become proud. I had never experienced someone "bragging on me" to this extent.

Then Hal said, "You do all the work of a servant well, better than I could have asked." Looking directly into my eyes, he went on: "There is only one problem. You don't have a servant's heart."

Tears shot from my eyes and I choked up. I knew that God was speaking to me through Hal.

Finally, I got out my questions: "What is a servant's heart? How do I get one?"

163

"I don't know, but you don't have it," Hal replied, his voice kind but straightforward.

I left that lunch in inner turmoil. I began to cry out to God to show me what a servant's heart was and to change me. The change came, but not suddenly.

There were three specific incidents over the next several months that represent milestones in that change of heart; however, looking back, I can see that the change actually began that day because God had begun to break something in me. The very feeling of being helpless to understand what was being asked of me, let alone to know what to do about it, began to break my dependence on my own abilities and gifts. To put it Scripturally (which I can do now), I was confronted with my weakness (in this case, an inappropriate self-reliance) so that I could become a candidate for God's strength to be manifest through me (2 Corinthians 12:7–10).

The first incident occurred a few weeks later after Hal, Jack, and Larry had returned from a conference with leaders of other ecumenical covenant communities with which we were connected. A day or two after returning, the three men met in the conference room next to my office. On this occasion they left the door open during a part of their meeting, and I could not help overhearing their discussion concerning the need to teach the members of the community to honor and serve as a part of our community culture. They talked about teaching people to stand up when an older person came into the room, and they talked about practical ways in which members in the community could serve their leaders.

As they talked, a war began in my mind. These leaders were Catholic. I was Protestant. I imagined them expecting me to do things comparable to kissing the Pope's ring.

In spite of my familiarity with the Bible, I did not know the command, "You shall stand up before the gray head and honor the face of an old man, and fear your God: I am the LORD" (Leviticus 19:32). I had not yet taken note of principles that Paul taught: that those who received spiritual wealth from others should share their material wealth in return and that leaders were to be shown honor as well as respected (Romans 15:27, Galatians 6:6, I Thessalonians 5:12–13, I Timothy 5:17). I resisted the idea of showing visible signs of respect and honor even though it is clearly Biblical to do so.

For several days I struggled with fear, with pride, and with rebellion about being a Protestant under the authority of Catholics. Then, on Saturday morning I went to my office to get alone with God. I cried out earnestly for God's help. In effect, I cried, "Get me out of here!"

As I prayed I had a vivid mental picture of two streams of water with a narrow strip of land separating them. I saw myself straddling the land, trying to walk with a foot in each stream. I was aware that the stream where my right foot stood represented the Catholic ecumenical covenant communities while my left foot was in the other stream, which represented those covenant communities led by the *New Wine* teachers, such as the Community of Hope in Lancaster, Ohio, of which my friend John Meadows was a member. I saw that both streams were flowing in the same direction. I realized that I felt I would be safe in the *New Wine* stream and that I had conditioned my commitment to my leaders in the Catholic-ecumenical stream on their relationship with *New Wine* teachers.

Then the Holy Spirit spoke very clearly to my spirit: "I want you to be in one stream or the other. I will bless you and use you in either. I prefer for you to be in this one [the Catholic-ecumenical stream]." Faith came with this word from the Lord. I literally lifted up my left foot, as though removing it from the *New Wine* stream; then I physically moved so as to dive headfirst into the Catholic-ecumenical stream on the right—stopping myself before I plunged my head onto the floor.

That settled the issue in my heart and mind. I had decided to trust God to take care of me and to use the leaders he had placed over me. If they taught something or asked me to do something I believed to be unscriptural, then we would have to work it out together. I was not leaving.

Ironically, just a few days later, the third New Wine Tape of the Month arrived in the mail, a message by Don Basham titled "Serving and Being Served." Don presented clear Scriptural teaching on the subject of serving. His message confirmed the word of the Lord to me, but after my encounter with God it was not the basis for my security in the community to which God had called me.

Later, I learned from John Meadows that some *New Wine* communities were emphasizing serving leaders far more than our community ever did. In fact, some of those communities were overemphasizing this practice to such a degree that it would produce negative repercussions several years later.

The second incident came not long afterward. Don Schwager, a servant from the Word of God Community in Ann Arbor, Michigan, came to visit us. All of us who had been designated servants met with him for several hours of teaching. Don taught us about deacons and servanthood from the Bible and from the writings of the early fathers of the church. He also taught us many practical attitudes and behaviors that servants needed to develop.

For example, Don talked about the need to wait—that is to be available to serve when called upon. He told us that a servant must learn to anticipate needs but also to learn not to jump ahead and initiate actions without authorization. He said we needed to learn to wait in peace, eager to serve, without being anxious about inactivity.

This really spoke to me. When I had times with no specific assignment to fulfill, I would often read a book while I waited for Hal to call on me. But if someone came down the stairs, my instinct was to hide the book and act like I was studying the Bible or like I was busy with some other "acceptable" activity. I had not understood that being available and ready when my current assignments had been fulfilled was in itself acceptable service.

The third incident occurred on a Thursday morning in the spring of 1968. I had come into my office a while before Hal arrived. As I waited, I opened my Bible and began to read the parables of the sower and of the growing seed in Mark 4.1–9, 13-20, 26–29. With no effort on my part, an outline for a teaching popped into my mind. And I knew it was a good one. I also knew that there was no speaker scheduled for the outreach prayer meeting that evening. And I strongly believed that the Lord had given me this teaching for that prayer meeting.

Quickly, I wrote out the outline, took it upstairs, and asked our secretary, Suzanne Perras, to type it up. When she finished, I took the outline into Hal's office and laid it on the center of his desk where he could not miss seeing it. Then I went downstairs, nearly trembling with anticipation. It had been a long time since I had had opportunity to preach or teach—and never in the Servants. This was the time, I was sure!

I heard Hal come in, greet the secretaries as usual, and then go into his office. A few minutes later he called me on the intercom to say that he was ready for our morning meeting. I went up into his office and sat down in my chair, trying not to grin.

Hal said, "Where did this outline come from?"

"The Lord gave it to me this morning," I replied.

"This is good," Hal declared. "I'm going to teach it tonight."

I froze up inside. I fought to keep a straight face. My face felt like it was on fire. Still, I tried hard not to show the disappointment and the hurt that I felt. I could barely wait to get out of that room.

It was a long day, and then I had to go to the prayer meeting. As Hal taught "my message," I could hardly stand the feelings of jealousy, anger, and resentment that were boiling inside me. I went home to a nearly sleepless night, wrestling with my thoughts and emotions.

The next morning as I drove down Pillsbury Avenue toward the office, just as I was turning left onto 48th Street, I cried aloud to the Lord, "What do you want from me?"

To my surprise, he spoke very clearly—again one of those times when his voice could not have been plainer even if he had spoken aloud. The Lord said, "I want you to take everything I have given you—your gifts, your abilities, your training, and your heritage—and use them to help Hal be the best man of God he can be."

With that word, I was free. Joy flooded me. I could think of nothing better to do with my life than to serve God by serving Hal.

At last I was beginning to see that God was indeed giving me a servant's heart.

****

A few months later, Hal was asked to move his family to St. Paul so that he could lead a district there. We both took it for granted that our family would move also. Patricia and I started looking for a house in St. Paul, and before long we put an offer on a duplex and it was accepted. Because our income was insufficient for us to qualify for a loan, a single brother named Brad Bye, a member of the community whom we hardly knew, applied for a loan with us and was to share ownership with us.

Plans changed, however, before we could close on the house. One morning in early June, Hal began to tell me that the head coordinators had been praying about me and discussing my future in the community. They had come to the conclusion that my primary calling was to be a pastoral leader; consequently, they believed that I should begin prepare to become a coordinator rather than to continue as Hal's servant.

He said that in order for me to develop as a leader, they thought it best for me to remain in Minneapolis, where I would become a district head in the newly formed East Central District. Hal said that I would need to find a new job in order to support my family. He also informed me that Larry Alberts would give me pastoral oversight and train me to be a coordinator.

I have no way to describe the anguish I felt upon hearing this news. I left the office, but I was in no condition to go home and talk about this change with Patricia. I drove over to a secluded place along the Minnehaha Parkway and parked. Leaving the car, I walked several yards to a tree, where I sat down, heavy in heart and mentally in turmoil.

Although from a human perspective there was more prestige and honor in being an elder than a servant, my heart felt as though I was being demoted. Serving Hal had become my joy and my ambition. I struggled once again to surrender my plans to the Lord and to embrace the steps that he had planned for my life. It took about twenty-four hours to work it through, but by God's grace I became able to embrace the change.

A few days later, Larry Alberts suggested that I talk to Chuck Downs, who, like me, was a fairly new member of the Servants. Larry told me that Chuck owned a screen printing business and needed to hire someone. Thus, I called Chuck and made an appointment to meet him at First Image, his shop out in Plymouth, a northwestern suburb of Minneapolis.

I found Chuck to be a jovial, friendly man. I knew nothing at all about screen printing; therefore, as we began to get acquainted, Chuck took me around the shop, explaining to me the printing process and showing me the equipment.

First, we went into the art room with its drawing table and dark room. There, Chuck briefly demonstrated how he would take art work and transfer each separate color into a positive photo image (the opposite of photo negatives) on transparent film. He then picked up a positive and a photo-sensitive emulsion-coated screen, consisting of fabric mesh (usually nylon) tightly stretched onto a wood frame, and he placed them on a light table. As the light passed through the blank areas on the film the emulsion hardened in the screen. However, because the light did not pass through the positive image on the film, the emulsion did not harden on those areas. Next, Chuck sprayed the screen with a gentle stream of water, washing out the emulsion that had not hardened, which left a negative image in the screen.

Next I watched one of the printers place a screen over a piece of plastic that he had laid on a table. He poured red ink onto the mesh. Then he pulled a rubber squeegee blade across the screen. The squeegee pushed the ink through the open mesh of the negative image, leaving a positive image on the plastic below. (Using this method one is able to print images, one color at a time, onto a variety of materials, including vinyl, paper, metal, plastic, glass, cloth, or wood.)

In addition to tables where this "hand screening" was done, Chuck showed me the two printing machines into which the screens could be placed. These machines accomplished the squeegee process mechanically. There were several racks in the shop on which the printing material was placed in order to dry. There was also a cutting machine for cutting and trimming print jobs.

Incredibly, I left First Image that day with a job. Chuck needed to focus on getting new business, and he needed to do the art work and make the positives. He hired me to oversee and manage all the printing work and also to do the shipping and delivery. It would be my responsibility to schedule the work, to oversee the printers, and to get the jobs out on time. I walked into that shop with absolutely no knowledge of screen printing. I walked out the newly hired shop manager.

One of my first responsibilities was to learn all the processes that I had been hired to oversee. Chuck trained me himself. During the training process, we hired another brother with some printing experience. When this brother saw the work on which I was learning, he told me that in any other shop I would not touch such complex jobs without five years or more experience.

It sounds foolish for Chuck to hire me to manage the shop without practical experience in the work. It does not sound less foolish that I took the job. However, Larry had recommended me to Chuck and had recommended the job to me. Such was our commitment to one another as brothers and such was our trust that God would lead us through leaders that Chuck and I acted on Larry's recommendations.

It worked well. First Image had been in financial difficulty due to moisture problems in the new building that Chuck had leased and because he was overextended as a result of trying to do so much of the work himself. The Lord blessed our obedience! Over the course of the next two years that I worked for Chuck, the business grew, the debt was repaid, and the profit margin increased substantially. Soon after I quit, Chuck was able to sell 90% of First Image to a larger company for an excellent price.

The Lord used my time working with Chuck not only to provide income for my family but also to teach me some important life lessons. For example, I learned that I derived satisfaction from finishing tasks; however, I had not learned to enjoy the work itself. I discovered that I got frustrated if there was never a time to "be finished."

Whenever we finished one job in the shop and delivered it to the customers, several other orders were still in process, and there were others to be started—at least there had better be if we were to meet expenses and make money. If our company were to prosper, we needed to have a continual flow of work. But my desire was to finish a job and then quit for a while so that I could do something I "liked to do," which to me mostly meant reading, listening to music, or watching a movie—in a word, escape from life.

I began to realize that life is not so much about "finishing" as about faithfully "doing." Life is not so much about "arriving," but about the "journey." In my assignments as husband, father, and pastor, it is rare to have times when there are not ongoing "jobs" to be continued. I saw that if I did not learn to enjoy the process of working, I was not going to have much fulfillment and a lot of frustration.

Although I did not immediately see the connection to my need to "finish" things, gradually I have begun to understand the importance of the Sabbath principle. God established a pattern for man in which on one day each week we are to say, in effect: "We have finished our work. Thank you, Lord, for what has been accomplished." For one day a week we are to set aside our unfinished jobs and, with thanksgiving to God, enjoy what we have been able to do in the previous six days. As we do, God refreshes us and helps us to reengage our tasks with energy and often with new insight into the work before us.

I know this with my head. Sadly, even now, all these years later, I still have a difficult time practicing it in real life. That is my own fault. I simply have not made a firm enough decision to set aside a specified time for rest and for giving thanks and to honor that time. Instead, I tend to continue in the rush of life until life runs over me.

In our American culture, we tend to fill even the weekends and our days off with frantic activity, often calling it recreation. However, I can see God's wisdom in establishing a set Sabbath day for everyone. I remember as a child growing up in central Ohio that Sunday was honored as a day of rest in our culture. In our small town, one filling station and one pharmacy would be open on Sundays—in case of emergencies; however, except for the churches, the town shut down. No one worked at their regular jobs except those who provided essential services. In our home, the big question was whether or not it was acceptable to play ball with the neighbor boys rather than to read or to take a nap.

There was strong encouragement in the Servants of the Lord to honor the Sabbath principle by making the Lord's Day a day of rest and celebration. Although there was no community rule requiring it, a number of households followed the example set by other communities, such as the Word of God in Ann Arbor, Michigan, and the People of Praise in South Bend, Indiana, where they had actually developed the custom of opening the Lord's Day on Saturday evening in the households with a family "ceremony" involving prayers, readings, lighting candles, and sharing bread, wine, and cheese. These communities also developed a short ceremony to end the Lord's Day on Sunday evening. The ceremonies were, of course, modeled on the Sabbath ceremonies customarily practiced in Jewish homes on Friday and Saturday evenings.

After we moved away from the Servants, where honoring the Lord's Day as a Sabbath was encouraged, I have found it much harder to build such a custom into my own life and into our family's life. Going against the tide of the culture to honor the Sabbath is much easier if several households decide to include it in their own pattern of life together, I have found.

The Lord began to teach me another life lesson directly through Chuck. He started teaching me to screen-print on a big job for the Musicland stores, a job that would take us over three months to complete. Musicland had contracted us to print 500 each of four cartoon-character figures: Spiderman, Mickey Mouse, Big Bird, and Winnie the Pooh. On a large press, we needed to print the figures onto sheets of a thick, plastic material about 3 feet high and 1 foot wide, printing the exact image on each sheet on both sides, only reversed so that, once printed, they could be die cut into the shape of the figure. Each figure had three to five colors; therefore, we had to print each sheet from six to ten times in order to print on both sides—all measured to exact specifications to align the colors properly.

Chuck taught me to print using an excellent discipleship method: (1) model the work for the disciple; (2) watch the disciple work; (3) have the disciple do the work and give feedback on the results; (4) release the disciple to do the work.

Chuck had me watch him work on the three-color Spiderman job. I did a little printing on that job but only under close supervision. Next, we did the four-color Mickey Mouse figures. This time Chuck taught me how to set up the press, and he watched me closely while I did much of the printing. Next, we started on the five-color Winnie the Pooh figure. This time Chuck watched me set up the press—making sure that I had it set up correctly. However, once the printing was going smoothly, he left me unsupervised for longer and longer periods of time. Then, when we started to print the Big Bird figure, Chuck left me largely on my own, only checking on me occasionally unless I asked for his help.

To print I had to pick up one sheet of plastic at a time from a stack on my right. I would then place the sheet onto the press table in exactly the right spot, marked by pieces of plastic (called registration) that I had taped to the table to mark the lower right-hand corner and the two edges extending from that corner. Once the sheet was in place I would press a button; the machine would lower the screen frame, already inked, and pass the squeegee across the fabric. After the squeegee had passed, the machine would lift the frame and I would pick up the sheet, placing it to my left onto a conveyer belt that took it through the drying machine.

At first it was exciting to work with much less supervision; however, the work soon began to become routine as I passed sheet after sheet through the press on the belt—520 sheets six to ten times each. I began to get bored. I had learned to work with the press set on automatic, a function that automatically raised and lowered the screen and controlled the movement of the squeegee according to a timer. After a while I began to experiment with various speeds.

At last I finished the first side of the Big Bird figure. Then one evening I finished printing the first color onto the other side of the sheet of plastic. The next day I started to print the second color. Significantly, these two colors did not touch each other at any point but were to be connected into a single image later by the colors applied later. About halfway through the run of the 520 sheets, I began to set the press speed faster and then faster and then faster. *I am really getting good at this,* I thought, grabbing up sheet after sheet, slamming each onto the press table and then thrusting it onto the dryer belt.

Whoa! I discovered that I had knocked one of the registration markers loose. My heart sank. I could only hope that I had discovered the problem right after knocking the registration loose, but I didn't know. Were the colors out of alignment? My eyes could not detect any problems. However, there would be no way to know for sure until I started applying the connecting colors. At that point the alignment, or lack of it, would be revealed.

Disaster! A few days later when I applied the next color, it was clear. The stripes on Big Bird's stockings were not aligned on fifty to seventy-five pieces. My heart sank. I had to call Chuck in and show him what I had done. As I talked to Chuck and as he looked over the damage, over and over I berated myself.

Chuck stopped looking at the work and glared at me. "Stop!" he said. "There is no value in focusing on yourself. We have a problem. Problems are an opportunity for problem solving. We need to focus on finding a solution." Chuck never did reprimand

172

me for my foolishness, which had caused the problem; rather, he corrected my attitude and response.

"Problems are an opportunity for problem solving." That maxim has stuck with me over the years; however, I am still trying to learn to approach life that way. My first response when I have made a mistake is usually to chew myself out. And, regrettably, that is often what I tend to do first when my wife or children make a mistake too. These days I often catch myself quickly—sometimes before I have spoken, but I am still working to make the lesson the Lord gave me through Chuck that day a way of life.

Thankfully, Chuck did find a way to salvage most of the damaged work on Big Bird.

****

In addition to what I learned while actually working at First Image, I also had a few memorable encounters with the Lord while driving the 20 miles (each way) to and from the job. One encounter took place as I was driving through the small tunnel on I-94 west near downtown Minneapolis.

While serving Hal I had made a settled decision about being in the ecumenical community instead of a community connected to the five teachers in the *New Wine* stream; even so, from time to time I still had questions concerning the Lord's purpose for placing me in a part of the Body of Christ where my comfort zone was often stretched.

On one particular day when I was wrestling with this once more as I entered the tunnel, the Lord spoke clearly to my spirit: "What if I have you here to be a bridge builder? What if I want to use you as a relational connection between two parts of my Body? Besides, in the *New Wine* stream, your gifts are a dime a dozen. Here, your gifts are more needed." That word settled something in me. I did not have to try to be somebody or something. The Lord knew what I needed, and he knew how and where to use me. All I needed to do was to be faithful where he had placed me in the Body.

A few months later I received another significant word from the Lord while driving to work, a word that brought adjustment to my way of relating to God's people.

Patricia had been having an ongoing battle with fear; she and I had not been able to get victory. Finally, I invited our district leadership team: Larry Alberts, Dan and

Joyce Driessen, and Anna Brombach, to come over on a Sunday evening to pray with us—or with her, to be honest.

After we had prayed a while, it became clear that God's agenda for that evening was different than mine. Someone gently suggested that it was I whom the Lord wanted to set free that night and asked if I was open to their ministry. I replied that I was. They asked if there were things in my life from which I wanted the Lord to free me. I named several areas of frequent temptation and some besetting sins that tended to trip me up. They did pray for me in those areas, a little perfunctorily, it seemed to me.

Then, after a time of waiting before the Lord, Larry told me that each of them had needed to be freed from certain strongholds associated with their church tradition, which in all their cases was Roman Catholic. They explained that along with much that was good in their heritage, the Holy Spirit had revealed to them that religious strongholds had also built up over time and that through these strongholds the devil manipulated and used people in the church for his own ends. (See 2 Corinthians 10:3–5.) They believed that the Holy Spirit was revealing some strongholds associated with my Holiness heritage, namely, judgmentalism and legalism.

This seemed accurate to me, so they prayed against these strongholds. They took authority over the work of the enemy, especially his influence on my attitudes and words, and asked the Lord to set me free. The prayer was straightforward, unemotional, and actually rather brief. There were no demonic manifestations. I had no spectacular experience. I had no particular awareness of any change. But I did have peace about the prayer. I simply decided to trust the Lord to do what needed to be done.

The next morning, I picked up my friend Ron Wolfe, who worked at a Sauder furniture factory about a mile from our shop. I dropped him off at the factory. Then, just as I turned out of the parking lot back onto the street to head over to First Image, the Lord spoke to my spirit: "I have freed you from a militant spirit and I am giving you the spirit of a farmer. I want you to lay down your sword and your shield toward the Body of Christ and pick up a plow."

Immediately I remembered a scene from a Saturday morning movie that I had watched several years earlier with some children whom Patricia and I were babysitting. The movie was about a boy about 12 years old whose parents were divorced and who were more interested in their own lives than in their son. For most of his life, the boy had been left in boarding schools, and he had become angry and bitter. The story concerned a summer that the boy spent on his grandfather's farm. Patiently, the grandfather loved on the boy and worked with him until, at last, the boy opened up his heart to his grandfather.

In the scene that came vividly to mind that Monday morning, the boy and his grandfather were sitting side by side under a huge oak at the edge of a freshly plowed field near summer's end. The boy looked up and said, "Grandpa, when I grow up I want to be a farmer just like you."

The grandfather reached down, picked up a handful of dirt from the field, lifted it to his lips and took a small bit onto his tongue. "A good farmer," he replied, "loves the soil. He can taste it and know its strengths and weaknesses."

Immediately, I knew what the Lord was saying to me. Because of judgmentalism and legalism, I was not making deep connections with many brothers and sisters in the Body of Christ, especially those whose theological heritages I did not trust. It was as though I shielded myself against their insights into God's truth and ways while trying to correct their erroneous thinking, using the Scriptures like a sword. The Lord was telling me that he had delivered me from the need to protect myself from his people. I knew that from that time forward, it would be up to me to choose, by the Spirit, to love my brothers and sisters, to choose not be afraid of their heritages or to be put off by their different beliefs, but rather, be willing to "taste the differences" and thus discover the good. If I was going to serve God's people, it would be with the love and patience of a farmer, not with the violent spirit of a warrior.

The Lord used Patricia's battle with fear to sneak up on me.

****

God blessed me with another life-changing encounter during that season as well, although it was not related to my work at First Image. Jack Brombach had asked me to speak at a camp sponsored by a small community in Staples, Minnesota, during the Labor Day weekend. A few days after Jack talked with me, I discovered that my friend Bill Bagby and his wife would be going to the camp too, and Bill asked if I would like to ride with them. Although I did not know it, the Staples group had contacted Jack previously and had asked that he send Bill as the speaker. For some reason, Jack and the other head coordinators thought I should go instead. However, a leader from the Staples group had contacted Bill directly and asked him to come. Bill did not know that they had approached Jack about sending him first, and neither of us knew that our leaders had thought it best for Bill not to speak at all.

After a pleasant three-hour drive on the Friday before Labor Day, Bill; his wife, Nan; and I arrived at the camp at about 4 p.m. Soon after I arrived and Bill had introduced me to his friends there, the facts became clear. They were looking for Bill, not for me. After some discussion, they asked me to speak only once, at the first meeting to be held at 8 o' clock that evening.

Finally, everyone arrived, and the meeting started—late. We had a time of worship in song and then a break. Afterward I was given less than 10 minutes in which to speak; then I was done with ministry for the weekend. I would have headed home, except that I had ridden with the Bagbys, who would not be leaving until Monday.

During the break between the singing and my mini-message, I met Bill Lemke. We talked for about 10 minutes upon meeting, enough for me to learn that he and his wife, Lou, were members of Daystar Ministries, a nondenominational charismatic community headquartered in Minneapolis, and that they were serving in a Daystar discipleship school called Eden, located near Weyerhaeuser, Wisconsin. Bill had a background in the Christian and Missionary Alliance churches, a denomination with a number of similarities to the Churches of Christ in Christian Union, and I had preached in a few CMA churches while in Bible college.

After my short message, one of the camp leaders introduced the Lemkes to the whole group, saying that they had a ministry of praying for people to be freed. Bill and Lou began their first prayer session about 11 o' clock that Friday night. I do not remember how they introduced the prayer, but I do know that I was the first one to respond to their invitation.

I remember Bill praying for me, although I cannot remember any specifics of his prayer. I do remember that it seemed like he had read my heart and my history. I know he prayed something about my relationship with my dad—his prayer obviously directed by the Holy Spirit, since I had told him little if anything about our relationship.

What I do remember with absolute clarity is what the Lord said in my spirit while Bill was praying: "You are not to look for acceptance and understanding from your dad. Look to me for acceptance and understanding. It is your responsibility to love your dad and to honor him and to serve him every time you have opportunity."

This simple, straightforward word from the Lord, along with the prayers, changed me! From that time on, I was free to love Dad unconditionally. I was able release him from the demand that he accept me and that he understand me. After that prayer session, I was able to listen respectfully to Dad to receive truth from him. Even when he said things that seemed critical and harsh, I was enabled not to argue or to take offense.

The work the Lord did in me during Bill Lemke's prayer was a big step toward the fulfillment of part of the word from Jeremiah 3:19, which I had received before moving to Richland Center:

> You shall call Me, My Father,
> And not turn away from following Me. (NASB)

It proved to be the turning point in my relationship with Dad. The changes became manifest gradually, but they were permanent.

14

Discovering Roots

During the summer of 1979, the coordinators authorized me to begin a Sunday morning service for nondenominational members of the Servants of the Lord.

Most Roman Catholic members of the Servants of the Lord believed that they were fulfilling the expectations of their parishes by attending a Sunday mass and giving offerings regularly. On the other hand, Protestant members of the community usually experienced tension between their commitment to their local churches and their commitment to the Servants, especially those belonging to evangelical, Pentecostal, and nondenominational churches. At the very least, these churches expected their members to attend two or three services each week, to serve in the ministries of the church, and to tithe.

Further complicating the picture, most nondenominational members of the community saw little, if any, distinction between our view of church and our experience in community. "Going to church" seemed artificial when we already felt that we were living "church life" in the Servants.

Why the emphasis on being members of a church anyway? A good question indeed, one that needs to be answered in the light of our call to community. We in the Servants of the Lord and members of similar communities believed that God had called us together to be a prophetic witness to the churches. We believed that our God-given mission included the call to model a fully Christian, ecumenical, Spirit-filled way of life, a life that would call the churches to repentance and renewal. If we all left our denominations to be in the community, then we would be only one more division in the already divided church. On the other hand, if we only went to our churches and did not live in community, then we could only talk about community; we would have no model that exemplified our vision. What is more, the call of God is to be obeyed not only by hearing it and talking about it but also by doing what we hear.

As we began to discuss the needs of our nondenominational members, we also looked at what similar communities were doing. The Word of God Community in Ann Arbor, Michigan, and the Work of Christ Community in East Lansing, Michigan, had started Sunday fellowships for their nondenominational members. Also, they were working with Roman Catholic, Orthodox, Lutheran, and Reformed church leaders in an effort to gain authorization to start Sunday fellowships for members from those churches.

178

The nondenominational groups in those two communities had taken the name Free Church Fellowship. I contacted Mark Kinzer and Ken Wilson, the leaders of the Free Church Fellowship in the Word of God Community, in order to discuss their vision and their choice of the name Free Church. Their vision was to have a fellowship in which nondenominational members could participate in the Lord's Supper and practice believer's baptism according to their understanding of Scripture, since we did not share the sacraments in the ecumenical communities. Their Fellowship gathered on Sunday to worship by singing, by sharing in communion, and by preaching the historical doctrines of the church according to their convictions. They also sought to reinforce the practical wisdom for Christian living given in the general community teaching.

Mark and Ken told me that they had decided that there would be two primary drawbacks if they were to identify their Fellowship as nondenominational: (1) They would be defining themselves negatively—by what they were not, rather than by what they were; (2) the word *nondenominational* could be construed as criticism of denominations.

After much thought and research, they had decided to identify with the free church tradition. This name seemed to have several advantages. The name "free church" historically referred to the churches not sanctioned by the civil government, in contrast to the state church. Since there was no state church in the United States, most Americans would not be familiar with the name "free church" (except for those who knew about the Evangelical Free Church denomination or those from an Anabaptist background). Therefore, Mark and Ken believed they could more easily define their fellowship for what it was without the name carrying its own meanings. In addition, like most of the historical free churches, they practiced believer's baptism rather than infant baptism; thus, this name actually did suggest continuity with some historical roots in church history.

After much discussion with the coordinators and a few interested nondenominational community members, we decided to launch our own Free Church Fellowship. Thus, in September 1979, seven adults began to meet on Sunday mornings in the living room of our apartment—Mike and Janetta Hynous, Duane Roller, Gary Meyer and his fiancée, Wanda Chaplin, Patricia, and I. The only children were our own, Elijah and Stephanie.

Over the next few years others joined us, so by the summer of 1983 there were about ninety members in our fellowship. We identified ourselves first and foremost as members of the Servants of the Lord community because the biggest part of our lives

179

we shared in common with the other members of Servants. The Free Church Fellowship filled out the smaller part of our lives that we could not share in common because of our convictions concerning a relatively few, howbeit important, Biblical truths and practices.

In the early 1980s, in an article written to explain the Free Church Fellowship for the broader membership of Servants, I set forth our view of the church: "A strong emphasis of the Free Church Fellowship is that the church is the community of believers who have entered into covenant with God in Christ through the work of the Holy Spirit. Because they have been joined to God by covenant they have also been joined to one another. They are meant to be the visible expression of God's kingdom on the earth in their love, faithfulness, and service, both to one another and to those to whom they are God's ambassadors of reconciliation."

For many other members of Servants, "church" primarily meant a historical institution that has been established. To us, "church" referred to all those related to God by the New Covenant instituted by Jesus, irrespective of historical institutions. To us, then, the community in essence was "church."

****

During our years in the Servants of the Lord, my priority was to grow in a way of life that would support my faith in Jesus and my walk in his kingdom. My focus was to grow as a man, as a husband, as a father, as a community member, and as a leader. However, my understanding of God's purpose, my vision for the church, and my awareness of the "cultural war" in my generation were also continuing to develop. In fact, the more I sought to learn a distinctly Christian approach to life, the more my thinking about the bigger issues began to take shape.

About the same time that we started to think about describing ourselves as "free church," some messages I heard on cassette tapes began to bring into clearer focus issues with which I had been wrestling since the Waite Park days. As I remember it, the first was a set of tapes by Charles Simpson in which he taught about God's covenant.

For several years the word *covenant* had been used to refer to committed relationships between brothers. The brothers in the *New Wine* stream had seemed to use it most often to describe the relationship between a "shepherd" (meaning a personal pastor) and his "sheep" (referring to those looking to the shepherd for care, accountability, and discipling). In the Catholic ecumenical communities, we used the word *covenant* to refer to a formal written statement setting forth the commitments that described a community and its life.[45]

I was aware that *covenant* was a Biblical word referring to a relationship between God and man, but I never had made an in-depth study of the matter. Brother Charles's messages brought much greater clarity to the subject than I had had before; more important, I was moved to begin a serious study of the matter for myself.

Brother Charles started in Genesis 15, the passage in which God made a covenant with Abram. Brother Charles then went on to describe the nature and development of the Abrahamic covenant. Next, Brother Charles discussed the content of God's covenant with the nation Israel. Finally, he set forth the key issues in the New Covenant in Christ. By the time I had finished these three messages I was more deeply moved than ever before by the surety of God's promises set forth in his covenants with man. I had a new and deep confidence that God was going to fulfill all that he had begun; what is more, I believed we were participants in a work of God that was to play a significant part in seeing his covenant promises come to pass!

The fourth tape brought a holy and healthy check after this "heady wine" that I had been drinking. In the message on the Abrahamic covenant, Brother Charles had said that the essence of covenant is not that one gives "something" but that he gives himself. When God, in the form of a smoking fire pot and blazing torch, passed between the pieces of the animals Abram had cut and laid out, God was committing himself to fulfill the covenant, which Jesus did as God and as man.

In the fourth message, Brother Charles powerfully declared that when all was said and done, more than anything else he wanted God's presence in his life, even if he did not see the promises fulfilled in his lifetime. I understood that it was vital for me to not lose sight of God, who made the covenants, while I was making a more serious search into the covenants he had made.

A few months later, John Meadows sent me tapes of the messages from the Covenant Life Conference that had been hosted by some of the *New Wine* teachers and held in Mobile, Alabama, in 1979. Many of those messages were a great help to me, but there were six in particular that have become part of my way of thinking (and hopefully of my living too).

---

[45] See Appendix Five for an example.

Bob Mumford taught a series on the foundational steps into the kingdom of God. His messages were rooted in the often-overlooked fact that the new birth has to do with seeing and entering the kingdom of God (John 3:3, 5). In the first message, Bob taught that we change kingdoms when, upon believing and repenting, we are baptized. With real clarity Brother Bob demonstrated from Scripture that water baptism is more than simply an outward testimony to an inward work, which I had been taught. Although the inward change—the new birth—is a reality, in baptism we leave the kingdom of darkness, renouncing its tyrannical king, Satan, and enter the kingdom of light, submitting to the gracious government of the Lord Jesus. God seals that work with the Holy Spirit.

Brother Bob went on in the second message to say the Holy Spirit will lead us at some point into a time of testing, just as, after Jesus's baptism, the Holy Spirit had led (Matthew 4:1, Luke 4:1) or had driven (Mark 1:12) Jesus into the wilderness, where he was tempted by the devil. This testing Bob called "undeception," describing it as a time in which God begins to show us areas in which we are deceived because we do not see our weaknesses clearly. Only as we see them clearly will we rely on God as fully as we must. Bob said, "It is better to go into life knowing I have only two ounces of faith than to go thinking I have a quart." Jesus's testing, of course, did not reveal deception; the devil was soundly defeated because there was nothing in Jesus that responded positively to the devil's enticement.

Brother Bob called the third message "The Eternal Yes." He called upon his listeners to make a once-and-for-all decision, up front, that "from this point on when the choice comes up I will always answer, 'Yes, Lord.' " Then, in any given situation, though it might not be easy and there may be struggle, one will have already predetermined to submit to Jesus. This greatly simplifies life. If, in any given situation one has to both struggle to find out God's will and to struggle with whether or not to obey, then one is bound to have much confusion and most likely many failures. However, if one has predetermined the outcome—"Yes, Lord"—then there is only one issue: "What does the Lord want me to do?"

Charles Simpson also presented three messages at this conference on the topic "The People of God." It would be hard to overemphasize the importance of these messages in the development of my views about God's purposes. As I listened to Brother Charles, strands of my thinking over the previous years began to come together to form a far more complete picture. I became much firmer in the conviction that in redemption through Jesus Christ, God was not simply saving individuals from hell but that in Christ, God is fulfilling his deeper purpose for mankind—to bring forth a people, a holy nation, a community of human beings with whom he will reign on the earth. I understood much more clearly that God is preparing his adopted children to "inherit the earth" along with the firstborn son, Jesus. It was through these messages that I began to realize that "inheritance" is a key to God's purposes. The new birth, I was learning, is far more than one's "ticket to heaven"; rather, the new birth brings us into God's family, where we are prepared to share in Jesus's inheritance (see Psalm 2).

As I listened to the third message, my old eschatology (that is, "the last things," the so-called "end times"), which had begun to change in 1975 when I heard Ern Baxter's message "Thy Kingdom Come," was completely blown away. First, Brother Charles set forth the Old Testament teaching, especially in Psalm 37 and some verses in Proverbs 10–12, that it is the people of God, the righteous, who will inherit the earth. Then, Brother Charles read the familiar passage in Matthew 24 which says,

> As were the days of Noah, so will be the coming of the Son of Man. For as in those days before the flood they were eating and drinking, marrying and giving in marriage, until the day when Noah entered the ark, and they were unaware until the flood came and swept them all away, so will be the coming of the Son of Man. Then two men will be in the field; one will be taken and one left. Two women will be grinding at the mill; one will be taken and one left. Therefore, stay awake, for you do not know on what day your Lord is coming. (Matthew 24:37–42)

Then, after a pause, Brother Charles asked, "Now, who was taken and who was left?"

All my life I had heard that passage interpreted as referring to the rapture of the church—that the church would be caught away to meet the Lord in the air, which according to 1 Thessalonians 4:16–17 is a fact. But for the first time I really examined the comparison Jesus was actually making in Matthew 24. In the flood of Noah's day, it was the evil who were taken away, while righteous Noah and his family remained—they passed through the flood safely and began to repopulate the earth.

Then Brother Charles turned to Jesus's interpretation of the parable of the wheat and the weeds (or tares) in Matthew 13:36–43, where he made it very clear that at the final harvest the angels will first take away the wicked and then the righteous will be left to shine like the sun.

Not too many years ago, the *Left Behind* series was best-selling fiction based on the premise that the righteous are taken away and the wicked are left behind. However, after hearing these messages by Brother Charles, I could no longer accept that premise. Rather I saw that God's purpose for mankind has always been to have a people who will "image" (that is, "re-present") God and serve as his rulers on the earth (Genesis 1:26–28, Revelation 5:9–10).

I know that some may react negatively to these statements, because to many evangelicals, what I have written will sound like heresy. At the very least some readers will have serious questions. I can only say that these ideas sounded almost like heresy to me as well when I first began to wrestle with them in the mid-seventies. However, through the teaching of such men as Ern Baxter and Brother Charles, the paradigms of my eschatology shifted. After processing their words and looking more closely at Scripture, I found that I needed to come to the Scripture using a different mental "filing system" to process and understand the Biblical material.

At this point in my journey, I am even more sure that the way I was taught to think about last things was Biblically inaccurate. There are a number of theories about eschatology that are taught as doctrines. It seems to me that there are strengths and weaknesses in the common theories. Over the years since listening to Brother Charles in 1979, I have come to hold a few strong opinions about eschatology. However, I have not settled firmly into one particular point of view. Frankly, I do not see any need to do so. On either side of the passage quoted from Matthew 24 Jesus made these statements:

> But concerning that day and hour no one knows, not even the angels of heaven, nor the Son, but the Father only. (Matthew 24:36)

> But know this, that if the master of the house had known in what part of the night the thief was coming, he would have stayed awake and would not have let his house be broken into. Therefore you also must be ready, for the Son of Man is coming at an hour you do not expect. (Matthew 24:43–44)

After Jesus's resurrection, the apostles asked him when the kingdom would be restored to Israel. (When the apostles asked about the kingdom of God, they were not thinking about "end times" in the way many of us do today.)

> So when they had come together, they asked him, "Lord, will you at this time restore the kingdom to Israel?" He said to them, "It is not for you to know times or seasons that the Father has fixed by his own authority. But you will receive power when the Holy Spirit has come

upon you, and you will be my witnesses in Jerusalem and in all Judea and Samaria, and to the end of the earth." (Acts 1:6–8)

Truthfully, I simply cannot understand why so many Christians spend so much time and energy speculating about how history will end up when Jesus himself said so bluntly, "It is not for you to know …."

Although the time of the end is not clear, our assignment is clear! We are to be witnesses to the ends of the earth; we are to make disciples of all nations, baptizing them and teaching them to obey everything that he has commanded us. He told us that the end will come only after "this gospel of the kingdom has been proclaimed throughout the whole world as a testimony to all nations" (Matthew 24:14). Whenever Jesus comes, may we be found doing what our Lord has assigned us to do.

There were other inspiring and insightful messages given at that conference. One given by Joseph Garlington as a "warm-up" for Brother Charles's third message on the people of God had an especially significant impact on me. In that message (still one of my all-time favorites) titled "We've Come a Long Way, but Now …," Joseph mentioned three books that had recently made an impact on him. The first book, Alex Haley's *Roots*, was important to Joseph, who is black, but it was also significant for me not only because it gave me more understanding of the history of African-Americans in our country but also because it stirred up my interest in my own heritage. The second book for Joseph was the Mobile, Alabama, telephone directory—but you would need to hear him explain why. The third book Joseph mentioned was Leonard Verduin's *The Reformers and Their Stepchildren* (Wm. B. Eerdmans, 1964), which I purchased and read soon thereafter.

****

Verduin's book deals with a number of reform movements throughout church history, most of which were labeled heretical by the Orthodox and Catholic churches. Some of these groups did end up in unorthodox belief and/or practice to some degree or another. However, Verduin points out that each movement also reemphasized points that the mainline church had ignored or in some cases points where the church had even erred. Even though these movements became isolated from the mainstream church and several have disappeared altogether, each emphasized something that is largely accepted in the church today, things such as preaching outside the church building and small groups meeting in homes.

Through Verduin's book I began to discover more of my heritage in church history, and it piqued my interest in the Anabaptist movement, which was significant in the development of the "free church" tradition. I wanted to understand more about that tradition because we were forming the Free Church Fellowship.

I began to research the Anabaptist movement. Prior to this research I had had only minimal contact with Anabaptists and Anabaptist thinking. Dad and I had fished a few times on a pay lake owned by an Amish man who lived in an Amish community near my Grandma Geiger's home in western Maryland. The owner of the lake was also a harness maker, and on one trip Dad had bought a side of harness ("side" meaning harness for one horse, contrasted with a set for two horses) for my horse, Dandy, to use when pulling our buggy or sleigh. On one fishing trip we had driven around that Amish community, stopping at several Amish farms to admire the work horses. In the late 1970s Dad pastored a church in an area of central Pennsylvania where many Amish and Mennonites live, and I had met a few of his Amish neighbors. I had been curious about their way of life, but I knew very little about their distinctive beliefs.

Several years previously I had read Mennonite John Howard Yoder's *The Politics of Jesus* (Wm. B. Eerdmans Publishing Co.), a book that had helped awaken me to the reality that Jesus's life and teaching, as well as the rest of Scripture, have implications for the social order and for civil government. I had found Yoder's book, as well as *Sojourners* magazine and the writing and tapes of black evangelist Tom Skinner in the early 1970s, a time when I was trying to sort out issues such as the Vietnam War, military service, and the civil rights movement.

These materials reinforced the shake-up of the politically conservative assumptions with which I had grown up. The radical ideas propounded in the 1960s had caused me to begin to question those assumptions, but through Yoder and these others I discovered that some Christians who took the Bible seriously were addressing many of the same issues that many youths had been raising in the 1960s. I was deeply moved by Yoder's call for a radical commitment to Jesus's teaching and to his strong concern for justice in the world. However, some of the Scriptural interpretations I found in Yoder's book and in *Sojourners* troubled me because they seemed to be heavily influenced by the ideology of secular socialists. Skinner, while using similar language, seemed to me more truly "evangelical" in his core beliefs.

While Yoder and those who wrote for *Sojourners* challenged my thinking and I found some of their beliefs attractive, much of the time I could not agree fully with their positions; however, I was not always sure why. A few years later, when I began to wrestle with developing a consciously Christian worldview, I started to understand more clearly what had bothered me in their approach, especially when I began to think through the way God works through several jurisdictions of government.

In 1980, I read several books by Anabaptist authors. Three of those books have been especially important for me: Harold S. Bender's booklet *The Anabaptist Vision*[46] (Herald Press, 1944), Robert Friedmann's *The Theology of Anabaptism*,[47] and Eberhard Arnold's *The Early Christians*[48] were especially significant for me.

The Anabaptists were the "radical reformers" of the Reformation period. The most commonly known descendants of the Anabaptists are the Amish and the Mennonites. These reformers were not willing to exchange the state-supported Roman Catholic Church for state-supported Lutheran or Reformed churches—but were known as "free churches."

The Anabaptists believed water baptism to be the sign of one's choice to put his or her faith in the Lord Jesus and to enter fully into the community of believers. They refused to acknowledge the validity of infant baptism on the grounds that infants are incapable of choosing to put their trust in Jesus. Rather, they insisted on baptizing only those old enough to believe for themselves, even those previously "baptized" as infants, from which they were labeled "re-baptizers" (Anabaptists). Furthermore, "Christian" civil governments in Reformation times mandated that infants be baptized, baptism having become a sign of national citizenship as well as the sign of membership in the church. Thus, when Anabaptists refused infant baptism, they were not only in conflict with the church but also were violating civil law.

Like the Anabaptists, we in the Free Church Fellowship also practiced believer's baptism, but we did not suffer for our belief as many Anabaptists had. They were persecuted (from their perspective), usually not directly by the church, but rather by civil authorities seeking to enforce church law in order to maintain social order. Scholars estimate that from 1525 to 1535, in Switzerland alone more than five thousand Anabaptists were martyred by Catholic and Reformed leaders. Quite often they were tied up and drowned—apparently a way of saying, "If you want to be

---

[46] Harold S. Bender, *The Anabaptist Vision* (Scottsdale, PA: Herald Press, 1944).

[47] Robert Friedmann, *The Theology of Anabaptism: An Interpretation* (Scottsdale, PA: Herald Press, 1973).

[48] Eberhard Arnold: *The Early Christians: A Sourcebook on the Witness of the Early Church* (Rifton, NY: Plough Publishing House, 1970). Originally the book was written in German and published in 1926. Plough Publishing's English translation was republished by Baker Book House in 1979.

baptized, then we will baptize you." The Anabaptists' willingness to follow Christ and their consciences even to the point of death was a challenge to me.

According to the Anabaptists in the time of the Reformation, the early Reformation leaders Martin Luther and Huldrych Zwingli were mostly reforming externals in the church. They were cleansing the church buildings of images and abolishing the mass, but because many of the people were not truly converted to become actual disciples of Jesus, there was no significant change in the level of Christian living among many Reformation people—there was no evidence of repentance in the lifestyle of most professing Christians. The Anabaptists believed that, although both Luther and Zwingli wanted to see people become true disciples, these Reformers also wanted to promote social stability; therefore, they thought it better to have the masses in the church, whether they were true disciples or not, and therefore they failed to make a radical distinction between those merely baptized and those who truly lived the Christian life. The Anabaptists rejected this "compromise."[49]

Harold Bender's book identifies the three major points of emphasis in the Anabaptist vision: "first, a new conception of the essence of Christianity as discipleship; second, a new conception of the church as a brotherhood; and third, a new ethic of love and nonresistance."[50]

The first of these two points especially resonated with me. Yes, Jesus made disciples, not Christians, and he commissioned us to make disciples also. Yes, truly following Jesus means actually working out our discipleship in the context of community, that is, within the brotherhood of disciples.

While the third point had merit, I could not fully accept the Anabaptist interpretation that Jesus's teaching on love was a "new" ethic since Jesus had summed up God's ethic with two Old Testament commandments to love God and to love our neighbor.[51] Jesus went on to say that all the Law and the Prophets (the Old

---

[49] I think it is worth noting that in evangelical circles today there are far too many people who profess to believe in Jesus as their Savior and claim to be born again, yet relatively few actually have *surrendered* their lives to the *Lord* Jesus Christ. Relatively few actively and consciously seek to be disciples. Relatively few truly manifest the fruit of repentance. Sadly, therefore, all too many of us evangelicals actually think and live more in conformity with the world system's values and ways than in conformity to Christ's values and ways.

[50] Ibid., p. 20.

[51] In the Old Testament, the prophet Micah had summed up God's requirement for us in the words in an "ethic of love": "He has told you, O man, what is good; and what does the

Testament) depend on these two commandments (Matthew 22:34–40), a point reiterated in the epistles. I also thought their interpretation of Jesus's teaching on nonresistance (Matthew 5:38–31, 42; Luke 6:27-31) went beyond Jesus's intent.[52]

The detailed presentation of Anabaptist belief and practice concerning the church, baptism, and the Lord's Supper in Robert Friedmann's book particularly got my attention then and has continued to influence me.

First, a diagram in his book helped me to picture the corporate nature of redemption and of the church's connection with God.[53] While his diagram is to some degree an oversimplification of all three positions, it does point out real differences in emphasis between three streams of Christianity.

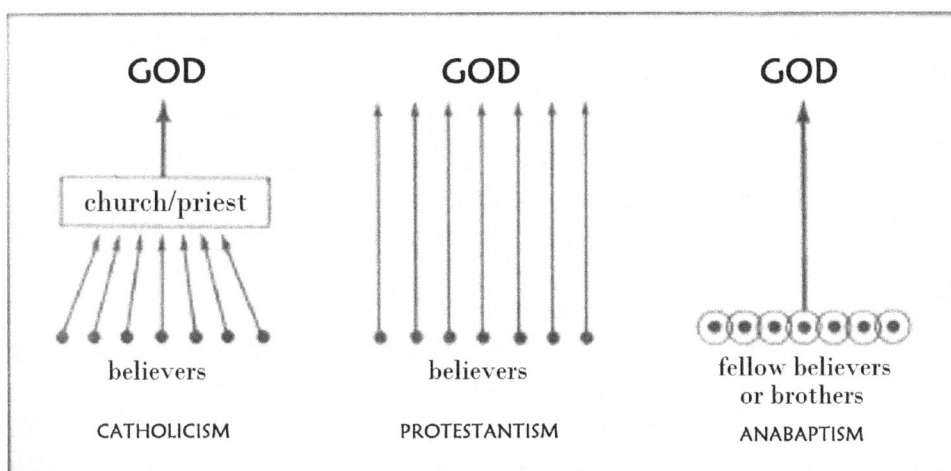

GOD	GOD	GOD
church/priest		
believers	believers	fellow believers or brothers
CATHOLICISM	PROTESTANTISM	ANABAPTISM

Over the years I have come to see a measure of truth in each of these pictures; however, I think the Anabaptist view is a needed antidote to the hyper-individualism of much evangelical thinking. In pondering this diagram, I began to understand more fully that, according to Scripture, God has designed us to come to him as a member of a people, the community of faith.

LORD require of you but to do justice, and to love kindness, and to walk humbly with your God?" (Micah 6:8)

[52] Jesus instructs us not to seek vengeance but rather to trust God to set things right, a teaching that the apostle Paul addressed in Romans 12:19–21, where he used Jesus's teaching and the Old Testament to make his point. I do not think Jesus was saying to never defend oneself, one's family, or others from evil.

[53] Friedmann, p. 81.

Every individual must respond to God's call to repent and to be baptized; however, those who believe and are baptized in the New Testament were *added* to the community of faith, the church (see Acts 2:41–47). This is not simple addition: adding onto the total number of believers; rather, it involved being placed into a visible, functioning community. The apostle Paul stated this truth clearly:

> For just as the body is one and has many members, and all the members of **the body, though many, are one body,** so it is with Christ. For **in one Spirit we were all baptized into one body**—Jews or Greeks, slaves or free—and all were made to drink of one Spirit. (1 Corinthians 12:12–13, bold print added for emphasis)

According to Scripture, we are baptized by the Spirit into the Body of Christ (1 Corinthians 12:13, 18), where we are joined to one another in mutually interdependent relationships under Christ Jesus's headship (Ephesians 1:22–23). To come to God in Christ is to become one of many "living stones [plural] … being built up as a spiritual house [singular], to be a holy priesthood [singular]" (1 Peter 2:4–5). In Christ we "are fellow citizens [plural] and members [plural] of the household [singular] of God. We are being built together [plural] to become "a whole structure" [singular], "a holy temple" [singular], "a place [singular] for God to dwell" (Ephesians 2:19–22).

Friedmann describes the Anabaptist ideal of church as a way of life together, a way of relating to one another: "It is in the present daily life that those islands of peace, unity of the spirit, and true communion (*Gemeinschaft*) are being lived and practiced…."[54] Later Friedmann says, "If the brothers are all genuine members of the one 'body of Christ,' then the 'unity of the spirit' is a natural corollary of this presupposition, and with it goes all the rest: internal peace, brotherly love, cooperation, sharing of material things, and concern of the preservation of the purity of the group."[55] These statements could easily have been a description of the ideals of the Servants of the Lord Community; thus, it is no wonder that those of us forming the Free Church Fellowship found this tradition confirming our own convictions and commitments.

While I was beginning to understand this Scriptural truth back then, I find that still today our culture's individualistic way of thinking and living is so deeply ingrained in me that all too often I think and act without enough regard for the community (family, church) of which I am a member.

---

[54] Ibid., p. 118.
[55] Ibid., p. 120.

Concerning baptism, Friedmann said that Anabaptists in the Reformation period often referred to Martin Luther's German translation of 1 Peter 3:21: "Baptism is a covenant [*Bund*] of a good conscience with God." According to Friedmann, "a covenant is a pledge which in Anabaptist thinking works in three directions: (a) a covenant between God and man; (b) one between man and God; and (c) also one between man and man, thus establishing the church or *Gemeide*. By accepting baptism the believer, a disciple of Christ, now enters the brotherhood as an equal to other members, or more specifically as a member of the spiritual 'body of Christ,' a quality shared with all other members."[56]

This covenant view of baptism was another point of connection between the Anabaptist tradition and things I was seeking to teach and build into the Free Church Fellowship. It helped provide us with a Biblically based explanation for our covenant relationship with the Servants of the Lord Community which, as I have said, we tended to view as "our church."

Friedmann's book also stirred me to think more deeply about the meaning of the Lord's Supper. The Anabaptists rejected the sacramental and spiritual interpretations of the Eucharist, agreeing with Zwingli that the Lord's Supper is a memorial (a remembering) of Christ's sacrifice; they saw both baptism and communion as ordinances, not as sacraments (means of grace). In itself, this was essentially the same viewpoint with which I had been raised. However, I learned that in actual practice the Anabaptists put an extremely high value on their practice of communion, just as they did baptism. "This eating and drinking in brotherly fellowship gave them strength and encouragement and the certitude of belonging to a company of redeemed souls, and of being part of the 'true body of Christ,' " Friedmann says.

And again, "such a profound symbol of brotherly love and togetherness provided a foretaste of the kingdom of God in the here and now ... of the inbreaking of a new transcendent reality. In this very real sense the Lord's Supper was more than *only* a memorial. In discussing the Anabaptist church idea, we spoke of it as a 'community of the unity of the spirit' and a fellowship at the Lord's table.' This meal ... gave the Lord's table the meaning of spiritual sharing and togetherness, the horizontal element in the Anabaptist church idea ...."[57]

Prior to reading these books, I had come to understand and had been teaching that the apostle Paul's teaching on the Lord's Supper in 1 Corinthians had to do with relating to God and to one another. Virtually all the numerous problems that Paul

---

[56] Ibid., p. 135.
[57] Ibid., pp. 139–140.

sought to correct through this letter have to do with wrong attitudes and behavior in horizontal relationships that were contrary to God's *agape*. The specific issues he addresses in 1 Corinthians 11:17–34 concerning the meal during which they shared bread and wine in remembrance of the Lord are relational in nature—namely, factions and those with food not sharing with those without food.

In this passage Paul strongly warned the Corinthian disciples and us that eating and drinking in an unworthy manner by not examining our own lives and by failing to discern the body is dangerous. The context of the whole letter and of this specific passage seems to make it very clear that "the body" Paul called us to discern is "the body of Christ"—not the nature of the bread they ate, but rather the state of the relationships they had with one another. Certainly this holy meal is God-centered. It is the Thanksgiving (Eucharist) meal. We share this meal together as a community of disciples, as the household of God. In this special meal we should reaffirm and renew the covenant relationship God has established with us by confessing sin, repenting, and receiving forgiveness of sin as needed. This covenant, which God first made with Abraham and then fulfilled by Jesus, is the New Covenant, which must be lived out in human relationships—relationships in which we are to love our neighbor as ourselves and to love one another the way Christ has loved us.

Furthermore, Friedmann also wrote about the Anabaptist emphasis that in the Lord's Supper we should recognize and embrace suffering as an integral part of the meaning of this meal, not only because Jesus suffered for us but also because our formation in the community of Christ involves our own suffering. He gave several examples from early Anabaptist history.

One example was part of a statement by Hans Nadler, an early Anabaptist martyr, in answer to questions about the Lord's Supper at his trial for heresy in 1529:

> With the bread the unity among the brethren is symbolized. Where there are many small kernels of grain to be combined into one loaf there is need first to grind them and to make them into one flour ... which can be achieved only through suffering. Just as Christ, our dear Lord, went before us, so too we want to follow him in like manner. And the bread symbolizes the unity of the brotherhood.

> Likewise with the wine: many small grapes come together to make the one wine. That happens by means of the press, understood here as suffering. (*Es zeigt uns das Leiden an.*) Hence, whoever wants to be in

brotherly union, has to drink from the cup of the Lord, for this cup symbolizes suffering.[58]

In another example, Menno Simons, spiritual father of the Mennonites, used similar imagery:

> Just as natural bread has to be kneaded of many kernels of grain broken in the mill, together with water and then baked by the heat of the fire, in the same way the church of Christ is made up of many believers, broken in their hearts by the mill of God's word, baptized with water of the Holy Spirit, and brought together into one body by pure and unadulterated love [at the Lord's Table].[59]

Not long after I read Bender and Friedmann's books, I discovered Eberhard Arnold's *The Early Christians: A Sourcebook on the Witness of the Early Church*. Arnold, who had founded the Bruderhof communities in the early twentieth century, opened his book with a stirring and enlightening "Introduction and Survey" that sets forth his view of the kingdom of God and the church. He then presented topically organized excerpts from the early Christian writings in order to show that his views were in harmony with those of the early fathers. Most of the *Didache* is in Arnold's book, including the model thanksgiving prayer to be offered over the communion bread. This early Christian source used the same imagery of the scattered grain being brought together in one loaf:

> We give thanks to Thee, our Father, for the life and knowledge which Thou has made known to us through Jesus, Thy child. Glory be to Thee into the ages! Just as this broken bread was scattered over the hills and became one when it had been brought together, so shall Thy church be brought together from the ends of the earth into Thy Kingdom. For to Thee belong the glory and the power through Jesus Christ into the ages.[60]

Quite likely the Anabaptists were drawing from this ancient source, whether from a written copy or from an oral tradition passed down through generations and centuries. Their emphasis on suffering as part of the growth together in community

---

[58] Ibid., p. 141.

[59] Ibid., p. 141.

[60] Eberhard Arnold, *The Early Christians: A Sourcebook on the Witness of the Early Church* (Grand Rapids, MI: Baker Book House, 1979 edition; original English translation - Rifton, NY: Plough Publishing House, 1970 & 1972). Original title: *Die ersten Christen nach de Tode der Apostel*, 1926.

probably stemmed from the intense persecution and suffering they were experiencing. This truth, like seed, was planted in me but germinated and came to fruition in my life only years later when I was in a season of grief and suffering.

When I read about the history of the Anabaptists and their beliefs, a chord seemed to have been struck deep within me, and it often seemed like I was being connected to previously unrecognized roots. I had worn a beard and mustache for several years by then, but I had such a personal sense of connection with the Anabaptist heritage that for several months I even shaved off my mustache like the Amish and the more conservative Mennonite men. When, a few years later, I discovered that my maternal grandparents had both descended from one of the early Amish immigrants, I could not help but wonder if that there was any connection between family heritage and the sense of roots I had found.

Arnold's collection of early Christian writings also added significantly to a sense of connection that I was feeling with the early church of the first few centuries. The idea that the writings of the early Church Fathers might be important had been first planted in me by my cousin, David Van Hoose, when he was my Church History professor at Circleville Bible College. This awareness had grown a little when Don Schwager had used material from those writings concerning deacons and deaconesses while teaching those of us who were identified as servants in the community. Mark Kinzer had also talked about the way the early church practice of the Lord's Supper as seen in the Church Fathers had developed from Jewish understanding and practice. However, this was another "seed" working in me that I would more fully recognize several years later.

I could go on and on concerning these things because they were so important for me; however, the point is that, while we were developing the Free Church Fellowship in Minneapolis, many themes with which I had been wrestling for several years began to form into a clearer picture. My vision and theology of the church continued to develop. I began to have a much higher view of baptism and the Lord's Supper. I could no longer think of them as only ordinances of the church, only outward actions pointing to inner realities and past events. Rather, I began to understand that baptism and the Lord's Supper were sacraments, channels through which God's grace came to me. In baptism and at the Lord's table, I have come to believe, something of real substance is happening.

Just as significant, I continued to see in virtually all of my reading the centrality of community in God's purposes. In the midst of the hyper-individualism of our secular culture, I was thinking, and trying to learn to act, more and more from the framework of God's corporate nature (three in one), which is manifest in all that God has created and in his purposes for mankind.

The changes in my thinking came out in the teaching that I did in the Free Church Fellowship over the next few years. Those changes have only deepened in the years following, as my reading has led me to the insights of other branches of the church, including the Orthodox. Sadly, I have not yet been able to communicate what I see in such a way that it is manifest very fully in the church in which I am a leader. However, I have great hope that the younger people coming up after me may well be able to lead our church into a new experience of God's grace through the sacraments.

****

Although Anabaptist thought was an important source in the development of my thinking, especially as it pertained to the development of the Free Church Fellowship, I was reading from other streams of Christian thought as well—sources that in the long run have had even more influence than the Anabaptists.

I have mentioned already the importance of the *New Wine* teachers in helping me develop in my understanding of the kingdom of God and of covenant. However, my desire to learn more about the kingdom and covenant led me to writings of more mainstream Reformed theologians as well.

Francis Schaeffer's work had already made a significant impact on me. However, Schaeffer, though a Presbyterian and clearly Reformed in his theology, usually did not write in typical theological language. Several of his written works were "evangelistic," and he typically used philosophical language in these. The works directed to Christians were for the most part instruction on living out the faith rather than about "doctrinal teaching," or they were written to awaken and mobilize the church to its cultural responsibility.

Among several Reformed books that I read during those years, Meredith Kline's *By Oath Consigned* and *The Structure of Biblical Authority* were important sources concerning covenant. About the same time that I found Kline's work, I also came across Herman Ridderbos's *The Coming of the Kingdom*, which opened my eyes to the centrality of the kingdom of God, not just in the gospel message but as the goal of all history.

Kline built on information gained from studying the archeological discoveries of ancient suzerain treaties in order to shed light on the structure of Biblical covenants.

The suzerain treaties were the means by which ancient Near Eastern kings established sovereign relationships with (and over) neighboring kingdoms. Kline showed that Biblical covenants follow that same pattern. Actually, it would probably be more accurate to say that the suzerain treaties are reflections of God's way of working through covenant—reflections that he preserved in fallen human culture as a witness to his way of dealing with man. God, the sovereign King of the universe, initiates relationship between himself and man by calling upon men to recognize his Lordship and to submit themselves to his covenant, which establishes, defines, and directs the relationship that God has designed for man.

Gradually I began to realize how significant it is that the Bible consists of two covenants, the Old and New Testaments (or Covenants). I began to see in the Old Testament a series of covenants that all led up to the everlasting New Covenant in Christ. It began to dawn on me that there was no way to really understand the Bible unless one reads it using the proper "glasses," that is, unless one reads the Bible through the lens of covenant and the lens of the kingdom of God.

Because Bob Mumford strongly recommended Rousas J. Rushdoony's *The Institutes of Biblical Law*, I began to discover the writings of Rushdoony; his son-in-law, Gary North; Greg Bahnsen; David Chilton; James Jordan; and other Reconstructionists who built on the presuppositional apologetic and theology of Cornelius Van Til. Although I was put off by the bombastic tone of some Reconstructionist rhetoric, it was not long before I realized that I would have to wrestle with the applicability of God's Law—not as a means of personal salvation, but as a tool for building a Christian social order.

Largely because of their writing, I had to reassess my views about politics. Even though I had a strong "conservative" heritage, I had been influenced by many "liberal" ideas from the sixties in my thoughts about war and government. Starting in 1978, I had begun to become more deeply aware of the influence of secular humanism in American culture. It became clear that there were humanists who had an agenda and a strategy to remake culture and society according to their vision.

Schaeffer's earlier work was the beginning of this awakening. His 1976 book *How Should We Then Live?* helped me begin to see the issues much more clearly. But it was the Reconstructionists who actually forced me to begin to deal with the dualism that has come to characterize most evangelicals.

The wars against Biblical authority, truth, and the supernatural had begun in the schools of higher criticism in the late 1800s; the Fundamentalist movement led by J.

Greshem Machen and other scholars arose in the early 1900s as a counter to higher critical thinking. The early Fundamentalists usually were balanced and intellectually sound—seeking to reemphasize the core beliefs of the Christian faith. *Fundamentalist*, however, came to mean something quite different as the decades passed, especially as more and more "Bible-believing" Christians embraced the premillennial dispensationalism that had arisen in the 1800s and that was popularized in the Scofield Study Bible, partly in reaction against the theological liberals' conception of the kingdom of God, which is more humanistic than Biblical.

Evangelical Christianity, as I had come to know it, was basically a pietistic faith, emphasizing personal salvation, personal morality, and a future kingdom after the Second Coming of Jesus. Most evangelicals whom I knew appeared to think that Christianity had little or nothing to do with politics and society beyond personal moral choices, usually defined by activities in which we were not allowed to engage—no drinking, no smoking, no dancing, no card playing, no sex outside of marriage, and so forth.

It was Schaeffer and the Reconstructionists, along with some of the *New Wine* teachers, who made me begin to wrestle with the implications of God's Word for all human beings and all of human life, including law, government, politics, education, business, economics, and art—not just the application of God's Word to Christians. Mind you, my understanding and approach to life did not change immediately. The truth is I am still in that change.

Sometimes things the Reconstructionists said sounded like American political conservatism. In fact, many of those evangelicals who did not draw their "political principles" from Scripture also sounded like political conservatives much of the time. However, gradually I began to see that truly applying the Bible to society and culture will ultimately challenge and even offend both conservatives and liberals, depending on the issue involved.

I will never forget hearing Bob Mumford on one of his tapes telling about a meeting in the mid-seventies when he was preaching in a Caribbean nation where Marxism was on the rise. Without forethought, Bob heard himself declaring: "Marxism is not the way. Capitalism is not the way. There is a third way; it's the kingdom of God." That declaration has stuck with me. I am still seeking to fully apprehend the third way!

Over time I came to see that it was not enough to find a Biblical position on various topics; I also needed to understand Biblical jurisdictions—that is, to whom God has delegated responsibility for what tasks. I came to see that God has chosen to make individuals responsible to govern themselves in some matters. He has given families responsibility for some things. The church is responsible for other things. And God has also given civil government certain responsibilities. And with responsibility, God also has given these several jurisdictions of government the authority to solve problems and to enforce compliance within their sphere. Understanding these Biblical jurisdictions, I believe, is an important key to properly applying Biblical truth to social, cultural, and political issues.

Along with changes of this sort, the Reconstructionists were instrumental in helping me complete my rejection of premillennial dispensationalism. There are several views that Christians hold concerning where God is going in history and the order in which events will unfold. I will not fight *for* any of the specific traditional theories. However, I do reject premillennial dispensationalism—especially when it is followed to its logical conclusions concerning the history, the church, and Israel. I believe the gospel is the power of God unto salvation for all. God, I believe, is not only redeeming individual people but he also is restoring every aspect of creation that was corrupted by Adam's fall. God is accomplishing that restoration through the incarnation, life, death, resurrection, ascension, and exaltation of Jesus Christ as proclaimed in the gospel of the kingdom by the church, Christ's body.

I reject the defeat of the gospel in history that characterizes premillennial dispensationalism. I believe that the victory of Jesus's resurrection is unfolding and will be manifest in time and space history! This victory will not be fully seen, I think, until the sons of the enemy are taken away and the sons of the kingdom are revealed (Matthew 13:37–43).

****

Although I will not expound on it at this point, in 1978 or 1979 I also read Robert Webber's *Common Ground: A Call to Evangelical Maturity* and *The Orthodox Evangelicals: Who They Are and What They Are Saying* (Robert Webber and Donald Bloesch, editors). In addition, I was following, as best I could from a distance, the journey of several former Campus Crusade leaders, including authors Peter Gillquist and Jack Sparks. These men had formed the New Covenant Apostolic Order in the early 1970s. A few years later their churches were renamed the Evangelical Orthodox Church.[61]

---

[61] One of the seven original leaders, Ray Nethery, along with several members of the church, chose not to become part of the Evangelical Orthodox Church. He and others formed a group called the Assembly of Covenant Churches, a group with whom I had

These books and the "journey" this group of churches was making were another challenge for me to look more seriously at the early Christian documents; however, unbeknownst to me, they were also sowing seeds that would later lead me to a high regard for much Eastern Orthodox teaching.

Not only was I living in an interdenominational, ecumenical community, but my theology was being broadened by exposure to a wider range of Christian thought. I had no plan to develop this way, but I have come to believe God had a plan and that he has been stewarding my development. I began to see the church as a many-faceted diamond, an image I have borrowed from Ephesians 3:10: "… the many-sided wisdom of God may now be made known through the church …." (MLB)

Other than in the matters directly pertaining to understanding covenant and the gospel of the kingdom (the latter primarily in the sense that I put primary emphasis on declaring the Lordship of Christ), I did not talk much about these issues in the Free Church Fellowship. I had little idea then of the theological journey that was unfolding for me.

---

contact a short time later. I discovered that the Assembly of Covenant Churches had produced the hymnal *My Lips Shall Praise Thee* (Mansfield, OH: Grace Haven Artisans, 1978), which we began to use in our Free Church Fellowship worship gatherings.

15

Expanding Household

Establishing the Free Church Fellowship was an important part of my work from 1979 through 1983. As I led the Fellowship, I was "forced" to begin to organize the changes in my understanding of the church, its beliefs, and its practices—changes that had been developing over the previous ten years. Forming the Free Church Fellowship also provided the opportunity for me to learn more about how to develop a leadership team. As it turned out, although we did not know it at the time, we were building relationships in the Free Church Fellowship that would prove to be far more significant than we could have imagined at that time.

However, the focus of my life was not on the Free Church Fellowship. Life in the Servants of the Lord Community was full, and what a wonderful life it was—rich in the awareness of God at work among us, rich in friendships, and rich in learning and growth.

Life in Christian community was "spiritual" but not "religious." Yes, we were active in prayer, worship, and evangelism, and we had great gatherings and teaching full of wisdom for living as God's people. However, just as important, we cultivated the awareness that our "normal" daily activities were as just as "spiritual" as the distinctively "religious" activities. Our family life was unto the Lord. Our neighborhood life was unto the Lord. Our recreation was unto the Lord. The distinction between "sacred" and "secular" all but disappeared. We were aware that God desired to be involved in every aspect of our individual lives and our life together.

Even as I write these words I realize that I am writing truthfully, and yet the story is incomplete. My experience of community and Patricia's had not been quite the same.

In the summer of 1980 Patricia and I made an offer on another house. Elijah was nearly 8 years old and Stephanie was 3; they needed separate bedrooms. We also needed a larger home in which to practice hospitality and to host meetings more easily.

An older two-story house went up for sale on First Avenue, about five blocks from our apartment building. A few other families had bought homes in the next block; some single women lived in an apartment on that block as well. It was a good area in which to buy since the houses were mostly in good condition and were affordable for first-time home buyers.

Larry Alberts had seen the house first and had suggested that we look at it. Because we did not have enough money to make the financial commitment alone, he suggested that we ask Tanya Sabellin, a single sister (who happened to be Russian Orthodox), to co-sign on our loan. The white clapboard two-story house, though not exceptionally fancy, had been well taken care of. It was solidly built and seemed lovely to us. Tanya agreed to co-sign, so we made an offer and it was accepted.

We had not said anything about looking at the house to others—in part because we had made the decision to look for a house quite quickly but also because we did not want to unsettle the others who owned apartments in our building until we were more certain that we were actually going to move.

Patricia and I had made the decision with no great show of emotion. We had walked through the house and both liked it well enough, but neither one of us said much about our feelings even when we made the decision to make an offer. To me it just seemed like the next step. I do not think either one of us realized the cost of moving until we came back to the apartment after the sellers had accepted our offer.

It was mid-afternoon when we parked behind our building and entered through the back door into the back stairway. As we started up the six stairs from the landing to our apartment, Patricia shouted out: "Anita! Mary Kay!" As usual, the doors were open to Dan and Anita Rosener's apartment, next door to ours, and to Dan and Mary Kay Gleason's apartment upstairs. They ran down the halls into the stairwell in response to Patricia's unusual behavior—perhaps worried that there was some emergency.

"We bought a house!" Patricia exclaimed. "And … ," she paused. When she spoke again her voice had changed; it was muted and mournful. "… And we're going to move." She began to cry.

There I was with three women—all of them crying and laughing at the same time.

We more fully realized the significance of that moment over the next few months. Up to that time, Patricia had lived in community faithfully out of her commitment to the Lord and to me, her husband. Living in community, however, had not been her personal choice. At times she dealt with some disappointment about not going into missions. Sometimes, in her words, her heels left skid marks because of fear and reluctance, especially in the earliest years.

After the incident with Mary Kay and Anita, we gradually discovered that Patricia had come to rest and peace in the place that God had placed us. The best way I can describe the change is that Patricia began to act like she was "at home" once she realized that she really did have "sisters" in the Lord. She had sisters whom she could count upon, sisters who knew her, who loved her, and she had sisters with whom she could work through the difficult times. Although we rarely see the Roseners or the Gleasons these days, the relationships are solid, and when we are able to get together it seems like we only need to catch up on details about our lives.

Since our community was organized geographically, most of the close relationships we made were with those who lived nearby. Sometimes we lived near people to whom we would not have been naturally drawn for friendships, and there were often rough spots in learning to know and to trust each other. Yet, sometimes the relationships we had to build by working through things became the most deep and solid.

I think that I learned something important from all this. Men, it seems to me, often enter into a commitment such as ours to the Servants of Lord Community because of vision, a sense of call, and a decision. I know I have done so. Afterward, it is the commitment to God's call that has held me in place through the inevitable times of testing and even disillusionment. Not all men hold their place in the difficult times, but they often can be strengthened when they are reminded of their call.

Patricia, on the other hand, and many other women, in my experience, may come into a commitment less because of their own personal sense of call and more because of their commitment to their husbands. But, if the woman's relationship with her husband is relatively healthy, once sisterhood has been established among the women, they seem able "to make a home," to come to a sense of rest and peace.

Just as the wife often sets the tone in the home, I think it is usually the women who set the tone for life in community. When most of the women are "at home," when they are at rest in their relationships, especially, the community tends to have a sense of peace and order. But when even a few women are insecure or disgruntled or cliquish, the whole community may experience a sense of unrest. To the degree that this is an accurate assessment, then it is important for the leaders of a group, as well as for the husbands, to do all they can to foster healthy, sisterly relationships among the women in the group. The "tone" of the group, which is so influenced by the women, can be an important gauge of the health of that group.

The importance of women in the life of a Christian community may well be one of the reasons that St. Paul gave specific instructions several times concerning women, even beyond the relationship between husband and wife. The New Testament specifically addresses women's participation in community meetings, and it addresses their daily life and relationships as well.[62]

Whether or not this digression about women is helpful or not, it was a good thing for Patricia to find her own place in the community. Had that not come about, it might have been more difficult for us to enter into a full covenant with the community a few months later.

Surprise! As with the house on which we had made an offer in St. Paul, we did not end up purchasing this one either. We really liked that house, but the more we thought it through, the more we realized that it was actually inadequate for all we needed to do. In it we would not have been able to have separate bedrooms for Elijah and Stephanie and still expand our household to include more single adults. And it would not have been adequate for the ministry of hospitality that we desired to do.

Therefore, we backed away, and Tanya bought the house herself; it became a wonderful home for several single ladies. A year or two later, Tanya and some other women made it the base for a sisterhood, a group of women committed to remain single and celibate in order to serve God and the community with less distractions.

****

During the time when we were looking at the house, Patricia and I were preparing to enter into a full covenant relationship with the Servants of the Lord Community. We had finished the mandatory courses by that time, and we also had clearly demonstrated our willingness to share fully in the committed life of Servants members. Patricia's realization that she had built true relationships with the sisters in our building was an important indication that we were ready to publicly commit ourselves to live the rest of our lives as members of the Servants of the Lord.

On the appointed evening we, along with several others, participated in a public ceremony in which we were received and prayed for by the covenant members. Several years previously, the Servants of the Lord covenant had been prayerfully and carefully written down by the coordinators and then had been approved by all the

---

[62] Consider such passages as 1 Corinthians 11, 14; 1 Timothy 2; 1 Timothy 5; Titus 2.

covenant members.[63] Therefore, in addition to a public statement of our commitment, we also signed the covenant document itself.

While I had been studying Biblical covenants, I had come to the conviction that there is only one central covenant relationship that God has established with all those who are in Christ and are members: the New Covenant. So, I had wondered, is this covenant legitimate? What is its nature? Is there a Biblical basis for it?

Clearly the Servants of the Lord covenant had to be subordinate to the New Covenant. Eventually I had come to the conclusion that the Servants of the Lord covenant was indeed legitimate. I saw that it was similar to the covenant of renewal made during Josiah's reign (2 Kings 23:1-25, 2 Chronicles 34:14–33) and even more similar to the one made under Nehemiah and Ezra's leadership (Nehemiah 8–10) in which the people made specific pledges to obey parts of God's covenant with Israel, which they had flagrantly disobeyed.

Our covenant with the Servants of the Lord was a commitment to a specific "household of faith" that was seeking to rebuild a way of life together consistent with the New Covenant. Certainly we needed to guard against becoming exclusive and prideful in a way that would be a barrier to our fellowship with the whole of God's New Covenant people, but that covenant must be lived out in a tangible way in actual functioning relationships. Our commitment to support ecumenism, both within the community and among the churches (or denominations), also called us to have a humble, serving attitude.

Since Patricia and I were putting down our roots in the community, a few months after backing away from the house on First Avenue, we began to hunt actively for another house. This time we were looking for one that would accommodate several single adults as well as our family. We had experienced household of a certain sort among those living in the apartments in our building, but we had also had opportunity to have single adults be part of our own household after the Driessen family moved. For about a year we were blessed to have Wanda Chaplin and Margie Graber share our home while they were preparing for marriage to men in the community. Not long after their weddings, Joe Hagens and Jay Rosengren moved in with us. We found that we enjoyed extended household life. Therefore, we began to look for a house big enough to accommodate our family and several adults.

---

[63] See Appendix Five.

Expanding Household

We looked at quite a number of houses in the spring of 1981 until we found one at 4003 Pillsbury Avenue, only three blocks away from our apartment building. It was right across the street from David and Deanna White's household. We knew we would have some good neighbors because the Whites had moved from Grand Forks. Our family had related with their household, and they had led the first men's group and women's group that Patricia and I had participated in.

The house, a story-and-a-half brick built about 1905, had a few drawbacks, the biggest one being that it was not light-filled, as Patricia would have preferred. There was barely more than a driveway's width between our house and the houses on either side. A large Dutch elm in the small front yard and a sun porch and another small room built across the front of the house blocked direct light from the living room. Small windows above a built-in buffet in the dining room allowed only a little sunlight into that room. The abundant woodwork was all stained dark, and the walls were dingy with old paint.

In spite of the lack of light, we saw that the house would work nicely for household. The living room and dining room were L-shaped, plenty large for small group meetings and a large dinner table. I could use the small room in front for my office, even though it would be hard to heat in the Minnesota winters since it was surrounded on two sides by windows. The upstairs would serve nicely for our family quarters; there was a very small room across the front where we could put little Stephanie, and two larger bedrooms: one for Elijah, the other for Patricia and me. Both of these rooms had doors in the rear leading into a large walk-through closet, behind which there was a large bathroom. There were two bedrooms and another bathroom on the first floor, quite suitable to house single ladies. The basement, though unfinished, was dry and large enough for us to build another bedroom and a bathroom for single men.

By today's standards the price was low, only $67,000—still a huge amount for us at that time. Interest rates had risen well above 10% at that point, so the mortgage payment would be large.

We were able to sell our 25% interest in the apartment building to another young couple for $7,500—just enough to cover a down payment and closing costs on a $62,000 loan. Still, our income of $1,000 per month was far too small to qualify us for a loan on our own. However, we were not on our own; we were in community. Thus, Randy Smith, a young, single electrician who had been living with Larry's brother Dave Alberts and his family, agreed to co-sign with us for a loan and to move into our household.

When we applied for the loan in April, the interest rate on a thirty-year mortgage from the Federal Housing Authority was 13.5%. By the time the loan was approved in late May, the rate had risen to 15.5% percent, plus the 0.5% that the FHA was adding back then to protect the investors who supplied the loan money. Our monthly payment would be $809—a huge sum to us, nearly four times what we had been paying for our share in the apartment building. What's more, we found out that less than $9 of the first month's payment would go toward the principal.

Thankfully, our realtor, a brother in the community, not only brought the amortization schedule for thirty years to the closing, but he also told us that if we were to pay only $35 per month extra on the principal we would be able to pay the loan off in twenty years instead of thirty. If we were to pay $80 per month extra on the principal, he said that we would pay it off in fifteen years. Because of this simple encouragement, we have always sought to pay extra each month toward the principal on our home loans—not only on that house but on the two we have purchased since then.

We moved into 4003 Pillsbury Avenue South in June of 1981. Within a few weeks we had six single brothers and sisters sharing our home. Besides Randy, there were Jay Rosengren, who moved with us from the apartment building; Jeff Gleason, whose mother and grandmother lived on that very same block; Jacquelyn Johnson; Joyce Wilhelm; and Diane Siever, who was engaged to be married later that year.

Each adult member of the house contributed a set amount to a household fund to cover his or her share of our common living expenses. We lived as one big family. I was the head of the household with final authority on things pertaining to our shared life. Patricia managed most details pertaining to care of the house and the meals, and she was most directly responsible for the pastoral care of the sisters. I worked with Patricia when needed in caring for the sisters, and I gave pastoral care to the brothers.

Although some households in the community handled their finances differently than we did, Patricia and I thought that since Randy had co-signed with us on the loan, then his name should be on the deed as owner with a one-third interest in the house. This arrangement worked well. Randy's sense of ownership as well as his heart to serve led him to move aggressively to build the men's bedroom and bath in the basement. Randy was not only an electrician but had all the building skills needed, whereas I had nearly none. By late August 1981, he and the other brothers had all but finished the basement room.

However, by that time, our community was experiencing a tragic division that would affect our household.

16

New Opportunities

The division in our local community was in large part the result of conflict among a circle of leaders outside our community. That conflict took me totally by surprise. I was surprised because there were things I simply did not know and had not been discerning enough to pick up on, but I was also surprised because I was idealistic and naive, not giving enough weight to human weakness and fallibility. Not only did the leaders whom we looked up to have weaknesses, but there were weaknesses in our own community that I had not perceived. I became aware of these weaknesses gradually over the next year as the divisions began to surface.

The Servants of the Lord Community belonged to an Association of Communities, an international network of ecumenical communities that had developed from the Charismatic Renewal in the Catholic Church. Leaders from these communities had joined themselves together seeking to develop a common identity among themselves and to share their wisdom and resources with one another as they worked together to build more stable communities, to become more effective in evangelism, and to develop new communities. Desiring to be a prophetic witness to what the church should be, they had sought to organize in a way that would give them more visibility and strength as they strove to build working relationships with the various churches to which their members belonged.

It had taken a few years for the primary leaders of the communities to agree on the structure of the relationships between the groups and on how they would define and govern their relationship and common work. One proposal had been to organize tightly into a *federation* of communities. However, they had eventually settled for a somewhat looser relationship, an *association*.

By 1977 the primary influencers within the Association came from two communities: Steve Clark and Ralph Martin from the Word of God Community in Ann Arbor, Michigan, and Kevin Ranaghan and Paul DeCelles from the People of Praise in South Bend, Indiana.

In addition, Steve, Ralph, and Kevin were also members of a group known as Ecumenical Council; other members of that Council were Lutherans Larry Christenson and Don Pfotenauer and the five *New Wine* teachers, who had widely diverse backgrounds. These men had joined together in a covenant relationship, agreeing to stand together and support one another as they worked within their own spheres of responsibility.

Along with the other coordinators of our community, in August 1980 I joined with coordinators from all the other Association communities around the world for a conference that was held at the Franciscan University of Steubenville in Ohio. Following that conference, I was invited, with several dozen others, to stay on in the Steubenville area for three weeks of special training and working together that would be held at a nearby retreat center.

There were two main themes in the presentations made during these gatherings. Both themes were developed at least partly in response to a number of prophetic words that had been given in recent years concerning hard times that the people of God and the world would be facing. One of the most significant of these words had been given at a huge Catholic Charismatic gathering in Rome in May 1975 and had been published in *New Covenant*, the magazine that served the Catholic Charismatic Renewal. That word, given by Ralph Martin, had included a warning that structures in which God's people had trusted would be shaken, an image suggestive of Hebrews 12:25–29.

At the Steubenville meetings, the brothers from the Word of God Community in Ann Arbor gave presentations on the theme "Stemming the Tide of Evil in the World." Their thrust was that the church and the world were in the midst of a major crisis in our generation and that it was highly likely that we had entered a time of judgment. They believed that God had raised up covenant communities like ours as a bulwark of truth to hold back the encroachment of evil. In one memorable presentation, Steve Clark talked about times and ways in which the Bible calls us to fight evil, at times to fight even with physical force.

The brothers from the People of Praise Community in South Bend talked about the theme "Being a Provident and Resourceful People." Drawing much from the Biblical wisdom literature, these brothers called us to develop a way of life that included practical preparation for natural disasters, such as storms and earthquakes, as well as preparation for economic and other crises. Their point of view was that from time to time difficulties do come in a fallen world, and that wisdom calls upon us to set aside resources to deal with such times. In addition, they called us to develop lifestyles in our communities that released resources, both human and material, to advance the cause of God in the earth.

Both themes were Biblically developed and made good sense. I did not recognize that these two themes also represented disagreement between leaders of the two communities as to how to interpret and respond to the prophecies, a disagreement rooted in some theological and philosophical differences. I was naive; I assumed we were just being given a fuller picture with these two emphases. In a few months, my assumption would prove to be false, but in the time before that I had opportunities to serve because of our connection with the Association of Communities.

Three specific things from the time in Steubenville were of special significance in my personal journey. First, one evening during that three weeks I had a private conversation with Ralph Martin. Let me say clearly at the outset, Ralph Martin is a man of God whom I respect. The Lord has used him powerfully as a prophetic evangelist. That being said, I did have to talk with him about a matter that had deeply troubled me.

Ralph had come to Minneapolis in the spring of 1980 in order to videotape a series of lectures called *A Crisis of Truth,* which were to be broadcast later on a Catholic television network. (In 1982 Ralph published a book with the same title.) The members of the Servants had been asked to attend, both for personal benefit and also in order to provide an audience for Ralph's presentation.

Ralph specifically addressed timely and important issues concerning the battle for truth in contemporary culture. His lectures were filled with documented evidence of the attack on the faith and teaching and morality of the church. This battle was then, and is now, a reality facing the whole Christian church. Ralph spoke specifically to Roman Catholics, even though there were a number of us Protestants from the Servants in the audience. Because I was a coordinator in the community, Patricia and I were seated near the front of the room.

I wholeheartedly agreed with what Ralph was seeking to accomplish in the lectures. The material he had gathered and his presentation were powerful; even so, I more than bristled at one of his key foundational points during the first lecture. Ralph repeatedly declared that there were matters on which Catholics could be sure that they knew the truth—absolute and without error. I agreed that there is absolute truth we can know; however, again and again, Ralph stated that absolute truth was to be found in the agreement between Scripture, the writing of the Church Fathers, and the official teaching of the Pope and the Magisterium of the church (that is, the Pope and the council of bishops).

The more I thought about this statement, the more I was bothered. Here was one of the primary leaders in our network of ecumenical communities proclaiming that absolute truth was to be found in the Scriptures *plus* ... Yes, I recognized that Ralph's words were consistent with Roman Catholic doctrine. However, I also believed that by emphasizing this definition of absolute truth Ralph was in effect shutting the door to meaningful dialogue between Catholics and Protestants over one of the main points at issue in the Reformation, that of *sola Scriptura*—the teaching that Scripture alone is the foundation for all truth. I wondered, *How are we to move toward unity in doctrine if one group already has the "absolute truth"?*

While Ralph was teaching, I had become so agitated that every time I saw a camera pointing my direction I slid down in my seat in hopes that I would not be seen and recognized by anyone when the lecture was broadcast on TV. *What if someone sees me and thinks I agree with that?* I fumed.

As soon as there was a break in the meeting, I had hunted up Larry Alberts and had begun to spew out my concern and frustration. Larry was taken back by my vehemence. Thankfully, he did manage to remind me of the deliverance that God had given me—"lay down your sword and shield toward the Body of Christ." During the next session, with the help of the Lord I managed to get control of my emotions and to settle down. My strong emotional reaction was a clear indication that Ralph's words had touched some insecurity in me that would block fruitful conversation.

Later that evening at a reception, Larry had brought Ralph to me and invited me to express my concerns. However, I was thinking more clearly by then, and I realized that Ralph was addressing such a necessary topic that it would be wrong for me to stir up confusion or dissension when he still had several lectures to give the next day. We decided to wait until a better opportunity. That opportunity came during the time in Steubenville when Ralph and I had the chance sit down together in a library at the monastery where we were staying.

I told Ralph my concerns about the way he had defined "absolute truth." He was perplexed by my concern. He told me that prior to the taping sessions in Minneapolis, he had given the presentation at an ecumenical gathering of Charismatic leaders and that it had been well received.

"You told the ecumenical leaders that the absolute truth is found when Scripture, the writing of the Fathers, and the teaching of the magisterium agree?" I asked.

Ralph replied, "I did not mean to imply that this definition applied to truth for Protestants. I was talking about absolute truth for Catholics."

"Ralph," I responded, "absolute truth has to be absolute. There cannot be absolute truth for Catholics that is different from absolute truth for Protestants." I went on to share my opinion that if Roman Catholics insisted on that definition up front, then there could be no possibility of dialogue toward unity unless we Protestants surrendered our view at the beginning.

I saw that my words struck a chord with Ralph, even though there was not much more to say. We left that room as friends, but we could not resolve the problem, because Ralph is a faithful Catholic, and the definition he used is the Catholic teaching. I think he might have been so familiar with the Catholic definition that he had not fully considered some of its implications. It was not that Ralph was ignorant at all, but on that point, he seemed not to have been conscious that the assumption he had accepted from his Catholic formation might be a major stumbling block to unity.

To tell the truth, I think we all have unidentified assumptions that are problematic, hindering conversation and making unity difficult. Certainly, my wife and I have run into some in our own ways of thinking through the years. Thankfully, not every unconscious assumption has such huge ramifications as that one.

I do not know whether Ralph has ever thought about the conversation again, but by 1983 I had come to see this matter of identifying the authoritative grounds for truth as an important issue for my own life.

The second important thing for me in those three weeks of training was the time spent brainstorming in small groups. I was assigned to a group led by Peter Williamson, a member of the Word of God Community and one of the editors of *Pastoral Renewal*, an ecumenical magazine for leaders of churches, communities, and prayer groups. Our group was assigned to identify some strategies that our communities could implement in an effort to "stem the tide of evil in the churches."

We recognized that the most important challenges facing the church in the latter part of the twentieth century were essentially the same for everyone who took the Bible seriously as God's revealed Word, be they Pentecostals, Charismatics, Evangelicals, Catholics, or Orthodox. In our discussions we sought wisdom about specific approaches to communicate better with each group. During several sessions we tried to come up with ideas to awaken God's people and prepare them for the battle.

One of the ideas our group discussed was to search out influential leaders from the various streams of the Christian church, leaders whom we had reason to believe were faithful to God, to the church, and to the truth. We discussed a number of ways to help these leaders meet one another and to become more aware of our common battle; we wanted to find ways to encourage them to network so that they could mutually encourage and help one another serve the Lord's purposes in the churches. Sitting on the lawn talking together on those hot August summer afternoons, I had no idea that I was participating in a conversation that was to have lasting ramifications in the church! But that comes later.

The third thing was that during these three weeks I was asked to accompany Mark Kinzer, from the Word of God in Ann Arbor, on a trip to Emmanuel Covenant Community in Brisbane, Australia, later that fall. We were invited there to help settle a problem between nondenominational and Catholic members in that community.

****

Shortly after returning home from the Steubenville meetings, I began preparations for the trip to Australia. The most urgent task was to apply for a passport since I had never traveled out of the United States, except for a few day trips to Nuevo Laredo, Mexico, and to Winnipeg, Canada.

While I was in the process of getting the passport, Jack Brombach informed me that the head coordinators wanted fellow-coordinator John Buri and me to participate in a theological colloquy in Ann Arbor, Michigan, in early October. I was not sure what a theological colloquy was; however, since my leaders had asked me to go, I never considered not doing so. I assumed that I was going because of my interest in theology. I did wonder why John, a psychology professor at St. Thomas College, was asked to go, but it turned out that psychology was the one of the topics that was taken up at the colloquy.

As it turned out, Mark Kinzer was to present a paper at the colloquy; therefore, we made plans to leave together for Australia from Michigan immediately afterward. Although the timing was close, my passport arrived soon enough, and I began to pack for the long trip.

As the time to leave drew nearer, Patricia began to be more concerned about me going so far away. That made it somewhat hard to leave, but the fact that I would be gone on her birthday made it even worse because birthdays had become important celebrations in our family. We celebrated the birthday in a small way before I left; however, I secretly gave money to one of Patricia's friends and asked her to host a surprise birthday party for Patricia on the actual day, Friday, October 10.

For Such a Time as This?

On the seventh of October, John and I flew together to Ann Arbor; that evening we attended the first session of the colloquy, the theme of which was "Christianity Confronts Modernity." To my surprise, as I began to learn who the participants were, the gathering seemed like a fulfillment of some of the ideas about which we had brainstormed in our small group at Steubenville. There were probably seventy-five to one hundred men and women there, among them Evangelical, Pentecostal, and Catholic theologians, pastors, priests, deacons, leaders of Christian communities, editors, psychologists, psychiatrists, professors, and students.

The next two days centered on the formal presentation of six papers, each presentation followed by two prepared responses. Following each paper and the responses, the three who presented them formed a panel and led a discussion of each topic, a discussion open to all the participants in the colloquy. In addition to these formal sessions, time had been built into the schedule for relationship building around meals and free time.

I recognized a few of the names on participants' name tags. The list of presenters included several more whose names I recognized. I knew of two of the editors: Kenneth Kantzner of *Christianity Today* and Stephen Board of *Eternity*. I also knew of the well-known English author J. I. Packer, an Anglican priest and also Professor of History and Theology at Regents College in British Columbia.

In addition to several esteemed Evangelicals, the list of responders included several Catholic theologians, a Catholic priest, and a Catholic deacon who was also a theology professor. Several of my friends from the Word of God and the People of Praise were scheduled to present responses. Also participating in the conference were well-known pastors and authors such as Charles Simpson, Larry Christenson, Robert Girard, and Howard Snyder—all of whom had made significant contributions to my life through their teaching, whether on tape or in books.

That left my big question unanswered: Why was I there among these scholars and leaders? I felt privileged, of course, to be around them, and certainly the topics to be discussed looked interesting, but I also felt out of my league.

The colloquy's theme was significant for several reasons:

1. It recognized that in our world there was a battle taking place between modernity (referring to ideas, attitudes, and practices that have developed out of the Enlightenment) and Christianity.

214

2. It recognized (by implication) that modernity presently had the upper hand in contemporary Western culture.

3. It suggested (again by implication) that Christianity ought to be on the offense confronting modernity, not simply on defense or in retreat.

The range of topics discussed at the colloquy is indicated by the titles of the main papers: "Christian Identity and Social Change in Technological Society" by Mark Kinzer, "Ideology Versus Theology: Case Studies of Liberation Theology and the Christian New Right" by Dale Vree, "The Course of Radical Change in the Churches" by James Hitchcock, "From a Secular to a Christian Psychology" by Paul C. Vitz, "Modern Approaches to Scriptural Authority" by Stephen B. Clark, and "The Challenge Facing the Churches" by Donald G. Bloesch.

Significantly, this colloquy took place in the same time period that the Christian New Right had arisen politically, about one month before a conservative, Ronald Reagan, would be elected president. In the years immediately preceding our gathering, a growing number of Evangelicals had begun to awaken to the cultural issues, to Christian responsibility, and to the weakened condition of the church. The awakening was welcome; however, in some cases, shallow theology and lack of spiritual and intellectual preparation were not providing a sufficient base for fruitful strategies and actions that would endure. The majority of those identified as the Christian Right appeared to be mostly interested in specific issues and seemed to think that they could change these issues by winning the seats of power.

While the colloquy touched on some of the same issues that had given rise to the New Right, the primary intent of this gathering was to expose the root problems, areas in which much of the church had been succumbing to modernism. Secondarily, these discussions pointed to the need to develop strategies for dealing with cultural issues that were theologically sound in the light of historic Christian faith and practice. In addition, the men and women participating in the colloquy had the opportunity to discover common concerns and to begin to establish relationships from which they could encourage one another, bring balance to one another's ideas, and hopefully even work together to develop and implement such sound strategies.

I have written about the way in which I had been influenced in the late '60s and early '70s by political and economic liberal ideas about social justice issues such as civil rights and war. Later, I had begun to see that some of those political ideas, which at a surface level appeared similar to Biblical teaching, were at a root level incompatible and sometimes even antithetical to Biblical thought. On the other hand, I had not been able to buy fully into political and economic conservatism either. I had come to the realization that the way of God's kingdom was neither liberal nor conservative in terms of its implications for politics and economics. Yet, I still was looking mostly at issues rather than at roots.

Dale Vree's paper, "Ideology Versus Theology: Case Studies of Liberation Theology and the Christian New Right," most directly addressed such issues. In Vree's view, the Marxist assumptions that underlay Liberation Theology were explicit and wrong, while the concern for moral absolutes that motivated many of those in the New Right were clear and most often right.

In my opinion then and now, Vree was more in touch with contemporary Roman Catholic theological perspectives than he was with Biblical thought on issues such as war. He rightly identified some of the problems stemming from dispensational premillennialism (which he called apocalyptic premillennialism), the most common eschatology held by Evangelicals; however, I thought that he did not understand Protestant thinking very well. Even so, Vree's paper caused me to ask questions that needed to be asked about my own assumptions.

The responses by Reformed theologian I. John Hesselink and Kevin Perrotta, a member of the Word of God community and also one of the editors of *Pastoral Renewal*, stimulated me to look more deeply at the theological foundations for political involvement. Perrotta's paper in particular clearly presented the need to apply distinctively Christian criteria to political ideologies. I was struck by Kevin's insight into the confusion that arises when it comes to considering the relationship between Christianity and politics in contemporary Western society:

> … Christian thinking of the past does not answer our questions about what is the right Christian response to the disorder and inequities of the global technological society which have arisen in the last couple of hundred years. Thus Christians are particularly open to the political ideologies which have arisen in the modern period to answer these problems. Christianity entered the modern period unprepared to deal with the systemic poverty generated by capitalism, for example, or with the complex processes of social decay in advanced technological societies; but ideologies such as Marxism and political conservatism offer diagnoses and cures. This accounts for some of the allure of the political ideologies: they analyze problems that Christians are deeply concerned about and offer solutions designed to fit contemporary circumstances.

> But what accounts for the confusion of these ideologies with the Christian message? How do they come to be seen as *Christian* approaches? The answer lies in the fact that these ideologies have learned from Christianity. Those on the left have derived a concern for the poor, a desire to see all members of society treated charitably; those on the right, a commitment to the integrity of the family and sexual morality. These attitudes seem to be Christian ones. In many cases, their source is the Judeo-Christian heritage of Western civilization. Thus Christians are faced with ideologies which, having adopted elements of Christian social thinking, are harder to distinguish from Christian positions than they would be if they plainly rejected goals that Christians cherish.[64]

This succinct statement summed up some of the conflict in my own thinking at that time: I was conservative when it came to morality and family issues. I also recognized that the liberals were correct in being concerned for the issues of social justice such as racism, poverty, and war. The Bible addresses all these issues, so how can we choose one set and ignore the others?

Over the following years, as my understanding of Biblical jurisdictions has grown, I have concluded that we must ask, "Which jurisdiction(s) has God made responsible to deal with the issue under consideration?" Then we can seek out how problems can be handled within the context of the appropriate jurisdiction.

In other words, since God has made individuals responsible to govern themselves in certain matters, then God's people must disciple individuals to handle those matters God's way. God's people must disciple families, business people, churches, and civil governments to handle *their* God-given assignments in their everyday world in God's way.

While I did not come away from the colloquy with all the answers to a Christian position on social and political issues, I did come away with deeper insight and a better set of questions to help formulate answers.

Steve Clark's presentation concerning interpreting Scripture had the most impact on my own calling. He identified three common methods of interpreting the Bible that

---

[64] Kevin Perrotta, "Response" to Dale Vree, in *Christianity Confronts Modernity: A Theological and Pastoral Inquiry by Protestant Evangelicals and Roman Catholics*, Peter Williamson and Kevin Perrotta, ed. (Ann Arbor MI: Servant Books, 1981), 86–87.

have been used by theologians: (1) the traditional, or theological, method, which puts the weight on authority and truth; (2) the secular-historical approach, in particular the historical critical method, which focuses more on assessing the historical validity of documents than on truth; and (3) the historical-biblical approach, which uses the tools of historical research while affirming the canonicity and authority of Scripture.

Steve elucidated a number of ways in which the historical critical method has been used by theologians to undercut the plain teaching of Scripture and the consistent understanding of the church in matters of morality and doctrine. This methodology starts with the assumption that the Biblical writings are relative to their own historical setting rather than true or false. The interpreter approaches the Scriptures "critically," undecided as to their validity and truth. Therefore, the technical skills and the reasoning of each theologian, in effect, has more authority than either the Scripture itself or the historical teaching of the church.

While interpreters may sometimes misuse the other methods of exegesis, it is vital that we who study the Bible approach our study trusting that the Scriptures are true and authoritative. We must not strip Scripture of its power and wisdom, but rather stand under its authority because the writers of Scripture were inspired by God's own Spirit.

The prepared responses by J. I. Packer and Michael Wrenn confirmed the core ideas in Steve's paper. J. I. Packer went beyond mere confirmation to declare, convincingly I thought, that in order to interpret Scripture properly it is necessary to use both the traditional, theological method and the historical-biblical method, holding them together, not as separate methodologies.

Since I was not at all on the level of most of the participants in that seminar in terms of academic training, intellectual ability, or leadership experience, up to that time I had listened to the discussions as an interested learner. However, upon hearing several responses from colloquy participants that defended a secularist approach to interpreting Scripture, I could no longer sit silent.

I went to the microphone. I told the other participants how I had become partially secularized in my own thinking because of the way I had responded to my Psychology class in Bible college and to the general culture of rebellion in the sixties. I told them that it had been my life in Christian community—a community consisting mostly of Roman Catholics—that had been playing a most significant part in reestablishing my life on the solid ground of the Bible and the historical Christian faith. Mine was not an intellectual appeal. It was the cry of my heart that God's people not be led astray!

Very possibly it came off as silly to many in that room full of scholars. No matter. I could not be silent.

Mark Kinzer had arranged for me to stay at the brotherhood house in which he lived during the colloquy because we were going to leave together for Australia after its conclusion. Thus, after the first session, I found myself in the back seat of a car sitting between the well-known evangelical Anglican pastor and author J. I. Packer and Harry S. Blamires, an Anglican theologian, literary critic, and novelist who had been mentored by C. S. Lewis. I freely admit that on that ride they talked over my head, both literally and figuratively.

That colloquy led to the formation of the Alliance for Faith and Renewal and to several Allies for Faith and Renewal conferences. Although I was not able to participate in the next two because of the conflicts that were soon to divide our Association of Communities, I was privileged to attend several more in the late 1980s, including one during which Charles Colson read the manuscript for his insightful and challenging book *Against the Night: Living in the New Dark Ages* before it was published.[65]

These gatherings had significant long-term impact on me. I was only a bit player, but it was a privilege to be involved. My conviction that God wanted some sort of unity among the churches was greatly strengthened. At first the unity of God's people seemed important to me mostly because Jesus prayed for that unity and because the Scripture teaches that he is preparing a bride without spot and wrinkle. However, because of the time in Steubenville and the colloquy, I came to see far more clearly that God's people will need to be unified if we are to be successful in dealing with the challenges to Biblical faith at this time in history.

The Alliance for Faith and Renewal conferences provided a forum for relationships to be established between leaders from a broad spectrum of Christian churches. Whether directly or indirectly, the Alliance was a forerunner of "Evangelicals and Catholics Together," the 1994 document[66] and subsequently the group that formed at

---

[65] The book was published in 1989 by Vine Books, an imprint of Servant Publications.
[66] The original document was published along with the names of those who prepared it and initially endorsed it in the journal *First Things* and can be read at https://www.firstthings.com/article/1994/05/evangelicals-catholics-together-the-christian-mission-in-the-third-millennium.

the initiative of the Baptist Charles Colson and the Roman Catholic Richard John Neuhaus.

Certainly, our little group of brain-stormers sitting on the lawn of a monastery in August 1980 are not responsible for all that has happened to foster the development of unity among Christians in the years that followed. Even so, some of those in that group played a significant role and the ideas we shared with one another played some part.

****

It was the God-given desire for unity that took me to Brisbane, Australia, with my friend Mark. At 5:30 p.m. (EDT) on Saturday, October 10 (Patricia's birthday), we took off from Detroit Metro Airport on the first leg of our journey to Australia. We arrived at Los Angeles International at 5:00 p.m. (PDT), a fact that has stuck in my mind because we arrived "before" we started.

Our 6:30 p.m. flight with TWA from LA to Honolulu had been canceled, so we were rebooked to take a Pan American flight scheduled to leave about 9 p.m. During that lengthy wait at the Pan Am gate, Mark decided to use part of the time to pray. To my surprise (truthfully, to my discomfort), he put a skull cap on his head and took out his Jewish prayer book and turned away to face a support pillar. Right there, in the midst of the crowded room, Mark stood, bobbing back and forth, his lips quietly pronouncing the words, praying just like Jewish men do at the Wailing Wall in Jerusalem. Mark's courage stunned and challenged me. I had to choose whether to stand close by, where it was obvious that I was with him, or to move away so as not to be identified with him. I chose to stay, but I am chagrined to say that I was still somewhat embarrassed.

As we got on the plane in LA, I heard people around us saying things like "Uh oh, the Australian football team! Things will be lively on this flight." I soon learned that those who play Australian football have the same sort of reputation for rowdiness as do those who play rugby, a similar game. The team was seated a couple sections behind us on the Boeing 747, so we did not see much of them on the flight to Honolulu, where we landed about 11 p.m. (Hawaii time) that Saturday night. (Meanwhile it was 4 a.m. Sunday back in Detroit.)

What was supposed to have been a short 45-minute stop turned into more than a 2-hour delay when a mechanical problem was discovered on our Boeing 747, and we had to wait for a different jet to be brought up so that we could finish our flight. We all had to disembark and wait in the terminal. There, I saw for myself that the footballers were indeed rowdy; these full-grown men ran all around that area of the terminal, jumping chairs, tossing various and sundry items back and forth, and basically being noisy nuisances.

We left Honolulu at 1 a.m. on Sunday and nine hours later arrived in Sydney at 7 a.m. on Monday morning, having skipped a day when we crossed the international dateline. Overall Coordinator, Brian Smith, and an Anglican coordinator from Emmanuel Community in Brisbane met us just outside the customs inspection room in the Sydney terminal and then flew with us on the two-and-one-half-hour flight into Brisbane.

Because Brisbane is about the same distance south of the equator as Tampa, Florida, is north of the equator, we left the fall colors of the upper Midwest and arrived to see the lilac-blue blossoms of the Australian jacarandas in springtime. I was struck by the many high-set homes—houses built several feet above the ground, often with lattice work around the base, built that way because it was supposedly cooler to have air under the house in summer. The fronts of downtown shops and pubs were quite often open to the street, and expandable gates were used to lock them up at night.

During our flight over, Mark had told me about the division in Emmanuel Community between the elders and the Pentecostals (used synonymously in Emmanuel for those we called nondenominational back home). Over an excellent lunch of fresh barramundi, the Australian brothers told us more about the problems in their community.

They had had a gifted Pentecostal coordinator in the community until a few months before when he and a number of the Pentecostals had left Emmanuel to start their own church. Because they left without fully processing the decision with the leadership, it had left a wound in the community. A number of the Pentecostals who had chosen to stay still had some distrust toward the leadership as well as hurt toward those who had gone.

According to Brian, there were no strong leaders among the Pentecostals who had stayed, certainly no one with a strong Biblical, theological foundation. Therefore, when a "theological" problem surfaced, there was no one grounded enough or secure enough to deal with it reasonably; instead, emotions had run rampant, and communication between most of the Pentecostals and the community leaders had broken down. Mark and I had been sent to try to help bridge the communication gap and bring peace to their relationships. On the one hand I wanted to laugh at the "theological" problem once I had heard it; on the other hand, how could I laugh when there was a serious breach in relationships among the brothers?

I was in Australia—by far the longest trip of my life—because of a comic book. Can you believe it? In 1979 tract publisher Jack Chick of Chick Publications had produced a comic book telling the story of Alberto, supposedly a former Jesuit priest who had been converted and had left the Roman Catholic Church. According to Alberto, the Jesuits actually control the Catholic Church, and the head of the Jesuits is a high priest of Satan. Furthermore, according to the comic book, Alberto had revealed that the Jesuits had a huge computer in Rome onto which they were collecting personal information about all Protestants. At a future time when the Roman Catholic Church had set up its one-world super-church, the Jesuits would then identify these Protestants and kill those who refused to convert. In the meantime, before his conversion, Father Alberto was purported to have been one of many Jesuits assigned to infiltrate Bible-believing churches and seminaries in order to disrupt them and to corrupt and destroy the leaders. The comic specifically identified the Charismatic movement and the ecumenical movement as two of the tools to be used by the Jesuits in creating this future super-church.

Still today, Chick Publications is propagating Alberto's story through the Internet, where they now offer six comic books featuring him. Never mind that he has long since been exposed as a fraud by a number of reputable sources, including *Christianity Today* (March 13, 1981) and the Christian Research Institute (February 25, 1983). However, in the fall of 1980 we had no sources like these to which we could refer.

It probably seems ludicrous that people would take a comic book so seriously. However, as one who grew up in a church context in which Roman Catholicism was considered a cult and the Pope had often been touted as the coming Antichrist, I had learned by experience that these sorts of charges could seem quite believable to sincere believers who had been steeped in some forms of premillennial dispensationalism. Many of the Protestants who had joined the ecumenical communities did not have solid theological and Biblical grounding. Since they were not solidly grounded in their own beliefs, they could easily become insecure when exposed to the differing beliefs of other Christians, and they were certainly ill-equipped to deal with accusations of conspiratorial plots, especially those that played to fears already planted by end-times sermons. Even the fact that they had become friends with Roman Catholics whom they believed to be genuine believers did not mean they trusted the Roman Catholic Church.

The comic book stirred up unrest as it was circulated among these Pentecostals in Emmanuel. Perhaps it was because they did not want to hurt their Catholic friends that they did not ask Emmanuel's coordinators about the truth in the book. Who knows?

It might not have become a big deal except that the coordinators made the simple decision to buy a computer for the community office. "So what?" we would ask today. However, in 1980, personal computers were in their infancy. Not all that many businesses even had computers, let alone churches or individuals.

When word got around that the community office was beginning to keep records in a computer, Alberto's accusation about the Jesuits collecting lists of Protestants seemed more than credible to a number of the community's Pentecostals. By the time Emmanuel's coordinators learned about the comic book, fear had already taken root, underlying distrust had been acerbated, and communication had become next to impossible.

Mark and I were there as Protestants to try and help reopen communication and to see if we could help establish an environment in which trust could grow. We did not get into the "theological" issue very deeply; rather, we focused on reconciling the relationships.

To tell the truth, Mark was the one who had the training and experience to be able to develop a plan for reconciliation. I was along "to be with Mark." He had been a member of the Word of God longer than I had been in the Body of Christ and the Servants of the Lord, and he had been a coordinator longer than I had as well. It had been primarily Mark to whom I had looked for practical wisdom and guidance in my efforts to establish the Free Church Fellowship. In addition, Mark had lived in the Word of God brotherhood with Steve Clark, one of the founders of the whole ecumenical covenant movement, and had been trained by him. I was there to support Mark and to learn from him.

I do think that I was able to contribute some to our mission. For one thing, it was probably easier for me to relate to the simplicity of the Pentecostals than it was for Mark, who had grown up in a Jewish home in Detroit. These folks were for the most part working people not too unlike those with whom I had grown up in the Churches of Christ in Christian Union. Because of this similarity in background, I may have helped us build a bridge of trust with them.

It turned out that in public meetings I was able to quickly establish a rapport with people. Every time I spoke before a new group, I was able to say only a few words before the people would break out into laughter. I can only think that that it was because of my accent—although Mark's Michigan accent seemed funnier to me. I have also wondered if they may have associated my accent with someone on television. The truth is, I never have figured out why they laughed, but it was obviously friendly laughter. It established some sort of connection that gave me confidence and seemed to make them receptive. After a couple incidents of this response, I began to play to it, deliberately trying to sound a bit "countrified." At the main community meeting, I opened with a joke about a hillbilly preacher who consistently exaggerated while preaching. It went over so well that I still try the joke from time to time, but not with the same results. Mark's wisdom was greater, but having a "comedian" along seemed to open the people's hearts to us.

By the time we left to come home, there had been significant reconciliation. Mark helped the Pentecostals and the coordinators draw up a written agreement to help reestablish their relationship and to set forth agreed-upon steps to take when their trust was tested in the future. Not only did they sign the agreement, but they also presented it to the whole body of more than 1,000 members at their community gathering. There was great rejoicing.

I came home from this apparent victory for unity only to become embroiled in a much larger conflict that was to come to light just a few months later.

17

Division

From my perspective, the Lord had called me to be a member of a significant work of the Holy Spirit. Many of us believed that the Holy Spirit was working through us to restore the whole church to the life described in the New Testament and to bring together the divided Body of Christ in answer to Jesus's prayer in John 17. Professing to believe that I had even a tiny part in a vision to change the whole church with its 2,000-year history sounds somewhat grandiose now. Even so, at the time I had not heard of any comparable movement in church history. To be a part of such vision was heady wine indeed!

The call to seek unity that I felt was strong. Vision for unity in the church had begun to awaken in me while I was still at Waite Park Wesleyan, where my farewell sermon in early 1974 was a call to unity with diversity. I had sought to build unity in relationships with other pastors while I was in Richland Center. Our experience in Wycliffe fed the desire and encouraged hope that Christians of diverse backgrounds could indeed work together in unity. Then my wife and I had begun to invest our lives into learning how to live in the unity of the Spirit with Christians from other denominations in covenant community. Uncomfortable and even frightening sometimes? Yes. But extremely exciting too—a call deserving of our highest sacrifice. I believed it was a special privilege to have such a call.

The importance of our ecumenical covenant communities seemed to be confirmed when I discovered that even the earliest stages of development of the communities had been noticed and mentioned, if only slightly, in *Eerdmans' Handbook to the History of Christianity*, published in 1977, the same year that we had moved to Minneapolis to be a part of the Servants of the Lord. In an article titled "The Pentecostals," James Dunn had written: "But the widening of the charismatic movement since the 1960s has brought with it a questioning of the classic Pentecostal categories, a desire to formulate the theology of the 'Pentecostal experience' more carefully, and *a renewed concern to let the life of the Spirit be expressed in new forms of community*" (italics added). Dunn also mentioned that in the view of some, "the charismatic movement is the best hope for a renewal of the church in the closing decades of this century."[67]

---

[67] Tim Dowley, ed., *Eerdmans' Handbook to the History of Christianity* (Grand Rapids, MI: Wm. B. Eerdmans Publishing Co., 1977), 622. [First published earlier in 1977 by Lion Publishing, Berkhamsted, Herts, England.]

I do not want to minimize the important work God had done to bring us together in community or the witness that the covenant communities and individual members (whether still in one of the communities or not) have had through the years. However, my perspective about what we were was overly idealistic. We had been greatly blessed by the grace of God and we had great potential to serve him together, but we were still human. We were redeemed in Christ yet still easily susceptible to temptation and sin. Idealism had to give way to reality and greater humility. Over the next several years, the divisions among the ecumenical covenant communities and between the five teachers in the *New Wine* stream would set back our ability to work as effectively as we could have for unity in the church; however, God's work did not begin or end with us. I am grateful that God is so committed to his purposes that he works with us and through us even when we are carnal and weak in ourselves.

****

One evening in early spring 1981, I came home later than expected from some meeting or another. As I walked into our apartment, Patricia informed me that Jack Brombach had been trying to contact me. She said that he had called several times; then he had shown up at the door and waited quite a while for me to get home. At last, when I still had not returned, he had asked Patricia to have me come to his house by seven o'clock the next morning, ready to fly to Chicago for the day. Clearly something unusual was afoot.

So it was that at 7 a.m. the following day I was sitting at the Brombachs' kitchen table drinking coffee. About five minutes later, Jack walked into the room and greeted me. His appearance startled me. Ever since I had known Jack, he had always worn a toupee. (Actually he had started wearing one when in his mid-twenties.) But on this morning, he wore no hairpiece. His head was completely bald on top and most of the back. What little hair he had was trimmed short on the sides and the lower back of his head.

Embarrassed, I looked away, thinking, "Should I tell him that he has forgotten something?"

Before I could speak, Jack put me at ease, saying simply, "I decided I do not need to cover up my baldness anymore." With these simple words, I realized that Jack had found new inner strength and self-confidence. Why or how, I had no idea. Once I got over the surprise and discomfort, I realized that Jack did not need the toupee. He looked better without it.

Jack informed me that the two of us were going to travel with fellow coordinators Hal Langevin, Bill Rademacher, Louis Grams, and John Buri, to Chicago, where we were to meet some of the elders from the People of Praise. Larry Alberts, our third head coordinator, would normally have been included in the group, but a few months earlier he had been sent on mission to help a community in Saskatoon, Saskatchewan, get established. By 10 a.m. we had flown into Chicago's Midway Airport and had caught a hotel van to a nearby Holiday Inn, where Paul DeCelles, Kevin Ranaghan, and a couple other brothers from South Bend greeted us. Together we walked into a meeting room that they had reserved.

It was here that I learned that there had been already, or was soon going to be, a separation between the Word of God Community and the People of Praise. Some communities in the larger Association would follow the lead of Ann Arbor, but the People of Praise would not, and they were looking to continue working with communities of like mind with them. The main substance of our discussion that day was to hear the ideas that the men from the People of Praise had for building together in the future.

As I understood it that day, the People of Praise brothers believed that the Word of God leaders were trying to build a tighter organization than we had had in the Association of Communities. From the beginning of working together, the Ann Arbor brothers had wanted the communities to form a federation with some measure of "central government," but after long discussions, the leaders of the communities involved had settled on the word *Association* to define our relationship as a network of self-governed communities who had chosen to build according to common values and structures and to cooperate together in mission.

We were told that the brothers from Ann Arbor were putting together something like a "community of communities," which they would call the Sword of the Spirit. To me it sounded as if the organization they were planning would be comparable to the many monastic orders within the Roman Catholic Church, except that this one would be ecumenical and would include families as well as celibates. It would have strong centralized government rather than continue simply as an association of autonomous communities.

The brothers from the People of Praise were considering two different ideas. The one they seemed to favor that day was to develop a fellowship of communities with an even looser structure than the Association. But they also mentioned that they had been considering building one large international community with "branches" in various locations, which sounded to me to be even more centralized than the Ann Arbor plan.

After batting these ideas around for a few hours, about 4 p.m. we headed back to Midway Airport to return home.

I was not totally surprised about these developments. There had been indications for several months that serious wrestling was taking place among the leaders of the Association. I remember that a few months earlier, when Paul DeCelles was visiting in Minneapolis, some of us had discussed some of the differences in thinking among leaders of the two communities. Although I had not discerned it at the time, these differences among the brothers led to the two distinct approaches to preparing for hard times that had been presented at the Steubenville meetings the previous summer. During this visit, Paul had told us that he and the South Bend brothers had serious concerns that the Ann Arbor men were taking the hard-times prophecies too literally and that, if they organized around the belief that hard times would be "cataclysmic," and if the prophecies were not fulfilled that way, people could be disillusioned and even hurt over time.

On the other hand, he had said the South Bend leaders had come to the conclusion that they had no way to know what or when or how hard times would come, but that, according to Scripture, God's people should live a provident and resourceful life, setting aside resources in times of plenty that would help them survive in difficult times, which are sure to come from time to time. Human history is replete with upswings and downswings in economies and social orders, he said.

Paul also had said that there were serious differences in how the two groups of leaders interpreted the Biblical teaching about brotherhood. According to him, Word of God leaders believed that only Christians are truly brothers, especially those walking in covenant, and that we are not brothers with those who are outside of Christ. Paul believed it important to emphasize the brotherhood of all mankind, while not denying that Christian relationships are special.

A third serious concern, he said, had to do with how the leaders and ecumenical communities should relate to the Roman hierarchy. He seemed to believe that they were in danger of losing favor with church authorities, and that it might cause the authorities to take action to take more hands-on control of the renewal communities. As I understood it, he believed that the People of Praise should build strategically in order to keep a good relationship with Catholic authorities on the one hand, and to continue the then-current situation in which the Roman Catholic Church had taken no direct authority over ecumenical communities.

In the days that followed, I had thought quite often about the matters Paul had brought up. Concerning hard-times prophecies, at that time I thought it would be a good thing if structures in which Christians trusted (especially denominational structures, I thought) were to fall down and there were to be a restoration of a church consisting of truly committed followers of Jesus. It certainly was not hard to believe that economic hard times were close upon us when interest rates had climbed well above 10%, inflation was rampant, and we had been through two energy crises in the '70s—to say nothing of the long-standing cold war between the Western nations and the Soviet Union, the hostages who had been held for months by the Iranians, and the instability of the Middle East. On the other hand, I was in the midst of a change in my understanding of eschatology such that I was learning to focus on living and building for the long haul rather than to live with all my hopes in an imminent rapture of the church. To me, both groups had something to contribute to the whole picture.

Concerning brotherhood, I recognized that all human beings are the children of God by creation since all descend from "Adam, the son of God" (Luke 3.38). However, there is also a clear Biblical distinction between how we believers are called to relate to those within the Christian community in contrast to how we are called to relate with people outside the community. For example, Galatians 6:10 reads, "So then, as we have opportunity, let us do good to everyone, and especially to those who are of the household of faith."

The Bible does teach that those who are in Christ are adopted by God as his children and, therefore, we are brothers to one another, not only in our humanity, but uniquely brothers in the redeemed community of Christ. God commands us to love our neighbor and even to love our enemy, but he requires many more specific acts of love toward "one another" in the family of God. After all, as St. Peter wrote, it is by God's doing that "... you are a chosen race, a royal priesthood, a holy nation, a people for his own possession, that you may proclaim the excellencies of him who called you out of darkness into his marvelous light. Once you were not a people, but now you are God's people; once you had not received mercy, but now you have received mercy." (1 Peter 2:9-10) We who are in Christ are the redeemed human race—a **people group** uniquely set apart as God's own. As such we belong to one another in a different way than we relate to those outside the covenant of God.

I was ambivalent concerning the matter of the communities' relationship with the Roman Catholic hierarchy. My deep-seated convictions that the denominations do not represent God's heart for a unified church, my own experience of having been expelled from the denomination of my youth, and my identification as a nondenominational all tended to make me think that a breach with the Roman Catholic hierarchy would equip us to freely pursue being the church of God's heart. At the same time, I believed that I had been called by God to work toward unity in the church along with brothers who were still connected to the denominational structures.

All in all, however, on most of these issues I would have to say that I was more closely aligned in my thinking with the brothers in Ann Arbor than with those in South Bend.

Still, I was surprised to learn in the Chicago meeting that these differences had led to serious division and that the dissolution of the Association was imminent. Still, these things seemed fairly far removed from the day-to-day life we were living in the Servants of the Lord. When it came to how to approach these trans-local relationships between communities, as a nondenominational, by conviction I clearly leaned toward a fellowship of communities rather than to a federation of communities or to one community with numerous geographically situated branches.

As we headed back to Minneapolis, one thing had become clear: we leaders of the Servants of the Lord would need to make a decision regarding which group of communities we would join with—or, we could make the decision to just stand on our own.

On the trip home, I talked with Jack about what seemed to me to be yet another viable option. If there was a split in the Association, I asked, could we not consider connecting with the communities in the *New Wine* stream rather than to choose between our brothers in Word of God and the People of Praise? Jack responded with something like "That's a possibility."

The old adage is "people hear what they want to hear." I certainly did. I came away from that conversation believing that we in Servants would seriously consider connecting with the *New Wine* brothers if the split came to full fruition. And a few months later when, tragically, our own community was dividing because of the split in the Association, I would seek to secure people—especially Protestants—in the Servants by telling them what Jack had said to me about the possibility of connecting with the *New Wine* communities.

The reality is that joining up with the *New Wine* stream was never more than a possibility—most likely quite a distant one at that—for Jack. And looking back, I realize that out of my own desire I wrongly, howbeit unwittingly, made more out of his words than he had any intention to communicate.

Although I did not realize it at the time, this situation was to going to show me a lot about myself that I had not seen clearly, including things in me that I needed God to change.

****

Fairly soon after the Association split, the Servants' Body of Coordinators, after deliberation, made the decision to remain neutral in regard to the Association conflict. We agreed that we would try to continue as friends with all, but not join a group.

Then Larry Alberts moved back to Minneapolis from Saskatoon, and it soon came to light that there had been tension among the three head coordinators about this decision. These men were aware of disagreement and conflict between leaders of the community in Ann Arbor and those of the community in South Bend well before I was. As far as I can remember, at that time the rest of us coordinators were not aware of the difficulties between our own leaders. There had been a legitimate need in Saskatoon, and Larry certainly was qualified to go help out. Therefore, when the head coordinators brought the matter to the rest of us, we readily gave our assent.

It was not so much that Jack, Hal, and Larry were against one another, although, given their very different personalities and approaches, they had to work at learning to trust each other fully—most certainly a common challenge in human relationships. The big problem that surfaced during the split was that they had different historical ties with the other two communities involved. Over the years, Jack had been more closely connected as a friend to the People of Praise leaders in South Bend, whereas Larry had been closely affiliated with Steve Clark, the overall coordinator of the Word of God and founder of the Servants of the Word brotherhood in Ann Arbor. In line with that relationship. Larry had begun a brotherhood in the Servants of the Lord that had close ties to Ann Arbor brotherhood. As events unfolded I came to the conclusion that on the level of ideas and methods, Hal had more affinity with Ann Arbor; however, he was joined relationally with Jack, who had been a mentor and spiritual father to him.

231

As the years passed, I came to realize that I have not had enough information to make a clear judgment as to who was right and who was wrong in the things that developed. It was too complicated then, and I cannot even remember the details well enough now. Besides that, unless I could help resolve relationships by sharing my memories and thoughts about it all, it would only be gossip to give a blow-by-blow account. There were plenty of misunderstandings and mistakes to go around. I am trying to share my story because of what I learned about God, about God's ways, and about my need to be changed, so I will focus on my own journey through one of the most difficult seasons of my life. Whatever else the prophesies may have meant, the warning that structures in which we trusted would be shaken had already begun in my life.

The summer of 1981 was tense from the beginning. Larry was back but had not resumed his responsibilities as a coordinator. The reason given for this was that it was a season for him to seek some needed change from the Lord. Understandably, Larry struggled with the feeling that he was being set aside because of his relationship with the Ann Arbor brothers.

Jack had become my personal pastoral leader when Larry had been sent out, but Larry was my friend. He had added much to my life, and I appreciated him and respected his calling and gifts. It was difficult to see him struggle, and it was difficult to deal with the tension that seemed to be over all of us leaders.

I remember on at least one occasion, when having lunch with Larry, I shared with him an illustration from Bill Gothard's teaching that I had received as wisdom when dealing with unjust suffering—if Larry was indeed being unjustly treated. Gothard, in his 1973 teaching about being under authority, read from 1 Peter 2 and then said, "God uses the hammer of authority and the chisel of unjust suffering to form the living stones that make up his spiritual house." I encouraged Larry to rest his case in God and to trust him to work through the coordinators. As I recall, Larry responded that I just did not know enough of the facts to understand. I probably didn't.

As far as I know, all the brothers involved, both in our local community and in the other communities as well, were doing the best we could in all sincerity to do what was right before God. Without doubt, none of us was perfectly aligned with God's perception of the situation. Surely, many of us had some measure of carnality in our viewpoint and in our actions. Clearly the situation was much more complicated than I had assumed.

Over the course of the summer, we came to what I thought was a mutual agreement that Larry would move to the brotherhood in Ann Arbor and become a member of the Word of God community. Before long, however, it became clear that Larry had felt coerced into the agreement, and tensions continued to grow even after Larry moved to Ann Arbor late in the summer.

In late August, several brothers and sisters around the community, including two men's group leaders in the district which I oversaw, came to the conviction that they needed to leave the Servants and follow Larry and the Word of God leaders. Several of them sought to influence others to do the same. And, most hurtful to me, the men in my district who were among my closest friends had made this decision and had taken their action without communicating with me about it beforehand. It became even more personal when Randy, who had co-signed on our home with us, moved out of the house to join with those leaving.

I think these brothers and sisters may have been trying to help rectify the problem. I think they may have intended their actions to be a protest concerning Larry's move to Ann Arbor and a way to influence the coordinators to align with the Word of God in the larger split. However, their actions only made it that much more difficult to consider seriously aligning that way at all.

Over the next three weeks I could hardly eat or sleep; I lost 15 pounds as I agonized internally and labored almost constantly to stem this "rebellion" (as I saw it), seeking to keep other members from leaving the Servants to join this "split" within our own community. I honestly tried hard not to speak personally against those who had left even while I opposed their actions in no uncertain terms.

Over and over again when talking with community members who were shocked and confused, having known nothing of these issues, I declared our position of neutrality in the larger split. Although I meant well, looking back I can see that neutrality was almost impossible by that time. What is more, I promised too many of the Protestants, especially, that we would consider alliances with groups other than those in the Association, namely with the teachers in the *New Wine* stream.

Neutrality became even more unlikely in mid-September.

****

During the same time that we had been trying to deal with these issues concerning the divided Association and Larry's relationship with our head coordinators, we had also been planning for a great ten-day celebration of our community's tenth anniversary in mid-September. We planned a community-wide picnic and arts festival and also special gatherings: one for covenant members, one for all the men, and one for all the women. The celebration was to begin with gatherings for worship and remembering our history on Thursday, Friday, and Saturday evenings, followed by a Sunday afternoon gathering with Ern Baxter, one of the great preachers of the twentieth century, as the speaker.

We seriously considered whether or not we should cancel the celebration because of the division and instead to call for a time of repentance and mourning. However, after taking counsel together, all of us remaining coordinators agreed that we should first celebrate God's goodness during the ten years of our life together.

During that discussion I reminded the brothers of the time recorded in the eighth chapter of Nehemiah when Ezra read the Law of God for the people who had returned to Jerusalem after the Babylonian exile. As Ezra read and translated the Law, the people began to weep—convicted because they had not been living according to God's Law; however, Nehemiah commanded them not to weep because that day had been consecrated "holy to the LORD your God."

Then Nehemiah instructed the people: "Go your way, eat the fat and drink sweet wine, and send portions to anyone who has nothing ready; for this day is holy to our Lord. And do not be grieved, for the joy of the LORD is your strength." (Nehemiah 8:10)

The next day, the people discovered God's command to celebrate the feast of booths (or tabernacles), and they obeyed. For seven days they lived in booths and read the Law daily, "and there was great rejoicing." (8:17)

Then, on the eighth day, they held a solemn assembly with fasting and mourning and confession of sin.

We coordinators came to the conclusion that the Lord was calling us to lead our community first to celebrate God's goodness and then to enter a season of seeking God with repentance and confession afterward. The brothers had me preach from this passage on Nehemiah on the first Thursday night of our celebration. The people of our community received this word, and we were able to have a real celebration of God's goodness during those following days.

Even so, the celebration was not without pain. First, we were acutely aware of those who had left us. Second, during the celebration, a group of men came from the brotherhood in Ann Arbor to Minneapolis, and along with some of those who had left the Servants, they began to contact members of our community in their homes in order to "tell Larry's side of the story," which they felt we coordinators had not disclosed as fully as we should. One evening they even showed up at a community-wide men's celebration in an effort to present Larry's case to all the men in the community.

Following the celebration, we did call the community to a season of seeking the Lord in prayer and fasting.

Later that fall, men representing each of the sides of what had been the Association of Communities made official visits to present their respective cases to the coordinators. Paul DeCelles and Kevin Ranaghan came and presented to all our coordinators their plan to form a fellowship of communities. Paul and Kevin offered our community friendship and continuing relationship, seemingly without conditions or a desire to be in charge. And it was obvious by this time that Jack Brombach desired to see us join in fellowship with them.

Ralph Martin from the Word of God in Ann Arbor and Greg Gavriledes from the Work of Christ Community in East Lansing, Michigan, came to represent the Sword of the Spirit, the community of communities, which had formed in connection with the Word of God. Their visit was friendly enough in tone, but they were absolutely clear about their terms. They said that we would remain in a relationship as brothers if we were to join the Sword of the Spirit or if we were to stay neutral (meaning that we would not join with either group). However, if we decided to join the People of Praise in a fellowship of communities, then they would consider us covenant-breakers and no longer brothers.

This approach to us was essentially the final straw. Any of us who had leanings toward the Word of God because of personal relationships and affinity with the vision and theological approach realized that there was no longer a chance that the Servants would continue in any working relationship with the Word of God and the Sword of the Spirit. We all knew that we could not respond favorably to what we saw as ungodly pressure. To relate to the Sword of the Spirit it seemed to us as though we would have to give up our responsibility to lead the Servants according to the direction of the Holy Spirit.

One good thing did come out of that visit. Because of the friendly way Ralph approached us, even when presenting the "ultimatum," we did gain some confidence in him personally. Therefore, Ralph Martin became our primary contact in the Word of God. Eventually, after months of work with Ralph, we came to a formal agreement to release all the people who had decided to leave the Servants of the Lord covenant into the care of the Word of God leaders with the condition that these people agree to move to Ann Arbor. Gradually, after that the tensions within our local community subsided.

****

Through this whole process, one thing became clear. I was the only one who had given any serious consideration to the idea of relating to some group other than the new Fellowship of Communities or to the Sword of the Spirit. This was painful to me. Because I had made this a part of my defense of the community during the time when people were leaving, I now felt like I had lost integrity. I also felt that to some degree I had been betrayed, since I had put so much weight on the conversation I had had with Jack about the possibility of aligning elsewhere.

Jack and I eventually worked this out, but it put a significant strain in our relationship for a season, so much so that in 1982 I began to relate to Bill Rademacher for pastoral care.

As I have said already, the problem was mine. I had heard what I wanted to hear. I had put far too much weight on that one conversation with Jack months earlier. Only years later, after several somewhat similar incidents, did I come to understand that, when talking with someone in authority, I have had a tendency to take their words too literally, and in a sense even too seriously. I have had to learn that, because of my desire not to be a rebel, I could be too compliant. I have had to face the fact that there is an unhealthy way to rely on the words of human authority without taking enough personal responsibility to hear God for one's self and without following the Holy Spirit's lead in responding to human authority.

My biggest regret about my own behavior as I look back is that I acted unwisely at times because of this orientation to take the things told me at face value. I assumed that those in authority over me were giving me all that I needed to know in order to make whatever decisions might be required.

I was convinced then (and I still am, for that matter) that there are different spheres of authority, and those with a wider sphere need more information to fulfill their

236

responsibility than those with a lesser sphere need. However, I now understand more clearly since it was not only the overall coordinator who was called to lead the community, nor was it only the head coordinators. Rather, it was the whole body of coordinators, acting in corporeity as one entity, who were ultimately responsible to govern the community. Because our decisions were supposed to be made in unanimity, we all needed to have the fullest picture possible in order to make the best decisions.

Now that I work with fellow elders of a church community, this same governing principle applies. Sadly, it took years and other conflicts before I finally saw that I had not pressed hard enough for everything to be put on the table when all involved were together. I was naive.

At this point I still believe that the men involved meant well. I believe they were trying to do the best they could. But by not insisting that everything be put on the table from all sides, I may well have failed my duty. There is even the possibility, however small, that if I had pressed harder, we might have gotten to the bottom line and actually resolved some of the deeper issues.

But whether we would have or not, I was naively trustful and gave my assent to decisions without full enough understanding. May God help me not to do so ever again. May God help me to foster an environment in our present community in which the elders can actually take the time and suffer the pain necessary to come to full unity concerning the wisdom and direction of God for the people over whom he has made us overseers.

I also struggled with how to pray about it all. Since the early '70s, I have found the Psalms a source of life, even at times when the rest of Scripture seemed dead to me. During that time of anguish I felt kinship with David when I read passages such as these:

> Even my close friend in whom I trusted, who ate my bread, has lifted his heel against me. (Psalm 41:9)

> For it is not an enemy who taunts me—then I could bear it; it is not an adversary who deals insolently with me—then I could hide from him. But it is you, a man, my equal, my companion, my familiar friend. We used to take sweet counsel together; within God's house we walked in the throng. (Psalm 55:12–14)

My companion stretched out his hand against his friends; he violated his covenant. His speech was smooth as butter, yet war was in his heart; his words were softer than oil, yet they were drawn swords. (Psalm 55:20–21)

Yes, I knew the feeling of betrayal.

Even so, I could not actually pray these Psalms in regard to my brothers who had left the community, because, as St. Paul wrote, our warfare is not against flesh and blood but rather against spiritual forces. Besides, I was very much aware that my brothers were probably inclined to pray the same thing about me. Hurting as I was, I recognized even then that only God could sort all this out; only he knew the whole picture, including the thoughts and intentions of all of our hearts.

18

A Big Change

Gradually, I realized that a season had changed. The late '60s and most of the '70s had been years when the Spirit of God had been awakening people to Jesus and to the gifts of the Spirit and to community. The Jesus movement, the Charismatic Renewal, and the rise of covenant communities had been God-initiated. In those years, evangelism was relatively easy. Multiplied millions of people around the world who were hungry for God and truth and spiritual life and had professed to be born again and/or filled with the Holy Spirit. Many churches and Christian communities that were open to the working of the Spirit sprang up in the United States as people sought for teaching and mentoring in the ways of God.

However, in the late '70s and on into the '80s, many of the churches, communities, and ministries that had been born during this time of awakening began to experience a season of testing. I have no doubt now about the validity of the "hard-times prophecies." It is quite possible that the prophecies saying "structures in which we trusted were going to be shaken" concerned the as-of-yet-future shaking of denominational structures, economic structures, and civil governments, as some of us had interpreted them. However, the first thing we should have done was examine the structures that we were trusting in— which for many of us were the leadership teams and the communities with which we identified.

Personally, I was as fully committed as I knew how to be to the purposes of God and the truths that he had called us to live, to the way he was working in us and through us to conform us to his mind and to his ways. Even so, it has become clear that I had in many ways become enamored with the structures that we were building; I had failed to focus *first* on the purposes and truths that these structures were meant to manifest.

For example, living in a "covenant community" was a practical, visible way to obey the commandments to love God and to love one another. However, when the structure of our community was shaken, I sometimes found myself fighting more for the survival of the community as an entity than I was fighting for the relationships with my brothers that the community structure was meant to serve.

The season of testing revealed flaws in us and in what we had built. I have concluded that this is one of the ways God often works. God calls us and works in us, and then he allows us to go through some kind of "wilderness" as Israel did after their great deliverance out of Egypt. In the wilderness testing, God exposed the unbelief and disobedience that the people of Israel had brought with them out of Egypt.

God called Abram out of Ur and promised him offspring. However, Abram went through thirty-five years of testing and waiting before God opened Sarah's barren, elderly womb and gave Abraham and Sarah the promised son, Isaac. After Isaac's birth, God gave Abraham yet another test by commanding him to offer that promised son as a sacrifice to God. From the human standpoint, Abraham could have raised all sorts of objections to this seemingly cruel test. However, this time Abraham's immediate obedience demonstrated clearly that his full trust was in the Lord his God, not in the promise or the son whom God had given to him.

God gave 17-year-old Joseph accurate dreams about his future, but Joseph was 30, having been betrayed, enslaved, and imprisoned, before his dreams began to be fulfilled. Only later did it become clear that God had sent Joseph ahead of his family in order to save them in the time of famine. The psalmist sang about the way in which the very word of the Lord that Joseph had received in the dreams "tested him" before it was fulfilled:

> When he summoned a famine on the land
>> and broke all supply of bread,
> he had sent a man ahead of them,
>> Joseph, who was sold as a slave.
> His feet were hurt with fetters;
>> his neck was put in a collar of iron;
> until what he had said came to pass,
>> *the word of the LORD tested him.* (Psalm 105:16–19, italics added)

Jesus, himself, after he had been baptized in water and the Holy Spirit had come upon him, was "driven," Mark wrote, into the wilderness to be tempted or tested. The difference is that Jesus passed the test; there was no flaw in him to be exposed.

Thus we, too, were tested—both as individuals and as a community. Much of the testing was directly related to the words of the Lord that we had heard—words such as *discipleship, community, covenant, kingdom,* and *spiritual authority.*

When the tests came, what would we do? Would we deal with one another faithfully in covenant love, or would we revert to our old ways? Would we hold fast to God, to our calling, and to our commitments, or would we turn to our own ways (sometimes even declaring that God was leading us to do so)?

Over the years since then, I have observed what seems to be a typical pattern in the way God deals with churches and communities that he has called together. Often it seems like people come together, sometimes without much human effort, for the first two years or so. Then some sort of test comes and there is a sorting out. Those who remain are the ones who are "foundation stones" in the group.

Then, about ten years or so into the life of the church or community, there is often another season of testing. In this time, as I see it, God allows the group to reap some of the mixed seed that has been sown. Because of our fallenness, there is almost always mixture in what we say and do, and what we sow in words and in deeds, whether pure or impure, will produce a harvest in due time.

God, because of his mercy, I believe, allows some of the impurities to manifest so they can be dealt with. At that point, one option is to repent of the mixture, hold fast to the truth, endure the testing, and go on as faithfully as possible. Another option is to refuse to repent and futilely try to hold onto everything. Some seem to react in yet another way: they give in to discouragement and disillusionment and settle for something less than the revelation and calling that they had claimed to have received. Sadly, some even seem to fall away completely.

The testing proved to be disillusioning for many of us. Someone has said, "You cannot be disillusioned unless you have first had illusions." It was the grace of God to show us our illusions. As Bob Mumford taught in the 1979 Covenant Life conference, it is better to know that we have only an ounce of faith, rather than to go on to face new challenges wrongly, thinking that we have a quart of faith. When disillusionment comes, the important thing is to press through to a deeper knowledge of God and his ways and not to let it drive us away from the call of God.

In the years following the breakup of the Association of Communities and the division in the Servants of the Lord, I heard of community after community and church after church that had been born in the '70s that were going through times of testing and shaking. Some survived. Some did not.

****

The immediate crisis in our community gradually passed. We began to adjust to the loss of our friends. There were seasons of grief in the loss. It was often awkward and sad when we came into contact with those who had left; however, we who remained went on living our life together as best we could. And I discovered that, even with the pain and loss, life in community was still far better than it would have been elsewhere.

Although disappointment, seemingly with Jack, but actually with myself, had created strain on my relationship with him for a time, we had not allowed the problem to grow into a rift between us; however, we did come to the conclusion that it would be better for Bill Rademacher[68] to give me pastoral oversight. It was not until later that I realized that the Lord was using my discomfort with Jack to "stir up the nest." God was preparing me for another major change that I did not foresee.

During 1982 and into early 1983, we continued to adjust to the new reality. Because of the split, we had lost at least fifteen adult members from the community. Those leaving included four coordinators as well as a number of small group leaders. At the same time, however, we continued to add new members steadily. We also recognized new coordinators and small group leaders.

The Free Church Fellowship continued to grow in numbers as the word about our Sunday worship gathering began to spread in the community. Some who came were nondenominational by conviction. Several others came because they struggled between fulfilling their commitment to the Servants and the commitment expected of the members by their evangelical churches. And a few came to us after making a decision to leave the Roman Catholic Church. By the spring of 1983 the fellowship had grown to nearly eighty people.

Because we shared a serious commitment to ecumenical unity with the rest of our community, the Free Church leaders worked hard to help people coming to us discern whether or not they really should identify with us. This meant examining with them their decisions to leave their former churches. It also meant that we diligently sought to instruct them in our way of understanding Scripture.

The cultural aspect of life together in the Servants continued to develop also. Some of the brothers and sisters began a dinner theater that added a dimension of the arts to community life—adding some "spice" to our life together. The dinner theater provided opportunities for community members to develop and exercise a variety of gifts, including organizing, administrating, cooking, singing, and acting. The dinner

---

[68] Bill and Louis Grams had begun to serve as head coordinators along with Jack. Larry, of course, had left the community and, for personal reasons, Hal was no longer serving as a coordinator.

theater provided a great place to bring people whom we were seeking to evangelize, a place where they could experience something of the "wholistic" life in Christ that we had together in community.

In the spring of one of those years, some of our gifted artistic people put together the "Spring Fling," a first-class variety show consisting of drama and music. The woman who directed it had actually had some theater experience on Broadway and helped the Spring Fling to be an expression of excellence as well as good fun.

While community life continued to be rich and full, the winds of change were blowing, even though I was unaware of it.

****

In October 1982, the Protestants in the Servants of the Lord held a conference celebrating our heritage. I opened the conference on Friday night, October 8, with an overview of church history from a Protestant perspective. Truth be told, it was primarily an Anabaptist or free church perspective since that is the tradition with which we in the Free Church Fellowship identified most. On Saturday morning a Presbyterian pastor and a nondenominational pastor gave presentations on the authority of Scripture. Then, in the afternoon, a Lutheran pastor and a Wesleyan pastor spoke on salvation by faith. We ended the conference on Saturday night with a banquet prepared and served by a number of our Roman Catholic brothers and sisters.

During this period, we coordinators began to develop our relationship with the newly formed Fellowship of Communities. In February 1982 and again in February 1983, several of us traveled to Tempe, Arizona, to meet with leaders of communities in South Bend, Indiana; Muncie, Indiana; Tempe, Arizona; Los Angeles, California; Augusta, Georgia; and Corvallis, Oregon. The first year we dealt mostly with organizational issues. The second year we brought our wives in order to deepen the fellowship, and we began to focus on our common approach to theological issues and to the cultural challenges we all were facing.

A few weeks before the 1983 gathering, I was asked to prepare for that meeting a paper concerning the distinctive beliefs of Protestants. I threw myself into the project for three weeks and finished the paper titled "What Is Protestant Orthodoxy?" just a day or two before Patricia and I flew to Tempe along with six other couples.

243

I had no idea the impact that working on that paper would have on me. I tried to give a perspective on the great variety of beliefs represented by Protestants. Near the beginning I set forth the two main issues that Protestants hold to be different than Roman Catholic teaching:

1. The Bible is the highest and final authority given by God. As stated in "The Formula of Concord," Scripture is "the only rule and norm, according to which all dogmas and all doctores [sic] ought to be esteemed and judged."[69]

2. People are justified before God by faith alone, *sola fide*, the Reformers proclaimed.

In his book *The Protestant Faith* George W. Forell[70] identified five key emphases in Protestant teaching: grace and the sovereignty of God, faith, Scripture as the rule of faith, the priesthood of all believers, and the fallibility of man and all human institutions. After introducing these central points in Protestant thought, I went on to discuss three matters about which Protestants, although not always fully in agreement with one another, do agree that the Roman Catholic teaching is wrong, namely, the full effect of original sin, the church, and the sacraments. I ended the paper by listing some ways in which Protestants and Catholics would have to be open to one another and open to change if we were ever to come to unity in belief.

The paper, though pretty accurate about Protestant thought, reveals that I did not have a fully accurate understanding of Roman Catholic teaching. The official teaching of the Catholic Church, especially as clarified in Vatican II, is not so very different than Protestant teaching concerning several of the points I tried to make. The Catholic leaders in the Fellowship of Communities appeared to take heart from my paper since the core disagreements are in a relatively few areas of the faith.

The more I thought about it, however, the more their response mystified me. What had begun to become clearer and clearer to me because of this project was that there was little chance of coming to substantive doctrinal unity among ourselves because of one foundational issue: What is the final ground of authority?

As long as Protestants hold to the Scripture alone as the final source of authority and as long as Roman Catholics hold the Roman Catholic Church's interpretation of Scripture to be final authority, I could see no hope that we could actually agree on

---

[69] "The Formula of Concord" as translated in Philip Schaff, *The Creeds of Christendom* (New York: Harper and Brothers, 1877), Vol. Ill, pp. 93–94.

[70] Published by Prentice-Hall in 1960.

certain teachings of the faith. Faithful Roman Catholics are required to accept certain teachings about which their church has spoken definitively, including the doctrine of papal infallibility, which defines the power of the Pope to speak *ex cathedra* (from the chair). Even though the use of *ex cathedra* is rare and bounded by strict limits, it has been used to reinforce Catholic traditions, such as the bodily assumption of Mary (1950), that divide Protestants and Roman Catholics.

Therefore, unless their church were to change its position on these matters, completely honest Roman Catholics, it seemed to me, would have to choose agreement with their church or ultimately would separate themselves from it. I knew that we could love one another as brothers and sisters in Christ, but how far could we go in building our lives toward the unity Jesus prayed for us to have if we were not looking to the same source as our ground of authority?

In the fresh enthusiasm of the move of the Holy Spirit that we had shared in the earlier years, it had been my impression, naive as it may have been, that *we were all open to moving toward something new*—that what God was after was a church like it was when it had begun in Acts, a church that was neither Catholic nor Protestant. I fully believed that God was "restoring the church of the New Testament." I did not seriously consider the arguments of the Roman Catholic Church and of the Eastern Orthodox churches that they are the legitimate continuation of that church in the New Testament.

The matter of the church's unity is vital. Jesus's prayer in John 17 that the church be one just as the Father and Son are one must be taken seriously. Jesus would not have prayed for something that cannot happen; in fact, because Jesus prayed for the unity of God's people, we know that there will be unity. This I believed then and I believe now. My naivety was not that God cannot and will not bring about unity. Rather, it was naivety that did not sufficiently recognize our human inability to bring about that unity and also naivety about where we were on God's timetable.

In the years since, I have come to see that part of the struggle I was having was rooted in my own immaturity as well as in my lack of faith in God's ability. I am still working to live out unity with my brothers and sisters in Christ—with those in our local community of faith, with those from other households of faith in Winchester, and with all those with whom I have relationships wherever they may be—including my brothers and sisters in Christ who are Roman Catholic.

And, yet, I believe God was at work in my weakness to make "the nest" uncomfortable because his plan was that I serve him in a different context.

For Such a Time as This?

****

I came home from the meetings in Arizona physically drained. I had felt extra weary for a few weeks, but I had assumed it was because of the intense energy that had been invested in writing that paper in such a short amount of time. I had noticed an aching sensation on the lower right side of my abdomen from time to time but did not take it seriously. After the conference, Patricia and I had stayed in Arizona for a few extra days so that we could drive down to the border town of Nogales, Mexico. We also spent a day in Tucson, where we had a brief visit with our long-time friend Phil Conrad and also drove out to tour the former movie site, Old Tucson. However, Patricia was frustrated by the fact that I felt so weary that I wasted most of one morning lying in the motel room bed watching a movie on TV—rather a dumb movie, in fact, titled *Take This Job and Shove It.*

Shortly after returning home, I went to preach on a Sunday evening at a black Baptist church in St. Paul for the anniversary of the pastor's ministry in that church. I remember the congregation's gift to him was a set of keys to a new Mercedes Benz. Their gift to me was an enthusiastic response to my message, a response that "pulled the sermon out of me" in such a way that by the time I was done I was totally spent— spirit, soul, and body—and had sweated clear through my clothing, even my suit jacket. I was so worn out that I had to drag myself out to the car to drive back to our home in South Minneapolis.

A few days later I went to see our doctor, who diagnosed me first with mononucleosis and then, a day or two later, after blood test results came back, called to say that I also had hepatitis A and B. How I contracted hepatitis, I do not know, but it may well have been by contact with some food handler in a Minneapolis restaurant. As politically incorrect as it may be to say it these days, several times while we were living there, hepatitis outbreaks had been traced back to homosexual food handlers who were not following sanitary procedures.

The bottom line is that I was really, really sick! There was no cure except to rest while my body fought the sickness and began to recover. The doctor's orders were that I not work at all for three months, and then, he said, I could try to work a few days a week. It was actually two years or more before I had the strength to do a full work week. During that time, I had time to read—and to think.

There was much to think about. The matter of authority was often in my mind. But there was more. In the early months of 1983, at the Fellowship of Communities meeting in Arizona, I believe, the leaders from the People of Praise informed us that

246

they had come to a decision to build one international community consisting of branches in many locales, and they invited the other communities in the Fellowship to become branches. They said they would continue friendly relationships and cooperation with all as they were able but that their priority would be to build the People of Praise.

When this vision and invitation were shared with all the coordinators of the Servants, a few were inclined to join with them, but most of us were not all that interested. Jack Brombach, our overall coordinator, seemed at best ambivalent to the idea of our becoming a branch of the People of Praise, but he also did not seem to like the idea of not being in a close relationship to these brothers who had become his close friends and advisors. However, after Jack returned from that year's National Catholic Charismatic Conference, held at Notre Dame in late May or early June, he told us that he had had an encounter with the Lord in which he felt a definite call to lead the community into the People of Praise.

My personal response to Jack's testimony was to think this is probably right for the community but, at the same time, I was not at all sure that I could serve as a coordinator in the People of Praise. From my perspective, the leaders of People of Praise in South Bend had a view of Catholicism that was strongly influenced by the teaching of Thomas Aquinas, whose work Francis Schaeffer had said opened the door to an overemphasis on human reason that had come to characterize Renaissance thought and had led to the Enlightenment. And, as I understood their vision, the authoritative teaching for the whole People of Praise would be coming from the leaders in South Bend.

I discussed my reservation and questions with my wife. *If our community joins the People of Praise and I remain a coordinator, wouldn't I be implicitly giving my assent to all the teaching?* I wondered. If we disagreed with any of that teaching, wouldn't I have to come home and try to "undo the teaching" with my children?

It is highly possible that in the context of these questions, the enemy who always seeks to divide God's people began to get involved. I began to think about questions such as these: What would we do if our children grew up and wanted to marry Catholics? How could we explain to them that even though these are our brothers and sisters in Christ, no, we can't approve of such a marriage?

Looking back, I think there were real questions that needed to be asked, yet some of my questions were mixed with concern about hypothetical possibilities. Whatever the truth of that may be, I was wrestling with what this all meant for me and my family.

Just about the time I was released to begin working again, it was time for a decision regarding our community's connection. A couple weeks after Jack's experience at the Notre Dame conference, all our coordinators gathered for a retreat at his lake cabin near Nisswa, Minnesota. I do not remember if other guests were present, but Paul DeCelles came from South Bend to help answer questions any of us might have as we prayerfully deliberated the course our community should take. Paul's presence was especially significant for me because the two of us walked to Nisswa and back in order to have a time to talk.

I opened up to Paul as fully as I knew how about all my thoughts and concerns. I remember at one point we were discussing the division in the former Association of Communities and the impact of that on the Ecumenical Council of which he had been a part along with other Catholic leaders, some Lutheran leaders, and the New Wine teachers. Paul told me that, even though there had not been public division, there were great differences and tensions among the five teachers from New Wine, just as great as those which had resulted in division among the Catholic leaders. It was a helpful talk.

When we returned to the cabin, I went directly to my sleep quarters to rest. I did more thinking than actual resting.

At that retreat, the coordinators made the decision that the Servants of the Lord would become the Servant Branch of the People of Praise. I assented to the decision. I said before them all that I thought it was the right decision for Jack and that it was best for the community, but I also stated that I was not at all sure I could continue as a coordinator.

A few days afterward, I wrote a long letter to Paul DeCelles in which, after thanking him for the talks we'd had on the walk, I reported on my thoughts in the days following the retreat and that I had concluded that it would probably be best for me to resign from serving as a coordinator. I did not get to talk all this over with Bill Rademacher because he and his family had gone away on vacation immediately after the retreat; however, I made a copy of the letter and left it on his desk for him to read when he had returned—at which time my family and I were scheduled to be away on our own vacation.

****

Our family had a spectacular trip to Wyoming for vacation. We had been blessed with the birth of our second daughter Andrea in March, 1982, so there were now five of us. Having loaded our suitcases and camping gear into a beige plastic carrier fastened to the top of our 1981 silver Volkswagen Dasher station wagon, we headed out on our great adventure. We drove across South Dakota and spent the night in Belle Fourche, South Dakota, near the Wyoming border. Then, the next morning we went on to Buffalo, Wyoming, where we had lunch with our friends Bill and Nan Bagby. After lunch we drove over the Big Horn Mountains by way of Ten Sleep Pass and Canyon and stopped for the night in the little western town of Ten Sleep. The next day we traveled through the wheat country of the Big Horn Basin through Worland and on northwest to Cody, where we visited the Buffalo Bill Museum. After a night in Cody, we drove up U.S. 14 along the Shoshone River past the Buffalo Bill Dam and Reservoir into the Absaroka Mountains and on into Yellowstone National Park.

There we met Bob and Kathy Catellier and a number of other friends who were members of the Shalom Covenant Community in Casper, friends whom I had had the privilege to teach at several conferences and retreats. We all planned to stay until Monday, July 4, but soon after we arrived on Friday evening, July 1, rain began to fall. It rained most of the time for the next twenty-four hours. Since it was our first trip into Yellowstone, our family spent most of that cold, rainy Saturday driving around the park to view the vistas and wildlife.

Thankfully, the weather cleared enough for us to enjoy a picnic supper with the Shalom folks on Saturday. However, waking up Sunday morning to find snow and ice on the tent was enough of camping in Yellowstone for us. We packed up the family, drove over to see Old Faithful, then out the south exit and down to Jackson Hole, where it was about 100 degrees! Since a blistering, crowded tourist town on Sunday afternoon held no attraction, we drove on through the wide open ranch lands in western Wyoming. Out in the middle of what seemed like nowhere we came across Sitzman's Motel on the edge of the village of Farson—a motel in a setting very reminiscent of the one where Mac, Robert Duvall's character, in the 1983 movie *Tender Mercies*, awoke from his drunken stupor.

On Monday we met the Shalom group at South Pass City, where two or three hundred people (an amazing number in such a sparsely populated area) gathered for an old-fashioned 4th of July buffalo barbecue and picnic. When the afternoon got too warm to be enjoyable, several of us took the "short" (for Wyoming) drive of 114 miles to Thermopolis in the Wind River Mountains for a "refreshing" swim in the mineral hot springs. After spending the night in Thermopolis, our family headed back toward

Minneapolis by way of the Black Hills, where we drove past Mt. Rushmore and then took time to stop a while in Deadwood, where Wild Bill Hickok had once been sheriff.

A few days later, back in Minneapolis, I was able to get together with Bill Rademacher, who said: "I read your letter. Now I understand the issue. You need to be in one of the communities related to the *New Wine* teachers, and I am going to see that you are able to make that change!"

It seemed so simple and right when Bill said it. But I had not considered that as an option, not after my experience of choosing streams in 1977 while I was Hal's servant. After all, my wife and I had made covenant with the community, so in all of this, I did not entertain any thought of leaving the community. The community was our home.

Besides, we loved living in Minneapolis, and we still had a number of friends in the Waite Park Wesleyan Church. Also, I had been asked to participate in a council of elders who represented a few dozen churches in the Twin Cities, and I was eager to keep up those relationships and to see what God would do through his church in the Twin City area. But now Patricia and I began to wonder what other options there were. Where did the Lord want us?

Soon after that talk with Bill, it was time for a campout with the Free Church Fellowship that we had planned previously. We had engaged a campground in western Wisconsin for a weekend retreat, and we had asked John Meadows to come from Kentucky to be our speaker.

There is nothing to say other than that it was a great weekend any way you look at it. We had great times of prayer, John shared some excellent messages, and we had some wonderful times of recreation and fellowship and entertainment. The camaraderie and joy in being together seemed palpable.

Although I had not yet talked with anyone in the community besides Patricia about the letter to Paul DeCelles and about my recent talk with Bill Rademacher, I did talk about it with John, whom I trusted and whose counsel I valued. Thus, on Sunday afternoon, as John, his wife Vicki, Patricia, and I were driving away from the camp, headed for a few days together at our friends' cabin on Ossawinamakee Lake north of Brainerd, Minnesota, John looked at me and said, "If you were to leave the Servants, most of the people in the Free Church Fellowship would leave with you."

"No, you don't understand," I replied. "The people in the *New Wine* communities see their covenant to be first with their shepherd (personal pastor). In our community we do not do it that way; our covenant is with the whole community."

"All I know," John answered, "is that the people in this group have the same kind of relational ties and spirit that we have as a flock (those walking together with the same shepherd) in our communities. If you were to leave, most of them will want to be with you."

This was interesting to hear from John, since he had moved from Lancaster, Ohio, to Lexington, Kentucky, in order to be near his shepherd. I knew that several groups from Ohio and Florida had been moving to Lexington with their leaders. But I did not take the remark seriously. That really was not the way covenant in the Servants was meant to work. Besides, I thought, we had just gone through that split with those who followed Larry Alberts. I was not going to be part of another division! No way!

****

After the Meadows returned to Kentucky, the members of our household joined us at the cabin for a short household vacation. Once back at home, Patricia and I began to discuss our future at length. With Bill leading the way, I also began talks with him, Jack, and Louis concerning the options.

One possibility I brought up was that any members of the Free Church Fellowship who desired to do so might form a local church that would have a relationship with the community as some sort of nongeographical district. The idea sounded good at first but after some discussion didn't seem very feasible.

Another possibility discussed was that I be released to be a part of the Way of the Cross Church located in Blaine, a northern suburb of Minneapolis. Don Pfotenhauer, the senior pastor who had been a Missouri Synod Lutheran pastor and had been disfellowshipped because of speaking in tongues, had founded the nondenominational Way of the Cross church several years earlier. Eventually, Don had begun to look to Ern Baxter, one of the *New Wine* teachers, for his personal pastoral oversight. A few years before, after we started the Free Church Fellowship, he and the Way of the Cross elders, after interviewing me, had authorized me as a minister to do weddings and other ministerial responsibilities that the Servants could not do since the community was not a church. Transferring to Way of the Cross seemed to make good sense.

The third possibility, the one I considered least, was that our family move to Lexington to become part of Covenant Church of Lexington, where John Meadows was serving as an elder. I still remember the August day when, while discussing these matters with Patricia in our kitchen, she said, "We are going to move to Lexington." I brushed that off, saying something about how truly unlikely that was. After all, we belonged in Minneapolis.

By September, we had talked about the change with the full body of coordinators but no one else in the community. During this time, the maintenance man for the Servants' office building, Duane Roller, whom we met in Grand Forks and who was one of the first members of the Free Church Fellowship, began to stop in my office frequently to talk about his own thoughts. The Servants' had begun mission outreach in Central and South America. Duane was excited for the community but had been struck by the fact that all the mission activity was among Catholics. Duane processed things by talking, so again and again he would rejoice that the community was active in missions but go on to say that he longed to be part of Protestant mission activity. Several times he said, "I wonder if I belong in one of the *New Wine* communities." Duane, who died from cancer while we were caring for him in our house in 2014, was a spiritually sensitive man, a very simple man in some ways, but a man who had an uncanny ability to hear from God, usually after a good deal of inner wrestling. Duane's thoughts, especially at this time, certainly got my attention, but in my own thinking I tried to keep his wrestlings disconnected from my own situation.

Bill, Jack, Louis, and I were close to full agreement that the best option was for the Servants to release our family to the care of Don Pfotenhauer and Way of the Cross. Therefore, Don and Tom Stewart, one of the elders, came to meet with us in the Servants' office building. It was a good meeting and, by the time it was over, we had agreed on a strategy for making the transfer, including me going with the Way of the Cross brothers to an early October meeting in Columbus, Ohio, where Charles Simpson would be speaking. We had ended our visit when, as we were leaving the room, in what seemed like a spontaneous afterthought, Jack Brombach said, "I don't think you should make this decision final without visiting your friend, John, in Lexington."

Therefore, since Jack represented authority, rather than ride in the RV to the Columbus conference with the Way of the Cross brothers, Patricia and I drove to Ohio in our VW Dasher so that we could go on to Lexington, Kentucky, for a visit the following week. According to our agreement, though, I met the Way of the Cross men in Columbus and spent the nights in their RV parked outside the hotel where the conferences was held while Patricia stayed with her sister, Kay, in the nearby town of Plain City.

During that memorable conference, I had a meal with Rob Reynolds, John's personal pastor, and a late-night snack with Paul Petrie, the senior pastor at the church in Lexington. I remember sharing my story with Paul. As I finished, he looked me in the eye and said, "It was written in your spiritual DNA—you belong with us." I took that to mean that he was saying that I belonged in the *New Wine* stream of communities. Maybe he did, but maybe he had foresight that I did not have—some sense about what was soon to happen.

****

When the conference ended at noon on Sunday, Patricia came to pick me up. We drove south on U.S. 23 to Portsmouth, where we spent the night with her mother before going on to Lexington late Monday afternoon, where we planned to stay with the Meadows until Friday.

We had good fellowship with John and Vickie and their family Monday evening. As it turned out, Covenant Church elders had their all-day elders meeting on Tuesday, so I had time on my hands. While Patricia visited with Vickie, I decided to drive around just to get "the feel" of the city. While I was driving, out of the blue, for no apparent reason, I simply came to *know* that we were to move to Lexington to be part of Covenant Church.

This conviction was so strong that, as I drove, I was wondering nervously how was I to tell Patricia that there was no decision to be made. I certainly had to do that face-to-face and not in the presence of John and Vickie. Therefore, in mid-afternoon I went back to the Meadows' house and asked Patricia to come with me for a ride. I took her to Gatti's Pizza, located near Lexington Mall on Richmond Road, and I told her as we were eating pizza and drinking Pepsi, one of her favorite meals. Her response was classic: "I know that," she stated firmly. "I told you already that we would move to Lexington! I don't know why we are here. What if we don't like it? We are going to move here anyway."

I had forgotten the August conversation in our kitchen. *At least I don't have to convince her*, I thought to myself, relieved. Thankfully, we were in unity about where God wanted us to be placed in Christ's Body.

The remaining days of our time in Lexington were spent learning more about Covenant Church and about Lexington, our future home. After we returned to Minneapolis I reported our decision to the coordinators. By that time, a Sunday early in November had been set when the Servants of the Lord would officially be received as the Servant Branch of the People of Praise. It seemed best for us to be officially released from our covenant with the community before that change was final. Generously, the coordinators decided to continue my salary for six months as severance pay to see us through the transition.

We had still not talked about the decision to move with community members other than the coordinators and the members of our household. In late October we called the people in the Free Church Fellowship together for a meeting in order to let them know first that we were to be released to move to Lexington. It was no big surprise when Duane Roller came to me within a few days to say he thought he should also move to Lexington and become part of Covenant Church. But it was a huge surprise when, over the next couple weeks, several others began to come to me saying the same thing. My immediate response to all was: "Don't talk with me about it. Talk with the other coordinators. If they release you from your commitment, then come talk with me."

When the whole community came together at the November meeting during which Servants of the Lord would officially become a branch of the People of Praise, I was invited to make a statement about our going. The coordinators requested that I announce our intention to move as a personal decision for personal reasons without talking about my personal concerns regarding the People of Praise. This approach seemed right to me since I had no desire to stir up undue turmoil for the community. In the long run, however, one inevitable consequence was that many members of the community, even close friends, came away with the view that we must have had some problem with our community, especially with the leaders, and that was the "real reason" we chose to leave. Some of them felt judged and even rejected by us. Thankfully, as the years have passed we have been able to get clarity in a number of those relationships, and today we still have deep friendships with friends in Servants.

After I had announced our decision and Jack had publicly released us with the blessing of the Servants of the Lord coordinators, the Servants of the Lord ceased to exist as an autonomous community with its own covenant, and the members officially became members of the People of Praise by committing themselves to its covenant.

Shortly after this we put our house on the market. Our family did not participate in People of Praise meetings, although we did continue participating in the Free Church Fellowship until just before Christmas when we left for Ohio to spend the holidays with our families there.

19

Moving to Lexington

The most memorable part of that holiday was hearing on December 26 that Minneapolis was having an unusually large snowstorm; 20 inches fell before it was over. We left for the drive back that evening, and after driving all night were able to make it to our house on the morning of the 27th, before another 16 inches buried us on the 28th.

Upon entering the house, we found part of our dining room ceiling had fallen. An ice bridge had built up in a valley on the roof, and heavy snow on top of the ice had caused heat escaping from the poorly insulated house to melt ice; therefore, with nowhere else to go, water had found a way into the attic and then down through the ceiling. Minneapolis had a record-breaking 109 inches of snow that winter.

After we repaired the ceiling, two of our friends from the Servants, Ron Wolfe and Bill Mitchell, professional painters, came over and, in one evening, made quick work of painting the ceiling of the living room and dining room area. We had listed the house with Steve Nichols, a realtor and another friend from community. He showed it as often as he could, but there were few lookers and no offers during that long winter.

In January, Bill Rademacher, a pilot, rented a plane and flew me to Lexington, where he formally turned over my pastoral care to John Meadows. There are no adequate words to describe the love and care Bill demonstrated during this transition process. I remain deeply grateful.

In addition to transitioning pastoral care, I had two other purposes for taking this trip to Kentucky. One was to go with Covenant elders and cell group leaders to Mobile, Alabama, for a week of pastoral training led by four of the *New Wine* teachers— Charles Simpson, Bob Mumford, Ern Baxter, and Don Basham. Before returning to Minneapolis, I also spent some time in Lexington beginning the search for a job.

I made two or three more trips to Lexington to hunt for a job between then and the end of March. I had one excellent interview at the Lexington office of Portman Equipment Company, which sold Clark forklifts and other material-handling equipment. They were looking for a person between the ages of 35 and 42, married, involved in church and/or other service-oriented social groups, and with no sales experience. That was me! Mr. Brooks, who interviewed me in Lexington, told me the company preferred inexperienced sales people whom they could train in their ways from the beginning. They preferred married people because they tended to be more reliable and stable long-term employees. And they wanted people who had an interest in serving the community. The interview seemed to go well.

A few days later, Mr. Brooks called to set up an appointment for me to go to the company's headquarters office in northeast Cincinnati to be interviewed by William Portman, the founder and CEO. It was impressive, I must say, to walk in the front door of the office building and to see, first of all, a sign welcoming me by name as a guest that day.

A few minutes later Mr. Portman took me to his office, an office most noticeable because it was simple and "countrified," not elegant and impressive, except for the mounted heads of several exotic animals that decorated the walls. That interview also seemed to go well. A key question was, "Why are you moving from Minneapolis to Lexington?"

This was a question I had prepared for. It did not seem wise to emphasize "religious-sounding" reasons for our move, but I could not be deceptive either. I told him that one draw was that we would be living closer to Patricia's aged mother and to my parents, who were getting older also. I went on to say that we had good friends in the Lexington Covenant Church, which had the same kind of emphasis on building strong relationships among the members as the Christian community we had been part of in Minneapolis. Rather than talk about theological matters, though, I simply said the Bible has a strong emphasis on living out our faith in strong relationships of love and service to one another and that we were committed to that kind of lifestyle. I left Mr. Portman's office without a job offer, but the conversation we had seemed to have been positive. He certainly seemed like the kind of person who would be a good employer.

In late March, Mr. Brooks called to say that Portman Equipment Company wanted to hire me, but that, as an entry-level sales person, they would not pay to move me there. He said that once I had sold our house in Minneapolis and had moved to Lexington I should come to see him and the job would be mine. Of course, that was gratifying, but there were as yet no prospects for selling the house, and the six-month severance pay was to end in April, so how were we to survive financially?

****

In the meantime, a number of people from the Free Church Fellowship had indeed been talking with the Servants coordinators and had gone on to ask for release from the community in order to move to Lexington. I heard bits and pieces of that but, for integrity's sake, did not engage in conversation about it. I did know, of course, that the three women and one of the men in our household, all members of the Free Church Fellowship, were involved in that process, but Patricia and I did our best not to influence them one way or another.

Around mid-March 1984, the coordinators sent letters to those asking to be released. The biggest part of each letter was common to all, appearing to be an official statement, basically saying we do not understand why you think you should leave, we do not think you need to leave, but the decision is up to you to make. The rest of each letter was personal and geared toward the individual recipient, and from what I heard some sounded more understanding than others.

The bottom line is that people began to come to me to say they had decided to move to Lexington with us to be part of Covenant Church. Although it was meaningful that people loved us and wanted to continue our relationship, it was not easy for me to hear. First, based on the experience of division when people left the community in 1981, it seemed likely that for most Servants' members this, too, would seem divisive. I thought it likely that people would think I wanted people to move.

Second, it was scary to think that I would have pastoral responsibility for a number of individuals and families moving 800 miles to a city and church they did not know. Therefore, when people came to me, in almost every case, my response after listening and asking questions was something like this: "This is a big decision. It will almost certainly have unexpected challenges and difficulties. The change in geography and culture may be hard, and the church will not be perfect. If God will let you do anything else besides move to Lexington, you should." However, not many were dissuaded, and over the next two years about thirty-five adults, along with more than thirty children, made the move.

In early April, John Meadows called with big news. Since I was moving to Lexington with pastoral responsibility for people, the elders had decided that our Minnesota group should come as a flock and integrate into the church as a flock along with the seven or eight other flocks into which pastoral responsibility was already divided among the elders. John said, "We decided to put you on the payroll right away so that you can be caring for the people as you all prepare to move and then are making the moves."

Wow! The house had not sold and we had not moved, but I had a job in Lexington! In fact, the first paycheck from Covenant Church came at essentially the same time as our last check from the Servants. I called Mr. Brooks, truthfully with some regret, to say that I would not be working for Portman Equipment. He wished me well and said that, if my situation changed, the opportunity would still be there.

****

Patricia and I had begun to look at houses on the early trips to see if there might be one we could purchase if and when ours sold. With our realtor, Jerry Galloway, a member of Covenant Church, we looked at many, many houses. But we did not think it wise to make an offer on any until our house in Minneapolis was at least under contract.

Near Memorial Day, a woman came to look. She did not seem like much of a prospect, but a day or so later she made an offer and put down earnest money on the house. Now it was time to get a house in Lexington—quickly; since Patricia was unable to make the trip, I went alone.

All the houses we had looked at previously had either been sold or were not the right house for one reason or another. I looked at several more. Then one day, while in desperation I was driving around on my own with a copy of the MLS listings, I came across a little 1½-story Cape Cod in Lexington's Southland area that had a "For Sale" sign out front. I called our realtor, who made an appointment for me to see it. Although it was not fancy, it was a nice house with four bedrooms and a walk-out basement with a finished room perfect for cell meetings as well as for family activities. It had only one bathroom, but it would be adequate for our family.

It was close to our price range, although a little high. To help us qualify for a loan, the Covenant elders gave us a small raise—before we had even moved, remember, and before I could take on any new responsibilities within the community. After consulting with Patricia by phone and trying to describe the house in words—no cell phone with cameras, no texting, and no emailing in those days—I made an offer and it was accepted, with a closing date on July 31.

Back at home we started to prepare to move. Then the woman who had made the offer on our Minneapolis house told the realtor she wanted to come back and look at it with her boyfriend. When they arrived and started to walk around looking over the property, both Patricia and I had the feeling that this was not a good thing; something about it just seemed wrong. So, while it was hugely disappointing, we were not too surprised when the realtor called later to say she had withdrawn her offer.

The only "good news" was that she did not insist on having the earnest money returned.

I've been sharing a long story here. Here's why. The Lord clearly had led us through the process of making the decision to leave the Servants and to move to Covenant Church. The Lord had stirred others to move with us. He had provided me a job and even a pay increase before we moved. I should have been able to meet this setback with faith and expectation of good, right? That's not what happened. Instead, I began to sink into despair and depression.

When the sale fell through, we decided to try to sell the house ourselves so that we could lower the price a little. We put up a "For Sale by Owner" sign. On a late Friday afternoon early in July, two men and a woman came by to look at the house. The impression we had of the man who seemed to be leading the group was that he was something of a fast talker, a high-pressure sort of person, like the proverbial used-car salesman. Before leaving he made an offer and wanted to give us earnest money. It caused us consternation; therefore, we took time to seek advice from a neighbor who was a lawyer. He offered to look over our paperwork at no charge. When he told us the paperwork was legitimate, we signed it.

On Monday, the buyer called to say he had changed his mind and wanted his earnest money back, which, by law, people in Minnesota can do within three days of making an offer. It was almost a relief to give his money back, but it left us with no prospects for selling the house with less than a month until we were to close on the house in Lexington.

We talked with our realtor in Lexington and decided to wait—and to pray diligently—until July 30 before informing the sellers of the house there that we could not close if no buyer came. That July was hot, hot, hot, even in Minnesota. Depression deepened. I was fearful and angry. I spent a lot of time in our basement, half-dressed, sitting or lying on a mattress that lay on the floor, because it was cooler, yes, but also because I was trying to hide from people and reality.

I tried to pray and read the Bible but got little relief. The only Scriptures that made sense were some of the psalms. Thank God for the honesty of psalmists who were not afraid to sing out their fear and frustration as well as their faith and hope. They expressed their feelings openly to God in words that I would not have dared to say to him myself.

My soul also is greatly troubled.
  But you, O LORD—how long?
Turn, O LORD, deliver my life;
  save me for the sake of your steadfast love.
For in death there is no remembrance of you;
  in Sheol who will give you praise?

I am weary with my moaning;
  every night I flood my bed with tears;
  I drench my couch with my weeping.
My eye wastes away because of grief;
  it grows weak because of all my foes. (Psalm 6:3–7)

Why, O LORD, do you stand far away?
  Why do you hide yourself in times of trouble?" (Psalm 10:1)

No one came to see the house or even ask about it until Saturday afternoon, July 29. Then a lady who appeared to be about retirement age came. She looked the house over and expressed interest in it, especially when she saw the bedroom space. She told us that her intention was to open a group home for special-needs people. We told her that we had to have an answer by the next day because we had to say something to our sellers in Lexington.

She made no contact that Sunday. Finally, late that evening, I called the realtor to say we had no deal. The closing there was set for early the next morning. He said that there was no way to contact the sellers so late in the evening; rather, he would have to tell them at the actual closing appointment.

I wish I could say I responded to this with great faith and trust. Not so. I tried to get it turned over to the Lord, but I was crushed!

At 8:30 a.m. on Monday, the lady called to say she was ready to bring an offer and earnest money. *That's just great*, I thought: *too little, too late.*

I called the realtor, who was already at the scheduled closing, where he had just told the sellers we had reneged on our deal. I told him that we had a new offer coming. He consulted with the sellers. They were already in the process of moving to Virginia for new jobs and since they had no other good option, they agreed to extend the contract to August 22, the absolute final day.

We signed the purchase agreement for the Minneapolis house. Because we had agreed to let the lady assume our FHA loan, at risk to ourselves if she defaulted, there was less red tape and she did not have to go through rigorous qualifying examinations. Closing was set for early morning on Wednesday, August 20.

****

We set about getting everything ready to move in order to leave immediately after the closing. We now had some hope, but still we knew everything could fall through anytime. I was quite aware that I was no superstar Christian.

Two things happened in the days just before the closing that are quite memorable. The first was wonderful. A few months after we had moved to that house, a couple with a young daughter had moved next door. Willie, the husband, was quite a few years older than his wife, whose parents we eventually discovered were members of the Servants of the Lord and lived not far away. Willie had worked for New England Bell for thirty years and retired. He had taken a job with Amoco Oil in Minneapolis.

Willie was a *character*. He had long, gray hair, not at all common for men his age in those days. He loved to set his stereo speakers out on his porch on sunny Saturdays and play music—really loud music—for the neighborhood. One of his favorite recordings was Willie Nelson and Leon Russell's double LP: *One for the Road*. In my memory, I can still hear their version of Hank William's "I Saw the Light" blasting out for all to hear.

Willie was devoted to marijuana and alcohol. Thankfully, he did not drive. He carried a flask to work in his hip pocket when he rode the Metro Transit bus to work and back. It was not unusual for Willie, on days when the weather was decent, to get off the bus at Nicollet Avenue South and West 40th Street and to go into Martin Luther King Park, where he would sit and enjoy a joint before walking the three blocks home. Eventually, I came to the realization that Willie had at least some alcohol in his system all the time, but on Saturdays and Sundays he drank freely.

Several times on Saturday afternoons, when well into his cups, Willie asked me to come over to his house, where he wanted to talk philosophy and religion. I learned that as a young man he had studied under Jean-Paul Sartre in France. Later he had dropped acid (LSD) with Timothy Leary. Willie really knew philosophy, especially existentialism and the modern philosophies of despair. I was able to carry on a conversation with him on these matters only because I had read Francis Schaeffer's work. Even so, I felt out of my league, but the insights gained from Schaeffer must have been the right ones. How well I remember Willie's words on one of the Saturdays. Leaning back in his chair, his eyes seeming to look into me, he said: "You amaze me. You've been through all these things I have, yet you still believe."

I had had no idea that he was talking with me thinking that I had journeyed experientially through the contemporary philosophies like he had. Reflecting on that conversation later, I realized that Willie drank and smoked pot not for enjoyment but to dull the pain of philosophical despair. He could not stand to live with no hope of there being "true truth" or any valid reason to have hope for a meaningful future without anesthetizing himself against the emptiness. His words revealed that he was a seeker who had come to believe there is nothing to seek. He saw that I had hope and that I had confidence in the one who is Truth and that I had someone and something to live for. Clearly, Willie wished he did too.

While we were trying to sell our house, I had purchased a copy of the *Good News for Modern Man* version of the New Testament and also a copy of Schaeffer's *Escape from Reason* and had given them to Willie. On the flyleaf of the Schaeffer book I wrote a note saying that Willie reminded me of the lyrics from a song that he had often played for the neighbors: "I've always been crazy but it's kept me from going insane" (Waylon Jennings) and that I had found Schaeffer's book helpful in understanding the hopeless plight of many in our culture.

Two evenings before we were scheduled to close on the house, Willie called to say he needed to talk to me. Even though our Free Church Fellowship friends were gathered at our house for a time of prayer and worship, I sensed that my priority should be to talk with Willie. He met me on his front porch, blurting out urgently, "I've been reading the book you gave me." I assumed he meant the Schaeffer book until he continued, "If a man really believed that book, he would have to give up everything he has!"

Then I realized that Willie was talking about *Good News for Modern Man* and that he was actually taking Jesus's words seriously in such passages as these:

> Once when large crowds of people were going along with Jesus, he turned and said to them, "Those who come to me cannot be my disciples unless they love me more than they love father and mother, wife and children, brothers and sisters, and themselves as well. Those who do not carry their own cross and come after me cannot be my disciples. If one of you is planning to build a tower, you sit down first and figure out what it will cost, to see if you have enough money to finish the job. If you don't, you

will not be able to finish the tower after laying the foundation; and all who see what happened will make fun of you. 'You began to build but can't finish the job!' they will say. If a king goes out with ten thousand men to fight another king who comes against him with twenty thousand men, he will sit down first and decide if he is strong enough to face that other king. If he isn't, he will send messengers to meet the other king to ask for terms of peace while he is still a long way off. In the same way," concluded Jesus, "none of you can be my disciple unless you give up everything you have. (Luke 14:25–33, GNT)

Then Jesus said to his disciples, "If any of you want to come with me, you must forget yourself, carry your cross, and follow me. For if you want to save your own life, you will lose it; but if you lose your life for my sake, you will find it. Will you gain anything if you win the whole world but lose your life? Of course not! There is nothing you can give to regain your life. (Matthew 16:24–26, GNT)

Nearly awestruck, I responded: "Willie, you are very close to the kingdom of God. I know many professing Christians who do not see this clearly."

We went on to talk a bit longer, and then I prayed for him to be fully enlightened and to be able to surrender himself to Jesus. As I left to return to the meeting with my Christian friends, my heart cried out for Willie to know the Truth! I have never been able to find out what followed in his life after we moved, but I truly hope I will see my friend when we gather around Jesus's throne in the age to come.

The second memorable thing happened the next night when several friends came over to help pack our belongings into the 26-foot Penske truck I had rented. Once it had been packed, one of the brothers started to back the truck farther into the driveway in order to get it clear of the street. There was an awful crunching noise— the truck had run into the gutter that went around the porch! The truck was not damaged, but the spouting and the eaves were. The brother driving promised to see that it was fixed after we moved, but there was nothing to be done at 10 o'clock that night.

****

The closing started early the next morning, August 20, at our lawyer neighbor's office. The first order of business was to inform the buyer that there was damage to the house and to try to assure her that it would be fixed quickly. We put our commitment into writing and she accepted it, understandably, a bit reluctantly.

When we got down to the business, we started signing the paperwork. All was well until it came time for her to give the down payment money; then she handed us a cashier's check for an amount that was more than $2,000 less than it should have been. When we asked where the rest of the down payment was, she offered some confusing rationale for why she only owed the amount she had given us. The lawyer tried numerous times to explain why the amount she had given was insufficient, but she just could not seem to understand. Meanwhile, Patricia and I were praying! After this had gone on for more than 30 minutes, I suddenly had an inspiration—from the Lord, I'm sure—about how to explain the matter, and this time she finally understood.

Then the woman started to write a personal check for the remainder. There was no way we could accept that! We had to get the money into our bank account and have it cleared so that we could get a cashier's check ourselves to take to the closing of the Lexington house on the morning of August 22! It took a while for our buyer to accept that reality also, but finally she began to scramble to get the rest of the money. It became clear that she simply did not have the funds on hand and that there was no way to get us cash that day.

Finally, our lawyer, who was serving us free of charge because we were neighbors and because our sons were friends, offered that if she could get money transferred to his law office's account, he would have his bank issue us a cashier's check.

Finally, the buyer made a call from the lawyer's phone, which I could not help but overhear, to her credit card company, Citibank South Dakota. After a long discussion, she convinced them to wire money to the lawyer's account. And they did, but it was after 2:30 in the afternoon before the transfer happened. There was no way for us to finish signing paperwork and drive to the bank before it closed at 3 o'clock. However, the lawyer contacted a bank officer, explained the situation, and was able to arrange for us to pick up the check at the drive-through window after the bank had already closed.

It was 3:30 p.m. by the time we got the check. We left the bank and went to pick up our children, who had been staying with friends, and then drove back to our former house to get the truck. It was 5 p.m. on Wednesday evening when we started the long trip to Lexington, with me driving the truck and Patricia driving our car.

Although it was about 100 miles farther, we had chosen to drive by way of Iowa, rather than to try to go through Chicago driving the two vehicles. We drove about as long a time as the children and the drivers could stand that evening before we stopped at an Iowa motel along Interstate 80 east of Des Moines. The next day we drove and drove and drove, but there were lots of stops with children and with both adults driving. Finally, about 1 a.m. on August 22, we arrived at the Meadows' home in Lexington.

Thankfully, the next morning our realtor was able to postpone our closing until early afternoon, giving us time to open a bank account and arrange to have the appropriate check in hand for the buyers.

Nothing had seemed to come easy in the move to Lexington. We never questioned that it was God's will for us to make the change; however, I certainly discovered my need for the fruit of the Spirit to come to maturity within me. Joy, peace, patience, and perseverance were often in short supply, and the lack showed up in relationships. It was difficult to act loving, gentle, and kind to others, especially to my family, when inside I was feeling pressured, anxious, and often angry about the seeming resistance, the disappointments, and the delays we faced.

Finally, we had arrived and we had purchased the house on Millbrook Drive without Patricia having ever been inside it. Thankfully, from the start she loved the place and quickly made it truly "home" for our family. We also arrived just a few days before Covenant Church's tenth-anniversary celebration began.

Although Covenant had purchased a building at 2700 Todds Road only a year or two earlier, these celebration meetings were held in Heritage Hall, part of the Lexington Center in the downtown area of the city. Many special guests traveled to Lexington to celebrate with us, including the guest speaker, Charles Simpson, one of the *New Wine* teachers.

At last we have passed through our wilderness and have come to the place of rest, I thought!

20

Testing Continues

I am not the person to write a history of Covenant Church in Lexington; however, some background is necessary to my own story. Therefore, based on what I have heard from others and from what I remember from my own experience, here is a little about this community of which we were now members.

Covenant *Church* was a relatively new name for the community there in Lexington. Until not too long before our visit in 1983, they were Covenant Community. Although this community was not ecumenical in the same sense that the Servants of the Lord was, it certainly did not have the history of a typical evangelical church— even of a nondenominational church. People came to it from all sorts of Christian backgrounds, and some had no Christian background at all. In the early years especially, a number continued to worship on Sunday mornings in whatever churches they had been participating in previously.

In 1968, Paul Petrie, his wife Rebecca, and several others had begun a ministry called Christ Center in an old school building near downtown Lexington, and a number of people actually lived there communally. The Petries and at least some of the others had been students at Asbury College (now Asbury University) in the small nearby town of Wilmore. Part of the inspiration for Christ Center was David Wilkerson's Teen Challenge, the ministry that had grown out of David's call to minister to members of New York City gangs.[71]

Christ Center was located on South Mill Street in the building that would some years later be known as Historic Dudley Square. The members of Christ Center actively shared the gospel with people from the streets, many from the counterculture and many involved in drug use. A good number of young people, both churched and also unchurched, were attracted to the ministry, and it became one of the early local expressions of the Jesus Movement—before the movement had been named or even recognized. In the early 1970s, Paul and Rebecca spent a couple years on mission in Europe and then lived for some time in Fort Lauderdale for more training as disciples after they became related pastorally to the *New Wine* teachers.

---

[71] David Wilkerson with John and Elizabeth Sherrill, *The Cross and the Switchblade* (New York: Pyramid Books, 1962). This book had significant influence and contributed greatly to the Charismatic Renewal and the Jesus Movement. Republished many times, it is still available.

In 1974, Paul moved his family back to Lexington where, joining together with some people from the Christ Center days and others involved in a nondenominational Bible study, they founded Covenant Community. Because words such as *church* and *pastor* have, over the centuries, taken on meanings and connotations well beyond the meanings in the Scriptures, this congregation, like many others in the discipleship movement, chose to use words such as *shepherd* (the actual translation of the Latin word *pastor*) and *community*, which is a fitting word for the life shared together by those who became followers of Jesus—the type of life described in Acts 2:42–48, for example.

By 1980, Covenant Community of Lexington was one of the "bright lights" among the "discipleship" communities, and several groups began to move to Lexington in order to consolidate their efforts, as had happened in the Servants in 1977 and 1978. The Meadows and another couple had moved from Lancaster, but a number of people from small churches in communities north of Lancaster also moved there with their pastors about that same time. In the early 1980s, groups from communities in Miami and Jacksonville and other locations in Florida also began moving to Lexington to be part of the community. While our group was in the process of moving from Minneapolis, a community from Norman, Oklahoma, began to move to Lexington as well. By 1985 there were ten elders in the church, most of whom had moved with a flock, all working full-time. Several were receiving part of their support from the tithes of leaders whom they were discipling in other cities.

During the early months that we were in the church, we were setting up about 550 folding chairs in the main room of our building on the first and third Sunday morning meetings each month, when all the flocks came together. It was common for the seats to be full, with as many as 25–50 more seated on the floor near the stage from which the worship team led us in singing and where speakers for any given Sunday ministered. Worship in song was robust! Church started at 10 a.m. Prayer ministry was available for people following the service. It was not unusual for us to get home at 2 p.m. or even later after praying with people. Excitement was in the air, at least for those of us who were new.

Each of the elders met with our own local flocks in a variety of locations on the second and fourth weekends of each month. Our flock usually met in the basement of our home unless we had a picnic in a park. We did not have meetings on the fifth Sundays, but we encouraged families and small groups to make the day special together. The flock structure helped those of us who had moved from Minnesota by providing secure relationships during the transition, but that structure also meant "meetings" were not the best means for integrating relationally into the larger community.

New Covenant Academy, Covenant's K–12 school, provided families another opportunity to be involved with each other. Some of our flock members became part of the worship team. Several members of the church went out of their way to be hospitable and to include people from Minnesota in their activities.

Overall, those first months were a positive time. Some from our group, however, were facing difficult financial times. One brother, for example, had been basically a stay-at-home dad, caring for the children and adding a little to the family income by giving music lessons while his wife worked at her accounting job. The couple had become convinced that he should be the family breadwinner, so he was doing everything he could to start a piano-tuning business, from scratch, in Lexington. For at least a little while, he came to Lexington alone and borrowed a phone in someone's office or home (no cell phones in those days!) and just started going through the Lexington phone directory seeking business. Then, for two or three months that first summer and fall, he and his family lived in a tent at the Lexington Horse Park campgrounds before they were finally able to get into a house. Talk about sacrifice to follow God's call!

Another brother who had a wife and four sons had worked as a loan officer in a St. Paul bank. Through some contact back in Minnesota, he was offered the opportunity to start a mortgage company in Lexington. So the family bought a home and moved, and he set up a full office for his company and began seeking business, all based on promises of financial support he'd been given—support that never came through. He struggled in that business for about two years before he had to declare bankruptcy both in the company and personally and then had to make a new start financially.

There were some who did well also. I remember one brother driving down with me to job-hunt on the trip when I came down alone to find a house for our family. In Minneapolis he had done maintenance work in a large office building. Before coming to Lexington, he had done some research and, as we drove out of downtown Lexington on South Main Street, he pointed out a sign identifying the site as a construction project of the well-known (but not to me) Webb Companies, owned by developers Donald and Dudley Webb.

"That's who I am going to work for," the brother declared. And he did. He got an interview with the company a few days later and soon moved his wife and their infant twin sons to Lexington, where he began to manage maintenance in several of the Webb Companies' buildings. Not only did he get a job with Webb Companies, but later he was able to help another brother from Minneapolis, whose first job did not pan out well, get a good position with the Webb Companies also.

For most of the families especially, however, it was a difficult move from a financial standpoint. I was very glad that I had not asked people to move but had encouraged them to move only if they were truly sure it was God's call. I tried to encourage and support them as well as I could.

My work those first months in the church, besides caring for the flock, was focused on teaching English and U.S. history at New Covenant Academy. In addition, I took part in the weekly elders meetings getting acquainted with my fellow elders, learning how they went about their work of praying and planning and leading in the church, and contributing when I could.

****

Gradually I became aware that not all was as well in the church as it had seemed to be. Just before the first of our people had moved to Lexington in early June, Covenant had begun the process I have described as "reaping the fruit of mixed seed sown." John Meadows had phoned me in May to say that he was sending a cassette tape of an important "family meeting" of people in the church. We had regularly been receiving tape recordings of Sunday services already in order to help us make the transition. This tape was different, he said; it was important because some issues had arisen in the church and that they had recorded the meeting of members during which the problems had been discussed. John did not want me and the others moving from Minneapolis to be surprised that all was not well. I listened to the tape, of course, but I did not have enough background information to truly understand some of the concerns people raised and certainly not the depth of hurt and offense that it turned out at least a few carried.

It turned out that it was not just Covenant Church of Lexington in which problems were surfacing, but similar things were coming to light in a number of the "discipleship" churches. The shepherding movement had been controversial, at first, largely among several nondenominational leaders who saw the growing number of people entering covenantal relationships and looking to the five *New Wine* teachers for leadership as a threat and competition.[72] Even by 1977 at the Kansas City

---

[72] Within a few years the discipleship movement, also often labeled the shepherding movement, was to grow quickly, but not without controversy. S. David Moore has written a definitive history of the movement in his book *The Shepherding Movement: Controversy and Charismatic Ecclesiology*. Moore, who in his younger years had personal experience in

conference, the controversy had become such an issue that it had led to two different nondenominational groups meeting in two different venues at a conference called to celebrate and foster unity among God's people.

Using terms such as *shepherd* and *community* had also become controversial, especially for people who had only a contemporary cultural, rather than a Biblical, understanding of what it means to be a church community. The word *covenant*, while a prominent theme in Scripture, had fallen into disuse among many evangelicals (as well as in the larger culture), and the use of the word *covenant* to describe personal relationships between brothers in Christ was simply not understood by many. Even the word *disciple* was not commonly used in many churches except when talking about the Twelve whom Jesus called to be apostles. Among evangelicals, the Navigators were among the few to use the term, and even they used it to talk more about helping someone get grounded in Biblical knowledge through Scripture memorization than to refer to mentoring relationships established to lead people into mature spiritual formation in Christ.

To complicate matters more, such words and the efforts made to live out these Biblical truths had been disparaged and treated pejoratively by Christian leaders who opposed the shepherding movement. Therefore, in the early 1980s, Covenant Community had bought a "church building" rather than continue to meet in rented facilities and had gone back to using the common American terminology *church* and *pastor*, in an effort to avoid misunderstanding and to counteract the accusations that they were cult-like.

Some leaders outside the movement had expressed deep concern, often using inflammatory language, that for people to have a personal shepherd (pastor) or to be a disciple of anyone other than Jesus was unbiblical, heretical, and an error that opened the door to spiritual abuse.

Truthfully, there were mistakes made. Looking back, as I see it the vast majority of leaders and people in the discipleship movement were young and inexperienced either as leaders or in following Jesus or both, hence the desire to be discipled that so many of us had. Inevitably, youth and inexperience and zeal did indeed sometimes lead to errors in the application of spiritual authority. As in any group of people, there were most likely some who were self-serving in the way they treated disciples. In

---

one of the churches connected to this movement, thoroughly researched and evaluated it and wrote it up as his doctoral dissertation. Therefore, there is no need for me to rewrite all that, even though it is important background to my own story.

Covenant Church and in the discipleship movement, at least some of the problems that surfaced appeared to have been related to immature and unwise leadership.

I had not been in the discipleship movement during the early days and so I cannot speak about such things from my own experience. My experience of pastoral care was positive; those to whom I looked as representing pastoral authority in Grand Forks and in Minneapolis did not mistreat me but rather served me well. Some were indeed young and inexperienced and had much zeal, but I profited from the leadership I received.

For example, the call to be a servant and to show honor and respect to leaders had been a life-changing reality in my life, something essential to my growth in Christ. But in the "discipleship" culture, too much emphasis was put on serving the one to whom a person looked for leadership. Serving, as it was understood, had in far too many cases been seen and experienced as an action that went in one direction, from the person "under" a shepherd "up" to the shepherd.

There is nothing Biblically wrong with a person serving the one who is discipling him; in fact, it is part of the training process. More than that, serving is at the core of what it means to be a human being reflecting the image and likeness of God. When the Son of God became a man, he became a servant because humans were created to serve God.

In the Upper Room on the evening before Jesus was crucified, Jesus plainly talked about servanthood being a part of discipleship, when he said to the Twelve he had chosen and trained:

> Greater love has no one than this, that someone lay down his life for his friends. You are my friends if you do what I command you. **No longer do I call you servants, for the servant does not know what his master is doing; but I have called you friends, for all that I have heard from my Father I have made known to you.** You did not choose me, but I chose you and appointed you that you should go and bear fruit and that your fruit should abide, so that whatever you ask the Father in my name, he may give it to you. These things I command you, so that you will love one another. (John 15:13–17, bold print added for emphasis)

However, Jesus also made it plain that it was not his goal to be served, saying, "... The Son of Man came not to be served ..."; rather, he went on to say, the Son of Man came "... to serve, and to give his life..." (Matthew 20:28).

Jesus is the ultimate example of servanthood in the way he served the Father and in the way he serves those he leads—by training and leading us, by protecting and overseeing us. His obedience in accepting death on the cross (Philippians 2:5–8) in order to save us who were under the tyranny of death and the devil (Hebrews 2:14–15, Colossians 1:13) is the ultimate example of serving motivated by love (Galatians 5:13).

To be a disciple of Jesus is to be a servant; to be a human is to be a servant. Jesus the "new Man," the "last Adam," is a servant. Since Jesus is also "the whole fullness of deity" dwelling in a body (Colossians 2:9), and since he is the "radiance of God's glory and the exact imprint of his nature ..." (Hebrews 1:3), we know that God also serves as the One who is Love.

Again, serving is not wrong. Serving is the high privilege of love. But if serving becomes the fulfillment of an obligation separated from an expression of other-centered love (*agape*)—whether on the part of the one being served or of the one doing the service—then serving has become something other than an expression of God's glory and is in vain.

In my opinion, the leaders whom I came to know in Lexington had not sought personal advancement or intentionally used people wrongly, but they apparently had not made it clear enough that "leading" in God's kingdom is simply a form of service, not some sort of exalted status and position of privilege. And I think it would have been wiser if they had made it clearer, by example, that no task was beneath the dignity of a leader, that all of us are called to "be" servants who serve in whatever way is necessary at any given time.

In the Lexington church, there was a further complicating matter. A number of the brothers who had started in the community early had become cell group leaders, and some had trained others who had also become leaders of cells. Some of these brothers had come to believe that once they were discipling and caring for ten men or more, they would become "full-time" leaders, supported by the tithes of those with whom they worked. It was disappointing and hurtful to some of them that, instead of becoming elders themselves, several leaders had moved to Lexington from other places and had become elders in the church. In effect, though I doubt consciously, some may have been serving for personal recognition and advancement, which is not "the way of the kingdom."

Another problem, it seemed to me, was that some people because of their immaturity had relinquished too much personal responsibility for their own decisions to the shepherd/pastor caring for them. By God's grace I had developed enough maturity in Christ that, when I began to look to another brother for pastoral oversight, I sought to listen to what he said as "unto the Lord." However, if I did not have peace with the counsel I was given, I would talk it through with that brother until we were in as much agreement as possible. I realized that I was responsible before God for my own actions and that I would need to give account to God myself.

Also, I came to understand that it was not wisdom, indeed it was not right, for me to use the counsel of my pastor as a way of putting my wife and family under obligation. It was manipulative for me to try to get the "right" response from my wife by saying, "My pastor says we need to ...." And it was not right for me to say to my children, "You cannot do that because our church says ...." God had made me the husband and father, the leader and caregiver of my family, not another. I needed to lead out of my own conviction and to allow my family to work through things with me, just as I needed to work through things with my leader.

Ultimately, we all belong to Jesus and we are each responsible to him; he is the one head of the Church, his body (Ephesians 1:22–23, Colossians 1:18). And Christ, Scripture teaches, is the head of every man (1 Corinthians 11:3, in which the context concerns the family).

****

Those of us moving from Minneapolis to Covenant Church did not have the same history, so we did not readily see the underlying turmoil at work among people who had been in the church for several years. We saw a building full of people worshipping God enthusiastically when we came to a Sunday meeting. We did not understand that some people were leaving the church offended and hurt, even while others were moving in. We did not see the losses clearly, but we were well aware that new people were being welcomed in. On the surface all seemed well to us.

Then a fresh working of the Holy Spirit began among us. Although I had not known the dynamics of it, I was aware that Rob Reynolds, one of my fellow elders, was going through a difficult time. However, not long after we had moved to Lexington, Rob attended a meeting where the late John Wimber, founder of the Vineyard movement, was ministering in teaching and in prayer, and Rob was deeply refreshed. At his urging, Paul Petrie made a trip to Little Rock, Arkansas, in the fall of 1984 near the holiday season in order to meet John Wimber and to attend one of his meetings. Without going into detail, I will simply say that Paul had a powerful, fresh encounter with Jesus at that meeting.

After Paul's return to Lexington, I remember well when we elders met with him in a secluded sitting room of his home where we sometimes had our elders meetings. He and Rob shared the testimonies of their encounters with the Lord at the meetings with Wimber, and they began to describe the phenomena which took place in these meetings.

Although I believed in the spiritual gifts and believed that the Holy Spirit sometimes moves in unusual ways, their description of people doing things like shaking violently, breaking out in loud laughter or weeping, and falling down in response to the Holy Spirit … well, I received their words cautiously, I must say. Although I spoke in tongues and I had seen healings and I had experienced other gifts of the Spirit, in my own experience and perception, these activities, while led by the Spirit, were done with the willful cooperation of the person being used of the Spirit and were not particularly connected with emotional feelings. Even when I shouted loud praises and clapped or even danced (tried to dance, anyway) to the Lord in worship, these were acts of obedience to the instructions of Scripture, typically not particularly connected to my emotions. What Rob and Paul described, at first anyway, sounded extremely emotional to me.

In some ways, that was an odd response; after all, I had grown up in a church culture in which people shouted and ran the aisles and did other unusual things. Once I had even seen a man jump up on the back of a pew and then run from pew-back to pew-back in order to get to the aisle so that he could run in the aisle as an expression of his joy and praise. I tended to trust those phenomena because I grew up with seeing them and knew many people who did those things. My own Grandpa Humble had been one of them. These responses, I had come to think, were emotional ways of expressing joy in the Lord because, based on my observation, people tended to do these things most often in response to songs about heaven or preaching about the hope to come.

Nevertheless, my first response to Rob and Paul was caution, or perhaps skepticism. Yet, I could not ignore Paul's personal testimony. When he talked about having stood for two hours, laughing, with his eyes closed and his hands and arms raised, all the while feeling he was being battered with light from above, I simply could not discount that. Paul is as sophisticated and self-controlled, in the best sense, as anyone I know. I had seen no sign that he was given to unrestrained emotional responses or odd behavior. And his testimony of the lasting refreshing and release from the weight of inner burdens that had come to him surely sounded wonderful and desirable.

Then, in a very calm manner, Paul suggested we pray. Simply and quietly he said, "Holy Spirit, come," as he had seen and heard Wimber do. The Spirit came! More accurately, I should say, the Holy Spirit was present already, as he always is, but I began to be consciously aware of his presence. In that manifest presence, things begin to happen among us—things that simply were not typical of our own normal responses. More important, I was fully aware that the Holy Spirit was moving quietly among us—even though our responses to his presence and working were not necessarily quiet ones.[73]

When Paul shared his testimony with the church the following Sunday, the Holy Spirit's presence was manifest in the same way and the same phenomena, and more, begin to take place—not only that Sunday but in a variety of gatherings and situations for weeks to come. Several people were dramatically healed of physical ailments too.

This was revival in the sense that many of us became aware of loving Jesus more, of anticipating the Spirit's work in us and through us. Many were refreshed in hope and faith.

Oddly, though, this revival did not stop people from leaving the church. In fact, I remember some long-time members being moved with powerful phenomena and great joy on a Sunday, and then we would not see them at our meetings again. I remember John Meadows saying it was like the Lord was giving us divine anesthesia—in the midst of a time of loss and even pain, there was refreshing and joy in the Spirit.

One Sunday evening in January, there was a gathering of teens in our basement. One of the long-time members of the church shared a simple message, and the adults present began to pray with the youth. The Holy Spirit moved among them strongly. The following day, during chapel at school, "revival" broke out. Repentance and confession and physical healing occurred as the students began to share with one another. Such a powerful working of the Spirit began in the youth that we ending up having no classes for the whole week in order to allow the worship and prayer and ministry to continue.

As word began to spread, adults came to be prayed for by teens. There were some amazing instantaneous physical healings, and a number were powerfully touched by

---

[73] I am not going to try to share in detail the phenomena that started among us that afternoon. There are many videos of John Wimber teaching and ministering available on YouTube. Also, his books *Power Healing* and *Power Evangelism*, written with Kevin Springer, are still available for anyone who wants to learn more.

the Spirit's hand. On Thursday we took a number of our students to Louisville so that they could share and pray and worship with students in a school there. More of the presence and working of the Spirit took place! Then on Friday evening we traveled with a group of students to share with a youth group in a sister church in northern Kentucky. Again, the Spirit moved powerfully among us!

Whether it was because we didn't stay in the posture of dependence and expectation or because seasons for "anesthesia" do not last forever, I do not know, but gradually the most obvious signs of the Spirit slowly began to wane. In fact, within a few weeks, according to my son, then a student in New Covenant Academy, quite a few of the students had reverted back to the way they were, and some may have become worse than before.

Among many of us adults, the obvious moving of the Spirit continued for at least several months. Even though most of the phenomena subsided over time, and the strong sense of the Spirit's work and presence among us diminished gradually, I experienced some substantive changes—a new confidence and delight in the Holy Spirit, for example—that have endured to this day.

In 1985, our church was led by the Spirit into missionary activity in a big way! It was exciting, and people from our flock were very involved in helping people pack their belongings for moves into various different places. Under Paul Petrie's leadership, a missionary sending agency, International Outreach Ministries, was established. In August 1986 we had our first commissioning service in which we commissioned forty-eight people to move to other countries for mission. And some left that year also to start or to serve a church in other places in the United States. This was exciting and yet had its sad side also, because people we cared about moved away.

People continued to leave the church from time to time for several years, seemingly in clusters of several families at a time. Although this was difficult, it did open a substantive way for our Minnesota "flock" to contribute to the good of the whole church. We had solid relationships with each other, a steady commitment to the church and its ministry, and a willingness to serve wherever and however we were needed; therefore, we were able to be a stabilizing presence in the midst of change and loss. I am convinced that our move to Lexington, from God's perspective, had more to do with him sending us to serve than it did with him sending us to be served. It seems like, in a completely unanticipated way, we were a gift from the Servants of the Lord that God sent to help strengthen Covenant Church when strength was needed.

Besides what was happening in our local church, most of us elders were stunned by an announcement the *New Wine* teachers made at a meeting for elders held in Chicago in April 1986. We Lexington Covenant elders had traveled together to Chicago for this meeting of leaders in the discipleship movement. Charles Simpson, Bob Mumford, Don Basham, and Ern Baxter had called the meeting since Derek Prince had decided to disconnect from his relationship with the other teachers in March 1984. In Chicago we were told that the other four teachers had decided that they would no longer try to work together. They said that they intended to continue in friendship with one another but would serve those in each of their relational networks separately.

However, the general statement made to the whole group of us did not disclose fully the tensions between some of the teachers.[74] Those, like Paul, who were pastorally connected to Charles, learned more of the facts; therefore, it seemed to me that Paul came away with the understanding that the "discipleship movement" (or "shepherding movement") was over. On the way back to Lexington after those meetings, Paul told us some of what he knew but was careful not to give details that could constitute gossip about the teachers.

There never was an attempt to gather "the movement" back together. Brother Don, who had edited *New Wine* magazine for a number of years, moved to Michigan once the publication ceased, and he died in 1989. Some of his books, including the classic *Deliver Us from Evil: A Pastor's Reluctant Encounters with the Powers of Darkness*, are still in print. Brother Ern died in 1993, but recordings of a number of his messages are available online.[75] His extensive library is preserved. After stewarding the library for fifteen years, Charles Simpson Ministries donated it to The King's University in Southlake, Texas, in 2015. Brother Derek continued in ministry until his death in 2003, but his ministry also continues in books and audio and on the Derek Prince Ministries website.[76]

A few years later, in November 1989, Bob Mumford released a public statement of repentance in which he wrote: "… Accountability, personal training under the guidance of another and effective pastoral care are needed biblical concepts. True spiritual maturity will require that they be preserved …. However, to my personal pain and chagrin, these particular emphases very easily lent themselves to an

---

[74] The teachers released a public statement about their decision in *New Wine* on pages 8–9 of the next to last issue of the magazine, November 1986, archived online at https://csmpublishing.org under Publications.

[75] See http://brokenbreadteaching.org under Ern Baxter MP3'S.

[76] http://www.derekprince.org

unhealthy submission resulting in perverse and unbiblical obedience to human leaders."[77] In one published interview, as I remember it, Brother Bob affirmed his belief that the teaching of discipleship was orthodox but that he repented for his part as a leader in those cases in which discipleship was practiced wrongly. The fact that Brother Bob apparently came to this decision without discussing it with the other brothers with whom he had served as a leader opened the door to misunderstanding. Misunderstanding and offense were also increased by the way his statement was handled by some in the Christian publishing industry at that time.

The story was not over yet, however. There was great rejoicing and God was glorified when Brother Bob and Brother Charles publicly reconciled with one another at a conference in Gatlinburg, Tennessee, in 2006. Many leaders who had looked to the five teachers for mentoring and leadership came together for that celebration of reconciliation.

Brother Bob and his son Eric are still working together to edify God's people and to advance God's kingdom.[78] Brother Charles and his son Stephen are also actively involved in serving the Lord and the church together. I have had the joy of participating in their annual "family gathering" in Gatlinburg several times in my later years. Their CSM website offers many resources.[79] The fact that the brothers who were our leaders continue to serve God effectively is wonderful to me.

The disillusionment that followed their decision to work separately was not wonderful. Many of us had been convinced that the "shepherding movement" was on the "cutting edge of the Spirit's work in our generation"—not without a measure of carnal pride, in me at least. And I still believe it was on the cutting edge—failures and mistakes notwithstanding. The restoration of the Biblical vision for making disciples, for building Christian communities, and for seeing the kingdom of God grow in the nations by the power of the Holy Spirit was critical for our generation. As time has passed, it is even clearer that we were hearing truly from the Spirit—no matter how weak and insufficient our ability may have been to be the agents through whom he worked. In the mid-1980s, however, time had not passed and hindsight was not clear at all to me.

---

[77] Quotation taken from S. David Moore, *The Shepherding Movement: Controversy and Charismatic Ecclesiology* (New York, NY: T&T Clark International (Continuum), 2003), p. 173.

[78] http://lifechangers.org

[79] https://csmpublishing.org

21

New Friends and Deep Change

Even during this season of testing in the community and in the church, there were many good moments. The fellowship shared among the members of our flock was rich and meaningful, and some who did not move from Minnesota were added to the group. I got to know some wonderful people from other flocks in the church too. Also, some relationships that were to prove very significant later in my life began with several leaders outside of Lexington Covenant Church.

I first remember beginning to get acquainted with Richard McAfee and Bill Livingston when I took several students from New Covenant Academy to Louisville Covenant Church's school in early 1985. Richard and Bill had moved from a church in Oklahoma City in 1984 in order to help Louisville Covenant through a difficult season following the loss of their senior pastor. These men were long-time friends of Paul Petrie and some of the other Lexington Covenant elders. In 1985 they began to come often to Lexington to join us in our elders meetings. Although they came mostly for personal strengthening and support, their gifts also contributed to our lives and often to our deliberations in that season. I had no idea that the Lord would soon use Richard powerfully in my own life, nor did I have any thought that Bill would one day be one of my closest friends and for a season would give me personal pastoral oversight.

I first remember meeting Dennis Cole during that school revival also, when I took students to Covenant Christian Church in Newport, Kentucky, where Dennis was serving as an elder. In the coming years, Dennis also was to become one of my best friends and is now the person I look to for pastoral oversight.

In 1985, John Meadows opened a door, a hugely important door, as it turned out, for me when he invited me to join him weekly in a time of fellowship and prayer with several pastors of other churches in Lexington. Billy Henderson, one of these pastors, has become one of my most faithful friends. Billy, when a student at the University of Kentucky in the late 1970s, along with some of his university friends, started a Bible study in a dorm. That Bible study grew and eventually became a recognized campus group—University Christian Fellowship (UCF).

Several members decided to continue as a community of disciples after they graduated; therefore, eventually Billy and the others began Lexington Christian Fellowship (LCF), while they continued their outreach on the campus through UCF.

The more I got to know Billy, the more we found that we had similar hearts for the kingdom of God and community and for making disciples. Even though our backgrounds and experiences were significantly different, we had much in common in how we thought and in what we longed to see in the local church. A big difference between us is that Billy's gift to reach people, to draw them together, and to establish a "community" with those who are willing to embrace the same mission and values is far greater than mine. On the other hand, Billy often says he has drawn on me for theological confirmation about truths and practices he thought should be developed in their church. I have learned more from him than he from me over the years though, I am sure.

In the summer of 1987, Billy asked me to teach one week of a thirteen-week Christian Training School (CTS) that LCF was beginning. In that first CTS, I taught five sessions on the subject "Servanthood." Those days together began to establish a strong connection between LCF people and me, ties that continue to bear fruit in my life and in my family's life to this day.

****

In 1986, the Holy Spirit directed us to send Paul Petrie and his family, along with several other people, to plant a church in Brussels, Belgium. Paul continued on as the "senior pastor" of Lexington Covenant, but he gave John Meadows the responsibility to preside among the elders and to represent the elders team to the church in Paul's absence.

There were men with more obvious "charismatic" gifts than John; however, he had been an elder in the Lexington church longer than most of us, and he was probably the most pastoral among us when it came to listening and caring for people as individuals. Besides, a brother with a more "charismatic" gift and a more "take charge" attitude might well have ruffled feathers at a time when the church needed to be settled and healed. Not only was John respected and loved by the elders, but he also was clearly a conciliar leader. We were all committed to following his lead since he represented Paul, but each of us was able to contribute meaningfully to the whole. John stayed in frequent contact with Paul by means of international phone calls. It was a gift to be able to have consistency in the overall direction of the church because Paul and John were communicating and because John understood Paul's heart.

By the summer of 1987, it seemed to the elders, in counsel with Paul, that there needed to be a consistent voice in the pulpit on Sunday. Some of the elders traveled many weekends. Others had various gifts and ways of serving in addition to caring for their own flocks in the church but were not as oriented toward preaching. It fell to me to be that voice, and I continued to serve in that role well into 1988. I presented a series titled "Loving and Serving One Another" in order to remind us and re-call us to the attitudes and behaviors that Jesus said demonstrate that we are his disciples and that build God's people together in a Christian community (John 13:34–35, 17:20–23). I also presented a long series of expository (more or less) messages from the book of Ephesians—all except for two passages that were covered by two other elders on Sundays when I had to be away.

It was clear by April 1988 that it was time for a more visionary leader to take the lead role among the elders. John had served faithfully and well through a difficult season in the church during which people continued to leave, a time when we were also transitioning from the direct leadership of the founding elder, Paul. Now, it became clear that the time had come for Paul to turn the church over to another leader who could, we hoped, lead us into the future.

Several of the brothers had been reading a good deal of the church growth literature that had been produced by people who had been influenced by Donald McGavran, well-known professor in Fuller Seminary's School of World Mission, the acknowledged "father of the church growth movement." Various ones of us read the works of Peter Wagner, Carl George, and others. Their writings stirred a great desire among us elders to be effective in evangelism and to see our community grow. Wagner's close friend, John Wimber, had already been used of the Lord to bring a reviving among us. We had profited greatly from Wimber's emphasis on signs and wonders in evangelism, and the church growth methodology seemed to some to be "right up our alley."

Even though people had continued to leave the church, there were still lofty hopes and expectations for growth in numbers and growth in influence in the city. One "prophetic" word even said there would be thousands in the church within a few years. It would appear that either the prophecy was wrong or that we did not follow the Spirit well enough for it to come to pass. It is also possible that we misinterpreted that word because we were only thinking about "the church" in terms of the little community that we called Covenant Church and not perceiving the church the way God intends it—the community of all believers in a locality.

There were several people who came to the Lord, even in our difficult days. Some, though, came to us ready to surrender to God, rather than us going to them. Still, the loss of people far outnumbered the gains. My best estimate is that there were about

250 of us who remained in the church that spring—less than half the number that had been in the church when we had moved to Lexington in 1984.

We certainly did not realize that more than a few of those who left would become leaders in a number of churches around the city. I first became aware that this was happening about the time we had begun to think about a new leader and the future. At one of the Greater Lexington Ministerial Fellowship's monthly lunches, a Church of God pastor, upon discovering my affiliation, said, "Your church has provided leaders for half the churches in the city." Although his was an overstatement, I discovered that there was actually some truth to his words.

As I reflected on it, my perspective gradually began to change. We had identified with the "discipleship movement," right? What do disciples do? Enter a permanent training relationship? No! Of course not. Jesus calls us to make disciples who make disciples. In a tangible way, through the relationships in Covenant Church, God had produced disciples in spite of weaknesses and failings. God had directed us by the Spirit to send people out by the Spirit. And God also had used human mistakes and failures to make people uncomfortable, dissatisfied, and ready to move.

In the Bible the pattern is clear. Sometimes it was the one who made disciples who moved on to make more disciples, as Jesus did. And other times, the disciples were sent out to make disciples as Jesus sent his and as the church in Antioch sent Barnabas and Saul when the Spirit spoke. But the New Testament communities were not static; they were not simply enjoying a nice, placid life together. Theirs were communities in which things were happening; people were coming and going.

In the Jerusalem church, God had used persecution to get the disciples moving out to make more disciples. The way Luke describes life in the first community of disciples in Jerusalem has stirred many of us to desire to be part of such communities (Acts 1:13–14; 2:1–11, 42–47; 4:23–36; 5:12–16). Who would want to leave such a "nest," even to fulfill a larger calling (Matthew 28:18–20, Acts 1:8)? Why, thousands from many nations had become new disciples and members of the community (Acts 2:41, 4:4, 6:7). To be sure, Peter and John had experienced some suffering, but didn't God also miraculously deliver them from prison (Acts 5:17–20)?

Then, following Stephen's martyrdom, great persecution was unleashed on that church and scattered the disciples, not the apostles, throughout Judea and Samaria. So much for the church, right? Wrong! Luke says simply: "Now those who were scattered went about preaching the word." Then Luke tells the amazing experiences of the deacon Philip, who had gone to Samaria because of the persecution, to illustrate the way God used the distress of persecution to expand the reach of the gospel through disciples. (See Acts 8.) Then, following the account of the conversion of Saul, the chief persecutor, Luke reveals the result of the disciples' obedience, encouraged as it was by persecution:

> So the church throughout all Judea and Galilee and Samaria had peace and was being built up. And walking in the fear of the Lord and in the comfort of the Holy Spirit, it multiplied. (Acts 9:31)

God also used difficult times to motivate his Old Covenant people. Because of famine, Jacob and his children moved to Egypt, where God had raised up Joseph. For many years while Jacob's children lived in Egypt, they had a good life because Joseph had favor with Pharaoh. But eventually a king came to the throne who had not known Joseph, and their "nest" became increasingly uncomfortable until they were ready to leave Egypt—in fact, they were crying out to leave. In Exodus 19, God compares the way he delivered them from Egypt in order to fulfill the calling he had for them as "bearing them on eagles' wings."

> The LORD called to him out of the mountain, saying, "Thus you shall say to the house of Jacob, and tell the people of Israel: 'You yourselves have seen what I did to the Egyptians, and how I bore you on eagles' wings and brought you to myself. Now therefore, if you will indeed obey my voice and keep my covenant, you shall be my treasured possession among all peoples, for all the earth is mine; and you shall be to me a kingdom of priests and a holy nation.' These are the words that you shall speak to the people of Israel." (Exodus 19:3b–6)

God motivated his people to desire to move into the land formerly promised to their forefather, Abraham, by making their circumstances increasingly miserable. Likewise, God used the hardship of the wilderness to expose their unbelief and rebellion and to raise up a generation that would follow him into that promised land. In the wilderness, God not only protected and fed his people, but he also had "stirred the nest" to get them to the wilderness.

Near the end of Moses's life, he sang a song summarizing the history of God's delivering and leading his people. In one part of that song, Moses picked up on the comparison of God's ways to an eagle's ways:

> But the LORD's portion is his people,
> Jacob his allotted heritage.

He found him in a desert land,
  and in the howling waste of the wilderness;
he encircled him, he cared for him,
  he kept him as the apple of his eye.
Like an eagle that stirs up its nest,
  that flutters over its young,
spreading out its wings, catching them,
  bearing them on its pinions,
the LORD alone guided him,
  no foreign god was with him. (Deuteronomy 32:9–12, emphasis mine)

The sermon outline for Deuteronomy 32:11 by nineteenth-century Scottish preacher James Orr sets forth a clear application to the way God works like the eagle in our lives:

The description is of a female eagle exciting her young ones in teaching them to fly, and afterwards guarding with the greatest care lest the weak should receive harm (Gesenius). In this picture of the eagle's treatment of her young, note -

I.   HER AIM. She aims at teaching them self-reliance. It is not God's wish that his children should go in leading-strings. They must be trained to prompt, fearless, self-reliant action. This was an aim of the discipline of the wilderness. Our action is to be in a spirit of dependence, but it is to be **active**, not **passive** dependence.

II. HER METHOD. She stirs up her nest. She does not leave her brood to the ignoble ease they would perhaps prefer. So God rouses his people to action by making their place uneasy for them. By placing them in trying situations, by removing comforts, by the stimulus of necessity, by the sharp provocation of afflictions, he goads them to think, act, and put forth the powers that are in them. It is not for the good of Christians that they should have too much comfort.

III. HER CASE. The experiment is not carried to the point of allowing the young to hurt themselves. She hovers over them, supports them

on the tip of her wings, etc. God tries us, but not beyond our strength.
- J.O.[80]

Although my own life circumstances have never been so dire as to be comparable to that of the people of God in Israel, still, I know from personal experience that at various times in my journey God has allowed the nest to get so uncomfortable that I began to desire and seek change. Sometimes circumstances have stirred me to desire external change, such as the way the Lord used the division in our community and misunderstandings in my relationship with Jack Brombach to help prepare me for the move to Lexington. Most often, unpleasant circumstances have stirred me to desire internal change, as, for example, God was doing at this time when he was bringing my weaknesses and failings into the light. Soon I would see that disillusionment, discouragement, and anger were motivating me to seek help.

It is not my intent, nor do I have the ability, to explain all the whys of my own journey, much less to explain the whys of the history of the Servants or of Covenant Church. Nor am I any more able than the apostle Paul to accurately evaluate with assurance either my own life or the lives of others (1 Corinthians 4:3–5). I do know, however, that in all things God was working to make good of all things, just as Scripture declares:

> And we know that God causes all things to work together for good to those who love God, to those who are called according to His purpose. (Romans 8:28, NASB)

I did not know that I was about to have a personal encounter with God that would change me. I also did not know that there would soon be a change in my responsibilities that was going to lead to a move for our family.

****

Financially, our family was not as well off as we had been the last few years that we lived in Minneapolis. My salary from Covenant Church was about the same as my salary from the Servants of the Lord, and I had the added advantages of being able to deduct household expenses from my taxable income; however, during the last years in Minneapolis, we had had six single adults sharing our household expense. Even though, most of the time, we had one extra adult sharing our home in Lexington, we

---

[80] James Orr D.D., "The Eagle (sermon on Deuteronomy 32:11), from the Pulpit Commentary Homiletics as found here: http://biblehub.com/commentaries/homiletics/deuteronomy/32.htm.

were also paying for our children's education. Therefore, when it became clear in 1985 that our son, Elijah, needed dental braces badly for the proper development of his mouth, we had to find supplemental income.

After due consideration, Elijah signed up to deliver the *Lexington Herald Leader,* our local newspaper, in our immediate neighborhood early every morning. The route was in his name, but from the beginning I worked along with him. We kept that route for six years. Most of that time we had at least one additional route, and for a period we had three routes. As we added routes, Patricia began to help us more and more regularly.

The income, usually $600–$800 per month, was in Elijah's name, but from the beginning we all saw it as a way to serve our family. Therefore, Elijah took about $40 per month for his own use, and from the paper-route money he paid for his own dental braces. We were also able to pay the children's school bill from that money. Blessings came from this family effort. Elijah learned to work, to handle money, and to serve the family unselfishly. We had the privilege of working together regularly. The orthodontist was so impressed when he heard about Elijah's efforts to serve the family that he deducted one-third of the price from the final cost of the braces.

The price we paid, though, was missed sleep and tired bodies. Our rising time was early—4:30 in the morning, no matter what time we had gone to bed the night before. We had the paper route while Elijah was in grades 7 through 12, a time of much rapid physical growth for a young person. He got to the point where he could go to sleep almost anywhere at any time. My night schedule could not be controlled well. I had to be available to serve individuals when their schedules permitted, and I needed to participate in the meetings and activities of the church. For six years, I averaged between four and five hours of sleep per night. One thing did help us. With the three of us working together, we arranged for each to have one day a week to sleep a little later while the other two took care of delivering papers.

Although we did not plan this with any spiritual discipline in mind, it served as one, since it helped us to develop a willingness to work and sacrifice in doing God's will, and it offered us an unforeseen means to build the godly attribute of "community spirit" into our family life.

There was another "benefit" that was not so pleasant. When I was tired, which was most of the time, my weaknesses became more apparent, especially impatience and irritability. Sadly, it was my family who took the brunt of these negative attitudes and the bad behavior that manifested accordingly. I also think the tiredness "helped" a deeper problem to be revealed. My tendency to flare up quickly in anger began to manifest more and more frequently. My first response to situations was often hardness and harshness. Although I did not like the way I behaved, recognizing that I could not consistently control my behavior did lead me to want change, even though I felt helpless to change.

Thankfully, through the years, Patricia and I had sought to take responsibility for our failures in relationships and to seek forgiveness quickly. We had made a habit of doing so with our children as well as with each other. The fact that we kept short accounts made a major difference. My wife and children were gracious to offer frequent and abundant pardon. Still, my wrong behavior produced consequences in them, such things as feeling the need to steel themselves against harsh words and to withdraw into themselves in the face of contention and confrontation.

Some good things took place, of course, even in this tough season. One of the greatest was an encounter Elijah and I had with each other when he was 15, during the spring of his freshman year of high school. Not only had I been irritable, impatient, and often angry, but quite often Elijah had been testing the limits (rather mildly in comparison to many) from age 13 to 15.

I often overreacted to his attitudes and actions. I tended to see much more rebellion than was actually there, because all too often I read into his behavior and attitudes my own rebelliousness during my youth. We had had some really tough moments in that season.

That school year we had some particularly bad arguments over his lackluster effort in algebra. In one rather ugly encounter, I attacked him verbally and really cut him down.

After he left the room, in guilt and frustration and helplessness, I cried out, "O God, I can't even be a good father without your help." This, of course, exposed a core issue: I was trying to do right without God's help! I broke in repentance before God.

As was my custom after screwing up, I soon went to Elijah and asked his forgiveness. I made clear that I was serious about his need to change his approach to algebra, but I also told him that my attitude, my judgments of his motives, my words, and my demeanor were inexcusable. I told him that I deeply desired his forgiveness. Elijah graciously forgave me and continued to love me. Keeping short accounts with one another and confessing our own sins and seeking and giving forgiveness were big keys in our relationship.

A few days afterward, Elijah and I went to a Hardee's restaurant for a Coke and a talk about these things. I was in a place of brokenness and dependence before God, who met us that day. I found myself scribbling on a napkin. I drew a line with an X on either side. The Xs represented Elijah and me, while the line was the problem between us.

I said: "Son, we have had these problems between us. We are both trying to deal with the problems. But as we slug away at the problems, we are slugging through the problems and beating each other up. From now on (I drew a circle around the X representing me and drew a line representing a curved arrow around the line, i.e., the problem, to a point beside the X representing him), I am on your side. Let's attack the problems together."

Immediately, tears filled both of our eyes. We were caught up in a profound "God moment"—a moment of wonderful intimacy, peace, and hope.

From that time forward, our relationship changed. We still had issues from time to time, but almost as soon as an argument would begin, one or both would "come around to the other side," and we would try to resolve the issue together and not allow it to come between us.

The next year, I homeschooled Elijah. I could not teach him much about mechanics or farming or woodworking or sports or hunting or fishing—all the things that I think about men teaching their sons—but I could help him build the conscious foundation of a Biblical perspective on life and history. I could offer him what I knew. And I did my best to do so.

Within two months, I realized that we were no longer simply a father and son. We had become the best of friends as well. Previously, I had understood something about the love of a father for his son, and I had understood something about the authority and submission that should characterize the relationship, but I had not realized that it was desirable or even possible for a father and son to be friends as well. But it happened, and through the next years, Elijah continued to be one of my truest friends. Over the next few months, we began to talk about how we could serve the Lord together in years ahead of us.

****

Would that all the things I had been messing up would have been "fixed" like that. By late 1988, I knew I was in trouble and that I was doing damage to our family. It is a good thing to be able to see one's weakness and failings, even when it feels terrible, if that "seeing" leads to repentance and change. In this case, I despised what I was doing, but I did not seem able to change. I knew it was cowardly, at best, to take out anger on my family.

I was not blowing up at my pastor, John Meadows. I was not taking it out on men who could "hit" back. I was taking it out on those who loved me and depended on me most. What business did I have pastoring and teaching leading God's people when I was acting so badly, so often? And, yet, what was I to do? I did not call myself to those ministries; God did, and he was not releasing me.

Gradually, I became aware that some of my anger had roots in the disappointments of the 1980s. When I was completely honest with myself, I had to admit that my quick temper had been a weakness for a long time. It was my typical response to adversity. Fear of my parents (some of it godly fear, some self-protective fear) had kept me from lashing out at my parents. But I had fairly often unleashed it on my younger sisters when they "provoked" me. However, anger had begun to manifest more often during the time that the Servants experienced division—the time when my idealism and grand expectations about the kingdom and community were first challenged seriously.

Disappointment grew still more as I began to comprehend more fully the depth of problems in Covenant Church, especially as the unsettledness, offense, and loss of people continued on from month to month and year to year. I learned that whether people left the church offended or were sent out in mission, it was still a loss. Not only were there fewer of us at meetings, but there were also fewer people to do the work and, for that matter, there were less finances to use in the work too. And, at some point, it was clear that unless things turned around, there would be loss in our personal income too.

Since Bible college days, it had not been my desire to be paid for working in the church, but now I was dependent on it. Money was not nearly as big a factor in my anger as the disappointments—the illusions that had been shattered. I deeply longed to wholeheartedly "seek first the kingdom of God and his righteousness" and to know that God was the one who would provide for all the necessary things, and at the same time it was fearful. Still, now that I had a family to support, had a monthly house payment to make, and had grown accustomed to at least a degree of financial freedom, I would not be honest if I were to think or say that the possibility of a bleak financial future did not matter. Yet, it was a shameful thing in my mind to lack trust in God to be our provider.

I had talked about these things with John Meadows on occasion and, in some measure of desperation, I began to talk about them more often. His counsel and prayers made some difference, but I still was not breaking out of the pattern. Finally, John suggested that he and I meet with our mutual friend, Richard McAfee, who was at that time serving in Louisville.

Richard had for a long time been effective in praying with people for healing from deep hurt. In fact, he had moved to Louisville to help the people of the Covenant Church there deal with their pain and hurt after a pastor fell scandalously. Although I tended to be, and still am, cautious about the "inner healing" ministry in general, I knew Richard and I trusted him as a man of God who ministered in the Holy Spirit's power; therefore, I agreed. John set up a time in late April for Richard to meet with the two of us at our church's building in Lexington.

I do not remember many details about that time with Richard and John. I do know that Richard asked me to share why I wanted prayer, which I did. I know he asked me some questions, and there may even have been more than one time of prayer while we were waiting before the Lord together. But one part of the ministry time I do remember! At some point Richard began to ask about my memories from earlier times in my life.

Richard asked me about my childhood and about my relationship with Dad. I remember that, at some point while I was talking, Richard came over to the chair where I was sitting and put his arms around me and began to address directly "the little boy I used to be," speaking to buried memories of times when I felt confused and hurt, specifically in my relationship with Dad.

While Richard was praying, however, I "heard" another voice—the voice of the heavenly Father—a tender voice, a loving voice, a delighted voice. The Father's words were as plain as if they'd been audible, even his tone of voice. As I write, I hear him again, now, in my memory, delightedly saying, "I like you, boy!" I wept at my Father's simple affirmation, and something changed within.

I had understood from Scripture that God loved me—after all, he loves everyone. Hadn't he demonstrated his love by sending his Son, Jesus, to rescue us by taking our sins and dying for us so that we could be forgiven?

But, *this* was different than that. My heavenly Father not only loves me—he likes me ... he delights in me as one of his children—"his boy." And not just when I do the right thing and say the right words. My Father liked "me" even at a time when I was angry and venting on my loved ones, when I was acting like a brat, so cowardly that my family had been receiving the brunt of my anger—not those who could "fight back" but those who were dependent on me, those who deserved and needed me to represent the Father's love to them. Even at this awful low point in my life, my Father "liked me." He was not just putting up with me. He wasn't just "using" me. He wasn't just using my gifts to minister to others. In spite of how messed up I was, my Father truly liked me.

My Father likes me! My Father really, really loves me and delights in me. In a way similar to the way Elijah and I had become friends, my Father also wanted to be my friend.

I write with tears today, because this is not simply an experience I had nearly thirty years ago. I hear my Father's delight again today, early on this Sunday morning, September 24, 2017. I hear his delight, even though yesterday I struggled unsuccessfully for a few hours to overcome frustration and to be patient when my wife was dealing with a vague (to me) dizziness and kept needing my attention while I was trying to diligently work on this book. My Father delights in me as his "boy" today, even though, last evening, I struggled with frustration because of the slow, very slow, service at the emergency room where I had taken Patricia to get help.

The word *like* has lost a great deal of its true meaning, in part, I think, because it is used so commonly and shallowly on Facebook. Sometimes I have asked younger folks, "Why did you 'like' that post when I am sure you disagreed with the content that so-and-so posted?" The most common response has been, "I wasn't 'liking' the content; I was expressing my affirmation for my friend who posted."

Certainly, when I heard my Father say, "I like you, boy," he was expressing his affirmation for me as a person, but he was not saying, "I like the way you've been acting out, boy." So, in some sense, there is a similarity to a Facebook "like," I suppose. Only what I heard in my very core that day was far, far deeper and more personal and more caring in its tone and meaning than any "like" button can express, because I "heard" his voice and his "tone" of voice. Those few words said everything that needed to be said.

My Father's "like" was much more than affirmation. It was a promise. His words said, "There really is hope for you, because you are mine."

Was my Father going to let me stay this way? Of course not! He is the Father of all fathers! Because of his love, he has disciplined me, and he still is disciplining me—

not with harsh anger, but rather out of his deep love for his 68-year-old "boy" whom *he* is going to bring to maturity.

Not only did my Father send his Son to rescue me from sin and death, but my Father has also sent his own Holy Spirit to abide in me, to take up permanent residence in me and to transform me, and to keep on transforming me—often little by little, it seems—from what I have been into the very likeness of his beloved Son, the one who lived among men as "the radiance of the glory of God and the exact imprint of his nature ..." (Hebrews 1:3).

The one and only eternal Son of God, God's very "Word became flesh and dwelt among us, and we have seen his glory, glory as of the only Son from the Father, full of grace and truth" (John 1:14), declared the apostle John. God's word to me that day was like a personal promise that he will finish what he started in me when I first became aware of being drawn to him when I was 4 years old.

That prayer time did not fix everything. The problems were still there. I was still "me" with my weaknesses and propensities to failure compounded by habitually not controlling my temper for several years.

Yet, I was different at the same time. From that time on, I have more easily been able to choose to turn away from disappointments and disillusionments when such feelings and thoughts arise and to turn with hope and trust to the Father's good plans for me. Instead of surrendering to bad habits I had developed over time by lack of self-control, I am now able to catch myself more frequently and to choose to look to the Spirit of grace, seeking for his help to build new habits of good responses.

The biggest change, though, was that there was substantial healing in the deep places, where shame and a sense of never being able to be good enough had been dominating my feelings. It had been about ten years before that the Father had said, "Look to me for understanding and acceptance." Now, I knew more fully that I really could look to him and that he really did understand and accept me!

22

Stepping Out

Paul Petrie had come back to Lexington for a few months in the spring of 1988. One day he called me into his office to tell me that he believed it was time to make the change to a new permanent senior pastor. Paul asked me to write out my vision for Lexington Covenant Church along with my plan for bringing the vision into reality. He also indicated that I was not the only elder with this assignment.

As I thought and prayed about it, I knew that my vision was not a match with a good deal of what I understood the church growth material to be advocating. I did not oppose their insights, but it was not my desire to become a "rancher" managing others who cared for the people, rather than to be a "shepherd" walking with and caring for a flock in a personal way. I did not have the inclination to preach to a congregation of "seekers" on Sunday mornings, hoping for converts who would later get connected into small groups of one sort or another for discipleship, fellowship, and service. Frankly, I really did not have confidence that Covenant's call was to be one big church with lots of small groups.

I was more inclined to see us emphasize the flocks we already had as the "primary" structure of the church. Although we still had flocks, we gradually had become more of a Sunday morning congregation that had small groups rather than a community consisting of several flocks.

I believed that by doing three things we could have unity and cooperation in the whole community. First, it was crucial for the elders to continue to maintain and build on the relationships of love and unity we already had among ourselves. Second, each flock leader needed to continue leading the members of that flock into honest, functioning relationships of love and unity. Finally, to the degree that love and unity characterized the mutual relationships of the elders and relationships among the flock members, then we could gather the flocks monthly or bimonthly in a gathering of the whole community in order to celebrate and worship before the Lord and to receive instruction together.

This was not a new vision. It was a proposal to become more like Covenant Church had been in the first two years after our flock moved from Minneapolis to Lexington. In an effort to hold the whole community together while people were leaving, we had tried to consolidate by having all of us together every Sunday and, I believed, had lost something vital in personal relationships and common life together.

Although I believed this to be the best direction for our church, I was not fully confident that I was the leader who could "restore" Lexington Covenant to what it had formerly appeared to be. I did believe that some of the flocks would prosper if we led the church in this direction, even if some flocks that had lost a number of people needed to integrate into one of the other flocks. In my written vision, I added that if our vision was to be a church of thousands with a big Sunday meeting, perhaps, among those elders fully focused on our local church, David Redish might be able to lead us in that direction.

I do not know what any of the other brothers may have shared with Paul. However, at our annual elders retreat in June, Paul announced that he believed it was time for him to step back from being senior pastor and that he was turning that responsibility over to David. We elders confirmed the decision. And the change took place in that retreat.

David's leadership did not stop the loss of members, however. In fact, as with most such leadership changes, some left who might have stayed even though David, along with the rest of us who were serving as the local elders, gave it his best and sought to lead the church into the new decade.

****

Charles Simpson had been coming to Lexington every year since I had been in the church to spend several days among us. Brother Charles was a close friend of Paul's and the one to whom Paul looked for his own pastoral oversight. Typically, Brother Charles would speak at a meeting for our cell group leaders and also at two or more meetings of the whole church. In addition, he also met with the elders, often for a meal, while he was with us.

In 1989 when Brother Charles came for his annual visit, David, John, Kent Ostrander, and I, the "local elders" whose focus had been on caring for Covenant Church hands-on, spent several hours talking about the state of the church with him. The four of us, along with two secretaries and a maintenance man, were by this time the only full-time employees of the church.

Kent had been an elder and leader of one of the flocks in the church since before I had moved to Lexington, but he also had always been active in the pro-life movement in Kentucky. He had worked hard and successfully to bring a number of different pro-life groups together into a functioning statewide coalition. At this meeting with Brother Charles, Kent shared with us his vision to start a pro-family organization in

Kentucky. He believed that such a group could serve to promote and advocate for legislation that would support and strengthen traditional Christian values across the state. He wanted to be released from eldership in order to pursue this vision full-time.

I remember that Brother Charles was positive about Kent's vision and the need for such work to be done, but he also expressed his concern that it is extremely difficult to raise and maintain support for such a work. David, John, and I also expressed our support for Kent's vision. To Kent's credit and God's glory, The Family Foundation, which he began, has become an effective organization and still serves the kingdom of God and the Commonwealth of Kentucky faithfully in the civil arena.[81]

That meeting was not significant only for Kent. Brother Charles addressed John and me about the reality of our own situation as full-time employees. Without mincing words, he pointed out the previously unspoken truth—that only David's job in the church, in terms of being a paid position, was secure. Brother Charles warned us that unless John and I actively and effectively helped the church grow in numbers and in ministry, inevitably we would need to find work elsewhere.

I left that meeting sobered and motivated to begin to seek the Lord diligently about what I needed to be doing, in part, admittedly, because my livelihood depended on it, but also (and to a greater degree, I hope) for the good of the church and God's kingdom. I wanted my motivation to be pure, not self-serving; therefore, I did everything I could to set my heart on serving God's kingdom at whatever cost to myself.

****

I was, in fact, already active in outreach in a couple of ways. First, one of the brothers in the church had recommended a local automobile repair shop at a time when I needed mechanical services. Over time, I had become friends with the owner, Bob, and with his employees and with many of his friends as well. To my knowledge, none of these people knew Jesus, and I had been investing a significant amount of time in building these relationships in hopes that these new friends would come to know Jesus and follow him.

---

[81] For more on Kent's work, born out of our covenant relationships, see http://www.kentuckyfamily.org.

In large part, my persistence in those efforts was due to something specific I had heard the Lord say to me. One day I was reading Paul's exhortation to Timothy regarding his work as a pastor when one charge grabbed my attention:

> I charge you in the presence of God and of Christ Jesus, who is to judge the living and the dead, and by his appearing and his kingdom: preach the word; be ready in season and out of season; reprove, rebuke, and exhort, with complete patience and teaching.... As for you, always be sober-minded, endure suffering, **do the work of an evangelist**, fulfill your ministry. (2 Timothy 4:1–2, 5, bold print added)

Do the work of an evangelist? How does a pastor, a shepherd of a flock, do that? I wondered to myself. Unexpectedly, from within I heard the voice of the Lord say: "Use the gift I have given you. Adopt some goats. Take care of them and pray for me to turn them into sheep."[82]

It seemed so simple. What "goats" did I know? *How about Bob and his friends?* I thought. After that I began to go to the shop two or three mornings a week before the shop opened, often swinging by Spalding's Bakery on the way in order to pick up a couple dozen donuts. Once at the shop, we would share coffee, donuts, and conversation until the guys began their day's work. Usually about midmorning, after their work was well under way, Bob would want to go to breakfast at Denny's, where we could talk freely and share our lives more deeply.

My time at the shop waiting for Bob to go to breakfast proved to have another benefit. Soon, there were so many people from Covenant Church who began to get their vehicles serviced and repaired at his shop that I was able to spend far more time visiting with them and actually investing in them than I would have been if I had been sitting in my office at the church's building.

In the end, my efforts to invest God's love and my gift into these men at the shop did not add members to Covenant Church, but a few years later some of them did come to profess faith in Jesus, which is, after all, the primary goal.

My second involvement in outreach was actually begun by others. While John was presiding over the church, a man named Stephen Johnson had come to the building wanting to talk with a pastor. John was available that day, and during that visit,

---

[82] I understood "goats" to be those who did not know and follow Jesus and, therefore, would not inherit the eternal kingdom, in contrast to the "sheep," those who follow Jesus and will inherit that kingdom (Matthew 25:31–46).

Stephen surrendered his life to Jesus. Following John's suggestion, Stephen joined a home group led by Kevin Metzler. Not only did Stephen become active in that group and in the church, but he also began sharing his newfound faith outside the church, including with his co-workers at the Comprehensive Care Center, located in the nearby town of Winchester, where Stephen worked as a counselor. Several of his friends there came to Jesus, and some began to attend Covenant Church too.

About that same time, Mort and Robin Trimble, members of Lexington Covenant, sensed a strong call to move with their family to Winchester. Prior to Stephen's conversion, Brent Goodrich and his family, who already lived in Winchester, had become members of Covenant Church and eventually had begun to look to me for pastoral oversight and had become a part of our flock. Another Winchester couple also had started attending Covenant. They had not known Stephen, but they joined Covenant not long after his conversion. In due time, a home group formed in Winchester, led by Mort under Kevin's oversight.

In 1989, however, Kevin needed to turn the oversight of the Winchester group over to someone else so that he could focus on personal responsibilities. I sensed a call to offer my services, and the elders assigned it to me.

I took the exhortation Brother Charles had given to John and me as a confirmation, so I began to pray more fervently for that group and to consider how to strengthen it. I was also asking the Lord what else I should be doing.

Soon the idea of planting two churches as outreaches of Covenant Church had developed in my thinking, an idea I believed to be from the Lord. One was obvious: to see the home group in Winchester grow and become an effective church there. The other was almost as obvious once I began to think about it.

Winchester is in Clark County, just to the east of Fayette County, where Lexington is located. Just to the south of both Fayette and Clark County is Madison County. One of the brothers who had moved from Florida to be part of Covenant Church in the early 1980s had bought a farm in northern Madison County and had started the River Hills housing development on that land. Several Covenant Church families had built homes in that development. My wife and I were also buying a piece of land in hopes of building our own home there at some time in the future. Several other Covenant people were planning to build there as well. It seemed right to encourage and help those people living in Madison County to plant a church there in order to reach people in that area with the message of Jesus and his kingdom.

Early on in the thought process, I presented these ideas to David and to John for prayer and consideration. Thus, at our 1990 elders' planning retreat, I was authorized to begin spending one-third to one-half of my time in trying to see churches begin in these two communities.

Later that year, Bill Camenisch, who had moved to Lexington in order to study under Dow Robinson and who was being pastored by David, sensed the call to move his family to Winchester in order to work with Mort and me to see a church develop. Bill's call was confirmed by the elders, and the Camenisch family soon moved there.

In 1990, I sought to lay the groundwork to plant the churches. The home group in Winchester continued to prosper. In late summer the people invited friends to join them for five Sunday evening services, which we held in the old library building at College Park. Several people who had not been part of the Winchester home group attended these meetings, which was encouraging.

We also had a few meetings with the people at River Hills in Madison County that year in order to pray together and to take counsel together about them developing into a church. The men in this group were truly dedicated to following Jesus and had demonstrated their radical commitment to follow the Lord and be active in the Body of Christ by buying land and moving there in the first place. And, they all were active in Covenant Church. However, they were members of various flocks in Covenant Church and had not come together as a home group, and they had not established a common identity as a group, other than that they all lived at River Hills. From the beginning, it was clear that several of them had their own strongly held, but quite different, ideas about what it would take to start a church and about what it would mean to be a church.

Two questions soon developed in my mind: Would the brothers at River Hills come together and lay down their personal ideas in order to develop a common vision and strategy? Was I the right person to be able to bring them together in unity?

By the end of 1990, we had laid plans to begin regularly scheduled church services in both Winchester and in Madison County the following year.

****

Sunday, September 30, 1990, was an unexpectedly significant day in my life. A few days earlier, on the 28th, David Redish had me accompany him on a trip to Louisville Covenant Church for a pastors' meeting with Dennis Peacocke. Bill Livingston, our mutual friend and the pastor of that church, had invited Dennis to visit their church and speak to them that weekend. I had heard of Dennis, the founder of Strategic Christian Services,[83] several times and, in fact, a year or two earlier, at Paul Petrie's suggestion, I had written Dennis a letter in which I asked for his input concerning *Humble Perspectives*, a newsletter I had begun to write and distribute from time to time. Dennis had graciously responded with helpful suggestions.

In that Friday gathering, Dennis presented a plan to bring positive, Biblically based change to our cities. He talked about the need to recognize the "elders in the city," a concept derived from Biblical passages such as Deuteronomy 19:12, Ruth 4:2, Job 29:7–24, and Proverbs 31:23.[84] Dennis challenged us to discover the elders in our own cities—those respected men from the civil, business, and church spheres who had both concern for the city and also influence in the city—in order to form a "city council" that would develop and implement strategies drawn from Scripture to the benefit of the community.

Before we left the gathering that afternoon, David invited Dennis to speak on the following Sunday evening at Lexington Covenant Church. Our family and most of the faithful members of the church came to that meeting in which Dennis expounded on some of the primary themes characteristic of his ministry—the state of the culture and the way the church (speaking primarily of people who professed to truly believe the Bible) had given the culture over to secularists by retreating into a religion of personal piety focused on "going to heaven when I die" rather than to be a people focused on praying and seeking to see the kingdom of God grow in our communities.

Dennis reminded us that Jesus had instructed us to pray, "Your kingdom come, your will be done *on earth* as it is in heaven" (italics added for emphasis). Dennis declared that our final commission from King Jesus, given shortly before he ascended to be seated on the throne of the universe where he been given all authority to rule heaven and earth, was the command for us to disciple nations and to teach them to obey his commands. Dennis emphasized that we are called to disciple nations, not just to make disciples of individuals within nations.

Dennis also told us that there were extremely difficult days ahead of us because as a culture we had rejected God's ways. Dennis went on to declare that God had given him a word of assurance: "You have time to obey me." Looking at it from the eternal

---

[83] Since then, SCS has been renamed Go Strategic, and information about the ministry can be found at http://www.gostrategic.org.

[84] This article gives further explanation from a Jewish archaeological perspective: https://www.haaretz.com/jewish/archaeology/.premium-1.643766.

perspective and from what we know God has promised to bring to pass, Dennis borrowed the words of a Rolling Stones song to proclaim, "Time is on our side."

Dennis challenged us to offer ourselves fully to God and, thereby, both to begin afresh to get our own lives, family, and community in order and to truly act like what we are called to be—the people of God's kingdom who seek to see God's will done on earth in our own spheres of responsibility and influence.

There was nothing truly new to me in Dennis's message. It was an excellent summation and declaration of primary themes the Lord had been building into my thinking for nearly twenty years. At the same time, it was a fresh word that pierced me to the core. During the testings of the 1980s, I had lost confidence in myself (a good loss) and in our ability to build strong communities or churches (a necessary loss). Although my theology had not reverted and I had continued to profess the same beliefs and goals, Dennis's message revealed that my faith had been shaken. I realized that it was not only my faith in myself and in our human ability to live the truth ("faith" that needed to be shaken because it was not rooted in reality) that had been shaken, but also my faith in God and God's ability, unbeknownst to me, had been shaken to some degree. My focus had turned too far from what God could do and was doing and it had turned too much toward what we could do and needed to do and were failing to do.

Dennis's word was Spirit-given, and it reawakened faith in me that God is true to his word and his purposes. I *knew* once again, deep within, that God's kingdom will indeed come! Confidence arose in me that we will see God's will done on earth as it is in heaven. Faith began to awaken that whatever small part I have been given by God's grace to contribute, I actually can contribute—in the Spirit's power, not in my own. I realized anew that it is not my place to insist on seeing the culmination but that I simply needed to give myself in obedience.

As soon as Dennis ended the message, I got out of my seat and called for my wife and children to accompany me to the speaker's stage. There, in front of my brothers and sisters in the community, I made my stand with the declaration: "What Dennis has said this evening is what I signed up for. As for me and for my house, we will seek the kingdom and serve the purposes of God."

By this declaration I was affirming the journey on which the Lord had been leading me through the years. I was especially recommitting myself to live according to the foundational truths that he had been opening to me. I was not committing myself to take a new path, but rather I was making a renewed commitment to stay true to the course to which the Lord had called me.

Sometime during that weekend, Dennis Peacocke mentioned that the following summer he was holding a special training course for young adults through his ministry, Strategic Christian Services (now known as Go Strategic). This "Intern Program," as it was called in the early years, was to be a three-year program. Each year, I learned, would start with an intensive: several days of teaching and activities for all who planned to participate in a year of study, small group accountability, and a community project under the oversight of a local mentor.

I knew this was something I wanted to do as a mentor for my son. Thus, in the summer of 1992, I traveled with Elijah and two of his friends, Matt Petrie and Joel Jirak, to Santa Rosa for the first Intern Program summer intensive. We continued in the program through all three years. It was one of the great blessings of my life to work with these young men, contributing what I could as we did the studies, read the books, and worked on the projects together.

****

On March 3, 1991, forty-three people came together at Hannah McClure Elementary School in Winchester for the first Sunday morning worship gathering of Winchester Covenant Church. We packed out the classroom that we had rented. Therefore, the following Sunday we met in the school's gymnasium. The gym was a big room for our small group, but it became our Sunday morning meeting place through September 1993.

I took an announcement about our first meeting to the *Winchester Sun*, the community's newspaper, for publication on the weekly church page. For some unknown reason, the announcement was never published. Nevertheless, new people began to hear about our Sunday gatherings. Over the next months, several came to visit, and a growing number came to stay.

By that time, I had begun to look to Paul Petrie for pastoral oversight. Therefore, while he was in Lexington for a visit in June 1991, I met with him to update him concerning my life and the work. I shared with Paul about Winchester Covenant's first few months and about the five or six new families who had become part of us. Paul's response was not what I expected: "It is quite clear," he said, "that these people are being drawn by your gifts and ministry. You need to find a house and move to Winchester."

Immediately, I realized that Paul was correct. We did need to move to Winchester—we belonged there. The fact that we were purchasing land at River Hills in Madison County was beside the point. God was establishing us in relationships with people in Winchester and Clark County, not with those in Madison County. In my heart and mind, it was decided. As soon as I got home, I told Patricia we needed to move, and I do not even remember that she questioned it. We began to prepare to sell our house in Lexington, a house she had come to love, and we prepared to look for a new house.

I was so convinced that this was God's will, having heard this word from Paul, my pastor, that I completely failed to make my fellow elders, David and John, a part of the decision. Rather, I informed them of the change that I planned to make. Sadly, it would be some months before I realized fully that I had dishonored them, and especially David, our lead elder, by taking this precipitous action.

When David pointed out the misstep to me later, I immediately admitted my wrong and asked his forgiveness. To his credit, he did forgive me. Not only that, but he and John generously gave their full support to the change, and together we came up with a plan that made it possible for our family to make the move and to get the church established with Lexington Covenant's relational and organizational support. The plan included a gradual change in financial support that continued into 1995, when we established a team of elders in Winchester and filed our own Articles of Incorporation with the Commonwealth of Kentucky.

****

It took several months to sell our house and then to buy one in Winchester. Once again, selling and buying a home became a trial of endurance and test of faith. We put the Lexington house on the market in the summer of 1991 and began searching for a place to make our home in Winchester. Mrs. Elizabeth Sphar, a 70-year-old, retired schoolteacher and lifelong Winchester resident, became our real estate agent and showed us dozens of homes over the next several months. Through Mrs. Sphar, we learned many things about the community to which we were moving.

It was difficult to find a house in our price range that was both adequate for our family and that would help us serve the church well. We were very cautious about how much debt load we should take on since it seemed likely that in starting a new church our salary would have to be reduced at some point. We did make offers on two different houses, offers that even went a little beyond the highest amount we had set as our limit. Both offers were refused. Ironically, both of those houses eventually sold for less than we offered. Looking back, we can see that God shut those "doors."

A few days before Christmas, interest rates fell and we received a reasonable offer on the Lexington house from a couple who were members of Lexington Christian Fellowship. By the time we could get to Winchester, however, the other houses we had been interested in had also sold as soon as the interest rates had gone down. We looked diligently, even desperately, but found no suitable house.

On a Sunday about three weeks before we were scheduled to close the sale on our Lexington house, Scott Sidwell, who with his family had begun worshipping with us, told us that his next-door neighbors had tried to sell their home in the summer of 1990 because they wanted to move to Florida. Although the house was no longer on the market, he believed they still wanted to move. He gave us the address and the owners' phone number. We drove by the house, and when we saw the house and the neighborhood, we were not at all hopeful that we could afford it. Still, we had to find a house, so we called that very afternoon. The owners, Mr. and Mrs. Mollenkopf, invited us to come and look that afternoon.

The house was more than adequate in space and layout, although it badly needed some updated paint, kitchen wallpaper, and new carpet. The 2,500-square-foot main floor had four bedrooms, two baths, a music room, a large kitchen, a large dining room, and a formal living room. The basement had been paneled and divided into three rooms: a laundry room with a half-bath and two carpeted rooms. Even though it was not a full basement, it was large, with one of the rooms having nearly 500 square feet. Patricia, especially, liked the openness of the main floor, with its large windows letting in lots of light and no hallway to chop up the space.

Quite obviously, we thought as we walked through, *this house is worth more than we can pay.* After the walk-through, we all sat down at the kitchen table in order to talk about the price, which, not unsurprisingly, was $30,000 more than the upper limit we had set for ourselves.

I responded: "Based on everything we have seen, that is a very fair price; however, it is well beyond what we can pay. Thank you for showing us your home. We are sorry to have wasted your time."
I walked outside with the husband, and the ladies came out behind us. After we got in the car, Patricia told me that Mrs. Mollenkopf had asked, "Couldn't you at least consider making an offer?"

Because we had nowhere else to go and our closing was coming up fast, I began to seek counsel about whether to try to buy something so far above our price range. Hoping that I would be encouraged not to make such a large financial commitment,

I talked with Paul Petrie, I talked with John Meadows, I talked with my friend Bill Livingston, and I talked with others too. Everyone encouraged us to make an offer.

Finally, I went to Tom Monroe, another friend and a great brother in the Lord. Tom had taken some big financial setbacks as he sought to follow the Lord, so I was hoping that surely he would give me the conservative caution I was looking for. He did. Was I ever relieved! Rather than leave well enough alone, however, I said: "There is only one thing that bothers me. What if God is wanting to stretch us beyond our comfort zone?"

"Now, that sounds like God!" Tom declared firmly.

On Friday, five days after Scott had told us about the house, we gave the owners an offer that was $15,000 less than they had asked—and $15,000 above our upper limit. In the written offer, we asked that they let us know their decision within twenty-four hours. Saturday passed and we heard nothing. Sunday passed; we still heard nothing. I was greatly relieved, even though it meant we had nowhere to go and our closing was coming up quickly. At least we would not be "biting off more than we could chew" financially, I was thinking.

On Monday morning I was with Elijah in the basement family room of our home when the phone rang. It was Mr. Mollenkopf calling to say that he and his wife wanted to accept our offer and that they wanted us to meet with them and their lawyer that afternoon to sign a purchase agreement.

When I hung up the phone, my first fear-motivated words were, "Oh, shit." We were going to have a house after all, and I was flat-out scared.

I called the man who was buying our Lexington house to tell him that we had nowhere to move before the closing. Since he and his wife were living in an apartment and were not required to move immediately, he graciously offered to let us rent the house until we could arrange financing and close on the house in Winchester. Thus, on April 7, 1992, we took up residence in our new Winchester home.

Even though it seemed clear that God had led us to that house, my faith was weak and I was very often anxious about the financial commitment we had made. Over the next eighteen months, I took Patricia to look at several other houses, thinking that we could sell the one we were in and get in a cheaper one. Nothing worked out. Finally, I was able to put it in the Lord's hands fully and I quit looking.

We never missed a payment on the house; in fact, we were always able to pay a little extra each month against the principal. We never missed a meal. All our bills were paid on time. To top it off, we were able to pay the house off in nineteen years instead of thirty.

Not only has that house served our needs well, but it also has provided office space for me, and for five years, from 1994 to 1999, we had our Sunday worship gathering in the large basement room. Each Sunday we sat up about eighty folding chairs in the room, and several times we set up seventy places at tables for church meals that we shared in that room.

We did, in fact, take a significant cut in pay, as I had thought we would. From the fall of 1993 until early 1996, I took a part-time job making deliveries for Rees Office Products, a local store owned by Margie and Rick Beach, who had become members of our church.

I had no problem working at a so-called "secular job," since from my youth it had never been my goal to be paid for "ministry." The truth is I enjoyed driving the truck and making deliveries in a number of close-by counties. I made it my goal to make a favorable impression for Rees Office Products. Even more I wanted to represent Jesus well with a cheerful serving spirit, even though it was not my place to stand around "witnessing" in words when I was on the clock. The part-time job did have an impact on the time I could give to study and other church work, of course, and it made it more difficult for me to build new relationships with leaders in the community and in the churches of Winchester and Clark County. Therefore, in early 1996, I quit that job and began to look to the Lord to fully support us through the church.

23

New Beginnings

From the beginning, Bill Camenisch and I, along with Mort Trimble, sought to work as a team in leading Winchester Covenant's development. Not too long after we moved to Winchester, Rick Beach also began to meet with the team. Rick and his wife, Margie, had begun to join in our Sunday worship gathering at Hannah McClure School during our first month of meeting there and had soon become part of the church family.

For several years, among my friends who were leading churches, there had been a great deal of emphasis on clarifying the mission and vision of our churches in written form in order to develop plans and strategies. Therefore, I worked hard to develop written materials from which I hoped to help our team clarify our vision during our times of planning. There was some value in this, I think, because we talked about what we believed and about the way we thought God was leading us to build together. Although we eventually agreed on certain statements, I was not a very effective leader when it came to turning the mission and vision (big picture) into strategies and plans (the steps) on which we consistently followed through. We did eventually agree on a "vision statement" that, with some modifications over the years, does capture something of our heart and intention through the years.[85]

It seems to me now that several of those early documents may have represented "my vision" more than "our vision," but the time I spent in this effort was worth it as a tool to help me clarify what was in my own heart concerning the church. For example, in the course of one of my first attempts in 1992, I came up with the motto "equipping people to fulfill their destiny." Although a few years later we would begin to use "building for the generations to come" as our church motto, the first effort really did capture what was in my own heart, as revealed in this 1992 statement of my personal sense of call:

> I am called to aid men and women to know God, teaching them to think his thoughts and live according to his ways, and equipping them to fulfill the purpose for which God created and redeemed them; and in this process encouraging and leading them to grow together into a covenant people who visibly live out the rule of Christ.

---

[85] See Appendix Six for a copy of that statement.

Also, in 1992 and 1993 I began to write a paper that I titled "The Church in Our Time." The first section[86] of that paper still quite accurately captures the "big picture" of what I think a church community needs to be, but I bogged down on the second section in which I intended to write out the specifics that we needed to work on if we were to become such a community.

Then, unexpectedly, the Lord gave me four "pictures" that represent the church's nature and mission. I am a word person, not a visual person. I think in words, not in pictures. What I read typically sticks in my mind far more readily than what I see. I am not given to visions. However, as I was wrestling with how to describe my vision for the church, one day these four "pictures" concerning Christ's church came sharply into my mind.

The first was of a seed that was buried in the ground and then germinated, sprouted, grew into a plant, and reproduced a number of seeds, which were either replanted to multiply again or were ground into meal and baked into a loaf that could be broken to feed people. I realized immediately that this picture was related to Jesus's words about himself and his followers in John 12:23–26 and also to his parables about the sower and the wheat and the tares (Matthew 13:1–43) and to the parable of the seed growing (Mark 4:26–29). The church started as the one Seed, Jesus, multiplied into many seeds through Jesus's death and resurrection. The seeds do not exist for themselves; rather, either they are ground together and formed into one loaf to be broken to feed others or they are multiplied through the death and resurrection process.[87]

The second picture was of a vine spreading its branches out to neighborhoods, workplaces, recreational venues, and all around the world. This picture I understood to be related to Jesus's identification of himself as the vine and his followers as the branches in John 15, to Old Testament passages such as Psalm 80 and Isaiah 5, and also to the parables Jesus told about vineyards, such as in Matthew 21:28–46. The church, according to this picture, is a living organism which, starting from the one trunk, spreads its branches everywhere so that the fruit is available for people to "taste and see that the Lord is good" (Psalm 34:8).

The third picture was different. I "saw" in my mind a *National Geographic* photo of an Amish barn building that I had seen as a child. This picture pointed to the reality that the church is God's community, a spiritual family made up of families within

---

[86] Appendix Seven is a copy of that musing with modifications that I have made across the years.

which single people also find family. This family exists to reveal and to share God's love through serving.

The fourth picture was of the broken loaf and cup of wine—that is, the Eucharist or the Lord's Supper. I understood the picture to represent the church as a worshipping community, a "holy priesthood" (1 Peter 2:4–5, 9), the people of the new covenant offering themselves to God as a living sacrifice (Romans 12:1).[88]

Almost twenty-five years after I first "saw" these pictures in my mind, I am more convinced than ever that they suggest essential realities about the church that Jesus promised to build (Matthew 16:18) and that they are especially pertinent to the life and witness the church needs in these present times.

****

Not long after we moved to Winchester, our friend Tim Mitchell and his wife, Susan, stopped by our home to visit. As was typical in our relationship, Tim and I began to talk about books we had been reading. Tim also brought a gift, a book by Jordan Bajis titled *Common Ground: An Introduction to Eastern Christianity for the American Christian.*[89]

It would be hard to exaggerate the impact Tim's gift had on me. The first two chapters challenged the way I had been taught to think about Scriptures as authoritative, seeming to undermine its reliability. But as I read on into the third chapter, I began to think that the Eastern Orthodox way of thinking holds the Scriptures in as high a place—if not even higher—than they had been in mine. Bajis's book opened my eyes to a different way of understanding "the tradition," that is, the teaching, whether written or spoken, received from Jesus and the apostles (2 Thessalonians 2:15, 3:6; 1 Corinthians 11:2; Jude 3) that has come down to us in Scripture through the church.

This book struck chords from my past exposure to "the journey" of Peter Gillquist, Jack Sparks, and others who had started as Campus Crusade workers and eventually had become part of the Antiochian Orthodox Church.[90]

---

[88] See Appendixes Eight through Eleven for English versions. In 2015, I added outlines to these pictures. Friends helped me to translate the notes into Spanish to use as handouts for church leaders on the island of Ometepe in Nicaragua.

[89] Light and Life Publishing, 1991 edition.

[90] That journey, Peter Gillquist chronicled in *Becoming Orthodox: A Journey to the Ancient Christian Faith*, Conciliar Press, 1993.

Eventually, I made personal contact with Jordan Bajis by contacting the publishers of *Common Ground*, only to discover that he been a member of the Work of Christ Community in East Lansing, Michigan. The Work of Christ was one of the communities in the Association of Communities of which Servants of the Lord had been a part. Jordan also, it turned out, had been associated for a season with Peter Gillquist and his friends before they joined the Antiochian church. Jordan and I became friends, and we stayed in contact for a season.

I began to read more and more books about Orthodoxy and books by Orthodox authors. So great was the influence that my wife and some of my friends became concerned that I might join the Orthodox church myself. I cannot say that I never thought about doing so, but I did not think about it seriously for three primary reasons. First, the Lord had established me in covenant relationships with members of his Body, and I was fully confident that, if Orthodoxy was God's path for me, then he would confirm that by leading my covenant brothers in that direction also. Second, Jordan Bajis, who had an Orthodox heritage and had actually studied at St. Vladimir's Seminary under some of the great contemporary Orthodox men of God whose books I was reading, shared with me his assessment—that the Orthodox church is truly orthodox in its teaching (doctrine), which is grounded in the apostles and the early Church Fathers, but that the structure and practice of the Orthodox churches has moved away from the practices of the apostles and early fathers, beginning in the fourth century. The third thing was that I did not have peace about the place given to Mary in Orthodox liturgy and prayer.

Common Ground, however, began what has become an increasingly helpful shift in my point of view, having helped to shake me out of a worldview that has been far more influenced by Enlightenment rationalism than I had ever realized. Additionally, Bajis's book fueled my interest in the early Church Fathers and the written material from the first few centuries after the apostolic period. It also led to me to several excellent books by Orthodox authors. One of the most important of these was Alexander Schmemann, whose book *For the Life of the World: Sacraments and Orthodoxy*,[91] although written from an Eastern perspective, seemed to connect with things I had learned earlier from Francis Schaeffer's work.

Several of Schmemann's books were of value, but none more so than *The Journals of Father Alexander Schmemann 1973–1983*, the published version of journals found and published nearly twenty years after his death. In his journal entries, I discovered the inner life and thoughts of a brilliant and highly trained scholar who was grounded

---

[91] First published by St. Vladimir's Seminary Press in 1970.

in real life. Schmemann seemed to have been deeply aware of God in whatever he might have been doing—whether talking with his wife, walking in the rain, taking note of a garden, conversing with Alexander Solzhenitsyn, meeting with theologians, or participating in the worship liturgy. There was no separation. The heavenly (or spiritual) realities were fully present in this material reality for him. I had no idea that Western dualism had been so deeply engrained in me.

John Zizioulas, another Orthodox author, also had a significant impact on me. His book *Being as Communion: Studies in Personhood and the Church*,[92] which Jordan Bajis recommended to me, was challenging to read (to say the least), and I am quite sure I did not understand it all; even so, it helped make a fundamental difference in my understanding of the Trinity and of human relationships. Although I cannot remember Zizioulas's words exactly, I came to realize in a far deeper and more real way than before that the one true God is Father, Son, and Holy Spirit existing in such a profound communion of love that the three persons are one being. The personhood of each is realized in that love. Likewise, we humans can realize our personhood fully only as we are united to God and one another in God's love by grace and thus share in their communion.

Clearly, this reality is far beyond my comprehension, let alone my ability to communicate about it clearly. My inadequate comments are doing the book a disservice. However, *Being as Communion* has both changed my perception of God and also fed my hunger to truly know and love him—to live in a much fuller communion with God and with the people of God through the reconciliation Jesus accomplished.

Several years later, I discovered that Zizioulas had published *Eucharist, Bishop, Church: The Unity of the Church in the Divine Liturgy During the First Three Centuries*,[93] originally written as his doctoral dissertation in 1965 at the University of Athens (Greece). I found this book as I was preparing a paper on this subject to read at one of the meetings of Kingdom Ministries International, the network of church leaders of which I was a member. We had been seeking to recover the full meaning and Biblical use of the Greek word *ekklesia*, which is translated *church* in English.

For a long time I had been saying: "The church is not a building and it is not a meeting. The church is the people of God, all those who have put their faith in Jesus and follow him." Zizioulas's book challenged my statement because he showed that,

---

[92] Published by St. Vladimir's Seminary Press, 1985.
[93] Published by Holy Cross Orthodox Press, 2001.

according to Scripture, the word *ekklesia* actually does refer to the people of God specifically **when they are gathered together as a kingdom assembly** (as in 1 Corinthians 11:18, Matthew 18:16–20).

In 1993, Thomas Nelson published *The Orthodox Study Bible New Testament and Psalms*, released in print while Jack Sparks and others were still working on the Old Testament. The notes in this Bible helped me gain some understanding about the Orthodox interpretation of Scripture, and the short articles about some key Orthodox teaching added insight. I appreciated even more two articles: "The Bible: God's Revelation to Man" and especially "How to Read the Bible." Also, I have often used the lectionary readings as part of my daily Bible reading in years since. However, it was the morning and evening prayers that became the greatest help of all.

Several years earlier, soon after becoming the leading elder of Lexington Covenant Church, David Redish had led the elders and wives to take a Christianized version of the Myers-Briggs personality test. Although I am cautious about such personality tests and other psychologically oriented evaluations, there was one result of that test that I had found intriguing—that my personality was best suited to using a set form of prayer, in contrast to the spontaneous prayer that is standard among the evangelicals and charismatics in my background. This result piqued my interest because I had desired to be faithful in prayer but had always found it difficult to be consistent in prayer.

Soon afterward, I came across *Drawing Near: A Guide to Devotion and Prayer*[94] by Kenneth Boa and Max Anders and bought a copy. I discovered that I did indeed find it helpful to have a "map" to follow in prayer. I was able to focus my mind better; therefore, following the suggested prayer guide left me with the sense that I had actually prayed meaningfully. However, the Orthodox morning and evening prayers, in a far greater way, seemed to help me present myself before the Lord and to present my intercessions for others to him. For several years, those prayers provided my daily prayer "map"—and for the first time my prayer life was consistent for a significant length of time. Although I have had long periods in the years since when I did not use the Orthodox prayers, in several seasons I have come back to that form of prayer, especially in periods when my life in God has needed to be renewed.

****

[94] Published by Thomas Nelson, 1987.

Elijah, who had graduated from high school in 1990, was very active in the Lexington Covenant youth group and often played the bass guitar for the worship team. Therefore, when the rest of our family began to worship in Winchester, he continued to serve our home church. When we actually moved to Winchester, Elijah moved with us and became a part of Winchester Covenant. At age 15 he had begun to work in the summers for the Davenport brothers, who had moved with us from Minneapolis and had formed their own company, laying block and pouring concrete. After that first summer, Elijah told us that he planned to continue working for a couple years after graduation in order to save money toward college and to learn the skills in that trade. "If I learn those skills I will have something to fall back on if I need it and, if not, I will have skills that I can use to serve others," he said.

Soon after we moved to Winchester, that company went out of business; therefore, Elijah took a job at a Winchester factory, a job requiring him to work twelve-hour shifts, from 7 p.m. to 7 a.m., spread over different days of the week, so that over the course of two weeks he would work at least once on every day of the week. It was a grueling schedule that left him without much of a life except to work and to sleep. Even on nights when he was not working, he would stay up all night so that he could sleep during the day. It was a great relief for Elijah, and for us too, when in late August 1992 the Beaches hired him to deliver office products—the job that I would take after he began his studies at Berea College in 1993.

Stephanie was a freshman at Lafayette High School in Lexington when we moved. In order to let her finish the school year in the same school, for six weeks she lived in a household with four single ladies who were members of Lexington Christian Fellowship, coming to stay with us only on the weekends. It was difficult to have her away from home, but it was also good to see her conducting herself with unusual maturity at such an early age.

Andrea moved with us and finished that school year in the fourth-grade class at Odell Gross Elementary School, where, even in 1992, the principal, Mr. Vermillion, had someone open the school day with prayer over the public-address system, which was connected to speakers in every classroom. Prayer and the character of the principal were the best things about the school, but the level of education she received was not very good. Patricia began to homeschool her again in 1994.

There were challenges in our marriage as there are in every marriage, but overall the next few years were good ones for Patricia and me. In 1993 one of the ladies in the church who worked for the local radio station encouraged Patricia to apply for a part-time job as a receptionist for the radio station. After she had worked there for about a year, Tom Nickell, owner of a Christian bookstore in the same building as the radio station, asked if she would work part-time for him.

Then in 1995, another woman in our church encouraged Patricia to apply for a temporary job at the University of Kentucky Medical Center. Patricia did apply and got the job. After working as a temporary employee for a year, Patricia became a full-time employee in the fall of 1996, a huge blessing for our family because of the benefits full-time employees received at that time. She could apply up to 5% of her earnings toward retirement, and UK would contribute double that amount. Plus, through UK we were able to get excellent healthcare insurance at a cost much lower than we would have been able to do with me as the sole employee of the church.

Once we moved to Winchester, I had begun to attend the meetings of the local Association of Churches because from the time I was a youth pastor in Minneapolis, I had always believed it important to try to build meaningful relationships with other church leaders in the community. When I started working part-time for Rees Office Products, I could no longer participate in those meetings because of my work schedule, so building those local relationships was slow. I did continue in close relationships with John Meadows, David Redish, Billy Henderson, and a few other leaders in Lexington with whom I had been praying for a number of years.

Soon after we began Sunday meetings in Winchester, David invited me to join in regularly scheduled times of fellowship with the pastors and wives of the covenant pastors and wives in our area. These times of fellowship with David and Sandra Redish, Bill and Barbara Livingston from Louisville, and Dennis and Sheila Cole from northern Kentucky quickly became a great source of fellowship and encouragement for Patricia and me.

Winchester Covenant grew steadily in numbers for the first couple of years until we had about eighty-five people fellowshipping together regularly. In some ways, this growth was not surprising to me, since I had observed that many newly started churches draw people in the beginning. I had known of several which, based on this early growth, had then gone into debt to buy or construct a building for worship, only to have many of the people leave after a year or two of attending.

Since we were not inclined to buy a building, we did not have a debt load, but in the fall of 1993, we did have some people cease to worship with us. That fall we tried a change in meeting place and schedule. I had developed a friendship with the local Episcopal pastor, whose church had a fellowship hall with a kitchen and several surrounding classrooms that became available to us on Saturday evenings. It seemed like a far more suitable place than the school we had been meeting in on Sundays. At Hannah McClure School, we were a small group meeting in a gymnasium that echoed and magnified every noise. Some of our children's ministry classes were actually sitting on the floor in the school hallways.

To have a more hospitable environment in which to gather seemed to offset the inconvenience of changing the time of our weekly worship gathering to Saturday evening instead of Sunday morning. Besides, in the early church, I had learned, it was common to open the Lord's Day with worship on Saturday evening following the end of the Jewish Sabbath at sundown, so I was excited that having a Saturday evening worship gathering would be a return to the way of our forefathers. We made the decision to make the change.

No strong objections were made when we announced the change. And when we met in the new location for the first time on the first Saturday of October, virtually every person who had been worshipping with us came. However, the attendance seemed to decline a little each week thereafter. Conflicts in schedule always seemed to come up on Saturday night for some families.

Part of the difficulty, I thought with some frustration, is that people have fixed cultural ideas about what church is and isn't and they just are not willing to change. Practically speaking, however, our families had a number of young children who seemed to come tired, restless, and even cranky on Saturday evening. It was harder for their mothers, too, after a full day of mothering and housekeeping, to come ready for worship.

In November, three families who had been with us nearly from our beginning decided to leave the church. That was difficult, to say the least.

Then the holiday season hit. The Saturday night schedule had proven difficult before, but once the holiday activities began, attendance really dropped. By Saturday, December 18, it appeared that there might be only five or six families left. I had anticipated that not all who came to the church in the early days would prove to be part of the church as time passed, but I had not anticipated this. It was test time:

First question: Is Winchester Covenant the Lord's church or mine?

Second question: If it is his, am I going to entrust the church to his care, or am I going to fight for "my own success"?

Third question: Is it time to recognize that I've failed and just give up?

Once I faced the questions, the answer was clear. The Lord had called me to this work. I was responsible to give my best, but the outcome was up to him. Everything did not become easy just because I had determined my answer, but at least I was not struggling with doubt.

At that meeting on the 18th, we adults talked it over. We decided that if those of us gathered that evening were all who remained in the church, we were going to go on seeking to follow and obey the Lord, who had brought us together.

To top it off, Christmas and New Year's Day fell on Saturday that year, and it became clear that scheduling a service on the evenings of those days would not work at all. Patricia and I did open our home for fellowship on Sunday evening the 26th. Three families came, all of whom had been part of the Minnesota group that had moved to Lexington, but only one of them had become part of Winchester Covenant. The other two were still part of Lexington Covenant at that time, although both families did eventually become part of our fellowship in Winchester.

It was a good evening of fellowship. Each family left us with a Christmas card. When we opened them after they had left, to our surprise they had included gifts of cash for us. We were encouraged with the fellowship and were helped by the money.

The leadership team by that time was Bill, Rick, and I. We called a meeting for Sunday morning, January 9, to be held in our home, and we sent invitations to everyone who had been identified with our church and who had not told us that they were leaving. We announced that we planned to talk together about our future as a church. To my surprise, at least one adult from every family who had been with us before the changes in October came to that gathering, except one couple, who were out of town for a funeral, and of course, the three that we knew had left.

Without being asked, Greg Dunteman brought a guitar, and we had a time of worship in song—a rich and meaningful time. It was clear in the discussion which followed that we were ready to go on together. We decided to gather in another home the next Sunday. So it was that for more than five years we had our Sunday worship gathering in our homes. For the first few months, we met in three or four different homes that had space to hold us. Then in April or May, we began to meet in our basement regularly.

I had been reluctant to schedule all the meetings at our house, only because the road is narrow and there is no place to park that does not hinder traffic. When we did meet at our house, I asked everyone to pull off the road and into the grass except for the four or five vehicles that could be parked in our driveway. I was concerned, though, about what would happen to the yard if we did that when the ground was wet from rain or snow. However, when it became clear that our house was the best place to gather, we made the decision to do so. After meeting there Sunday after Sunday—every Sunday except one when we had 13–15 inches of snow—and after parking in that yard no matter what the weather, five-and-one-half years later there were no ruts in the yard. It was undamaged!

****

The summer of 1995, although very busy, was a very special time in our family. Stephanie, who had been homeschooling using the Christian Liberty Academy curriculum, graduated from high school and planned to enter Berea College as a student that fall. Elijah also came home for the summer to work in the maintenance department at the Clark Rural Electric Cooperative (now called Clark Energy), as he had for two previous summers. And we had a wedding coming up. He and Jenny Nelson had set their wedding date for August 11.

Elijah and Jenny had begun to date during his freshman year at Berea and were engaged the following summer. From the first time he had brought Jenny home to visit the family, she began to connect deeply with us. In fact, before that visit had ended, I took her aside and said, half-jokingly, "Jenny, you do not have to marry Elijah, but you do have to be our daughter."

Jenny came to live with us during that summer. Jenny's mother lived in North Carolina and her dad lived in Arizona. Since she and Elijah had met at Berea College, the friends they had in common were from the college. Both also had strong connections with our church family too; therefore, it seemed best to them to have the wedding in Winchester. Jenny and Stephanie were roommates and both took jobs at Quality Manufacturing, a local company that made printer cartridges. Jenny fit right into the family.

During the year I had homeschooled Elijah, he turned 16. Not only did he and I become closer and closer, but his relationship with his mother began to grow stronger the older he got. Of his own volition, he also began to reach out in friendship to Stephanie, who was four-and-a-half years younger, and a strong bond developed between them.

I am convinced that Elijah's influence helped Stephanie to mature more quickly than most do. In eighth grade she had written an essay for school about why teens need not rebel—and lived it! It was that maturity which had given us the courage and trust to allow her to live with adult women in Lexington for six weeks after we moved to Winchester. When she was 15 we hosted a party at which we presented her to our church as a young woman and asked that people receive her as such. With no prompting from us, Stephanie began to reach out in friendship to Andrea, who was nearly five years younger.

The summer flew by. I was working in the church and for Rees Office Products. Patricia was working part-time at Bethany Bookroom; Stephanie and Jenny had wearisome jobs at Quality. Elijah not only worked hard at the electric co-op, often outdoors in the summer heat, but he also took a part-time, late-night job, mostly washing dishes, at the local Wendy's restaurant.

Even with all that, it was a great summer with the family all together. And it was capped off by the wonderful wedding celebration on August 11 when Elijah took a bride and Jenny officially became part of the family.

There was one difficult thing I remember from that summer. Not long after the wedding, it came time for Stephanie to leave home for college. I can only say that it was far harder for me to release a daughter to leave than it had been to release a son. For the first time, besides some assignments in school, I tried to express my feelings in a poem: "Much Music left my house today …," it began. The actual poem expressed honest sentiments, even though they probably got somewhat lost in my overworked metaphor of an orchestra. I can say, though, these days when Stephanie comes with her nine children, it's like the whole marching band has arrived.

****

In early 1996 I quit the delivery job and, trusting that the Lord would meet our financial needs, began giving myself full-time to the work of the church. Our relationships as a church community seemed stable, but I wanted to be more active in trying to reach new people. I began to get involved in the Association of Churches again.

Then Elijah died.

24

Grace Working in Grievous Loss

It was difficult enough to process Jenny's call[95] summoning us to the Berea Hospital because Elijah had apparently had a heart attack. The initial shock that followed Dr. Gresier's telling us that Elijah was dead stunned me so completely that I could not respond emotionally for about 30 minutes.

We had seen Elijah and Jenny briefly that morning. On their way from their home in Berea to Lexington, where they were to spend the day working at a lemonade stand during Lexington's 4th of July parade, they had swung over to Winchester and had come to our house in order to pick up a package of fireworks that I had purchased for Elijah when driving through Tennessee a few days earlier.

It was a short visit, ending as was our custom with us saying "I love you" to each other as Elijah and Jenny headed out the kitchen door. Now he was dead!

According to my journal,

> At some point we began to ask what happened.
>
> Jenny and Elijah had gone to Tom and Susan's to set off the fireworks he had gotten from me earlier in the day. Elijah had gotten tired, so tired that he had to sit on the porch steps. Then he had gone into the house to use the bathroom.
>
> He was gone too long, and Tom went to check on him. Elijah answered weakly that he was not feeling well. Tom got Jenny and she went in and found Elijah collapsed on the floor between the toilet and tub. He roused to ask them to help fix his pants back up. They tried.
>
> Tom went to call 911, and Jenny held him in her arms and talked to him. He roused at least once more and asked, "What's going on?" Then, she says, he convulsed once, his face turned pale, his lips turned blue, and he was gone.

Once the paramedics arrived, Jenny told us, for twenty minutes they had tried to revive Elijah. Then, after his body arrived at the ER, Dr. Greiser told us that he had

---

[95] See the introduction for that account.

also worked for 20 minutes trying to revive him. Dr. Greiser went on to say: "It was such a massive heart attack that I don't think he could have been saved even if it had happened in the hospital. It is almost certain that it was caused by a defect he had had since birth."

While we waited for our daughters to arrive at the Berea Hospital, I began to make calls to our family and some close friends. I had already called our friend and pastor, Bill Livingston, to ask for prayer while I was waiting for Patricia to dress after the phone call from Jenny.

Even after just a few days, I was not able to remember the exact sequence of calls to record in the journal, but I did reach Bill Camenisch and asked that he would get hold of our daughters and bring them to Berea as soon as possible.

I called my brother, Wes, and asked him to call our parents in upstate New York, where Dad was preaching at a camp meeting. I cannot remember if I called my sisters or if Wes did. Patricia or I called one or two of her sisters and asked them to get the bad news around to her siblings.

I called my good friend Billy Henderson, and I asked him to contact John Meadows, whom I had not been able to reach.

In the journal entry for July 16, I wrote,

> Everyone we talked to was stunned. It was so hard to process the reality. It was almost funny to me that a couple of people responded first with "You're kidding?" (as though any sane person would kid about such a thing). I knew they were only trying desperately to grasp Elijah's death as a real possibility.
>
> After some period of time, after some calls, after some efforts to comfort others, after some prayers, and after some pacing in the hall, I broke into sobs and weeping for the first time; periodic bursts of hard crying and deep sobs that came forth seemingly of their own will became commonplace from then until Sunday afternoon.

Although I am not one to cry easily, in this circumstance I did not hold back but poured out my pain unchecked. I suspect this was better in the long run than trying to hold it in. It was 1 a.m. or later before Bill was able to reach Stephanie and Andrea and get them to the hospital. Bill and his wife, Gina; our fellow elder Rick Beach and his wife, Margie; our close family friend, Joyce Wilhelm; and Stephanie's boyfriend, Daniel Loveland, all arrived together.

Once the girls had arrived, Patricia and I were escorted back to see our son's body, something I recalled in some detail in my journal. For now, I will simply share these few sentences.

> I released him to the Lord with tears of deep sorrow yet mixed with joy that there was no doubt that Elijah had lived for the Lord, that he was now with the Lord, and that I was choosing to offer the Lord a good offering, the best that I had to give. It was a strange mixture of thinking of him in past tense and knowing that he was still alive in the present tense, though absent from us and from his body. I remembered holding Elijah in the delivery room and, along with Patricia, dedicating him to the Lord. He was too big to hold up in my hands now, but we offered him up in death in the same spirit as we had at his birth.

After worshipping and praying together in the emergency room waiting area, we all headed back to our house. We arrived about 2:30 a.m. to find John and Vickie Meadows and John's mother, Dorothy, parked in our driveway waiting for us. Before long, Billy Henderson arrived also, and not long afterward, to our surprise, Bill and Barbara Livingston arrived from Louisville. We spent a couple hours together in our family room weeping and crying. Sometimes we laughed a little too, after someone would bring up some special memory.

Of course, we talked about things leading up to Elijah's death. For a couple of months, Patricia and I had been noticing that he had gained a significant amount of weight. We had also seen him experience shortness of breath a couple of times. We were concerned because he did not look healthy, but we assumed it was because he was eating too much of the wrong foods and exercising too little. After all, I was significantly overweight too. Two Saturday evenings before his death, Elijah, Patricia, and I had talked together about our weight issues while sitting at our picnic table with some cold drinks.

For two weeks before dying, Elijah had made a few visits to the student medical clinic because of respiratory problems. We learned that he had even had at least two EKGs. Because the first one showed a small abnormality in the heart, he had another test several days later. When both tests were identical, the examining doctor concluded that the abnormality was Elijah's "normal."

Now that Elijah had died, we remembered how the weight he had gained made him look puffy and wondered if that had been a sign that his body was holding water because of heart issues. We talked about the trip Elijah and several men from our church and from Berea had taken to a Promise Keepers Conference held at the Charlotte Motor Speedway just three weeks earlier, and especially about Elijah and his friends sitting on the unshaded grass under a blistering hot sun all day to be near the speakers' stand. We discussed the 100+ degree heat that Elijah had worked in that very day during the parade in Lexington. We recalled an incident when, two Sunday evenings previous, while playing ping pong in our basement, Elijah had become so breathless that he had had to stop and lean against the table for a while before he could play again. We wondered if that might have been a small heart attack, maybe even the cause of the heart abnormality that had shown up on the first EKG a day or two later.

Patricia told us about the time when at age 4 Elijah came and asked her to pray with him that Jesus would forgive his sins and come into his life. We recalled how a few months later he asked that on his fifth birthday he be baptized in water and that he be prayed with for the baptism in the Holy Spirit.

We laughed as we remembered how, when he first had talked about water baptism, he had wanted to wait until he got to heaven so that Jesus's cousin, John, could baptize him. And we laughed as we remembered that on his birthday, he forgot about baptism in the Spirit. He could barely get through the water baptism. His eyes were on a great big, wrapped-up box that Mike and Janetta Hynous had brought for him.

On July 19, concerning that time of sharing, I wrote,

> At some point I remembered a phrase from Revelation 22:5, " ... And his servants will serve Him" (NKJV). The apostle John made this comment when describing the bride, the city coming down out of heaven from God, that city where the water of life flows out from the throne of God and of the Lamb. The water of life is a river with the tree of life standing on each side, yielding fruit monthly, its leaves providing healing for the nations. There is no curse in that city, no night, no need for the light of the sun. In that city are no tears, no death, no mourning, no crying, no pain. In that city there is no separation from one another or from our God. In that city, Elijah and I indeed will serve our King together and reign with Him forever more, I declared to the others. Every good thing here is only a foretaste of that which is coming and which will remain. This is our hope, our faith, and our confidence. *Amen. Come, Lord Jesus.*

With only relatively few ups and downs, Elijah had walked with the Lord, and the evidence in his life was plain to those who knew him.

After a time, Billy Henderson and Bill Livingston got on my computer and began to send emails to those in my contact list, spreading the news about Elijah's death.

Finally, about 5 a.m., everyone had gone. Patricia and I got into bed. She refused to lie down, choosing to sit up against the headboard. I snuggled close and tried to sleep. I don't know if Patricia even dozed. I did a few times, for what seemed like seconds at a time. We did get quiet and rest a little until just about 6 a.m. Then Patricia began to weep again, and I held her. Just as her weeping subsided, I started sobbing, and she held me.

After crying together for a while there in our bed, Patricia and I went ahead and got up. I cannot remember details. I do know I made some coffee and wandered back and forth between the kitchen and the family room. Every little while, one of us would break into tears again. The other would quickly move over and hold the one crying until the tears had stopped again and the immediate wave of grief had subsided. It was still hard to believe that this was all true. Yet the deep pain we felt testified that it really was.

By 8 a.m. friends began to show up, usually with food. Concerning those first days until Sunday afternoon, I wrote,

> Something of a pattern began to emerge which continued into Sunday afternoon. I would all of a sudden break out in crying, often with hard sobs, a few times with nearly a keening sound which reminded me of the wailing that characterizes mourning in some other cultures. I never tried to cry but I never tried not to cry either. The crying spells were unpredictable. I simply refused to analyze my behavior. Somehow, I sensed that for once I simply must experience life, not figure it out. Later as people came in to us I might weep with them, or I might hold them and comfort them as they wept. It was not unusual for me to try to put them at ease saying, "My fountain of tears is dry at the moment. But don't worry it will fill up and spill over at any time."

****

I don't know how we could have made it through the next few days without friends. Joyce Wilhelm and Gina Camenisch came to serve Patricia, especially by coordinating the kitchen and managing hospitality. Bill Camenisch took a day off work (a real sacrifice for one who is self-employed in a one-man business) just so that he could be available to help with whatever needed to be done. I have no idea the number of errands he ran, of details he covered, and of phone calls he handled. Others of our church family stepped up and helped selflessly without recognition in uncounted ways. So many people helped in so many different ways that there is no way to mention all, even if I could remember such details.

Billy Henderson was back at our house again by midmorning in order to accompany Patricia and me to Scobee Funeral Home, where we met Jenny and her mother. Together we made the arrangements for the visitation on Sunday evening and the funeral and the burial on Monday morning. Next, we drove to the nearby Winchester Cemetery, where we purchased a grave plot.

At some point, with help from Billy Henderson and Bill Livingston, we did plan the funeral itself. But mostly Friday and Saturday were like a blur—a seemingly endless line of friends coming by to mourn with us—plus phone calls, flower and food deliveries, lots of weeping, and countless stories remembered.

Three of Patricia's sisters, Norma, Reada, and Kay, came from Ohio to grieve with us and to help us through those days. Her sister Freda came on Saturday to stay with Patricia for a week. What a gift that was.

Billy was there much of the time, overseeing the visitations, helping to control the traffic flow in the house so that we would not become too overwhelmed, and dealing with phone calls. There was a constant flow of people on Friday and Saturday until about 8:30 p.m. each evening, when Billy would encourage everyone to leave and began to urge us to go on to bed while he took care of phone calls.

My brother had reached my dad and mom by phone soon after I called him on the night of Elijah's death. Elijah was their first grandchild, and they had a close bond with him, even though our geographical separation and my parents' ministry travel schedule had meant that they could not be together all that often. After Wes called, Mom and Dad tried to go back to bed but soon realized they were not going to be able to sleep; therefore, they got up in the wee hours of the morning and made the eleven-hour drive back from New York to their Circleville, Ohio, home. Once home, Dad called and offered to come on down that Friday evening, but I encouraged them to rest at home. On Saturday morning they drove to Winchester, arriving at our house in the early afternoon, and they settled into the rooms in our basement.

It meant the world to have them with us. I found myself torn, though, since they did not know our friends and were more comfortable keeping their privacy. I wanted to be in the basement where Mom and Dad were with my sister Marvene and her family, who had arrived a short time after my parents. Yet I also wanted to greet all the friends who came to grieve with us and to support us.

One huge surprise from that Saturday afternoon is etched into my heart and mind. About 4 p.m. Mitch Ramey, one of my two closest childhood friends, called to ask for directions to our house. Although Mitch had suffered with muscular dystrophy since early childhood and was wheelchair-bound, that day, accompanied by one of his great-nieces, he made the three-and-one-half-hour drive in his handicapped-equipped van. We were able to get his motorized wheelchair into our walkout basement where my parents were so that we could visit. Mitch and his niece were able to stay for only an hour before they had to load back up and drive back to Circleville. "What love and sacrifice! It was overwhelming," I wrote a few weeks later.

Sunday morning was quieter for a while. Our church family met at the Beaches' house to worship and grieve together. We stayed home and had a time of prayer with the family. I wrote about our prayer time in my journal:

> The family prayer time was quiet but very meaningful. Dad shared some Scriptures and some of his thoughts with us. Then others of us also shared Scriptures and comforting words. We sang together and asked for strength and mercy for the day ahead.

> Marvene and John wanted to visit Berea to see the college and also Elijah and Jenny's house. They wanted to be able to identify a bit more with the last three years of his life. Dad decided to go also. With the young people, we were too many for one car; therefore, Stephanie rode with John, Marvene, and Chris while Dad, Rachel, Andrea, and I rode together.

> We drove in from the southern exit and went through town and drove through the college. Then we went past Elijah and Jenny's first apartment. I told how they worked so hard moving alone over New Year's weekend in order to surprise us when they were able to find a small house to rent. I wanted to stop and look at the house. Dad paused but then drove on, saying that might be too hard. I got pretty quiet and tearful after a while, and he reached over across the seat and just held onto my hand. It was a tender act of fatherly love.

I began to share about my relationship with Elijah, about our friendship and hopes of working together. These were tender and precious moments for me. At the same time, they must have been as hard for Dad as they were for me since both of us would love nothing more than to have had the same deep fellowship and friendship and working together that Elijah and I had tasted. Our relationship, however, has been a complicated one. We have always loved one another and wanted to be closer to each other. The last several years we have grown much closer, but there has been a serious issue between us since the mid-1970s. Our spiritual journeys differ; our spiritual perspectives and experiences also differ, but I believe that in our common loss of son and grandson there is also a deeper healing taking place between us. Anyway, the closeness of those shared moments is precious to me, even now, as I write, nearly a month later.

I remember that Dennis and Sheila Cole came and served us that day. Not too many besides our relatives came to visit on Sunday afternoon. My cousin Dick and his wife had come from their homes south of Atlanta, and the other of my two closest childhood friends, Don Benner, had come with his family.

To our surprise, Colin Lavergne, a good friend since our days with the Servants of the Lord, came from Minneapolis. A little more than two years earlier, Colin had lost his wife after a long battle with cancer, leaving him with eight children and great grief. We were able to sit down at our picnic table with Colin for a brief but deeply meaningful conversation. He offered us encouragement and wisdom about dealing with grief.

In the journal I wrote about that Sunday afternoon:

> For me, however, the afternoon was hard. I was very tired. My heart seemed to literally ache; there was an almost physical ache in my chest. I dreaded the visitation. Sometime around 3 p.m. I went downstairs where Dad, Mom, and Marvene's family were. Dad suggested I go and lie on the bed he and Mom had been sleeping in. A little later, Marvene began to play Jenny's piano, which is there in the basement. Her music ministered peace and strength to my weary soul. I found encouragement in just being near Dad and Mom at that time. And Dad always seemed to have just the right words to keep me going.

My sister Debbie and her family and my brother, Wes, with his family arrived in the middle of the afternoon.

****

We left home at 4:15 to go to Lexington Covenant Church's building for the visitation. I wrote about the visitation and the funeral in a letter, dated July 11, 1996, to Paul Petrie who, with his family, had moved back to Brussels, Belgium, earlier that year:

> We drove to Lexington Covenant Church and Bill Livingston prayed with us before we entered the auditorium to view Elijah's body. As Jenny, Patricia, and I; our daughters; and Mom and Dad started down the aisle toward the casket, the Holy Spirit filled us with strength and comfort. Afterward we discovered that Jenny and I especially were aware of three very strong emotions—excitement, peace, and overwhelming joy. Many times I felt almost apologetic as we stood there greeting and comforting others for hours.
>
> Hundreds came to mourn and to comfort us. Some stood in line for 2½ hours in order to see Elijah's body and to hug us and to cry with us. However, none of us in the family had many tears that evening, and I had none. I was filled with elation that Elijah was with his God and that the kingdom was in some intangible way being advanced significantly in all this.
>
> The excitement, peace, and joy prevailed through the evening, through the night, and all through the day of the funeral. Patricia was not experiencing those same emotions, at least not so intensely, but she was full of faith, hope, and comfort, even though physically weakened and faint at times because of the stress and lack of food (she has found it hard to eat until yesterday). The girls were serene and trusting and towers of strength. My parents were stately and imparted encouragement, strength, and hope to us.
>
> Just before the funeral began on Monday morning, God gave us insight into these "strange" emotions. Elijah's high school, senior year, Bible teacher, Joe Bray, came and gave Patricia and I copies of an essay, in the form of a letter, that Elijah had written in the school year '90–'91. Mr. Bray had found the paper in his files the day before Elijah died, and then he remembered it upon receiving word of Elijah's death. I have enclosed a copy for you—misspellings and sloppy writing included. The assignment was to spend time alone in a cemetery to ponder death

327

without the hope of our Faith.

You will see that the excitement, peace, and joy we were experiencing were God's way of letting us share a special gift and revelation with Elijah.

Dear Mr. Bray

First off I want to say thanks for this opportunity. It was GREAT! My experience was very different from the rest of the class, to my knowledge. To begin with I heard several people say it would be freaky, or scary to walk alone in a cemetary. I didn't ever feel this way. I was kind of excited about the trip from the beginning. When we got there you asked us to be silent and serious in our walk. You also asked us to try to forget heaven and the promises of God and act like we knew nothing of the afterlife. Sorry Mr. Bray but I failed you in this. I really really tried to do it but it just didn't work. Looking at the gravestones I understood the hopelessness people who don't know God has. I felt sorry for people who tried to "make it all better" by pretending the dead are sleeping or are just on a trip. Personally, I think this is wrong, it tries to bypass some very real emotions that should be expressed. I firmly believe we shouldn't be run by our emotions, however,

Jesus himself cried bitterly, even to the point of anger when Lazarus died. Anyway, I understood others points of view about death. For myself it was different. I felt the peace and solitude almost as soon as we were in the gate; but the longer I was there the more exited I became. I felt God's presence as soon as I started walking, not among the graves but on me, and this overwhelming sense of joy fell on me. Also as I walked around God showed me how foolish other religions are. No other religion gives people a way to correctly handle their thoughts, feelings, and emotions surrounding death. Christianity does. Through Christ we've been given victory over death. That victory is who gave me joy and made me excited during the walk.

I hope I've covered your assignment, but this is what happened and I'm glad it did. Oh, I did get scared one time. I leaned down to clean off a head stone and it fell over. I thought I was in trouble. Enlightened an victorious

Elijah G Humble

Great work. PTL!

Hundreds filled, to standing room only, the LCC building, including the foyer. We have no way of knowing how many never got in. There we worshipped, offering up our son as a sacrifice of thanksgiving, to our Lord and God, who is worthy of all. I am enclosing a copy of our invitation to worship. Billy Henderson read comments about Elijah from family and friends, and we learned that our son was far deeper in his wisdom and understanding and far more effective in his influence and ministry than we had ever imagined. Some key words were "without guile, wisdom, discipler, mentor, friend, deeply spiritual while fully engaged in this world."

Bill Livingston preached an absolutely profound and superb message on embracing fully the pain and the joy. My brother, who is a student of preaching and not ineffective himself, reportedly said later, "I guess I'll have to quit preaching now."

It took close to half an hour to get all the cars into the cemetery (not including the drive there) and all the people to the gravesite. On the way, we shared Elijah's essay with Jenny and my parents. While we waited, we could not mourn. Frankly, Jenny and I wanted to get up and dance on the green carpet where they were going to set the casket. Knowing that would be scandalous to some, we held ourselves to wriggling and grinning in our seats. Then we had the inspiration to have Bill Livingston read Elijah's essay at the beginning so everyone would know what we were feeling. He read it masterfully. We all laughed, and as he finished the crowd broke into applause.

Then he read two comforting passages of Scripture and prayed. Jenny started to sing, but John Meadows got there first, singing out as declaration, "The steadfast love of the Lord never ceases ... ." As that ended, Jenny began what truly expressed our thoughts and feelings: "This is the day that the Lord has made; let us rejoice and be glad in it." We sang and clapped and rejoiced, and I think I know what Peter felt when he said, "Let's build three tabernacles here." Even now, three days later, I have excitement, peace, and joy at just the thought of visiting my son's grave.

Occasional tears and the lonely ache are again with us, but so far there has been no moment when that taste of eternity has not also been present with us. Yesterday was Patricia's and my 25th anniversary. God

331

graciously granted us a day of his presence, of painful sweetness and joy, and only the occasional tear. This morning I woke to hold my dear wife as she cried one more time.

We do not know, of course, what the path of grief and suffering will be in days ahead, but we have tasted heaven and are sustained by the Father of all comforts who comforts us in our distresses. We are surrounded by family and friends who are carrying us in love and prayer. And we are surrounded by a great cloud of witnesses, which includes our beloved son, Elijah, who is cheering us on and calling for us to overcome.

I hope this does not sound to you like whistling in the dark or like sweet platitudes, but I must declare: "God is good. God is faithful. God does all things well."

In the years since, I have shared many times with others about the way my dad seemed to set aside his own deep grief in order to strengthen me in mine. His care for me in those days continues to be a testimony of true fathering in action. Dad cared for me with the Father's heart.

25

Walking in that Lonesome Valley

Elijah's death was a devastating loss for Jenny, for our immediate family, for our extended family, for our spiritual family, and for Elijah's friends.

Each member of our family has a unique story about the immediate days following Elijah's death. I can share only mine.

On July 28 I wrote this in my account of those days.

> One thing that has happened is that Stephanie, Andrea, Patricia, and I have in many ways grieved separately. The girls especially got very tired of all the people and the endless rounds of weeping. Eventually, they more or less withdrew to the living room and their bedrooms, each with one or two friends.
>
> I don't know if this was good or bad. It happened. It has left Patricia and me with the concern for whether or not they have processed their grief fully enough. We have had a special concern for Stephanie, but we keep talking with her about it and she seems to be doing all right.
>
> We are aware that, to some degree, we have not had the time to grieve as a family unit. I don't know if we can schedule it or whether it will happen naturally as the next few months pass. We are aware of some probable tender moments ahead:
>
> > August 12: Elijah and Jenny's anniversary
> > September 3: Jenny's 25th birthday
> > October 10: Patricia's birthday
> > November 6: Elijah's birthday
> > November 28: Thanksgiving with several of Patricia's family
> > December 25: Christmas with my family

While I did not know how to evaluate the fact that we grieved separately, at the time, as stated above, I was tending to see it as the girls pulling away from all the activity and people. In hindsight, however, Patricia and I have come to the conviction that we failed by not carving out time for our family to be alone and to process things together. Had we known better, we would have set aside times and places for that soon after Elijah's death.

Yes, each of the girls had their own friends with whom they shared their loss, but as parents we should have taken responsibility to pull the family together, but we were caught up in our own grief and caught up in greeting and visiting with our extended family members and friends. I do not say that with self-condemnation, for we did the best we knew at the time.

Amazingly, the sense of excitement, peace, and joy—the euphoria—that I experienced during the visitation and funeral continued to a great degree for two or three days. Certainly, there were times of weeping, but hope prevailed in me—for those few days. I remember going to the cemetery with a folding camp chair early in the morning on several days immediately following the burial so that I could sit facing east by Elijah's grave with my chair placed near his head. I had read somewhere that it was an old tradition to bury people with their feet pointed toward the east so that in the resurrection they would arise facing east, from which direction it was believed Jesus would come. Although we had not purchased the gravesite with that in mind, Elijah's grave lies that way.

On those hot, July mornings the haze was thick to the east, and sunlight seemed to be coming through a veil. The lit-up haze seemed like a veil on the other side of which things were brighter and more real than on this side, and it seemed as though I could simply reach out, part the veil, and slip on through into the "world to come."

Those seemingly mystical experiences did not last long. Even those few days included plenty of times of deep weeping, pain, and loneliness. Within four or five days after the funeral, the numbness I had often felt in the previous days was replaced with a gut-sick ache most of the time.

On July 27, I wrote,

> This week, July 21–27, has been one of the toughest. There were tears and sobs the first weekend, but there was also the numbness and the incredulity. And in the midst of the crisis, faith came easily and God seemed to pour out his grace on us. We were surrounded by people and there were decisions to be made.
>
> Now that kind of activity has ended. Life is returning to normal. But what is normal? Our son is gone from us. Jenny is trying to make their house into her house. Stephanie and Andrea no longer have a big brother to whom they can look and with whom they can talk.

And I am the only male in this immediate family now. Home for me changed a lot when Elijah went to school and then got married. A household of women is different than a mixed house. I love my wife. I love my girls. We have good relationships, I think. But that is a whole different thing than having male companionship, not a bad thing, not a lesser thing, but a completely different thing. Now I can no longer look forward to being with Elijah on Sunday, or holidays, or other special occasions. I cannot call and hear him on the phone. I cannot share my interest in music with him. There is no one here who is interested in what I think about or read about. Most of my interests are either boring or threatening to my female family members.

Life has lost a lot of color for me.

My journal entries witness to the fact that I kept turning to that simple directive: "Trust God. Entrust Elijah to God. Take a posture of worship." Some of the things I wrote now seem to indicate that I was trying to make a stand on Biblical truth and theological concepts. That is not all bad, of course, but I soon discovered that grief must be acknowledged and dealt with.

****

At the risk of sounding morbid or hung up on Elijah's death, I am going to write about some of my experience and about what I learned while walking through the valley of the shadow of death. It is, after all, a part of my spiritual journey.

On the Saturday evening following the funeral, Patricia and I went to the basement to set up chairs and get the room ready for Winchester Covenant's worship gathering. Bruce and Kathy, our neighbors, came over just in time to help out. As we worked, Bruce, who is a member of our church, Patricia, and I were talking about Elijah and about the funeral. The conversation focused on faith and hope and the presence of God. Kathy was a faithful member of another church but did not profess a personal relationship to Jesus at that time, although in more recent years her growth in faith has been wonderful to see. During that conversation, she held her tongue for a while and then burst out, "Well, I think Elijah's death was shitty!"

Without thought I responded: "Kathy, you're right. Elijah's death is the shittiest thing that's ever happened to me. The only difference is that I believe God turns shit into good things."

The shock and pain and loss of that first week was indeed bad—it was shitty, if you will. Still, though I thought I knew something about grief, I was yet to learn how much the grace of God had carried me through to that point. Later, I would think that it had been almost as if God had given me a dose of anesthetic that made the pain somewhat bearable for a while. But anesthesia wears off, and the long journey through deep muck had only just begun. God never left me, I know. Grace was always there, though I often could not feel it, and there were times when my choices revealed that I had refused it. Grace held me when I could not hold myself. I do believe that God was at work doing good, although I still do not have the full picture of his good purpose in it all.

In mid-July Jenny brought us copies of Elijah's medical records from the clinic where he had been seen and the EKGs had been made. Reading through them was difficult. A few weeks after Elijah's death, I took copies of those test results and the records of those visits to our former family doctor, Dr. Wayne Marlowe, a good friend from Lexington Covenant. After looking at the documentation closely, Dr. Marlowe told me that he would have almost certainly come to the same conclusion, that the "abnormality" that appeared on the EKG was "normal" for Elijah. That assessment helped me greatly, freeing me from the concern that human error might have kept Elijah from receiving treatment that might have saved his life.

By August of 1996, I was experiencing depression more and more often. I would have to fight to turn to God and fight to take hope. I remember a day in early August when my daily Scripture reading included "Draw near to God, and he will draw near to you" (James 4:8). That directive and promise stood out as if printed in bold relief.

I recognized that this exhortation was a personal encouragement to me, and some part of me received it with gratitude. Yet I also found myself struggling with this word. "Draw near to God"? Come up close to the very One who could have allowed our son to live and could have spared us from this pain? Sometimes I obeyed; sometimes I gave in to the depression. Either way, there was pain. However, I found that giving in to the depression usually led to seeking an escape, which led me into temptation and then often into sin. The consequence of sin was worse pain, destructive pain.

When I obeyed and sought to turn to God, that also hurt, because he could have kept Elijah alive; however, when I continued setting my mind on the Lord and remembering his works of grace and mercy and his promise that everything would work for the good, although there was pain, I began to realize that it was productive pain.

From the first, I was never angry with God, not any form of active, conscious anger anyway. I struggled with why he allowed this tragedy to befall us, but I did not accuse him or curse him or rail at him. I began to realize over time, though, that much of the depression I was dealing with was actually anger turned inward. Rather than fighting outwardly against God, I was struggling not to shut him off from within and simply give in to passivity.

That battle was difficult, but as time went by, healing slowly, oh so slowly, began to come, and my trust in God began to grow a bit at a time.

Once I did cry out a question to God: "Why my son?" I had driven Stephanie to her job at Clark Rural Electric one morning later that August. On the way home, I turned left from Winn Avenue onto Main Street. As I crossed the railroad track, I yelled, "Why my son?" with no expectation of an answer. But God spoke! It was not audible, but it was clear, even the tone was clear—firm, Fatherly, and filled with tender love, "Why not your son?"

Yes, why not my son? I thought. We live in a broken world filled with broken lives and broken families. Why should I be spared from sharing in the pain that so many of us face in life? Isn't that what my Master did? He came among us, became one of us, in order to embrace and bear in himself the agony of our brokenness so that we, by grace, may share the glorious love and community of his life with the Father and the Spirit. Why should I be spared? I worshipped and that morning was filled with gratitude that I could follow Jesus by embracing this cross in my life.

Still, the pain of grief was intense. Although it gradually, oh so gradually, subsided, after a time there was the sense of loss and the disorientation. The gut-wrenching pain began to hit me more infrequently. The insidious thing was that the hard, agonizing moments of pain would hit (and I do mean "hit") at unexpected and unpredictable moments. Even now, more than twenty years later, those moments of pain will come, but not with the same intense agony.

Special days were especially hard that first year. Actually, the dread that always built up for a week or two leading up to the special days was the worst part. Usually the actual days were redeemed by time with the family. Soon after the funeral, my sister Debbie, who worked for a funeral home in Waverly, Ohio, had given us some material about dealing with grief that her employers had gathered. One simple suggestion we found to help immensely. Patricia began to purchase a candle for those special days, particularly when the family gathered for meals. At the beginning of the meal we would light the candle in honor of Elijah's memory; afterward we often shared some other memories. Then, having acknowledged our son and the loss, it was much easier to go ahead with the meal and be more fully present to one another.

It was not unusual for my mind to just slip away from the present moment, either to a memory of Elijah or to a fresh wave of sorrow and pain. Many times it happened right in the middle of a conversation, even when I was the speaker. I would start a sentence … and just drift off. It also happened when I was driving, and several times I simply drove through a red light or stop sign without awareness. Thankfully, I did not cause any accidents.

My perspective on Psalm 23 changed dramatically in this season also. Always before, when I read about walking with the Shepherd through the valley of the shadow of death, I had pictured the Shepherd comforting and protecting the person dying. I am sure that is true, although in Elijah's case the time when he was aware of walking in that valley, if he was at all, was very short. It was we who loved Elijah who were left in the shadow of his passing and who needed the Shepherd's faithful care and comfort so badly for a long time. The Lord has indeed been our faithful Shepherd.

In contrast, just a few years later it became clear to our family that my mother had Alzheimer's disease. Her mind was "dying" long before her body died. Both she and her family were walking in the shadow of death for at least ten years before she died. Mom died of a heart attack in November 2008, by God's mercy we believe, or her journey in the valley of the shadow could have been several years longer. Dad, however, not only walked with her on the journey to her death but also was left in the valley of the shadow when she had gone on into "the world to come." He continued to walk in the shadow of her passing for five years until he died in August 2014. The Shepherd was faithful to see them both through.

Based upon my own experience and upon my observation of the experience of others, I have come to the conclusion that there is no one "right way" to deal with grief. There are ways of dealing with grief that are helpful, and other ways that are not helpful, perhaps even harmful. Still, everyone has to find his or her own path through that valley of the shadow of death—as bluesman Mississippi John Hurt put it, "You got to walk that lonesome valley, you got to walk it for yourself." It helped me greatly to share with others who are also in that valley. It was also very helpful to receive encouragement from people who have been through it already. Each journey is unique, but the Good Shepherd is always there to guide and guard those who look to him.

We were blessed to have people who encouraged us. I usually didn't find that the words people said to us were that helpful. Frankly, most of the standard lines people utter in times of loss, I found, were not helpful all. It was hard not to react to some of them. But I did realize that people wanted to be helpful. The best words, it seemed to me, were simple ones like "I am so sorry." If the relationship was close enough, sharing a hug and even tears soothed the pain.

The biggest help was for people to simply be there. Often, the fewer words, the better, it seemed. Some simple things helped immeasurably, especially in the long, lonely days that followed the funeral. My brothers "in ministry," such as John Meadows, Dennis Cole, and Bill Livingston, touched base often, usually with a phone call or an email. For several weeks, Mitch, a brother in our church, would stop by two or three evenings each week on his way home from work. Sometimes we'd have a cold drink together. Usually he would just stay a few minutes, long enough to see if I wanted to talk, and that was long enough for me to know that I was not alone. Darrin, another friend from the church, understood how much Elijah and I had loved to listen to music and talk about it together, so he came over several times in the next months just to listen to music with me.

My wife was wonderfully encouraged when Billy Henderson came from Lexington one day just to plant a little herb garden outside her kitchen door. Dennis Cole's son Jeremiah, who was a little younger than Elijah, asked to spend several hours with me one day just to have me share about my relationship with my son. Brent, Gary, and Mitch, who all traveled around Kentucky doing sales and service for Bluegrass Kesco, a water treatment firm, each invited me to ride with them for a day, getting me out of the house and providing me with meaningful companionship during the first months of grief.

Our good friends Dan and Faye Smithwick, from whom we had been estranged for several years but with whom we had been reconciled in 1995, were faithful to visit. Phone calls and emails (no text-messaging in those days) from friends and family who lived in other places communicated love and concern. One such friend, Jim Zielinski, who lives in central Ohio, to this day calls sometime around July 4th and often on other holidays just to say that he remembers Elijah and cares about us. A few others sent cards of remembrance on the 4th for several years afterward.

In early November 1996 my brother, Wes, came down from central Ohio in order to go with me to a Bela Fleck concert as a way to remember Elijah on the first birthday after his death. The previous January, Wes and Elijah had discovered a common interest in Bela Fleck's music. I had not been familiar with his music, but doing something with my brother that Elijah would have loved meant the world. (The music Bela and his friends made was outstanding too.)

Speaking of music, before Elijah died, our daughter Stephanie had purchased tickets to an Emmylou Harris concert scheduled in mid-August as anniversary presents for us. She was almost apologetic to give us those tickets to do something fun on our anniversary, only two days after her brother's funeral. But we went to the concert. Two couples from the Fellowship of Believers, Stephanie's church, were also going and offered us a ride with them—a simple, kind act that showed care and may well have encouraged us to step out and do something.

The Kentucky Theater concert venue is small and intimate. There are no bad seats, but our seats were great, on the eighth row, right on the outside aisle to the right of the stage. Although it was not a distraction, it was notable that several people, all dressed in dark clothes, came up the aisle and stood along that wall once the music started. A few songs into the concert, Emmylou began to sing plaintively,

> When I go, don't cry for me
> In my father's arms I'll be
> The wounds this world left on my soul
> Will all be healed, and I'll be whole
> Sun and moon will be replaced with the light of Jesus's face
> And I will not be ashamed, for my savior knows my name
>
> It don't matter where you bury me
> I'll be home and I'll be free
> It don't matter where I lay
> All my tears be washed away ...[96]

A knot, not a lump, formed in my throat. I looked at Patricia and saw her crying softly. I put my right arm around her and she leaned against my shoulder. One of the people leaning against the wall noticed. She came over to us, leaned down, and gently asked: "Is everything all right? Is there anything I can do?" When we assured her that we were okay, she went back to her place.

A few songs later, in her most wistful voice, Emmylou began,

---

[96] Julie Miller, © Warner/Chappell Music, Inc., 1993. Later I discovered that Julie wrote the song to commemorate the death of Mark Heard, one of the Christian musicians whose music Elijah had appreciated. Ironically, Mark had died from a heart attack in 1992 at age 40.

See what you lost when you left this world, this sweet old world
See what you lost when you left this world, this sweet old world ...[97]

Again, the knot, the tears, the hug ... and again the woman noticed and came over and asked, "Are you sure you are all right?"

"Our son died last month," I replied this time. "We are a little tender these days, and these songs touch the tenderness."

"Emmylou's father died a couple years ago. I think that's why she sings these songs," the woman said.

Later, Emmylou took a break backstage while Buddy Miller and the rest of Emmylou's Spyboy band sang and played. Out of the corner of my eye, I noticed that the woman who had been concerned about us went backstage. A few minutes later, she returned and came over to us.

Leaning down, she said quietly: "This is the next-to-the-last concert of a world tour for Emmylou. She is tired and is not receiving guests backstage, but I told her about you and your loss. She asked me to invite you to come back and meet her if you want."

With a little reluctance because I never know what to say to "celebrities," after consulting briefly with Patricia, we accepted the kind invitation. Immediately following the concert, our "angel in black" came and escorted us backstage, where we saw a few others were waiting also, but she took us to the head of the line. Emmylou, seated behind a table on which there was a large fruit tray, was talking with a man whom our escort told us was a reporter. While Emmylou was being interviewed, our new friend told us her story of being a longtime fan and how she had become friends with Emmylou.

Before long we were standing in front of the table. For me, it was as awkward as I had thought it would be, but Emmylou asked us a few questions about our son and expressed her condolences. She signed our programs and we left. The simple concern of a stranger and the kindness of a well-known but weary musician were balm in our time of sorrow.

****

---

[97] Sweet Old World lyrics © Warner/Chappell Music, Inc., 1992.

Soon after Elijah died, I realized that I was measuring time by Elijah's death. Things either happened before he died or after he died. That event had become the central event of life in the season. A year later, about three weeks after July 4, I realized that I was no longer measuring time that way. Elijah's death was beginning to take its proper place in the timeline of my life. Soon afterward I told Patricia about this change, and to my amazement she said her experience had been very similar.

Perhaps the agonizing grief had something to do with the season of physical difficulties we began to face. Just a few weeks after the funeral, while Patricia was doing something in the flower garden outside our kitchen, she began to experience great difficulty breathing and became deeply concerned that it might be a heart attack. We called for an ambulance and they took her to the hospital. The tests did not point to a heart issue. The doctor told us that extreme grief sometimes leads to hyperventilating and to symptoms that could suggest a heart issue. That was not the only time she had that fearful experience, nor was it the only time we went to the emergency room because of such an experience.

Although no heart issue was identified during those incidents, there came a time a number of years later when she needed an echocardiogram. After looking at the results, the cardiologist asked, "When did you have the heart event?" When she said she did not know of one, he told her that the test had revealed scar tissue from a heart attack, probably a silent one. She may well have had an actual heart attack during the intense period of grief.

In January 1997, I had the first of several health problems, which led to more than a few hospital stays and surgeries and other issues, a season that continued into the early months of 2009. No one needs to read a recital of all those ills. But some were directly related to my spiritual journey.

I had experienced some abdominal discomfort for a few days, but by the time I came home from our worship gathering on Sunday, January 19, the discomfort had increased. I tried to get relief by using a laxative, to no avail. The increasing pain continued into Tuesday, when I could no longer deny that I had serious pain and yielded to my wife's urging to seek medical help at Clark Regional Medical Center's emergency room. There, tests revealed a serious enough issue that I was admitted, and they began pumping my stomach. After more examinations and tests, the diagnosis was Crohn's Disease, and a local gastroenterologist was assigned to my case.

After two days of treatment with IVs and pills, I was reintroduced gradually to food, beginning with a liquid diet. It appeared that the immediate problem was being dealt with and it was time for me to learn how to live with Crohn's. On Friday evening, I was given my first meal of solid food, and the plan was to send me home on Saturday. All I remember about that meal was that it included cooked carrots. My wife and all visitors left about 8:30 p.m. that Friday evening, and I was preparing to a get a good night's sleep—one without IVs and periodic interruptions for blood pressure tests and the other things nurses do to keep waking a patient up over and over through the night.

At 9 p.m. pain started and then increased and increased. The point came when I thought I could not stand anymore, so I asked for pain medication and a nurse gave me morphine. It did not seem to help. I had no roommate that night, so I paced the floor. Several times I even bumped my head against the wall, hoping, I guess, that pain in my head might help me not feel the pain in my belly. That didn't help. I walked the halls—anything to try to distract myself from the pain. I had to wait two hours for more pain medicine. When I did, the nurses offered to call the on-call doctor. I refused because of some misguided notion that I did not want to disturb a doctor's sleep.

By morning I was desperate, and at 6 a.m. I asked for a doctor. To my surprise, the on-call doctor was Dr. Bill Greiser, the same surgeon who had tried to save Elijah. Dr. Greiser gave me another kind of pain medicine in addition to the morphine that I had already been taking. From that point of the day I was drowsy, and my memory is fuzzy. I do remember having several different tests, but the details that I do remember are not ones I care to tell.

At about 5 p.m., after a C-T scan, I think, Dr. Greiser came to the conclusion that there was infection in the small bowel and that he must do an emergency surgery to remove a section. I was taken into surgery at 5:30 on that Saturday evening. I awoke to the news that 18 inches of my small colon had been removed, and that an abdominal hernia had been repaired, but without using mesh because a substance foreign to my body would likely cause infection.

My parents stopped by the Medical Center to visit on Sunday morning on their way from Circleville to some church where Dad was scheduled to minister. While they were visiting, I was sitting in a chair when fluid began to leak from the incision. I had no idea about the implications of this leak but soon was told that the leaking part of the incision would have to be left open and cleaned carefully twice daily, and that healing would need to be from the inside out. This meant that Patricia would need to clean the wound twice a day and that I would be restricted in activity for at least two months.

Dr. Greiser and the other doctors were still thinking that the infection was related to Crohn's Disease, and the plan was to deal with that by a changed diet and medication. According to normal procedure, however, the diseased tissue removed by surgery was sent for lab analysis. To the doctors' surprise, the results determined that the issue was not Crohn's but rather that part of my small bowel had died because of ischemia, a lack of blood supply to that part of the colon.

Why? Nobody knew, and there was no way to find out. The doctors' best guess was that I might have been infected by e-coli bacteria, but there was no way to prove or disprove it.

A few years later, my friend Gary Gurwell told me in a letter that intestinal issues could be related to grief. I have never seen research that shows a link between them; however, my wife and daughters have expressed their belief that my intestinal problem was related to the way I grieved. There is, of course no way to know whether or not it was the stress of grieving for Elijah that weakened my system and led to that intestinal issue. I do know that for many years, in times of great stress, I seemed to have problems in my digestive system.

What is clear to me, however, is that the complications of the ischemia, if untreated, could have caused my death. Elijah had died at age 23, but for some reason, rather than die at age 47, I was going to live a while longer. Why? I could not answer that question, but I could reaffirm my commitment to do what I could to serve young people as Elijah and I had wanted to do. I had prayed that at the time of his death that somehow, in some way, his death would impact many, many others who would have been reached had he lived.

God had now spared my life. Now it was my time to offer the life I had been given to God for him to use in reaching people, especially young people.

****

Thus, when the opportunity arose not long afterward, I began to teach at Lexington Christian Fellowship's Mars Hill homeschool co-op. The first year I taught two English classes. The next year I began to teach a Biblical worldview class for seniors, and for nearly a dozen years, I did the best I could to help prepare young Christians to go onto college campuses ready to advance the faith among their professors and classmates. I longed to help equip them not simply to survive the assault against the faith that most would face in college but to serve effectively as representatives of God's kingdom in that often-hostile environment.

As part of my ongoing efforts in that class, in 2000 I read Robert Webber's *Ancient-Future Faith: Rethinking Evangelicalism for a Postmodern World*.[98] Because of the worldview class, I read several books that had to do with postmodernity after I discovered that a number of authors were wrestling with how the church could be more effective, given the changes in the cultural assumptions and beliefs that had taken place, especially among the younger generation. Webber was one of these authors.

Around 1980, not long after we had begun the Free Church Fellowship, I had read Webber's book *Common Roots: A Call to Evangelical Maturity*,[99] and it had helped me be far more appreciative of the church in the first few centuries after the apostles. It had also helped me be more appreciative of the church traditions to which most of my brothers and sisters in the Servants of the Lord were connected. In addition, that book had made me curious to know more about the writings of Church Fathers.

A primary impact that *Ancient-Future Faith* had on me came from Webber's emphasis on "Christus Victor," the understanding about Christ's atonement, which had been the primary way Christians had viewed it for the first thousand years of church history (and is still the view of the Eastern church). This view of Jesus's work on the cross focuses on his triumph over the principalities and powers (sin, death, and the devil) as the primary accomplishment of the atonement. I began to pursue a better and more complete understanding of the victory Jesus had won by his death and resurrection. One Biblical statement about Christ's victory that had intrigued me for a long time now began to make more sense:

> And you, who were dead in your trespasses and the uncircumcision of your flesh, God made alive together with him, having forgiven us all our trespasses, by canceling the record of debt that stood against us with its legal demands. This he set aside, nailing it to the cross. **He disarmed the rulers and authorities and put them to open shame, by triumphing over them in him.** (Colossians 2:13–15, bold print added for emphasis)

A process of change began in me that increasingly has pulled together my previous study and insight and wrestling with spiritual realities such as the gospel and the kingdom of God and the covenant. Because of Webber, I began to see much more

---

[98] Published by Baker Academic, 1999.

[99] First published by Zondervan Publishing House, 1978. It has been republished after Webber's death as an e-book with the title *Common Roots: The Original Call to an Ancient-Future Faith*, (2009).

clearly that the truths I, along with many others, had been wrestling to understand and to live were vital foundations for the young people coming along behind us.

Webber's book helped stir me up to pray frequently and fervently, "Lord, show me your vision for the church of the next generation!"

This prayer became a primary cry of my heart over the next years. It was never far from my consciousness, no matter whether I was trying to sell office products (which I did for a few years) or leading the church or teaching at Mars Hill or involved in a conference or reading a book … or at any time.

A short time after I read Webber's book, my friend Dennis Peacocke asked the church elders with whom he had influence to read N. T. Wright's *What Saint Paul Really Said*. Although I soon recognized that this book was significant, I had no idea who Wright was or what he had already written, let alone the many books he was to write in the years since. I certainly had no idea that Wright's work was to play a major role in expanding and shaping my understanding of the message of the gospel of the kingdom of God. While the Lord used Webber's book to "open a door" for me, Wright's prolific work has helped me "to explore the house."

One summary passage from Wright's book brought together in a few words truths about the gospel of the kingdom of God that I had been wrestling to understand and live and teach for years.

> My proposal has been that "the gospel" is not, for Paul, a message about "how one gets saved," in an individual and a-historical sense. It is a fourfold announcement about Jesus.
>
> 1. In Jesus of Nazareth, specifically in his cross, the decisive victory has been won over all the powers of evil, including sin and death themselves.
>
> 2. In Jesus's resurrection, the New Age has dawned, inaugurating the long-awaited time when the prophecies would be fulfilled, when Israel's exile would be over and the whole world would be addressed by the one creator God.
>
> 3. The crucified and risen Jesus was, all along, Israel's Messiah, her representative king.

4. Jesus was therefore also the Lord, the true king of the world, the one at whose name every knee would bow.[100]

This, I realized, was an excellent summary of the good news Peter proclaimed on the Day of Pentecost (Acts 2:14–36) and that he shared, reluctantly it seems, to Gentiles gathered in Centurion Cornelius's home (Acts 13:34–43). Wright's four points also sum up the gospel proclamations Paul made in the synagogue (Acts 13:13–41), before King Agrippa (Acts 26:1–23), and to pagan philosophers in Athens at Antioch in Perga (Acts 17:22–31), although in Athens Paul reframed his message for people unfamiliar with the Jewish Scriptures. What's more, it is this understanding of the gospel that underlies the content of the letters (the epistles), which Paul wrote to those who already had believed that message and had been called to live as citizens of that kingdom.

A few years later, I read Wright's *The Challenge of Jesus: Rediscovering Who Jesus Was and Is*,[101] which helped me to understand even more clearly that the good news which Paul proclaimed was indeed the same good news that the Old Testament prophets had announced ahead of time, the same good news that John the Baptist called people to prepare for, and the very gospel that Jesus lived, proclaimed, and fulfilled through his birth, life, death, resurrection, and ascension.

The opportunity to teach a Biblical worldview course was a "God-send" for me during that season of grief, in part because it helped me focus on something other than grief. More important, it also provided a tangible way for me to seek to serve the younger generation. It challenged me to not be overcome and stopped by loss but rather to keep learning and growing for the sake of others.

---

[100] N. T. Wright, *What Saint Paul Really Said: Was Saul of Tarsus the Real Founder of Christianity?* (Grand Rapids, MI: Eerdmans, 1997).

[101] Published by InterVarsity Press, 2000.

26

New Paths

There is simply no better image of the years following Elijah's death other than to think of them as a time of "walking through the valley of the **[long] shadow** of death." As is true of things that are in the shadows, many details about those years are fuzzy in my memory. Some, however, stick out boldly.

Attending a regional meeting of a group called the Fellowship of Christian Leaders, which was held in Hopkinsville, Kentucky, in October 1996, is one such sharp memory. Bill Livingston was becoming more involved with Dennis Peacocke at that time. Dennis, of course, had made an impact on my life with his message to Lexington Covenant in 1990, and his influence continued through the Intern Program. I decided to go with Bill, partly to see Dennis and meet some of the leaders who were working with him, but mostly just to be with Bill and to have some face-to-face fellowship in that lonely, lonely season.

To my pleasant surprise, Ted Sandquist and his wife, Dawn, were among the people in Hopkinsville. I had never met Ted but had loved his music and profited from cassette tapes of his teaching on worship. He had been a long-time elder in Covenant Love Church since the 1970s, when the community was known as Love Inn—the community of Jesus Freaks led by Scott Ross of *The Scott Ross Show*.

In those meetings, Dennis's theme in teaching was "Building with Sons." Three months after Elijah's death, it was excruciating to listen. While I clearly understood that Dennis was primarily talking about spiritual sons (sons in the kingdom), he and Ted and some others in that room were clearly working with their own physical sons, who also had become spiritual sons. But my son was dead! My hopes and dreams of working with him had been smashed!

Yet, it was not all bad. It gave me another opportunity to trust God, to entrust Elijah to God, and to take a posture of worship. Out of that posture came a freshened and strengthened resolve to invest in younger people, in part as my tribute to Elijah.

****

Especially in the first months after Elijah died, the people of our church, as well as many in our spiritual family who were not part of our local fellowship, walked with us in the grief. For a season, many of them seemed to feel the loss nearly as deeply we did, but not for such a long time as us, I think, which seems only natural. Most of them have seemed very aware that our journey would be a long one and were patient and supportive even after their own lives had moved past that season. There were some others who did not appear to understand about the length of our painful journey. How could they be expected to understand, unless they had experienced such a loss themselves or had been close to someone who had? A few seemed to lose patience after months rolled by, and a very few even said things that demonstrated their lack of understanding and impatience.

For the first month or two, the "sermons" I presented in our church were mostly sharing from my heart thoughts that were the direct outcome of trying to deal with my own grief. I remember, for example, sharing one Sunday in August from James 4:8: "Draw near to God and he will draw near to you." Obviously, the message was for me, perhaps more for me than anyone, as may be seen in the wrestlings I described above as that directive and promise from Scripture continued its work in me for months afterward.

I remember (mostly because I have sermon notes saved from that period) that I taught a series on covenant that fall. There is some good material in those notes, and I certainly desired to feed God's flock from the Scripture. Some of that material would probably still be worth developing into something to share with others; however, I suspect that at the time I was in part turning to a "theological study" as one of the ways of trying to get relief from the grief.

Not long afterward, I began to preach about the kingdom of God and what it meant to be "rebuilders," to be a people who are giving themselves to seeing God's will done on earth as it is in heaven, starting in their own lives, in their own families, and in the church, but also extending that work into whatever sphere of influence they had been given, at work and in whatever social groups in which they were involved. Certainly, I believed that and still do. But in some ways, studying and thinking and teaching about it then was, in part, my way of "surviving" and of holding on to hope for the future.

In those years, I laid aside most of my efforts to clarify the vision and to establish the best "structure" for our church community. Those were still concerns, certainly, but they were not a big focus. Supporting one another and encouraging one another, even simply holding on to one another, I believe, was something of an accomplishment. Yet it was more than a simple accomplishment, I think, in that that's not a bad representation of the heart of what Jesus wants to see—his people living by his new commandment and living toward the fulfillment of his prayer as our primary witness to the world around us:

A new commandment I give to you, that you love one another: just as I have loved you, you also are to love one another. By this all people will know that you are my disciples, if you have love for one another. (John 13:34–35)

As you sent me into the world, so I have sent them into the world. And for their sake I consecrate myself, that they also may be sanctified in truth. I do not ask for these only, but also for those who will believe in me through their word, that they may all be one, just as you, Father, are in me, and I in you, that they also may be in us, so that the world may believe that you have sent me. The glory that you have given me I have given to them, that they may be one even as we are one, I in them and you in me, that they may become perfectly one, so that the world may know that you sent me and loved them even as you loved me. (John 17:18–23)

During that period, I did produce a document titled "The Covenant Ideal of Winchester Covenant Church," which the elders discussed and adjusted. That document begins with another statement of our vision and then is organized around the commandment to live in covenant love by living out nine values, each of which is listed along with references to supporting passages in Scripture. The nine values are these: to be a worshipping people, to be a humble people, to be a serving people, to be servant-rulers, to be a faithful people, to be a people of peace, to live in community, to be a people who share the good news of God's kingdom, and to be a mission-oriented people. If we who follow Jesus were even to come close to being that kind of people, what a community we would be. Any progress at all we have made in that direction has been only by God's grace and has been altogether worthwhile.

I can only hope some people were helped through my efforts to serve the Lord in those difficult days. Simply because God is the person God is, some probably were helped. It is God's way to use weak and broken people as channels of his Life for others. After all, what other kind of people are there for him to use when we face reality? But the most Life comes through people who know and admit their weakness but still offer themselves freely to God. Second Corinthians is one of the clearest descriptions of God working that way in the apostle Paul's life, and it had long been one of my favorite books in the Bible. In those days, I got to practice that way of life—"in spades"—and trust the Lord to make what good of it that he would.

****

It has never been a goal for Winchester Covenant to own a "church building" or to be a church providing for people's needs through programs of one kind or another. Our primary goals have always been to be disciples, to make disciples, and to build strong families who fellowship and work and serve together as a community of disciples.

After five years of meeting for Sunday worship in our home, I came to the conviction that it was time for us to gather in a more public, visible way as a part of our testimony. On the first Thursday in May 1999, the annual National Day of Prayer, during my prayer time "out of the blue" another of those rare pictures appeared in my mind. I saw a storefront in the downtown area with a sign identifying it as "The Meeting Place." It did not look churchy at all. Immediately, I thought such a place could be a gathering place for people in the downtown area and that we could even make it a place to which people could bring their sack lunch and have Bible studies or other gatherings.

After I shared this "vision" with the elders and after we gave it due consideration, we elders decided to look for a suitable place to meet, preferably in downtown Winchester. We asked our people to keep their eyes open for a possible site. A few weeks later one of the women in our church suggested a place on East Broadway Street, just around a corner from the central downtown area on Main Street. When I drove by and looked in the window, I could see that the space had been divided into several rooms for offices. *That will not do at all,* I thought.

The sister was persistent, though, and brought it up again. This time she told me who owned the building where the place was located, and she gave me the phone number to contact him. I drove by again. This time it struck me that next door there was a place called "A Taste of Jazz," a banquet room associated with Jazz Man, a popular downtown restaurant. *That room would be big enough for Sunday meetings if the space were for rent*, I thought, *but it's not.*

A week or two later, on a Friday, our friends Dennis and Sheila Cole came down from northern Kentucky for an overnight visit. On Saturday morning Dennis and I went for a ride during which I showed him around our county. As we passed through downtown and we happened to drive by the rooms on East Broadway, I offhandedly commented: "Those rooms are for rent and might be a good place for our church office. For two cents I would talk to the owners of Jazz Man about renting that banquet room to us on Sundays."

About an hour and a half later, Dennis said, "Sheila and I would like to take you and Patricia out to lunch at the Jazz Man." We agreed to that quickly enough. Jazz Man was one of our favorite local spots to eat.

After we had been seated at our table, been given our drinks, and ordered our meal, Dennis said, "Well, are you going to talk to them or am I?"

Huh? It took me a few seconds to recall my earlier comment about renting the banquet room, but when I did, I replied, "I'll do it."

I walked over to Paulette, who with her husband, James, owned the restaurant, and I asked her if they would consider renting the banquet room to our church on Sunday mornings. Somewhat to my surprise even then, Paulette quickly answered: "I think we probably would. James is not here today. Why don't you stop by on Monday afternoon and ask him about it?"

After lunch, the four of us walked around the corner and across the street. The huge windows across the front were covered halfway up with black curtains, but we saw that there was a ledge below the windows on which we could stand and look in. As we approached, I looked up and noticed the words stenciled in the upper right corner of the first window: "A Taste of Jazz" in big letters, and below them in smaller letters I read: "Banquet Room and Meeting Place." The Meeting Place? No, it was not the same front I had seen in my mind three months earlier, but there were the words. That was confirmation enough for me.

It was no surprise when James Baker immediately agreed to rent us A Taste of Jazz on Sundays, and for only $30 per week. By that time, some of us had gone through the rooms in the space next door. There were five rooms. Some repair was needed, but nothing major. With a some repairs, some painting, and a thorough cleaning, we had an office, a conference room, rooms for children's ministry, and a restroom, all for a very reasonable monthly rent.

We met there for a year and it served us well. The Taste of Jazz was decorated with painted scenes of the French Quarter in New Orleans. One of the pictures, a large one in the center of an end wall, appeared to be a "lady of the night" and she was not wearing "church clothes," not even those of an informal church like ours. So each Sunday we hung a banner with a symbol of the kingdom over her. And we faced the chairs to the other end of the room. In this way we protected young men (and older ones too) from any temptation that might have arisen.

It was great on Sundays to pull back those curtains. Not only did it let lots of light in, but it made our worship quite visible to passersby. It was actually fun to open the door on warm days and allow the sound of our praises and messages go out into the streets. With a growing number of teens among us and the door wide open, we would often heartily sing out the call to proclaim the good news, as in song by the group called Delirious?.

> Men of faith rise up and sing
> Of the great and glorious King
> You are strong when you feel weak
> In your brokenness complete
>
> Shout to the North and the South
> Sing to the East and the West
> Jesus is savior to all
> Lord of heaven and earth[102]

We met in those rooms for about a year. Marian Englebrecht, who had played piano for us the first few months we had Sunday services, was at the time attending a church that met in an old building about a block and a half away from us on the corner of Buckner and Broadway. She came to the conviction that the Lord was directing her to invite my wife and me to her house in order to have dinner with her family and with the pastor of that church, Jesse Acosta, and his wife. We enjoyed our time with the Acostas, but we did not become close friends.

A month or two later, though, Jesse urged me to visit them during some special revival services. Wanting to be polite, I went to a Sunday evening service. A crazy thought hit me as I was walking into that building for the first time: "Ask him to give you this building." I tried to squash that thought immediately. After all, we were not looking for a building; we did not even want a building. The thought kept intruding into my mind throughout the service until I began to think, *How would I ask him such a thing, even if I wanted to?*

After the service Jesse was at the door shaking hands with people as they left. I approached the door somewhat uneasily, wondering what to say. Before I could say anything, he said to me, "I have to talk with you." We set a time to talk at my office one afternoon the following week.

---

[102] "Shout to the North," Martin Smith ©1995 Curious? Music UK.

The time came. Jesse came into the office and sat down. After we had greeted one another, he said: "The Lord told me you are supposed to have our building. Our group is merging with a church in Richmond, and we will be having our services in their building. If you are interested, I will talk to the landlady. I am sure she will want to rent to you."

"Let me talk to our elders," I replied, "and I'll get back to you." The bottom line is that we moved into the building a few weeks later. It was an old building that had once been a house and service station, then a grocery, then a laundromat. We became the third church to meet there. The building needed work. We did what we could to make it presentable and usable for our needs, and we met there for four years.

To top it off, one day after I had set up my office in that building, I walked up Broadway toward Main Street to pick up something at a shop. As I started past The Taste of Jazz, I noticed a man painting a sign on the window of a little bar across the street. The man, with his long hair and long beard, looked like a cross between an old hippie and a motorcycle gang member. On a whim I crossed the street and began to talk with him while looking at the painting he was doing. *That's not bad,* I thought.

"Would you like to come by the building where our church meets and give me a price for doing some painting on our window and on a sign out front?" I asked spontaneously.

"Sure," he responded. "I'll come by later this afternoon."

He did. I described what I would like to have painted. In the window at the front corner of the building, which was approximately 4 feet by 4 feet, I said I would like to have the words "The Meeting Place" in big letters curved around a picture of a loaf of bread, broken in half, with stalks of wheat and some wheat seeds lying between the halves. Immediately below the picture I wanted the name "Winchester Covenant Church" in smaller letters, and below that, our motto: "Building for the generations to come." On the sign, which was mounted on a pole between 15 and 20 feet high, I wanted to have the words "The Meeting Place" along with the picture of the broken bread, wheat stalks, and seeds.

"Could you design something like that and paint it? If so, what would you charge?" I asked.

"Let me sketch something out and I'll show it to you and give you a price," he answered. A few days later he came back with sketches of the two signs.

"That's it!" I exclaimed. "How much would you charge?"

"How about $225?"

"Let's do it!" I agreed quickly. And within a week or two there was a building and a sign that was quite reminiscent of the picture I had seen that morning in May 1999.

Our building never became a drop-in place as I had hoped. It did not become a place where downtown groups could get together or have meetings or Bible studies. My desire to see us become effective in reaching out to unchurched people was not fulfilled—and has not been fulfilled to this day.

There was one exception. A homeless man named James quite often stopped by for a cup of coffee. He told me he was usually called Hammer, because at some time or another he had threatened to hit someone with a hammer. I had several opportunities to talk with James about Jesus, including one when he was in jail because he had accidentally set an old, empty shed in someone's backyard on fire. He had gone into the shed to escape the cold and had tried to cook over a charcoal fire when the shed itself began to burn. James was taken on to a prison, and I have never seen him since. I do pray that some seed of the good news has taken root in him.

I learned later that there were city leaders, such as the lawyer who was then mayor, who were watching us, taking note of the healthy families among us and our willingness to serve. That season seemed to give us a place in the city—not a prominent place, but we did gain some respect. On one occasion the mayor even told me that he believed that having our church meet near the downtown area was a positive thing for the community. I probably should have asked him why, but I'm usually not quick on my feet in responding to such unexpected statements.

I do believe that our somewhat odd and seemingly disorganized church community has offered a needed picture of a church that is not all about buildings and programs but of one that is instead a people committed to follow Jesus together as a way of life. Perhaps we have been at least a shadow of the life of the church that we glimpse in the New Testament.

****

Shortly before Elijah's death I had begun to look to Bill Livingston for pastoral care, following Paul Petrie's return to Belgium. Bill and I were part of a group of leaders we had called the Association of Covenant Ministries (ACM) since its formation in the early 1990s. All of us in this group were associated with Paul Petrie and his friend Robert Grant. Bill, however, had begun to connect more and more with the leaders in the Fellowship of Christian Leaders (FCL), which Dennis Peacocke led.

These two groups were two among several that began in the years after the *New Wine* teachers had decided not to keep working together. The various groups were not splinter groups from an organization that had broken apart, since there had been no organization as such. The discipleship, or shepherding movement, had been a large network of relationships held together by brotherhood and pastoral care, given and received. The names of these new groups were new, and some were more organized than others, but the relationships at the heart of them had decades-long roots.

Each group had its distinguishing characteristics reflective of the personalities and callings of those involved. FCL had been formed by Dennis Peacocke, Ted Sandquist, and some other men who had continued in the regular fellowship of friends after Bob Mumford, to whom they had looked for pastoral oversight, repented for his involvement in the shepherding movement. After a few years, they had sensed the leading of the Lord to invite others into their fellowship. Some of those who began to fellowship with them had similar histories in the shepherding movement; others did not. But all had been gripped with a desire for the kingdom of God.

I had come into contact with some of these brothers through my involvement in the intern program. I had met some others at the meeting in Hopkinsville in October 1996. My friendship with Bill opened the door to more fellowship. A few months after the Hopkinsville gathering, my wife and I, along with Bill and his wife, Barbara, traveled to Vincennes, Indiana, where we spent several hours fellowshipping in the home of Bryce and Bobbie Anderson. The couple from the church in Hopkinsville that had hosted the October meeting were there also. Bryce and Bobbie soon became special friends.

After I had attended a few more meetings with FCL people, Dennis Peacocke invited me to participate in a weeklong gathering they called the Builders School, held at Duquesne University in Pittsburgh during July 1998. Dennis asked me to prepare a paper about the sovereignty of God to present during the school. However, I wrote only a short, informal paper and did not expect to read it at the Pittsburgh gathering after having a conversation with Ted Sandquist, who told me that since I was not actually a member of the group, Dennis should not have invited me to present a paper. As it turned out, I did present the paper, but that is a different story.

That conversation with Ted was significant and memorable for a very different reason. In late May 1998, Ted was going to pass through Winchester while on a trip. He called and asked if we could meet for lunch at a Winchester restaurant; therefore, a couple hours later, I met him at El Rio Grande. It was the first time the two of us had been together for a personal conversation, an enjoyable opportunity to get better acquainted.

In the course of sharing some of my story, I mentioned the close ties that I had maintained with David Redish, John Meadows, Billy Henderson, and other church leaders in Lexington with whom I had prayed weekly for many years. At that time we were spending a good deal of time and energy trying to help one of the men who was going through a difficult time. Ted began to encourage, or perhaps exhort, me to untangle from my history in Lexington and to give myself more fully to building relationships in Winchester and to take opportunities to serve our local community.

Just as Ted finished what he was saying, a man neither of us knew and who had been eating at a table across the room, came up to our table. "I'm Dr. Mark Miller," he stated. Looking straight at me, he went on, "I don't know what this man is saying to you, but the Lord wants you to know that what he is saying is from the Lord."

That certainly got my attention and led me to keep on pondering Ted's exhortation later. I became convinced that Ted had been speaking as the Lord's representative. My friendships with brothers in Lexington are still important, but my focus turned to our local community in a new way.

Interestingly enough, ten years later I became personally acquainted with Dr. Miller, and now he is a friend and regularly gives me chiropractic care.

Later in 1998 I became a member of FCL after seeking discernment and agreement from my fellow elders and the people of our church community. A year or two later, Dennis Cole also joined FCL, and for a while our three churches, along with the church Bryce led in Vincennes, became one of the regional groupings within that network.

One blessing that has come from relating with the brothers and sisters in FCL (later renamed Kingdom Ministries International [KMI]),[103] has been the emphasis on "generational transfer." That emphasis on sharing the journey from generation to

---

[103] KMI still exists as an international fellowship of leaders who lead groups of leaders. However, the group has now multiplied into several groups, based on geography. Those of us in the United States are now called Kingdom Ministries USA.

generation and working together with brothers from multiple generations of course struck a chord within my own heart.

****

Life continued for our family, of course. A few months after Elijah died, a young man whom Jenny had known at Berea before Elijah entered the college moved back into the area. The two of them began to see one another and were married in January 1998. They now have three sons and live in Tennessee.

Stephanie continued at Berea College for two more years. Like Elijah, she had begun working summers at Clark Rural Electric in the summer of 1996 following her freshman year at Berea. She continued working there in the summers the next two years and then took a full-time job with the Co-op. Rather than finish college, she decided to work full-time in order to save money in preparation for her marriage to Daniel Loveland, who would still have a couple years of college studies to complete after they were married in December 1999. In the fall of 2000, they presented us with our first grandchild, Elijah Wolffe Loveland, his first name in honor of his uncle.

Andrea graduated from Mars Hill in 2000. After working full-time for a year at Rees Office Products, she entered Morehead College for the fall semester in 2002 and graduated in December 2005. Like Elijah and Stephanie before her, she spent her college summers working for Clark Rural Electric Cooperative. In June of 2005 she married Daniel Rake.

I think it was in 2002 that I began to work for Rees Office Products again, this time as a sales person. It was my job to go out into towns in several surrounding counties to take sales orders from some established customers and to seek to establish new accounts. I was motivated in some ways by that old desire to be a Christian ministering (i.e., serving) in the everyday world rather than to be simply "in the ministry," as it is generally understood in our culture. I wanted to have opportunities to meet and serve people outside the church. Looking back, I wonder if this was also an effort to step outside the routine, something of a new beginning out of the "valley of the shadow."

My early efforts did pay off in some increased sales for the company, but after a time of training in which I had an hourly wage, I went on straight commission, and it soon became clear that sales was not my calling. In spite of a great deal of effort, I never was able to have much success at establishing new accounts, which was neither good for the company nor for me in terms of income. Ironically, the biggest account I had

358

a hand in gaining for Rees Office Products was actually landed by Rick Beach after I quit in early 2006. That account proved a great blessing for the company during the difficult financial time that started in 2008. Beyond that, even though my earnings were not large, the period during which I worked for Rick and Margie Beach did indeed help me get a new start in engaging the world beyond grief more fully again.

Trained by Grace

At times I have been deeply discouraged and nearly in despair over the discrepancy between what I believe that I understand and the way I find that I am living. It is a testimony to the grace God and the work of the Holy Spirit that I have continued to hunger and thirst and seek the kingdom of God through the years in spite of my weakness.

The spring of 2003 was one such difficult time. As Easter, which fell on April 20 that year, approached, I began to consider again Paul's message in Romans concerning the victory that Christ had won in his death and resurrection, a victory that, according to Paul, provides the way of victory for God's people. I wanted to have the Lord's message for the people of Winchester Covenant, but I am sure that my own need for encouragement and renewed hope also motivated me to read and meditate on Romans 5–8.

That Easter the primary word of hope I sought to proclaim was Paul's declaration that when we were baptized we were baptized into Messiah (Christ) Jesus's death and that we had been buried with him by baptism into death in order that we could be raised with him **"so we too may walk in a new way of life"** (Romans 6:4, HCSB).[104] According to Paul, we are set free from slavery to sin and death, and by the Spirit we have been set free from sin.

During that sermon, I read Romans 6 to the church. Even though I was emphasizing the truth that we had been resurrected so that we could live a new way of life, I distinctly remember that words from verse 14 caught my attention, even though I could not stop and ponder those words right in the middle of delivering the sermon. **"… We are not under law, but under grace,"** Paul had written. Over the next few days that statement kept popping up in my mind. I would think about it for a bit and then turn my mind to other things.

On the Wednesday morning following Easter, I headed north out of Winchester, drove through Paris, then headed northeast on U.S. 68 on my way to the small town of Carlisle to visit several of my customers. Not far out of Paris, as I began my way through an area of horse farms, the implications of Paul's words finally got through

---

[104] I was using the HCSB translation for my reading and praying in that season. Some translations such as the NASB and ESB say something like this: "… walk in newness of life"; others such as the NIV translate it "… we may live a new life."

to me—"I am not under law, I am under grace!" Immediately I was filled with nearly overwhelming joy. The morning spring sunlight seemed to be bursting on the fields, fences, and trees, and the grass and leaves seemed to sparkle in rich and brilliant green. Spring had awakened the land and spring had come to me! I wanted to get out of the car, jump a fence, and frolic in the fields!

Romans 5 and 6 began to come alive in my thinking, with several statements standing out in my mind as if they were in bold print—

> "… How much more will **those who receive the overflow of grace** and the gift of righteousness **reign in life** through the one man, Jesus Christ." (5:17b, HCSB)

> "… Where sin multiplied, grace multiplied even more so that, just as sin reigned in death, so also **grace will reign through righteousness** …." (5:20b–21a, HCSB)

> "… **Do not let sin reign** in your mortal body, so that you obey its desires…. For **sin will not rule over you**, because **you are not under law but under grace.**" (6:12, 14, HCSB)

One thought after another filled my mind: grace is a dominion! Grace is my ruler! The Lord has taught me how to submit to authority; I can submit to grace!

Then I remembered an exhortation from the epistle to the Hebrews: "Let us therefore come boldly to the throne of grace, that we may obtain mercy and find grace to help in time of need" (4:16, NKJV). *"The throne of grace"—it's a possessive*, I thought, *that could be read "… come boldly to Grace's throne!" Grace is a person!* I exulted. *God is Grace! Jesus, God who became a human being, the only Son of the Father, came full of grace and truth* (John 1:14). The thoughts came tumbling. And joy increased.

Later at home, I decided to look up the Greek word for *grace*. It should have been obvious, but it had never dawned on me that in Greek the words for *joy* (*chara*) and *grace* (*charis*) come from the same root word, a word that according to one Greek-English Lexicon suggests the picture of lambs frolicking in the field. I identified with those lambs!

Not only am I under Grace's authority, but his dominion, his kingdom, his realm is over all. Therefore, the apostle Paul opened Romans 5 by drawing the conclusion, based on the previous chapters, that since we have been justified by faith, through Jesus, "we have also obtained access **into this grace in which we stand.**"

Our God and King is Grace, and his realm in which we may now stand (and live) is described as grace; therefore, Paul goes on, "… We rejoice in hope of the glory of God" (Romans 5:1–2). Paul then describes the process by which, in the realm of Grace, God's glory is produced and made visible in our character.

> Not only that, but we rejoice in our sufferings, knowing that suffering produces endurance, and endurance produces character, and character produces hope, and hope does not put us to shame, because God's love has been poured into our hearts through the Holy Spirit who has been given to us. (Romans 5:3–5)

For several weeks I continued in that overflow of joy, a gift that I still treasure. But whether I experience the same feelings of joy or not, what a difference it makes to know the Creator and King of the Universe is Grace personified. What a joy it is to know that I can come confidently before His Grace's throne to receive mercy and grace!

****

In April 2006 Bob Mumford and Charles Simpson worked together again in an annual conference sponsored by Brother Charles's ministry in Gatlinburg, Tennessee. The theme was reconciliation. It was the first time the brothers had worked together after being personally reconciled with one another. Many who had been involved with the discipleship/shepherding movement came to those meetings. I was privileged to be there. Even though I had not been directly involved with the movement in its heyday in the 1970s, it still felt like a big homecoming. Reconciliation was the word for that season.

A year before, when I was visiting my brother Wes in Newark, Ohio, I realized that Paul Petrie and the brothers in the Association of Covenant Ministries were having their annual "family gathering" nearby in downtown Columbus. Most of those brothers I had not seen since I had joined FCL. Wes agreed to go over with me for a session. Even though there had been no estrangement and thus no need to be reconciled, I had not been in any of their meetings since 1996, just before Elijah died. After his death, I had begun to develop closer ties with Dennis Peacocke and the leaders who were involved with him.

Three things were important about that short visit to their get-together. First, I realized that these brothers truly were friends whom I had missed more than I had realized. Second, I was thrilled to see how many sons came to that meeting with their fathers. Third, I saw that their emphasis was on the kingdom of God, and I got a glimpse into the way the Lord had opened doors for various ones of them to make a kingdom impact in places all over the world, including reaching people high in government circles and people in Muslim nations. It was inspiring, and in the years since then, I have been blessed to be with this "band of brothers" a number of times. These renewed relationships have added strength, inspiration, and wisdom to me.

Late in 2003 and on into 2004 I was privileged to have a part in helping to bring reconciliation to a relationship between brothers in Winchester whose relationship had been broken twenty years ago. The details of that story are for those involved in the broken relationships to tell. I became involved when a brother who had been involved in the controversy that led to that break had moved back to Winchester with his family and had begun to attend our worship gatherings. The relational split had occurred in a Winchester church with whom I had meaningful ties.

When it became clear that there was a willingness to seek reconciliation, although there was not strong confidence that it could actually happen, that brother and two leaders from the church involved began to meet periodically to try to work out their differences. I met with them because of my connection with both, hoping that I could contribute something toward facilitating the potential reconciliation.

Whether I should have or not, I experienced great stress in the days leading up to each meeting. My digestive system, as was typical for me, seemed to take the brunt of the stress. I really don't know that the stress of reconciliation caused my digestive issues, but I do know that I seemed to be experiencing more pain in the days before each meeting.

I know that there was spiritual warfare involved. Quite obviously, one of the last things the devil desires is to see unity restored among God's people. Jesus prayed for our unity. The devil, whom Jesus called the thief, "comes only to steal and kill and destroy" (John 10:10). That enemy of God works hard trying to divide and conquer the people of God.

After the surgery in 1997, I had had two more surgeries: one in January 1998 to repair the "repaired" abdominal hernia, which had not held, and one in October 1999, an emergency appendectomy. After a few years of relatively good health, by early 2004 I was frequently experiencing abdominal discomfort. In late February I ended up in the hospital with a very painful case of diverticulitis. When another serious episode took place in early April, the doctor said I was in danger because another such attack could breach the wall of my colon and dump infection onto other organs. Therefore, in August I went back into the hospital to have the sigmoid colon removed.

The good news is that the reconciliation happened. Whether it had anything to do with my physical troubles, only God knows for sure. I do know this: as in the past in difficult times, the apostle Paul's account of his struggles in 2 Corinthians helped me endure with whatever measure of courage and faith I may have had.

During that time, another account of Paul's sufferings took on new meaning for me. Here are Paul's words as translated by N. T. Wright:

> Right now I'm having a celebration—a celebration of my sufferings, which are for your benefit! And I'm steadily completing, in my own flesh, what is presently lacking in the king's afflictions on behalf of his body, which is the church. I became the church's servant, according to the terms laid down by God when he gave me my commission on your behalf, the commission to fulfill God's word. This word declares the mystery that was kept secret from past ages and generations, but now has been revealed to God's holy people. God's intention was to make known to them just what rich glory this mystery contains, out there among the nations. And this is the key: the king, living within you as the hope of glory!
>
> He is the one we are proclaiming. We are instructing everybody and teaching everybody in every kind of wisdom, so that we can present everybody grown up, complete, in the king. That's what I am working for, struggling with all his energy which is powerfully at work within me.
>
> You see, I'd like you to know just what a struggle I am having on behalf of you, and the family in Laodicea, and all the people who don't know me by sight. I want their hearts to be encouraged as they're brought together in love. I want them to experience all the wealth of definite understanding, and to come to the knowledge of God's mystery—the Messiah, the king! He is the place where you'll find all the hidden treasures of wisdom and knowledge. (Colossians 1:24–23)[105]

---

[105] Wright, N. T., *The Kingdom New Testament: A Contemporary Translation* (Kindle Locations 9102–9116), HarperCollins, Kindle Edition.

As I read and thought about this passage, several things began to stand out to me. First, Paul said his sufferings were for the benefit of the disciples in Colossae. A few sentences later, Paul said that he was struggling with all the king's [that is, Christ's[106]] energy to present everybody grown and complete in the king [in Christ]. Then, Paul clarified who he meant by everybody—the whole family of Jesus's disciples in Colossae, those in the neighboring city Laodicea (cities and church communities which Paul had never visited in person), and all who did not know him by sight.

You and I are included. After all, we don't know Paul by sight. Somehow in the economy of God, Paul's struggles were helping to accomplish God's work in other people's lives, including yours and mine. That, then, is what Paul meant when he made this incredible statement: "I'm steadily completing, in my own flesh, that which is lacking in the king's afflictions on behalf of his people."

Wow! I began to consider the possibility that my own little sufferings could count for the good of someone else. I could ask for relief or healing or deliverance, and I should. After all, Jesus provided for it in his suffering and death. But what if it did not come right away? Could I also offer myself and my struggles to God for the good of others? Paul did. When, for Paul's own good, God sent a "messenger of Satan," "a thorn in the flesh" to harass Paul, he asked for deliverance. Three times he asked.

Then God spoke: "My grace is sufficient for you, for my power is made perfect in weakness" (2 Corinthians 12:9a).

And what was Paul's response?

> Therefore I will boast all the more gladly of my weaknesses, so that the power of Christ may rest upon me. For the sake of Christ, then, I am content with weaknesses, insults, hardships, persecutions, and calamities. For when I am weak, then I am strong. (12:9b–10)

I have come to the conviction that I can and I should offer myself and my struggles—whether spiritual, emotional, or physical—in God's service for the benefit of others. In fact, I believe that this is part of our calling to follow Jesus. How does it work? I do not know. It is part of what Paul called "the mystery of Christ" at work in us.

No wonder Paul could declare,

---

[106] "King" is an accurate way to convey the actual Biblical meaning of the Greek word *christos* (the anointed one, Christ, Messiah).

Indeed, I count everything as loss because of the surpassing worth of knowing Christ Jesus my Lord. For his sake I have suffered the loss of all things and count them as rubbish, in order that I may gain Christ and be found in him ... —that I may know him and the power of his resurrection, **and may share his sufferings**, becoming like him in his death, that by any means possible I may attain the resurrection from the dead. (Philippians 3:8–11, bold print added for emphasis)

****

Still, I was not asking for another chance to suffer. (Or was I?) The chance to suffer physically again came with the surgery to remove the sigmoid colon in August 2004. For a couple weeks I appeared to be recovering well, even though the wound from the incision was not closing correctly again, so Patricia was again doing the twice daily cleaning, packing, and re-bandaging procedure that we had been through before. But all in all, things were looking up.

Then, one morning about two weeks after the surgery at about 4:30, our dog, Zeke, began to whine and I got out of bed to take him outside. As I was walking through the family room to the garage door, things begin to get dim and fuzzy and I could not stand up. When I became aware again, I was on my knees leaning over the coffee table. My wife was in a panic. She could not rouse me at first, and she thought I had fallen onto the surgical wound. She was trying desperately to call 911 but without her glasses was not being successful. At last she got through.

By the time Patricia got from the phone to me, I was attempting to get up, and she helped me into the nearby recliner. Apparently, instinct had kicked in when I passed out and fell, or more likely the Lord had spared me, and my arms had slowed the fall. There was no damage to the incision.

Soon the EMS team arrived. By then my head was clearing and I was not feeling bad, mostly just weak. As they checked my blood pressure and other things, they asked me some questions. I had had surgery recently, I told them. No, I had not been feeling bad, other than the evening before when I took some medicine because I thought my chest was getting congested, I said.

They began to prepare to take me to the hospital. I resisted. They insisted. Something was not right and needed to be checked out, I was told. So, into the ambulance and off to the Clark Regional ER I went.

In the ER, they did the usual protocols and then took me back to radiology, where I had a chest X-ray followed by a C-T scan. Back in the ER, someone—a nurse, I think—said: "You've had a pulmonary embolism. We will be transferring you to the University of Kentucky." I did not know how to spell *embolism*, let alone know what it meant. Oddly, I don't think I asked. Since I did not know what it meant, I was not worried. After all, I was not feeling very bad.

I did call my parents. When Dad answered, I told him I was in the ER and that they were saying I had had a pulmonary embolism. The phone got really quiet for a while. I reassured Dad that I was feeling okay, even though I would be going on to UK.

A few days later I found out that my call had frightened Dad badly. Not only did he know the seriousness of a pulmonary embolism, but when he was 15 his own 49-year-old mother had died because of a pulmonary embolism following abdominal surgery. Although I had heard that my grandmother had had surgery and had died because of a complication after surgery, I did not remember ever hearing it referred to as a pulmonary embolism or even a blood clot.

Surprisingly, as a pastor I had never been called to the bedside of someone who had had one either, I suppose because most of the people for whom I had provided pastoral oversight were as young as or younger than me.

At UK I got the full explanation: a blood clot had formed in my leg and the clot had broken loose, lodging in my pulmonary arteries. It never dawned on me to ask how the clots had gotten through the right side of my heart in order to reach the arteries to my lungs.

In the early afternoon that day, they did an ultrasound on my legs in order to see if a clot was still there. To everyone's surprise, my legs were "full of clots." The attending doctor became really serious. "At any time, those clots may break loose and cause your death. You need to have a filter inserted in the main vein of your abdomen to slice up any that do."

Therefore, before long I was taken to a room for the procedure. Because there were so many clots in the legs, they could not do the procedure in the normal way, inserting the filter by going in through the groin. Instead, the tech told me, the filter would need to be inserted and put into place by going through the jugular vein. All the details are not necessary. I'll just say that I was given medication that was supposed to keep me from feeling pain for half an hour. UK is, however, a teaching hospital, and a new doctor needed to learn do the procedure, so I was "appointed" to

367

provide his training. It took him nearly 45 minutes to get it done. The last 10 or 15 minutes got quite uncomfortable as the pain medication began to wear off, I must say. You can bet, though, that I was sitting really, really still with my jugular vein open and a wire going down into my abdomen.

A few weeks later during a follow-up visit to my primary care doctor, I was examined by a resident who had been serving on the cardiology unit where I had been, following the embolism. He told me in vivid terms that my case was special. "Before I came into your room that first day, I looked at your C-T scan from Clark Regional. I was amazed that you were alive. I had never seen such a big clot in a living patient. Then when I walked into your room and saw you sitting up chatting, I could not believe my eyes."

"The left artery was completely blocked and the right artery was all but closed off with a clot about the size of a quarter."

"How big is the artery?" I responded.

"About the size of a quarter." After a pause to let that sink in, he continued his examination.

Once again, I have no doubt that the Lord kept me here in this life for whatever his purpose may be, rather than take me into the world to come.

A few weeks later, it became clear that the incision simply was not healing correctly. After examining it, my surgeon, Dr. Paul Kearney, discovered that infection had bonded with the mesh that had been put in back in 1998 during the hernia repair. By 2004 that brand of mesh was known to be associated with such problems.

There was no quick solution to my problem. The wound could not heal until the mesh was removed, and the mesh needed to be removed in order to deal with the infection. I could not have surgery to remove the mesh because I was going to be on blood thinner for at least six months to be certain that the blood clots reabsorbed. In the end, that wound remained open and the twice-daily cleaning routine had to be continued for more than seven months.

At the end of April 2005, I finally was able to go into surgery again. Dr. Kearney removed the mesh. Later, wisely I think, he told me that he had also dissected and removed as much scar tissue as he could. Because of the danger of infection and other complications, he had needed to repair the hernia without mesh.

There was one benefit to the surgery. A huge scar had developed in my abdomen where incisions had been made three times already. I had lost a little weight, enabling Dr. Kearney to clean up much of the ugly scar when he closed it up for the fourth time. The incision healed correctly that time! Now I have a joke to tell if someone happens to see my belly: "Some people have six-packs. But I have two vertical quarts, one on the right and one on the left."

A year later, the hernia redeveloped. Another surgery was in the works so that another brand of mesh could be used to fix it. By this time, I was convinced that at least a part of the reason I was prone to these recurring hernias and that it was so difficult for incisions to heal was the size of my overweight abdomen. I had gained back all the weight I had lost before the 2005 surgery and had added more.

After trying many diets over the years, I had absolutely no faith that I could take weight off and keep it off. Patricia had been trying to get me to try Weight Watchers, but I had no hope. Then one day in June 2006, I seemed to hear the Lord say, "If you will train yourself with this discipline, then I will help you with the disciplines that really count." With that word, faith came. I started the Weight Watchers program, and weight began to come off.

The following year, Dr. Kearney was able to reinsert mesh and fix the hernia. Because of the truly significant weight loss, this time he was able to do the surgery laparoscopically. In comparison to the others, it was a breeze.

I do not know all that God was doing in me through these years of physical difficulties. However, working on the discipline of weight loss was worth a great deal. Plus, Dr. Kearney and I became friends over the course of three years. Not only is Dr. Kearney one of the very best surgeons in his field, but I have never had a doctor (and I've been blessed with some wonderful doctors) who was more accessible to me when I needed to contact him in between appointments. He took an interest in theologically oriented books that I would bring to the office to read while waiting to see him. This led to some meaningful conversations, and he wanted to receive the occasional "Humble Perspectives" that I would send out.

In more recent years, Dr. Kearney has had some big challenges of his own to face. Not only did his wife die from cancer, but he also went through much-publicized legal difficulties related to his work. I was able pray for him and still do from time to time. I hope the Lord used me to make some small contribution to his life, maybe even something that has helped him while facing his own issues. If so, then that alone would make the physical suffering I faced worthwhile.

I have had no serious difficulties with those sorts of physical ailments since that time. That in itself is something that I have reason to believe is a blessing from God. The hernia repair in January 1998 had been done Dr. Stacy Harbin, then a partner in the same office as Dr. Greiser, who by this time had left the practice to serve in medical missions. A few days after the surgery, just before I was released from the hospital, Dr. Harbin stopped by during his rounds. "I have been thinking about your case," he said, "planning how to get in the next time."

Startled, I asked, "Are you saying another surgery is possible?"

"Not possible, probable," he responded, rather bluntly, it felt to me. "It is likely that you will need a colostomy at some point."

Immediately, self-pity arose. "I don't want to be an invalid," I groaned.

"Stop that!" Dr. Harbin commanded. "That is an insult to all those who live full lives with colostomies, including more young athletes than you would be able to guess."

His rebuke, though blunt, was a blessing. Not only did it kick me out of the self-pity mode, but it led me to turn to the Lord to whom I offered myself, my health, and my future one more time.

****

About 2002, the Alzheimer's disease that had begun in Mom began to seriously limit her abilities, and the impact on both Dad and her was huge. By 2005 Dad was having to curtail his ministry schedule a great deal. As the time passed, I made more and more trips to Circleville in order to support Dad and to help care for Mom, even during the time when I was dealing with my own physical issues.

The brunt of helping Mom and Dad, however, fell upon my sister Debbie. Therefore, in 2005 while I was recovering from surgery, Dad and Mom moved 35 miles south from Circleville, Ohio, to Waverly, where Debbie and her family lived. After I quit my job with Rees Office Products, my schedule was more flexible. I began to travel to Waverly as often as possible in order to help care for Mother and to offer what relief I could to Dad and Debbie. Usually I would stay over for a night or two. One time I stayed with Mom almost a week so that Dad could get away and minister in central Pennsylvania.

Speaking frankly, the fact that Mom had Alzheimer's offended me. I had not expressed anger to God about Elijah's death, but I did about Mom's battle with Alzheimer's. My complaint went like this: Mom had given her life to Jesus at age 8. She had been faithful to God ever since. She had weaknesses, as all of us do, but if there had ever been a more godly woman, I did not know who it would be. I thought: *Mom does not deserve to go out whimpering in a fetal position like my Aunt Ruby did! Mom deserves to go out in a blaze of glory!*

My anger was based on faulty thinking, of course. I knew the truth in my mind: none of us deserves anything but death because of sin. None of us is good enough to deserve God's mercy, let alone the blessing of dying "in a blaze of glory." It is God's love that motivated the Father and Son to rescue us. It is God's grace alone that brings mercy to us. Unthinkingly, I had an illusion when it came to Mom. Although it took many months, I finally was able to fully surrender the illusion and the anger to the Lord and to begin to trust Father's plan.

God had the last word, as it turned out!

Under the influence of Alzheimer's, Mom was a "roamer," a person who was always moving and doing something, even harmful things. She had to be watched virtually all of the time. It was too much for Dad to handle, even with Debbie living only a mile away. In the summer of 2007, we made the difficult decision to move Mom into an Alzheimer's unit at Traditions in Bristol Village, which was only a half-mile from their home, making it easy for Dad to be with her daily.

In November 2007 Mom had a stroke, which took her eyesight. From that point on, she became much less restless. While her memory was all but gone, she knew Dad and continued to remember many gospel songs. There are stories that I could tell about the testimony her life was to those who worked in the unit.

Then, in November 2008, she was rushed to the emergency room with what appeared to be a heart attack. Dad and Debbie arrived quickly, and they were standing by Mom's bedside when a nurse entered to say that Mom had had a heart attack and would likely not make it. Years before, Mom and Dad had made the decision not to be "kept alive" in such a situation. Whether Mom heard and understood the nurse or not, we do not know. However, according to Dad and Debbie, Mom *looked* to their left and declared, "The Lord is here with me." Those were her last words. Less than a minute later, she died.

A blind woman with Alzheimer's saw and recognized the Lord as she lay dying. *That* is "going out in a blaze of glory!"

****

There was another surgery, one which I did not anticipate. Over a period of several years, I had gradually developed a limp in my right leg. I adapted to it as just a nuisance without much concern until the "discomfort," mostly in my knee, became pain, which made it difficult to sleep.

Around 2007, my daughters talked me into going to a chiropractor for treatment. A chiropractor? Oh yes, I had met one, Dr. Mark Miller, the man who had given me a word from the Lord at El Rio Grande back in 1998.

Dr. Miller's X-rays of my back showed that a compressed disc was causing pressure on the sciatic nerve. That seemed to account for the pain. Dr. Miller treated it with adjustments and decompression, which really made a difference for a while. Eventually, the pain began to grow again.

Finally, in 2008, I told my primary care doctor, Dr. Charles Griffith, about the pain during my annual physical. After having X-rays taken of my lower body, Dr. Griffith saw that there was arthritis in my knee—and in my hip too! Dr. Griffith sent me to Dr. Jeff Selby, a sports medicine doctor who specializes in joint replacements.

My appointment with Dr. Selby came on the day Mom died. I remember that day well since my mind drifted to Mom's death while I was driving on Midland Avenue near the Lexington Herald Leader Building on my way to the clinic. Next thing I knew, I heard a siren and saw red lights flashing in my rearview mirror. I pulled over as soon as I was in a safe place. Grief turns out to be no good excuse in the eyes of the law. The officer soon handed me a speeding ticket—a $175 fine.

Dr. Selby talked with me and watched me walk across the room. Then he sent me in to have more X-rays taken—of my right hip.

"What about my knee? That's where the pain is greater," I protested.

"All right, we will have pictures taken of the knee too," he said.

Soon I was back in his office. "Your right hip needs to be replaced," he concluded.

Again I asked, "What about my knee?"

"I think that if we replace the hip, you will find the knee will be fine. There is some arthritis in your knee, but most of the pain is radiating from the hip," he replied.

I was skeptical, but we scheduled surgery for January 5. Doctor Selby was correct. The hip replacement took care of the pain and the limp. Ten days later, when I went to his office for the follow-up visit, he was very pleased with my ability to walk across the room without even using the cane I was carrying. What's more, he was obviously pleased and a little surprised to see that my legs appeared to be exactly equal in length.

Two days later, early in the morning, I passed out in our bathroom and once again found myself in the hospital because of a blood clot in the leg. This one, we discovered, was one huge clot from the groin all the way down my right leg. The good news is that if any of it broke loose, the filter worked. There was no embolism this time.

Actually, I may have helped the blood clot develop. I was so intent on sticking to my Weight Watchers diet that I even refused fattening hospital food following surgery in favor of a chef's salad from the deli. Tests showed that I had become malnourished as well as dehydrated, never considering that my body might need more sustenance to do the work of recovery. The blood clot slowed progress a little, but by July I felt better than I had felt in years. "I feel like I have gained ten years of my life back!" I exclaimed often.

****

On Sunday, March 8, 2009, while I was still recovering, the Holy Spirit spoke to me once again about grace. That Sunday I was listening to Dirk Goodrich give a message on prayer. He had my full attention, and I was looking up each of the Scriptures as he gave the references and made his comments.

All of sudden, a thought intruded emphatically: *"The grace of God teaches us to say No."* The words were as clear as if Dirk had said them; however, he had said nothing about grace.

I immediately recognized that the word I had heard was from Scripture, but I did not immediately remember where it was found. The word was so clear and strong that I ignored Dirk and began to look for the reference. Eventually, my memory kicked in and I realized that it must have been from a passage in Titus, which I looked up. The Bible I was carrying that Sunday said something similar, but not those same words.

> For the grace of God has appeared, bringing salvation for all people, training us to renounce ungodliness and worldly passions, and to live self-controlled, upright, and godly lives in the present age. (Titus 2:11–12)

As before when the word about being under grace came to me, so it was this time, that for the next few days that word kept coming back to mind: "The grace of God teaches us to say 'No.'" Finally, I started looking through the various translations of Scripture in my library, and I found it, ironically, in one of my least favorite modern translations, the NIV.

> For the grace of God has appeared that offers salvation to all people. It teaches us to say "No" to ungodliness and worldly passions, and to live self-controlled, upright and godly lives in this present age, while we wait for the blessed hope—the appearing of the glory of our great God and Savior, Jesus Christ, who gave himself for us to redeem us from all wickedness and to purify for himself a people that are his very own, eager to do what is good. (Titus 2:11–14)

"The grace of God has appeared …. It teaches us … "! Grace not only teaches us to say "no" to ungodliness and worldly passions, but grace also teaches us how to live. "The grace of God has appeared …. It teaches us … to live self-controlled, upright and godly lives in this present age …."

Having seen that several other translations use the word *train* rather than *teach*, it occurred to me that I should look up that Greek word.

I had been aware for a long time of the Greek word *didaskalia*, translated *doctrine* or *teaching* in Titus 2:1 and 2:10, because it had been eye-opening when I noticed the word *doctrine* was used concerning the practical, everyday life instruction found in Titus 2, rather than doctrine in the sense of theological concepts, which was the way I had previously thought about it.

But this Greek word translated *teaches* or *trains* in 2:12 turned out to be another word altogether, the word *paideuo*, which I discovered meant to "train, teach, correct, chastise." This word is not about teaching in the sense of imparting information but rather about teaching in the sense of disciplinary instruction.

I found multiple instances where this word is commonly translated by forms of "discipline" and "correction" in modern translations of Hebrew 12:5–11. It is also the word Pilate used when he wanted to teach Jesus a lesson by chastising or flogging or punishing (*paideuo*) him and then releasing him (Luke 23:22).

Grace rules! The joy of that lesson was stirred up as I remembered the Lord showing me that! Now I was seeing more: Grace teaches! Grace trains! This Grace is not impersonal; rather, it is our God, His Grace, who has adopted us as his sons and daughters and, therefore, trains us in the way to live. Grace is not only my King; Grace is my Spiritual Trainer; Grace is my Father!

The same God who had told me twenty years earlier "I like you, boy!" was now helping me, at age 60, to see more of his Fatherly love and care.

It was about this time also that the Holy Spirit gave me an unexpected answer to my heart's cry: "Lord, show me the church of the next generation." Since 2001, that had become my frequent prayer. In 2009 the Spirit responded clearly and pointedly: "No, I am not going to give you the vision for the church of the next generation! Old men dream dreams and young men see visions. I will give the vision for the church to those who will build it."

This answer has put things into a different and more proper perspective. My prayer changed to "Lord, raise up young men and give them the vision for your church in their generation! And give them the ability to bring many of their generation into living that life."

Along with that changed prayer, I have greatly longed to contribute at least something to the lives of some of those who will receive God's vision. Now I am far more at peace with the small part I have played in God's big purposes. When I view things from the proper perspective, it is a privilege beyond words just to be included in God's family at all! How much more of a privilege it is to have even a small part in his purposes.

Compare it to being in a movie, for example. What if I had had a bit part or even been an extra in some well-known movie? Wouldn't that be something! How much more wonderful that God would make a place for me—any place at all—in his family and his purposes!

As Eugene Peterson translated the song of David,

Oh yes, you shaped me first inside, then out;
    you formed me in my mother's womb.
I thank you, High God—you're breathtaking!
      Body and soul, I am marvelously made!
      I worship in adoration—what a creation!
You know me inside and out,
    you know every bone in my body;
You know exactly how I was made, bit by bit,
    how I was sculpted from nothing into something.
Like an open book, you watched me grow from conception to birth;
    all the stages of my life were spread out before you,
The days of my life all prepared
    before I'd even lived one day. (Psalm 139:13–16, MSG)

The apostle Paul added: "For we are God's masterpiece. He has created us anew in Christ Jesus, so we can do the good things he planned for us long ago" (Ephesians 2:10, NLT).

Still, it often takes some time, some reminding, and some disciplining for me to remember that it is Grace who is directing my life and training me. It is Grace who before time "wrote the script." Quite often I don't like the training regimen. It often takes some effort, or even some failure, before I get my perspective right.

Grace has brought me this far and Grace will lead me on!

Interested Beginner

Following Ted Sandquist's exhortation in 1998, I increasingly became involved in our city and county. The first step was renewed involvement in the Association of Churches. Most of what I called the more "conservative, Bible-believing" (evangelical) pastors had ceased to participate in the Association during the years when I had been delivering office products and then grieving Elijah's death. I never knew exactly why, although I did hear that there had been a dispute about abortion at some point.

As usual, I was reluctant to take on leadership responsibility. But around the year 2000, I allowed the Association members to elect me vice president. When the president took a different job and resigned, I ended up becoming the president (shades of my experience as a sophomore in college). I developed three goals for the Association that I hoped to bring about while president. First, I wanted to see pastors from the more evangelical churches get involved again. Second, I wanted to see pastors from the black community become active in the Association. Third, I wanted to see small groups of pastors committing to regular times of prayer together.

There was not much visible progress toward these goals made while I was president. I resigned as president soon after I began selling office products and, therefore, I was not able to be at many of the Association meetings. In August 2005, I began an effort to become a regular participant again. Dale Hanson, a Southern Baptist, was president, and I was surprised to see how many evangelicals had gotten involved. At that first meeting I attended the primary discussion concerned a city-wide tent meeting—The Great Hope Revival—which was to be held later that month.

One part of that conversation is unforgettable. A question was put forth for discussion: "Should we have an altar call each of the three nights, or should we have an altar call on only one of the nights?" I assumed that this question was motivated by a desire to be sensitive to the less "evangelical" pastors. Before discussion could start, the voice of the Catholic priest, Father Norman Fischer, a young man who was fairly new to the community, rang out: "Of course we will have an altar call every night. We are praying for people to be saved, aren't we?" Father Norman was leading the prayer team for those meetings, so he knew what they had been praying for! No one dissented after his declaration.

Father Norman is Afro-American, so at least one black pastor had become involved! Eventually he became president of the Association, and the effectiveness of the group that had begun to grow under Dale Hanson's leadership grew even more. Within a few years, Rev. Sam Peoples from Broadway Baptist, one of the largest churches in the black community, became involved, and later he also served as president.

It is worth noting that it has been hard for many of our Afro-American brothers to participate, even when they want to, because so many are part-time in church ministry. Several, I learned, were not only leading churches and holding down jobs but also were taking seminary classes. That would be a load for anyone, but on top of that, quite a few had children to raise as well. I am encouraged that there are Afro-American brothers currently leading churches in Winchester who seem clearly to be called to make a significant impact in our whole community.

In January 2009, while I was dealing with the hip replacement, Clark County Coroner Robert Gayheart sensed a strong urge to call together pastors to pray for the community. Several began meeting to pray every Tuesday. As soon as I heard about the group that April, I began to pray with them. As many as eleven or twelve have prayed together at times, but five of us are still meeting regularly, more than eight years later. There may well be other groups of leaders I do not know about who are praying together in our community.

For quite a number of years, Winchester's Mayor Ed Burtner and Clark County Judge Executive[107] Henry Branham have called a community prayer meeting on the first Saturday of each year. The intent of this gathering is to bring Christians in the community together in unified prayer in which we seek to pray for every sphere of responsibility in our community as the first "order of business"[108] for the year.

None of these things took place while I was leading, but progress has come about in all three things that I had wanted to see come to pass!

In the spring of 2005 I saw a front-page article in the *Winchester Sun,* our local newspaper, about a meeting that had been called by an 83-year-old retired black pastor, Rev. Henry Baker,[109] and a white business man, Roger Hurst. The purpose of

---

[107] Judge Executive is the highest executive position in Kentucky's county system.

[108] This is not an official meeting of the government, but it is a recognition of God's government over all.

[109] It's difficult not to tell Rev. Baker's story. He pastored Broadway Baptist for 40 years. He the primary mover in integrating Winchester, without outside help. He was the first Afro-American to serve as a city magistrate. And after 2005, I had the privilege to become his friend. When Rev. Baker died at age 91, I lost a friend, and our community lost a prayer warrior and a hero.

the meeting, the article said, had been to gather Christians together to deal with pervasive drug issues in our community, a problem that was killing about twenty people each year in our county of 35,000. As I read the article, I sensed the Lord saying clearly that I was to get involved; therefore, I was present at the next meeting.

Eventually I was asked to serve on the board of the group that was formed and named the Clark County Drug Coalition (CCDC). For several years I served as president of the group. Among a number of activities that we led over the next several years, I think the most important were public prayer gatherings we held. In the course of one week in October 2010, we prayed in two city parks, on the grounds of an apartment complex, and in one of the local federal housing "projects"—all four of these locations had been identified by city officials as centers of drug-related activity. Then, in the spring and summer of 2012, we prayed in locations near to the "four corners" of the county. We held one of those gatherings just outside the property line of a "pain clinic" that was known to be a source of easy-to-get pain pill prescriptions, the major drug to which our citizens were addicted at the time.

It's often hard to prove the specific effectiveness of prayer. All I can say is that by 2012 the number of drug-related deaths had dropped to a half-dozen or fewer and stayed at that low level for several years. More than one civil official has attributed the decline in addiction deaths to those prayer meetings. I can also report that the clinic was investigated and soon closed down.

Early in 2012, Jim Corbett, an acquaintance and former Cincinnati Bengal, called to set up a lunch appointment with his friend Chad Varga[110] and me. At lunch, I learned that Chad had been raised by an alcoholic and drug-addicted mother who, with her two children, had lived with one abusive boyfriend after another. Chad had been dramatically saved by Jesus at age 14 and had become a basketball star. At the point when his professional basketball career was about to become truly lucrative, Chad felt called of the Lord to leave basketball in order to reach young people with a background like his. Now he makes presentations in schools all across the country, motivating young people to believe that they can build good character in their lives even if they have a background as terrible as his.

A few times a year, Chad will work with churches in a community to plan an event to which young people can be invited following the assemblies. At these events they can hear his testimony about Jesus. Jim believed that it would be good for Chad to come to our area. After hearing from Chad and Jim, I told them straightforwardly

---

[110] For more on Chad Varga's story and ministry check out http://www.chadvarga.com.

that I was skeptical about the fruit of event-type evangelism. Still, over the next few days, I became convinced that God was leading CCDC to call the churches together to sponsor such an event in our community. The CCDC board agreed.

Suffice it to say, in six months Chad and I spent eleven Sundays visiting twenty-one churches in three counties. In each church, Chad presented his testimony and the vision for the event. Gradually, volunteers from the churches came together to form an effective team to plan an event at our local high school, which we called "COLLIDE! at GRC." People in the churches Chad and I visited also gave enough money for us to prepare more than 1,300 follow-up packets at $10 per packet, and nearly a thousand of them volunteered to staff the event. Individuals and businesses in the community contributed $25,000 dollars to pay for hundreds of prizes, free food, music, and games.

At the beginning of the 2012–2013 school year, on August 27–29, Chad made his presentations in all the public high schools and middle schools in our county and in two neighboring counties, Montgomery and Powell. He addressed about 8,000 students in seven schools. It was amazing to see the young people respond to his speech and then to see many line up afterward in order to meet Chad and, for a dollar, purchase the book, *If You Only Knew ...*, which told his story in more detail. It was heartrending to hear even a few of the stories they told him about their lives. Later, Chad received hundreds of private Facebook messages in which teens from those schools not only opened up about the horror in their lives but also about the hope he had inspired in them.

At each school we offered free tickets to COLLIDE! at GRC. Chad informed the young people right up front at the end of each assembly that he would be sharing his testimony about Jesus at the event. Each ticket had an area to be filled in with the student's name and contact information so that when the student came to the event we could collect that part of the ticket in order to follow up with him or her.

On Wednesday evening, August 29, about 3,500 students came to COLLIDE! at George Rogers Clark High School. After food and games, we gathered the students into the gymnasium to hear Chad share more of his story. Toward the end of his testimony, he completely surprised the students by introducing and calling to the stage his mother, who had become a believer and had been living free from addiction for about twenty years. Right before their eyes, those young people saw a living example of redemption and reconciliation.

After a short, clear presentation of the gospel message, Chad said: "Now, I don't want you to look at your neighbor. I don't want you to follow the lead of anyone around you. If you have a desire to make Jesus Lord of your life and to receive him as your Savior, then stand up right now."

Hundreds stood immediately. It was "electric." As I write these words, tears are welling up in my eyes as I remember that moment. At Chad's direction, most of those who stood came down in front of the stage, where he took time to look directly at each one (literally) and then led them in a prayer of confession and repentance. More than 800 of the students filed over to the school auditorium and to the cafeteria, where we prayed with each of them and gave each a follow-up packet.

I do not know whether or not the saints in the heavens join Jesus in interceding for us (Hebrews 7:22–25) or not, but if they do, I am confident my son Elijah had joined his Lord in praying for us and for all those young people and that he was rejoicing with the angels that night!

****

About midnight, Patricia and I got home from COLLIDE! after going to Don Señor for a late dinner with Chad. I was weary but elated! What a great victory God had brought about! And there was some satisfaction in having a part to play in it all, I must admit.

Then I noticed that Patricia was not elated and did not appear to be happy. I began to question her—most likely pressing too hard, which is one of my weaknesses. When my wife began to talk about what she was feeling, my emotions turned upside down.

She had retired from her job earlier that year, and the change in schedule had allowed her to volunteer her help with some of the COLLIDE! preparation. I had been all caught up in "my work" on the event and missed the signals altogether. Understandably, she had felt there was no place for her. Then some things happened that caused her to be offended. Patricia, sincerely seeking to spare me from extra burdens while I was working so hard on the event, had carried these things alone, holding them in. Something had taken place that evening while we were out to eat with Chad following the event that had brought everything to the surface. Although I cared about the hurt she was carrying, I did not care enough. I was disappointed and offended, more concerned about myself, if I am fully honest.

That evening we entered one of the most difficult seasons in our whole marriage—maybe even the most difficult. While there were many wonderful moments along the way, for more than two years both Patricia and I were in a difficult place. From the beginning we had been in this marriage for life. That was a settled issue. What kind of life it would be was the question. More than once I despaired.

Several times we sat down with our friend Dennis Cole, who would draw us out and help us to hear and think through what we were feeling ourselves and what we were communicating with each other. Those times I found to be very helpful. Toward the end of the two years, Patricia and I read *Power Christian Thinking: Changing Hopelessness to Faith, Hope, and Love*, a book by Dr. Gary Sweeten, a counselor and church consultant from Cincinnati, Ohio.[111]

The book helped to bring together several things the Lord had been working on in me during that season. In early 2015, Patricia and I visited with Dr. Sweeten for a couple hours in a coffee shop. The time was encouraging for me.

One of several key moments in that season took place while we were singing during our Winchester Covenant worship gathering in December 2012, as I recall. I had a strong sense that God was speaking to me. I grabbed my phone and typed in the words I was hearing:

Harden not

Let suffering not make me hard but tender/do not focus on my wounds and protecting myself but concerned with Pat's hurt.

I have taken offense: I didn't deserve this. I've had wrong done me so I've put up defense so that what is said will not cut me.

I've tried to be strong (hard) rather than be weak and let the hurt **hurt** so that I can be a vehicle of healing.

Lies:
Only the strong survive
The good die young—the opposite of which would mean the evil, hard, tough endure.

---

[111] Dr. Sweeten is a good friend of Dennis Cole, and much of the wisdom Dennis shared with us had been gained in his association with Dr. Sweeten, who founded Sweeten Life Systems. More information may be found at http://www.sweetenlife.com.

Those words may not make sense to you, but they did to me, and as I chewed on them in the days to come they became even clearer. God was working with me to help me make myself vulnerable. He wanted me to be free to be available to Patricia and more concerned with her than with myself. He wanted me to allow myself to hurt so that he could bring the kind of comfort to me that could then flow through me to others. God was reminding me and assuring me that, in God's kingdom, his strength really comes into action when I am weak and content to be weak in myself if, in my weakness, I turn to him and allow him to enable me, by grace, to do for others what I cannot do by myself. He was reminding me that dying to myself is the path that releases his life in me and through me.

Christianity 101, I know. But I seem to have to go back and repeat the early grades often. But that is that the way of discipleship—the method of any discipline. For example, when an athlete gets into some kind of slump, he does not try to learn new and more complex things but rather focuses once again on the fundamentals. So those simple words, "jotted down" that Sunday, became a big part of my practice routine for the next two years.

God gave us another special gift during that time. Not many weeks after it felt like our world was exploding, God sent a young couple to us in order that, of all things, they could receive help for their marriage. We began to meet with them regularly.

It seemed as though prior to every time we met, usually shortly before, Patricia and I would "hit another knothole" in our difficulties. We might have worked through it or might still be working through it when the time came to get together with the young couple. It seems as though every time we met, our struggle provided some wisdom or encouragement for the younger couple. In the course of our times together, we became real friends.

God did a miracle in their relationship. It looked like it might be broken beyond repair for a while. But with great courage and determination, they each kept turning to the Lord and he restored them! In our weakness …

God also did a miracle in our relationship. We still do not have "the perfect marriage," but we love each other more than ever and we are slowly learning to work together more fruitfully than before.

****

As awesome as the things the Lord was showing me and working in me back in the 1970s were, in the last twenty-five years he has led me to look again into these foundational truths. The "opportunity" to work on marriage again is one example.

While my understanding of these truths is, I fully believe, much greater than it was, I must add this confession: I now know more than ever that my ability to build on this understanding and to impart it to others and build it into the life of our church is much weaker than I could have known.

In recent years, once again the Lord has been emphasizing the truth that he created us and redeemed us and **calls us to be disciples who make disciples**. I was sure I got this point way back when! Yet now I know that my understanding of even this basic truth has been quite incomplete, to say nothing of the level of discipleship I have lived. Discipleship, I see more clearly and deeply than ever, is not a program, nor is it simply a way of life. Rather, discipleship is the process by which we are transformed from the inside out by the Holy Spirit.

In a way, I was driven by my weaknesses to wrestle again with what it means to be a disciple. In the spring of 2015, I was in a season of discouragement and stress, perhaps even depression. It seemed impossible to resist the temptation to be discouraged about the difficult things Patricia and I had been working through, in spite of the fact that much good had come in those struggles and that season was ending. I also had been dealing with concerns and anxiety having to do with Winchester Covenant for a number of months, in spite of the fact that there was much about our life together that was wholesome and good.

Once again, the Holy Spirit used books, this time to stir me to ponder the purpose and means of Biblical discipleship. Without thinking out why I was doing so, I responded to an ad offering me two free audible books if I would sign up to be a monthly subscriber to Audible books (audible.com). I had never been inclined to purchase audible books but, for some reason, that day I began to look at what was available. To my surprise, two books grabbed my attention, and I took the offer. The first book I chose was N. T. Wright's *Simply Good News: Why the Gospel Is News and What Makes It Good*, which I had recently read and thoroughly appreciated. This book, along with two previous books, *Simply Jesus: A New Vision of Who He Was, What He Did, and Why He Matters*[112] and *How God Became King: The Forgotten Story of the Gospels*,[113] distill some of the fruit of Wright's academic theological work in a format far more accessible to a less academic reader. The

---

[112] Published by HarperOne, 2011.
[113] Published by HarperOne, 2012.

greatest thing about this book is that it brought into sharp focus conclusions about Jesus and the gospel of the kingdom that had been developing in my own thought for years, as well as opening many insights that I had not perceived.[114]

The second audiobook was Dallas Willard's *The Great Omission: Reclaiming Jesus's Essential Teachings on Discipleship*,[115] which I began to listen to first. It was Willard's emphasis on the spiritual disciplines—such disciplines as prayer, memorization, meditation, and silence—as primary ways God has provided for us to be transformed that struck me to the heart and stimulated me to hunger for more of the kind of transformation that he was describing.

Dallas Willard's work is not new to me, nor was the topic. My friend Dr. David Lanier had given Willard's book *The Divine Conspiracy: Rediscovering Our Hidden Life in God*[116] to me on my 50th birthday, and I had even used the third chapter as a reading in the Mars Hill worldview class. Several years after receiving that gift, I had been deeply touched and helped by Willard's *Revolution of Character: Discovering Christ's Pattern for Spiritual Transformation*,[117] a book co-written with Don Simpson. But in 2015 the time was right according to God's script for *The Divine Omission*. A new season began.

While I was still listening to this book, Amazon began to tempt me with ads for other books, triggered by my purchases. In this way I became aware that Willard had been involved in the production of a study Bible on the theme of transformation, *The Renovare Spiritual Formation Bible*,[118] and I bought a copy. Frankly, I do not like some of the introductions to the books of the Bible very well. I do appreciate the list of disciplines with related Scripture passages listed in the back; however, the opening essay, "The With God Life," by Richard Foster, author of the well-known book *Celebration of Discipline*, was worth the price of the Bible for me. This essay, I discovered later, is expanded in *Life with God: Reading the Bible for Spiritual*

---

[114] While I find Wright's teaching about the gospel of kingdom of God in the teaching of Jesus and Paul to be the best available, I do not share all of his views about how to work out the kingdom in contemporary culture, especially when it pertains to present day social issues. As with all books and teaching except the Bible, "eat the meat and spit out the bones."

[115] First published by HarperOne, 2006, the audiobook version was released in 2009.

[116] Published by HarperOne, 1998.

[117] Published by NavPress, 2005, this book was something of a simplified version of his 2002 book, *Renovation of the Heart: Putting on the Character of Christ*.

[118] First published by HarperOne, San Francisco, 2005. Later versions are called *The Life with God Bible*.

Transformation,[119] which I recommend highly. Eugene Peterson was also a part of the Renovare project, and his *Eat This Book: A Conversation in the Art of Spiritual Reading* was a great help at that time to me as well.

The first spiritual discipline that I thought I should practice was to memorize and meditate on Scripture. I started with the Sermon on the Mount, which Dallas Willard had recommended. Whether because of my age or some other reason, I soon discovered that memorizing, especially retaining what I worked to memorize, is far more difficult now than it was in my younger years. I began by trying to memorize Matthew 5:1–16. I still have to review the passage to get the words correct unless I go over it nearly every day. However, that need to go back over it again and again has actually helped me to meditate on (to chew on and ponder) the meaning.

I believe that the Holy Spirit prompted me over the next couple of months to add John 15:1–17 and 1 John 1:1–2:6 as passages for memorization and meditation. I do not have adequate words to share what these passages have meant to me, except to say that I continue to be moved by the depth of God's desire for us all to enter into real fellowship (*koinonia*—communion, participation) into a relationship of true love with God and with all the members of God's family.

The stress and anxiety I was experiencing at that time would wake me up in the middle of most nights. Unable to sleep, anxious thoughts kept racing in my mind. I learned that if I would get out of bed, go to the chair in my office, and begin to meditate on these passages, then before too long peace would come, and I could go back to bed and sleep. What I gained in these meditations far outweighed lost sleep.

I am sure that it was also the Holy Spirit who prompted me to work on memorizing and meditating on Ephesians 4:1–16. The first six verses, especially, began to direct my heart, my mind, and my behavior as I faced the stresses related to our church. Again and again, I was reminded that my primary responsibility is to be a disciple— to live in a way that honestly reflects the attitudes and way of life of my Master and Trainer, a way of life that is the fruit of abiding in fellowship with God in dependence on the Holy Spirit.

When I went to the doctor for my annual physical in late July that year, I was just beginning this practice of memorizing and meditating on Scripture. My primary care doctor is a teacher in the University of Kentucky's School of Medicine; therefore, I normally am interviewed by a medical student, an intern, and/or a resident before I

---

[119] Richard J. Foster with Kathryn A. Helmers (Renovaré Inc., 2008).

see the doctor himself. I try to be as open and forthright as possible with the student doctors and interns in the hope I may contribute something to their training. Thus, on that visit I opened up a little about the loss of sleep, the stress, and discouragement. I think the intern who saw me must have been excited and thought, *Now, I've got one!*

When the doctor came in after talking with the intern, he was wanting to send me to a counselor and offered to give me medicine to help me sleep. I refused. Still, he urged me to schedule a follow-up visit in October.

His response jarred me to take my condition more seriously. Within a day or two of that visit, I made a written list of everything I could think of that might be a source of anxiety, stress, or depression. Prayerfully, I entered into the presence of His Grace, and there before his throne I presented that list—more than once, I should add. I also got together with Dennis Cole, to whom I look for pastoral care. And I continued meditating on those passages (trying to memorize them, or mostly simply to remember them). By the time I went back to the doctor in October, I could truthfully say that I was sleeping well most nights.

Through prayer and meditation, I had gone to the great Counselor, the Holy Spirit, who helped me. My wife and Dennis were also praying for me, and the Counselor was releasing the peace of God in me.

Then, early one morning in December, whether in a dream or in that odd state between sleeping and awaking, an incomplete phrase came sharply to mind: "internal transformation → external _____." Immediately, I had a powerful sense that God was speaking to me.

The arrow I recognized as a symbol we had used in linguistics, meaning "rewrites as" or "generates." I knew immediately that this was an important phrase even though the last word was missing. For at least two weeks I pondered and prayed about that phrase, seeking for the right word to complete it. Finally, it came: "internal transformation → (generates) external reproduction." It struck me that this word, *reproduction*, has a twofold application:

> 1. To the degree that the core of my being (my heart, my inner man) is being transformed into conformity with the life of Jesus (conformity with his attitudes, thoughts, and character), to that degree the same kind of attitudes and thought and character will be produced in my external behavior. The fruit of the Spirit will develop and mature on

the branch (to use the image Jesus gave in John 15). His fruit can become reality in my life and will be available for others "to taste and see that the Lord is good."

2. Fruit carries seed; therefore, seeds can be spread to the people who taste the Spirit's fruit through my life. As that seed germinates in those who "taste and see that the Lord is good" (Psalm 34:8), they also may become fruit-bearing disciples of Jesus.

****

The seasons have changed—certainly for Patricia and me. It seems clear to me that in my lifetime, the season has changed for the church (church in the full sense, the whole body of Christ), for our nation, and for our world. That change, for the most part, is not in a good direction. No, I am not yearning for a return to the 1950s of my childhood and I am not yearning for a return to "America the way she used to be."

I yearn for the future! I yearn for the coming time, the time the prophet foresaw, when "the earth will be filled with the knowledge of the glory of the Lord as the waters cover the sea" in fulfillment of God's promise to Moses: "… Indeed, as I live, all the earth will be filled with the glory of the Lord." I yearn for the time when there is "a mighty flood of justice, an endless river of righteous living," "the time of the restoration [restitution (KJB)] of all things," the time when the prayer is fulfilled and God's kingdom has come and God's will is done on earth as in heaven.[120]

Our life in Winchester Covenant goes on. I am extremely grateful for the brothers and sisters with whom I have been privileged to share life in our fellowship, as well as for those in the larger spiritual family who have shared their lives with us over the years. We have now worshipped together, lived our lives together, fellowshipped together, rejoiced together, and wept together. Children have been born among us, they have grown up among us, and several of them now are raising families of their own among us. Sadly, we have lost some children together also. Some we have lost to death, yet we will see them again! Others we have lost to ways of the world, but their stories are not yet complete, and we persist in praying that we may see every one of them restored in the kingdom of God and the community of disciples.

We are by no means "the model church" for anyone to follow, but there are several ways in which our life together, I think, can serve as a faithful witness and a good

---

[120] References in order of use: Habakkuk 2:14, ESV; Numbers 14:21, NASB; Amos 5:24, NLT; Acts 3:21, CSB & KJB; Matthew 6:10 ESV.

testimony to other church communities as well as to our city and region, especially in these changing times.

The culture has changed. We no longer live in a "Christian" nation as was assumed when I was a child, and unfortunately, still is assumed by too many. People who identify themselves as "Christian" may still be in the majority, but those who actually live as "Christians," those who actually seek to follow Jesus as Lord and Master of the whole of life and history, are not in the majority. What's more, by any definition of *Christian*, the mind-set in our culture and the voices that actually drive us are not "Christian"; rather, the driving forces of our world are decidedly anti-Christian.

The church, the body of the Messiah (the Christ) who has all authority in heaven and on earth, desperately needs to rediscover what it means to be "*a people*," a community who belong to God and who, by our way of life together, are a "light in the darkness." Winchester Covenant is not a big light, and we, by no means, "have it all together." Still, our efforts to be "a people" who live distinctly as the people of God, the disciples of Jesus, though often feeble and incomplete, have, I think, been headed in the direction that is so necessary in these times.

****

These more recent years have not been uneventful for our family! After working sixteen years for the University of Kentucky's hospital, Patricia retired in 2012.

Together she and I have gone through long seasons when I was dealing with health issues and surgeries. We have had wonderful seasons of joy in our marriage, and we have also had challenging seasons when we have had to work out the unity of marriage in Christ. Having now completed nearly forty-seven years of married life together, I know for sure that marriage is a great gift from God, a gift into which it is more than worth investing my very best in the hope that we may become a more faithful "picture" of Christ and the church.

Our daughters, after marrying godly men, have now given us fourteen wonderful grandchildren.

Stephanie and Daniel have given nine of them: Elijah Wolffe in 2000, Gillen Jude in 2002, Kylie Grace in 2003, Augustin Daniel in 2005, Jesse Sackett in 2007, twins Lucy Arwen and Daisy Suzannah in 2010, Zane Isaac in 2012, and finally Ever Jane in 2014—until the quiver was full (Psalm 127:3–5). Their family is fully involved with our friends in the Fellowship of Believers, the church in which Daniel grew up. And they live only a mile and a half away.

Daniel and Andrea have given us five more: Benjamin Asher in 2006, Carolina Jane in 2008, Josie Karis in 2010, Justice Ryan in 2012, and Shiloh Eden in 2015. Their family is active in Winchester Covenant, and they live right in our house.

What a wonderful gift God has given me in our own family—a third generation into whom I can invest love and with whom I can share what God has done in my life. More than that, there are three generations of us, so far, who now have the opportunity to follow Jesus together and to offer ourselves in service for his kingdom purposes.

This year I have stepped back from serving as presiding elder, having handed over that responsibility to Bill Camenisch. I am not actually retired, but I am now 68 years old, I'm drawing Social Security, and my work responsibilities as an elder in the church are changing.

I do not know what the future will be like. I do not have a clear vision for what will unfold in this new season. Dad died in August 2013. Our friend and intercessor Duane Roller, who was only a few years younger than Dad, died in June 2014 after spending the last few weeks of his life in our home, where we had the privilege to care for him.

Like the leaves falling in the autumn, so more and more of our own generation are passing from this life into the age to come. In December 2009, I had the sad but great honor to be with one of my closest brothers in Christ, Bob Catellier, and his family when he went on to see his Lord. Colin LaVergne, a good friend from the Servants, died in 2015. My two closest childhood friends have now died: Don Benner in November 2015 and Mitch Ramey in 2016.

I know that my body is slowing, and aches and pains are increasing. But my journey in this world is not over yet. I do not know how many days I have left, but God has something for me to contribute while I am here, and I pray that whatever he has given me and has made of me will contribute something of his life and his ways to at least a few of those who will be helping to lead the way for God's people in the years ahead. Most of all, I long to know my Father better and to be transformed much more than I have been so far into the image of Jesus my King.

Quite often the words of a gospel song from my childhood come to mind:

Many things about tomorrow I don't seem to understand;
But I know who holds tomorrow, and I know who holds my hand.[121]

Most of the time I trust the One who holds my hand. Sometimes I still forget and need to make the choice afresh to be "… of good courage. We know that while we are at home in the body we are away from the Lord, for we walk by faith, not by sight" (2 Corinthians 5:6–7).

****

Years ago, I heard my friend, Dennis Peacocke, share the wisdom his karate instructor gave after Dennis had just received his first black belt: "Now you are an interested beginner." At different points in my journey, I have realized that this statement was true of me. Now more than ever, I know I am still only an "interested beginner"! That realization would be devastating indeed at my age "if in Christ we have hope in this life only" (1 Corinthians 15:19), as the apostle Paul put it. However, Paul did not stop there:

> If in Christ we have hope in this life only, we are of all people most to be pitied. But in fact Christ has been raised from the dead, the firstfruits of those who have fallen asleep. For as by a man came death, by a man has come also the resurrection of the dead. For as in Adam all die, so also in Christ shall all be made alive. But each in his own order: Christ the firstfruits, then at his coming those who belong to Christ. (1 Corinthians 15:19–23)

The apostle John also told us about our true hope:

> See what kind of love the Father has given to us, that we should be called children of God; and so we are …. Beloved, we are God's children now, and what we will be has not yet appeared; but we know that when he appears we shall be like him, because we shall see him as he is. And everyone who thus hopes in him purifies himself as he is pure. (1 John 3:1–3)

My friend the late Dr. Dow Robinson challenged commonly held cultural ideas represented in mantras such as "reach your full potential" and "be all you can be" when he said: "These are lies if we hear them as philosophies for the present life. We

---

[121] Ira Stanphil, "I Know Who Holds Tomorrow," 1950.

were created and redeemed to grow in the knowledge of God and in his life for eternity. We will die having only begun our development."[122] There is hope, even for a person like me who has often been a slow learner, especially when it comes to working out in life what I know in my head. In the life to come the battle with sin will be over and I will fully and truly become what God has purposed me to be.

Finally, what is it that I hope and long for concerning you who have read my story? Eugene Peterson has expressed it well in *The Message.*

> So here's what I want you to do, God helping you: Take your everyday, ordinary life—your sleeping, eating, going-to-work, and walking-around life—and place it before God as an offering. Embracing what God does for you is the best thing you can do for him. Don't become so well-adjusted to your culture that you fit into it without even thinking. Instead, fix your attention on God. You'll be changed from the inside out. Readily recognize what he wants from you, and quickly respond to it. Unlike the culture around you, always dragging you down to its level of immaturity, God brings the best out of you, develops well-formed maturity in you. (Romans 12:1–2)

It is my conviction that the journeys on which the Holy Spirit has led me and many comrades of my generation, are not primarily for our benefit. Rather, our journeys are meant to benefit you who are younger. I have written this book as a prayer that you who read my story will discover and fully embrace the journey for which God has created you.

May you too hear the Master's call: "Follow me! Come, learn from and know my Father." May you be enlightened and empowered by the Holy Spirit to reflect the Light of God for the sake of your own generation that so desperately needs the hope of God's good news and the sure purposes of God's kingdom. May we cry out to our God as one people: "May your kingdom come in this broken world. Let your good will be done here on this earth in the same way it is done in the heavenly realm."

> "So now I put you in God's hands. I entrust you to the message of God's grace, a message that has the power to build you up and to give you rich heritage among all who are set apart for God's holy purposes." (Acts 20:32 VOICE)

---

[122] Although I have presented Dow's words as a quotation, I do not remember his exact words, but I well remember this thought that took root in me through his words.

Appendix One
Dad's Preaching Record

After my dad died, my brother Wes found that Dad had recorded this event in a notebook in which Dad had kept a record of the sermons he preached.

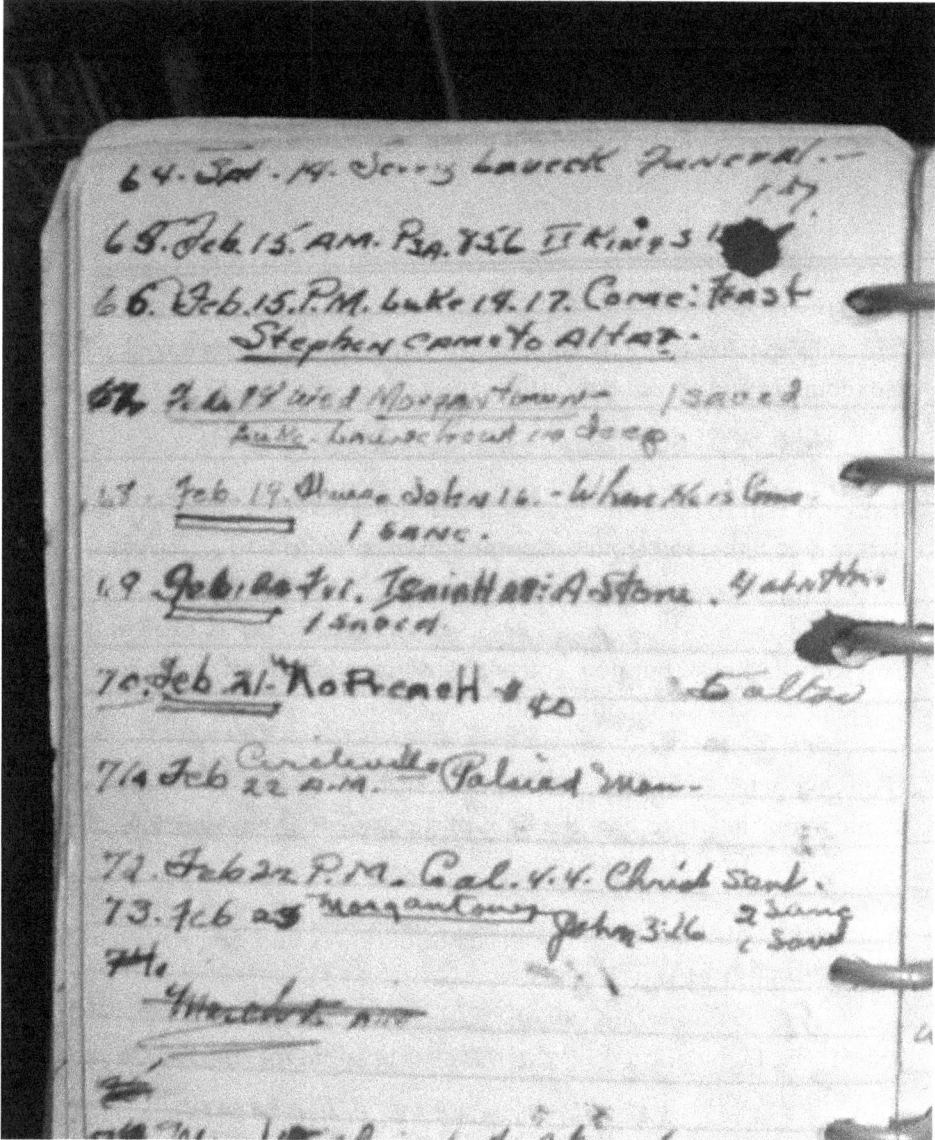

Appendix Two
See? A New View

"Let this mind be in you which was also in Christ Jesus."
Phil. 2:5

I. When we come into Jesus Christ and the life He offers, all things change. The difference is as great as that between night and day.

    A. "... old things passed away; behold new things have come." (2 Cor. 5:17–21)
- a new relationship
- a new job
- a new position

    "He delivered us from the domain of darkness and transferred us to the kingdom of His beloved Son." (Col. 1:9–12)
- a new government

    Paul was sent to open the eyes of the Gentiles, "so that they may turn from darkness to light, and from the dominion of Satan to God ...." (Acts 26:18)
- a new ruler

    B. "You were darkness, but now you are light in the Lord; walk as children of the light, trying to learn ...." (Eph. 5:8–10)

    "For God, who said, 'Light shall shine out of darkness,' is the one who has shone in our hearts to give the light of the knowledge of the glory of God in the face of Christ." (Col. 4:6)

    "Let us therefore lay aside the deeds of darkness and put on the armor of light." (Rom. 13:12)

    Jesus is the Light (John 8:12); he makes it possible for us to see, to perceive God and His ways.

II. The mind is the traitor through which Satan keeps us from seeing God. God's power and tools work in our lives to tear down and rid us of the teachings or viewpoint of Satan— found in his world system.

" ... the god of this world has blinded the minds of the unbelieving that they might not see the light of the gospel of the glory of Christ who is the image of God." (2 Cor. 4:2–4)

With divinely powerful weapons, "we are destroying speculations and every lofty thing raised up against the knowledge of God, and we are taking every thought captive to the obedience of Christ." (2 Cor. 10:3–5)

III. Knowledge is stored and used in the mind. The mind must be changed.

A. " ... be not conformed to this world, but be ye transformed by the renewing of your mind." (Rom. 12:1–2)

Also, Phil. 2:5; Rom. 8:5–8.

B. The new mind is knowing God

"This is eternal life, that they way know Thee, the only true God, and Jesus Christ whom Thou hast sent." (John 17:3)

Also, I Cor. 2:10–16.

IV. We must have a new vision—eyes of the heart (Eph. 1:18)—in order to perceive life as it really is in God's reality.

A. "The light of the body is the eye; if therefore your eye is clear, your whole body will be full of light. But if your eye is bad, your whole body will be full of darkness. If therefore the light that is in you is darkness, how great is the darkness." (Matt. 6:22–23)

B. A few of the high points of the new view—of God's system rather than the world system are found in these passages:

- Matt. 5, 6, 7
- Luke 6:20–49
- Luke 11:1–36
- Luke 14:25–35
- Mark 8:34–38
- John 13:12–17

- Rom. 6:4–7:11
- Gal. 2:20
- Col. 3:1–3
- Gal. 5:20–26

Unity and Division Article

Unity and Division

REV. STEVE HUMBLE*

The church at Corinth is often considered Paul's problem church. However, the main problem at Corinth was not an adulterer in the group, or misuse of spiritual gifts, or selfishness at communion, or eating meat offered to idols, or marriage relationships. All of these hassles, I believe, resulted from the division caused by their carnal attitudes. In I Corinthians 1-3, Paul exposes clearly their carnality in the context of divisions over spiritual leaders.

Jesus makes clear that love and unity are the characteristics of His church that will demonstrate to the world who His disciples are and the love of God for man.

1. ". . . love one another; as I have loved you. . . . By this all men will know that you are my disciples, if you have love one for another" (John 13:34, 35).

2. "Sanctify them in the truth; Thy word is truth . . . so that they may all be one, even as Thou Father art in Me, and I in Thee, that they also may be in Us; that the world may believe that Thou didst send Me. And the glory which Thou hast given Me I have given them; that they may be one just as We are one; I in them; and Thou in Me, that they may be perfected in unity that the world may know that Thou didst send Me and didst love them, even as Thou didst love Me" (John 17:19-23). (New American Standard)

These are the basic conditions for an effective demonstration of Christ's Body, and Satan puts much effort to disrupting God's plan for the church.

This oneness — this unity — is not a oneness or sameness of spiritual leaders as is made clear in I Corinthians 3:3-10. Ephesians 4:11-13 shows us that our Lord has given the church a variety of ministries and ministers in order to equip the saints for the work of building up the Body with the goal of reaching the unity of faith and knowledge of the Son of God (theology), of becoming a perfect man measured by the fulness of Christ. When the church as a whole is perfected, we will, as one perfect man, demonstrate to the world the likeness of Jesus Christ even as He showed the likeness of the Father. This oneness — this unity — is not of experience. In the Old Testament three different men met lions in the power of the Spirit. Samson turned his lion inside out with his bare hands. David killed his lion with a stone flung from a slingshot. Daniel took no action and God sent an angel to shut the lions' mouths. Could Samson call David and Daniel cowards? Could David and Samson

*Pastor, Richland Center, Wisconsin

say to Daniel, "Faith without works is dead"? Could Daniel accuse the others of a lack of faith? Of course not. God has an infinite variety of methods to work among men. Experience does not unify — we are individuals and God deals with each of us differently according to our need and His plan for us.

The only essential unity is one of the Spirit (Ephesians 4:1-6). He calls us to the one hope, puts us into the one body, glorifies our one Lord, teaches us of the one faith, one baptism, and one God and Father of us all. That teaching comes in different order, at different times, and in different ways to each but we are headed toward one goal — the likeness of our Lord Jesus Christ.

How can we preserve the unity of the Spirit in the bond of peace (Ephesians 4:3)? How can we avoid division? There are eight keys which follow:

EIGHT KEYS TO AVOID DIVISION

1. Do not form groups within the church around doctrines or experiences. Test all doctrines and experiences by the Word.
2. Get to know one another before allowing yourselves to get upset over someone else's doctrine or experience.
3. Then do not be afraid to discuss your doctrines and experiences with one another,
   a. looking for the common factors,
   b. attempting to understand the differences,
   c. and not trying to do the work of the Holy Spirit in leading someone "into all truth."
4. Be humble. Be honest enough and wise enough to realize that you, too, have probably not yet been led "into all truth" — there are gaps in your doctrine, and your experience is not finished.
5. Do not hold things against one another. Confess your misunderstandings and faults to one another.
6. Cultivate a relationship in which you can suggest advice to one another (even as "from the Lord") without being hurt when it is not followed.
7. Pray for one another, and especially when you sense division is possible, blessing in your prayers —not criticizing or correcting.
8. Serve one another. Go out of your way to give service in love to those with whom you differ.

"Now I beseech you, brethren, by the name of our Lord Jesus Christ, that ye all speak the same thing, and that there be no divisions among you; but that ye be perfectly joined together in the same mind and in the same judgment" (I Corinthians 1:10). "I . . . beseech you that ye walk worthy of the vocation wherewith ye are called, with all lowliness and meekness, with longsuffering, forbearing one another in love; endeavoring to keep the unity of the Spirit in the bond of peace" (Ephesians 4:1-3).

Appendix Four
Affirmations Concerning the Blood of Jesus

In 1973 I heard a Derek Prince tape, "God's Atomic Weapon: The Blood of Jesus." The following material comes from that message.

"Then I heard a loud voice in heaven say: 'Now have come the salvation and the power and the kingdom of our God, and the authority of his Christ. For the accuser of our brothers, who accuses them before our God day and night, has been hurled down. They overcame him by the blood of the Lamb and by the word of their testimony; and they did not love their lives so much as to shrink from death.' "

Derek said that the way to overcome the devil is to testify to the devil what the word of God says that the blood of Jesus does for us. He gave the following statements. I recommend that one meditate on the Scripture verses and then proclaim these declarations out loud in faith, often, as one way to "put the devil to flight."

According to Psalm 107.2 and Ephesians 1.7, through the blood of Jesus I have been redeemed out of the hand of the enemy.

According to Ephesians 1.7, through the blood of Jesus all my sins are forgiven.

According to 1 John 1.7, through the blood of Jesus I am continually cleansed (in accordance with the Greek verb tense) from all sin.

According to Romans 5.9, through the blood of Jesus I am justified—that is, I am made righteous, "just-as-if-I'd" never sinned.

According to Hebrews 13.12, through the blood of Jesus I am sanctified—that is, I am holy, set apart as God's possession to fulfill God's purpose.

According to Hebrews 9.14, through the blood of Jesus my conscience is cleansed from dead works—that is, from acts that lead to death.

According to 1 Corinthians 6:19–20 I have been bought at a price, the blood of Jesus, and I therefore belong to God body, soul, and spirit (KJV, NKJV).

Therefore, Satan, because of the blood of Jesus you have no place in me and no power over me!

Appendix Five
Servants of the Lord Covenant

We have been called by God to be a holy and righteous people, a nation, a family, a servant people set apart for His purpose. He has called us individually and personally and through His grace and His Holy Spirit has transformed us and joined us together as community.

Our response to His call is made through aspiring to personal holiness and perfection while entering into and strengthening our relationships with our spouses, families, and brothers and sisters in the Servants of the Lord Community.

Our covenant is first and foremost with God, and then, in accordance with His plan and the teaching of the Holy Spirit, with our brothers and sisters in the Servant of the Lord Community.

—Isaiah 42:6–7, Acts 2:42–47, Philippians 2:1–18

In response to these words, expressing God's call to unity, humility, and servanthood, I covenant myself to God and to the Servants of the Lord Community and pledge:

To live a life of service to God and the establishment of His Kingdom.

—Exodus 19:3–8, Philippians 1:3–6

To constantly seek to perfect my praise to the glory of the Lordship of Jesus Christ through the power and gifts of the Holy Spirit.

—Ephesians 2; I Corinthians 12; Romans 8;
Revelation 4:11, 5:12, 7:9f

To pray regularly, celebrate as the Lord leads, and to study and read Scripture as the Word of God.

—I Thessalonians 5:17, II Timothy 3:16

To serve and care for the brothers and sisters whom the Lord calls to the community.

—Romans 12:10, 13; Galatians 6:10

To accept and support the ongoing authority, order, and patterns of life of the community (e.g., structure, ecumenism, mission).

—Hebrews 13:17, Philippians 2

To meet with the community whenever it gathers.

—Hebrews 10:25

To support the community spiritually, emotionally, physically materially, and financially.

—Acts 2:42–47, II Corinthians 9:6–15

I recognize that while relocation or departure is a possibility with community discernment, my commitment to the Servants of the Lord is one of life, love, and service.

—Matthew 28:18–20, 22:37–39

I want to publicly accept the covenant our heavenly Father is offering and promise to live it out as a member of the Servants of the Lord.

Appendix Six
The Vision of Winchester Covenant Church
"Building for the Generations to Come"

Winchester Covenant Church is a community of disciples who are seeking to build our lives together in a way that pleases God, that is consistent with Biblical revelation, and that honors and values our roots in historical Christianity and in the "covenant movement" of the 1970s and 1980s. We have determined that, by the grace of God and the power by the Holy Spirit, our life together in Christ will be effective and fruitful as we prepare to enter the 21st century.

Mission Statement:

Winchester Covenant Church is a people called by God
- to know and to love Him
- to learn to live His way
- to manifest His Kingdom through our words and deeds

Vision Statement:

We are a people joined together by the hand of God; therefore, (1) we are seeking to share our lives with one another as fully as we can; (2) we are offering our lives and relationships to represent to God's transformation process in order that we may reflect God's character, thoughts, and ways; (3) we have resolved to obey our Lord's commission to evangelize and disciple our families and the unchurched.

We will do this by developing and using our leadership skills, gifts, and resources to build and multiply small groups networked together for accountability, shared resources, celebration, and corporate witness. We will expand these small groups through neighborhoods, friendship and family ties, shared-interest groups, and school and work environments.

We will seek to be Biblically sound in doctrine and life, both personally and corporately. Our goal is to win and incorporate the unchurched into Christ and his body. We will seek to serve people with and without church backgrounds who cannot connect with the traditional American churches that center on buildings and in-house programs.

We will work to equip every person whom God joins to us to serve God's purpose. We want each individual to fulfill the plan of God for his or her life. We want each one to serve God effectively in his or her sphere of influence. We want to equip and encourage each person to seek for the growth of God's kingdom by offering himself or herself to be God's agent of change within his or her God-ordained sphere of influence.

Values:

Love expressed in
- Humility (brokenness, self-denial, crucifixion with Christ)
- Worship (obedience, praise, thanksgiving, adoration, intercession)
- Service (servant leadership, everyone contributing)
- Faithfulness (loyalty, perseverance, endurance)
- Peace (right relationships, God's order)
- Accountability (discipleship, care)
- Fellowship (community, small groups, a full life)
- Evangelism (loving the unchurched, proclaiming the kingdom, incorporating people into the body)

An alternative statement of our values:
Winchester Covenant Church: A people focused on
- Being worshippers
- Embracing the cross
- Maturing as God's sons and daughters
- Fulfilling the New Covenant
- Living as servant-rulers
- Seeking God's reign

Winchester Covenant Church is deeply committed to serving within the larger body of Christ. We want to fellowship and work with the other households of faith in Winchester and Clark County.

We also are connected to an international network known as Kingdom Ministries USA (formerly Kingdom Ministries International). Along with the other KMUSA churches and ministries we are committed to walk in mutual submission to God's word, to build relationally and in mutual accountability, and to confront the world system with God's demand for justice in all things, seeking first the kingdom of God and His righteousness.

The Church in Our Time

Stephen G. Humble

1992/1993[123]

Introduction

What is the church? What did God intend the church to be? Is what we call "church" really "church" from a Biblical point of view? At a deeper level, is the American Evangelical model of the church so culturally ingrained in our subjective inner consciousness that we are unable to do more than give lip service to another model? Is it so vital to our livelihoods that we find it next to impossible to seriously consider another model?

These kinds of questions have plagued me for years. Therefore, I am attempting up front to reveal my internal struggles and biases before attempting a more objective discussion of the Biblical church.

I grew up in a Christian subculture—the non-Pentecostal holiness movement. Our group was "conservative" in that we stood for a high view of Scriptural authority and the necessity for personal conversion to Christ, and we were "conservative" in that our faith was lived out in terms of "high standards" regarding clothing, hairstyles, jewelry, entertainment, and the like. We "went to church" and had "church services." However, because of the cultural elements, our lives tended to be separate from the broader society and even from other Christian groups.

Our "church life" spilled over into our daily living—though we did not call the daily living "church" and had no intellectual conception of the church as a community. We had a strong group identity and, to some degree, "took care of our own." We were evangelistic toward individuals, seeking to see them converted to Christ and our way of living, although our actual effectiveness in evangelism could be seriously questioned, at least during my lifetime. We scorned societal involvement and awaited an immediate rapture to get us out of this sinful world. As I moved into an adult commitment to Christ, I rebelled against the cultural rigidity of this background.

At the same time that I was growing up in this Christian subculture, I was also growing up in the Baby Boom generation. I lived in a world that was disillusioned with structure in the arts, in education, and in institutions; a world which feared nuclear annihilation; a world which seemed to leave the individual alienated and unimportant; a world which fought apparently meaningless wars without a will to win; a world which idolized technological advancement and scientific knowledge; a

---

[123] Edited and developed in 1999 with some additional editing in 2014 and 2016

world which was breaking apart at its most basic social units. Multitudes in my generation sought to reject our heritage, our social order, absolutes, authority, and the emptiness of materialistic lifestyles, and they attempted either to re-order the world or bail out of it. While I did not enter fully into either response, I was deeply influenced by both.

It was in the context of that cultural milieu that I came into contact with the unstructured fervor of the Jesus movement, the non-institutional house church movement, and the subjective, experientially-oriented Charismatic movement. Each of these movements deposited seeds of the reality of God's kingdom in me. And each appealed to the "rebel," to the searcher, in me. These movements opened my eyes to a God at work in powerful ways outside the "religious" institutions and activities. In these movements, I made contact with the King who is actively at work in the apparent chaos of this world, gradually subduing it to his rule. During that time, God exposed and dealt with my rebelliousness so that my motivations began to become more pure.

The steps I took toward missionary service with the Wycliffe Bible Translators further opened my eyes to the reality of dedicated, educated, fervent Christians from denominations that I would have written off before. It served to begin to open me to a cross-cultural mindset by which I began to look more critically and objectively at my own little world.

Then the hand of God steered me into the Catholic-ecumenical covenant community movement. The teaching of the Christian Growth Ministry brothers started me in that general direction, but God led me into a context from which my heritage should have kept me. In the covenant community movement, the inner hunger for a tangible expression of God's rule among a people began to be met. In community we led a corporate Christian life outside the institutional churches, without rejecting them; a life that was rich and real, down-to-earth and heavenly—until our own carnality "caught up" with us.

Idealism reigned in me. I thought the Kingdom of God was being manifested in unprecedented power among us, but personal points of view and ambitions and weaknesses tore our leadership apart relationally; we found ourselves fighting for control and maintenance of our organizations, rather than for our relationships with God and with one another.

When the Lord moved me to Lexington and the covenant church movement, I found essentially the same struggles repeated with different faces and over somewhat different issues. Again we appear to have fought to keep our institutions (and our livelihoods too, I fear), but have largely lost our peoplehood and spiritual family.

In all fairness, most of us sought to stand on principle and as leaders sought to protect the flock. However, the line between protecting that which was entrusted to us as a stewardship and protecting ourselves has seemed to me quite fuzzy, especially in looking back.

It is, then, as an idealist whose idealism has crashed against the shoals of human carnality and spiritual warfare; as one who still hungers for the ideals of God's kingdom without being fully confident that he even perceives them; as one still suspicious of institutions though convinced of their necessity; and as one compelled to seek for the rule of God among men yet questioning our willingness and ability to fully submit to it, that I set out to grapple with the subjects of the kingdom of God, the church, and the human institutions that supposedly promote and model them.

What about the New Testament Church?

How are we to view the church as seen in the New Testament in Acts and the epistles? Is it the pattern or model that God intended us to emulate? After all it was shaped and led by those whom Jesus, the founder and builder of the church, personally trained. Is it a "seed" which contained the life and "genetic code" that was to germinate, grow up in a different form and produce fruit in which that "seed" would be multiplied again and again? Is it the "primitive" beginning from which the more sophisticated forms would evolve? Has the Holy Spirit revealed the ideal form and life of the church in Scripture or has he revealed its essential nature and left it to history and leadership to express that nature in appropriate forms?

Are we to study the New Testament church as a distinct entity complete in itself? Or should we see it in relationship to the Hebraic womb from which it was born? How important are we to consider the Greco-Roman world into which it spread and took root? Do we take seriously the leadership and liturgical structures that were, at the very least, clearly developing by the time of the apostle John's death around 100 A.D.? Were these developments mere aberrations from the simplicity of the New Testament beginnings of the church, or were these the structures that the Apostles themselves had established?

I sometimes wish that God had revealed the answers to these questions, as well as answers to a number of others, with unmistakable clarity! Instead he has required his people to depend on the Holy Spirit for insight and application as we search the Scriptures and search for the mind of Christ.

At this point in my life, I view the church as seen in the New Testament as *a pattern* in that it reveals the essence of the church. In the New Testament, the Holy Spirit reveals to us the normal response to the gospel as believers begin to live together under the Lordship of Jesus. The heart of the church is revealed by the emphasis given to the relationship of believers to God and to one another, by the distinctive way of life that believers are to live in contrast to the unbelievers, by the fervent spreading of the good news in response to the church's commission, and by the warfare believers face in themselves, among themselves, and toward themselves as they begin to spread the victory of Christ.

However, in the New Testament, issues pertaining to structure in meetings, leadership, and organization are cloudy at best. Description of and direction for the activities of the churches when gathered as churches are noticeably limited and inconclusive.

I believe, therefore, that we need to know the Hebraic roots of New Testament church life and practice in order to understand what the first believers did, and why they did what they did. I believe, as well, that we would be much better off to understand the way in which Hebraic activities such as Passover and Sabbath meals, synagogue worship and leadership appear to have been adopted and adapted into even the "Gentile" churches. There is much wisdom to be gained from this knowledge.

Although most evangelicals seem to readily dismiss the writings of the early church fathers, I find it difficult to do so for two primary reasons. First, it seems very clear to me that, in view of the high regard that the early fathers had for authority and for tradition, the early churches after the New Testament period were more likely to have crystallized and institutionalized apostolic practice than to have innovated upon it.

Secondly, I believe that Paul's instruction recorded in 2 Thessalonians 2:15 gives us reason to consider seriously the teaching and practice of the early fathers. "*So then brothers, stand firm and hold onto the teachings we passed on to you, whether by word of mouth or by letter.* There was, in fact, authoritative instruction given to the early churches that is not recorded in the New Testament.

The book of Acts documents the spread of the gospel, largely through Peter's early ministry and through Paul's ministry. We can derive a measure of understanding about what the apostles built and what they taught, but are given few details. The epistles certainly contain both doctrinal instruction and building instruction;

however, they were written primarily to address specific problems or to give encouragement. If the epistles clearly lay out the complete content of the "*whole counsel of God*" which Paul says that he had declared, then we are, at best, left to try prayerfully and carefully to piece it together. This is especially true when it comes to how the church is to be governed and to worship. Isn't that why we have so many different theologies, all based on the same Scriptures?

Many of us put great weight on the theological insights of Luther or Calvin or Wesley or Hodge, or Ladd or one of the many others who have studied the Scriptures 1500 or 2000 years later. Some of us even put the most weight upon our own personal insights and conclusions. Shouldn't we at least take very seriously that which we can learn about what the apostles said and built through the writings of those who were taught by the apostles, those who were much closer to the earliest expression of the church? We have accepted fully the work which those churches and their leaders did to determine the canon of the New Testament, and to set forth core truths of the faith such as the nature of the divinity and humanity of Jesus and the mystery of the Trinity. Yet most of us seem to readily ignore what the early fathers have to say concerning the way in which the apostles established the government and the worship of the churches.

I fear that this is arrogance on our part. I fear that the spirit of this age has had a great impact on our thinking and on our approach. I think that we have all too often exalted our own reasoning. I think we are deeply influenced by individualism as well as by the contemporary tendency to reject or discount authority and tradition. I think we have unwittingly bought into an evolutionary view in that we act like we have developed into a more knowledgeable generation than any in the past.

Therefore, I strongly believe and advocate that we need to carefully examine and consider the evidence concerning what the Holy Spirit produced through the apostles as reflected in the early generations, and we need seek out how it may apply to today's churches.

Nevertheless, there is a Biblical canon. We have been given the Bible as the inspired and authoritative word by which, according to the leading of the Holy Spirit in the churches, we are to measure what we believe and what we do. The lack of Biblical emphasis on structure in the New Testament churches leads me to believe that the Holy Spirit must have intended for us to have a significant measure of flexibility in meetings, leadership structures, and organization.

There are big issues that we face, including these:

- How do we build so as to foster the same heart and life that the New Testament church had?

- How do we build so as to effectively evangelize people in our generation and culture to Christ and into his church?

- How do we build church communities that demonstrate the way God intends for people to live?

- How do we build so as to overturn the works of the enemy in our day in order that we may fulfill our commission to disciple the nations?

- How do we build to produce these results in the power of the Holy Spirit without ignoring the historical church, its worship, life and structure as irrelevant?

The big question we must ask ourselves is this: "What must we do to build churches which equip, enable, and release believers to be the people of God and to expand his kingdom in our day?"

Living as the People of God

God created mankind to be "human beings". By living obedient lives as humans, men were to serve God, honor God, represent God, and fellowship with God. Adam fell and with him mankind fell from the ability to fulfill the purpose of their creation as well as from fellowship with God.

Jesus came as a man to redeem mankind. He came to live and die as a man, and to be resurrected as a man in order to undo the consequences of mankind's fall. He is forming a *new mankind* of those who are called out of the fallen race and who come into Christ by believing in his name—by entrusting themselves to him as their Lord and Savior.

Jesus restores this *new mankind* to the place intended in the beginning. It is through living obedient lives as humans that the *new mankind* is to serve God, honor him, represent him, and fellowship with him. *Church life* is the life of this *new mankind.* The life of the church, then, ought to encompass the full scope of human life, lived by redeemed humans in obedience to their Creator and Savior.

The life of God's people should not center around an organization or its meetings and activities. It should be *normal* human life with all the activities necessary to obey God. The church is not the church only when its members step apart from "life" to gather in church meetings.124 The church should *live life*, a life that includes times of gathering for various purposes and in various configurations.

I believe the model (or type) that God gave for the church is Israel. Israel was the "holy nation" of the Old Covenant, called by God to be his light to the nations, rooted in a specific geographical locale. The church is "the holy nation" of the New Covenant, called by God to be his light in the nations, rooted in Christ the vine, but spread throughout the nations.

The primary model for the early church was Israel. After all, the earliest Christians were Israelites (Jews). I do not mean that the church is to set up a national structure like Israel. Nor I do not mean that the church is to hang onto specifically Jewish customs or to adopt them. However, our heritage goes back to the same source as that of the natural descendants, the children of Israel, to God's covenantal dealings with his servant and friend and prophet Abraham. Because of their efforts to be faithful to the Torah and to the tradition handed on to them starting with Abraham, the Jewish people have been successful to an amazing degree in keeping their distinct identity. They have remained remarkably distinct even though they have spent many centuries dispersed into a multitude of cultures, most of the time without a homeland.

Why have the Jews survived as a distinct people? By the grace and will of God, of course. However, I think some credit must be given also to their loyalty to the Torah, as they understood it, and to their faithfulness to maintain their customs (some received in the Torah and others added later). These customs include celebrating Passover and other feasts which regularly reinforced their present identity in relation to a common history and place in God's future purpose. The Sabbath celebration also has served to regularly reinforce their identity and commitment to God, to the Torah, and to their common history and destiny. The feasts of Israel and the Sabbath were centered in the life of the family.

God made human life to center around family!

---

124 As I read this again in 2014, I realize that revision is needed at this point. In my paper "Assembled in the Presence of the King" (KMI SAT, 2007), I first set forth my growing conviction that the word "*ekklesia*" specifically refers the people of God assembled to represent the government of God on the earth especially through intercession and proclamation in words and actions.

The typical church structures (not buildings) that we see today in the U.S. are, I believe, left over from a Christian social structure. When *all* of life was lived from an essentially Christian base built on essentially Christian presuppositions, the whole culture was essentially Christian. That is not to say that every person was Christian or that every social structure, every value held in common, and every activity was fully harmonious with God's revelation for human life in the Bible. But not too many years ago the culture in Europe and the United States was much closer to that than we are today. In an essentially Christian life context you could have distinct "church" activities centered in a "church" building without implying that the other activities of life were less spiritual or less Christian.

In addition, in keeping with the Christian base, the family was much more clearly the basic structure and center of life in that essentially Christian society. Even if not always for Biblical reasons, at least for economic reasons, the family was central. The U.S. was different than Europe, however, in that the country was vast and empty and through migration the family had more of a tendency to separate into nuclear units rather than to experience transgenerational community in extended family units. The technological revolution has only increased this breakdown and helped extend it even to the breakdown of the nuclear family unit, as the economic center has shifted from the home, small business, and farm. First, fathers left home to work for large blocks of time; then the mothers also began to leave home for the marketplace. Divorce is now nearly more the norm than remaining married. Since the 1960's marriage itself has become completely optional. And now we are dealing with a complete redefinition of marriage and family to the point that virtually any arrangement qualifies.

The loss of a Christian base for society and the breakdown of the family have implications for God's people and the way we need to structure and live our lives today. *We need models of the church that will work in a dispersion, not those of Christendom.*

First, since the basic culture is not Christian, if we continue with *church* activities that center in *church* buildings and *church* meetings, then we are giving support to the prevailing view that *church* is separate from, if not irrelevant to, the daily realities of human life. We need to live out our life as the church in the midst of the totality of human life, not primarily in special buildings and special meetings.

Second, in order to be faithful to God's creation of mankind, in order to testify to the unity of life in God and to the centrality of family, and in order to survive, we need to build our life together as God's people explicitly around the basic human structure

410

which God established, the family. I am not saying that we should have more *church* activities that include the family or even support and strengthen the family, although these may help. I am saying that the church, the people of God, should build their life as human beings, who are redeemed and who are a *new humanity*, around the key human structure that God has given us and by which he has ordered heaven and earth (Ephesians 3:14-15).

Again, a look at the Jews will help. It is not the priests and temple worship which have been the source of Jewish continuity. It has been the family, and the fact that the primary acts of worship and remembrance are family-centered. The priests and the temple worship took care of sin; and this whole system has been fulfilled in Jesus. But the events that have passed on stability and continuity, the heritage and destiny, have continued in the family. The synagogue (building or no building) reinforces the family by teaching and by incorporating the family into a community of those who believe and live the same way.

The New Testament church did not take the temple as a model. The synagogue service became the source of the liturgy of the word, not temple worship. The elders representing families and cities became the community government, not the priests. And the breaking of bread, the Eucharist, took place in homes, at least for a time, as had the Sabbath and Passover and other feasts. Later, to our detriment, elders became "priests", rather than community fathers.

The New Testament says very little about the structure of church meetings. However, the record of the New Testament and of the earliest church fathers strongly indicates that the gatherings were probably conducted quite informally even though there was a basic pattern of worship. It is clear that all the believers were expected to participate in the gatherings by ministering to the Lord and to one another in prayer, in singing, and in the use of spiritual gifts — not just by filling a seat and giving some money.

Over time the churches gradually began to meet in special buildings, so that worship and spirituality began to be separated from the mainstream of life. The Lord's Supper gradually became a great mysterious event administered by priests as a *temple sacrifice* at the altar, instead of a family and community feast led by fathers and elders.

It is very important to clarify that I am speaking about a new society and a redeemed humanity in Christ. Otherwise, we will over-emphasize the natural family, and may even make it an idol. The family in this new society certainly includes, but is not limited to, the nuclear family unit. In Acts, we see that it was not uncommon for whole households to believe and be baptized at one time. These households almost certainly included not only parents and children but also other relatives and even servants.

The *new mankind*, however, consists of the redeemed. Often the redeemed family units will not be simply the physical extended families that we see in natural Israel. Jesus said that his family, his mother and sisters and brothers, are those who do the will of God. He said that the gospel of the kingdom would at times divide natural families. Jesus said that his disciples have to give up their natural family as the primary loyalty in their life in order to be committed to God in an exclusive sense. In fact, Jesus said that he and his message will actually divide families. Jesus also said that those who do give up natural family will be given one hundred times as many family members in the redeemed kingdom family. No one should interpret these statements outside the context of the whole of Scripture. It is clear that God's purpose includes the redemption of natural families; however, natural families can only fulfill God's purpose as they are surrendered to God and then reestablished within the redeemed community.

I am also not suggesting that, in the modern technological world in which we live, many of us can rebuild the same kind of households which were common in the Greek and Roman world of New Testament times.

We can, however, make a priority of living geographically near to brothers and sisters in Christ with whom we can share a good deal of ordinary human life. And if some cannot live in neighborhood communities we can still make other lifestyle sacrifices necessary to build functioning family relationships with brothers and sisters in Christ. We can make commitments to one another to live out the instruction of Scripture regarding human relationships and values and priorities. We can celebrate together at the appropriate times on both the natural and spiritual calendar. We can agree to raise our children similarly according to Biblical principles applied in practical ways. We can agree to support one another, and to exhort and admonish one another in thinking and living God's way in the daily affairs of life. We can commit ourselves to serve one another and to care for one another in ways that make life worthwhile, in ways that make outsiders say, "They really do love one another." We can seek to build a life together that is not dependent on the ups and downs or the fads and fashions of the culture around us.

And, in our neighborhoods, in the marketplace, or in special interest associations, a few Christians committed to life together can eagerly welcome unbelievers to share their life, and through this shared life introduce them to the LIFE who is life.

Four "Pictures" of God's People on the Earth
The Seed

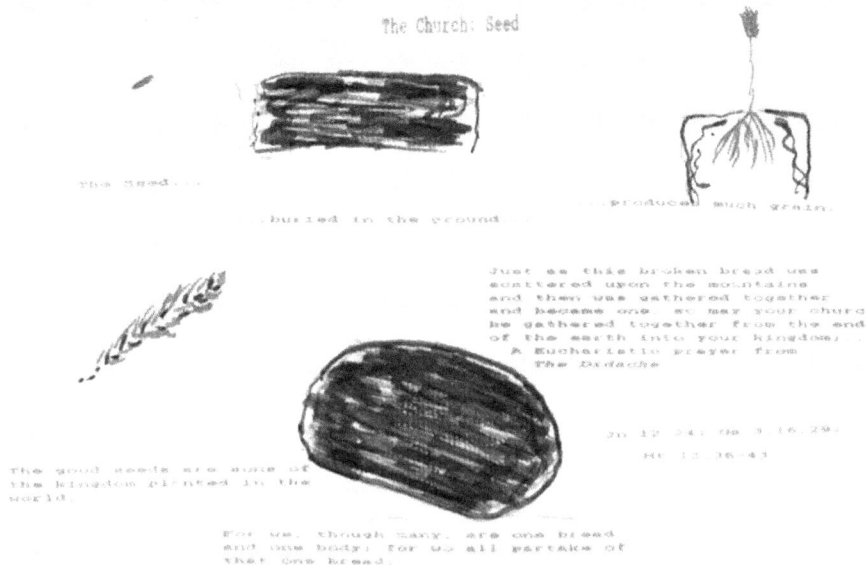

The Church: Seed

The Seed....

...buried in the ground

...produces much grain.

Just as this broken bread was scattered upon the mountains and then was gathered together and became one, so may your church be gathered together from the ends of the earth into your kingdom. A Eucharistic prayer from The Didache

The good seeds are sons of the kingdom planted in the world.

Jn 12:24; Ro 5:15-21; Mt 13:36-43

For we, though many, are one bread and one body; for we all partake of that one bread.

Seed and Sons

Jesus commanded for us to pray, "Your kingdom come, your will be done, on earth as it is in heaven." This petition is at the very heart of what God is doing in history.

The Seed

Key Scripture: John 12:23-33 in which Jesus compares himself to a grain of wheat.

Jesus told five parables about the kingdom that have to do with seed.

1. The parable about the sower who sows seed (Matthew 13:1-23; Mark 4:1-20; Luke 8:4-16).
2. The parable about the good (wheat) seed and the weed seed (Matthew 13:24-30, 36-43)
3. The parable about the mustard seed (Matthew 13:31-32; Mark 4:30-32; Luke 13:18-19)
4. The parable about leaven mixed into flour, which is crushed-up seed (Matthew 13:33; Luke 13:20–21)

5. The parable of the mysterious growth of seeds (Mark 4:26–29)

The Sower
The angel sowed the good news of the kingdom to shepherds (Luke 2:9–11).
John the Baptist sowed the good news of the kingdom (Matthew 3:2; Luke 1:16–17; John 1:19–27).[125]
Jesus sowed the good news (the word) of the kingdom (Matthew 4:17, 23; 12:28).
The apostles and the believers sowed the good news of the kingdom.

- Peter sowed the message of the kingdom on the day of Pentecost (Acts 2:32–36).
- Unbelievers recognized that Paul's message about Christ was about a king (Acts 17:1–9).
- Paul sowed the message of the kingdom all the way to the end of his life (Acts 28:23, 30–31).

God sowed the Living Word of the kingdom when he sent his Son Jesus. (John 1:1–18, 3:16; Hebrews 1:1–3; 1 John 1:1–3; Revelation 19:11–13)

The Holy Spirit planted God's "seed" in the womb of the virgin. (Matthew 1:18; Luke 1:30–35)

Jesus was the promised seed of the woman. In obedience to the Father, Jesus offered himself, like a grain of wheat, to die in order to conquer the serpent and all other rulers and authorities of darkness. On the cross our debts were cancelled. Because the "seed" died and was buried, and because he overcame death and was declared to be the Son of God in power by his resurrection, the seed has multiplied and many sons of the kingdom are being brought to glory. God had vowed that he would fill the earth with his glory. After dying and rising from death, Jesus took the throne of the universe. Through the declaration of the good news about his kingdom, King Jesus has been sowing his sons of the kingdom, like seed, all across the world. (Genesis 3:15; Colossians 2:13–15; Romans 1:1–6; Hebrews 2:5–17, Matthew 13:37–43; 1 Corinthians 15:20–28)

The Purpose of God
God created human beings to be sons in order to reveal his kingship on the earth. [Genesis 1:26–28; Luke 3:38; Psalm 8:4–6; Hebrews 2:5–9; Malachi 2:13–15; Matthew 6:10]

---

[125] "The Christ" is not a title referring to Jesus as God. It refers to the Messiah, that Son of David who the prophets had declared would take David's throne and to whose reign all nations would submit, the son who was promised in passages such as Isaiah 11:1–5.

Immediately following the fall, God declared that the seed of the woman would win "the war between the two seeds" (Genesis 3:15). The rest of the Bible is about that war—about how God's victory was won by the man Christ Jesus, and about how Jesus' victory is being worked out until "his enemies have become his footstool" and his inheritance, the nations, has been secured. At that time every knee will bow and every tongue will confess that King Jesus is Lord. (Psalm 2; Psalm 110; Acts 2:34–36; Romans 1:5; Romans 16:25–27; Philippians 2:511. See also Galatians 3:16–29; Romans 4:13–18; 1 Peter 1:18–21.)

We, the sons of the kingdom, are to follow Jesus in laying down our lives like grains of wheat so that the sons continue to multiply. God has adopted us as sons and intends for us to be conformed to the Son's image. By the work of the Spirit, as we all behold the glory of God in the face of Jesus, we will be indeed be transformed into the Son's image and the earth will be filled with God's glory. (John 12:23–26; Romans 8:29–30; Ephesians 1:5; 2 Corinthians 3:16–4:15; John 1:14)

The good news about Jesus and his kingdom is seed. That good news is the power of God unto salvation. And we have been called to proclaim that good news! (Matthew 28:18–20; Acts 1:8)

Appendix Nine
Four "Pictures" of God's People on the Earth
The Vine

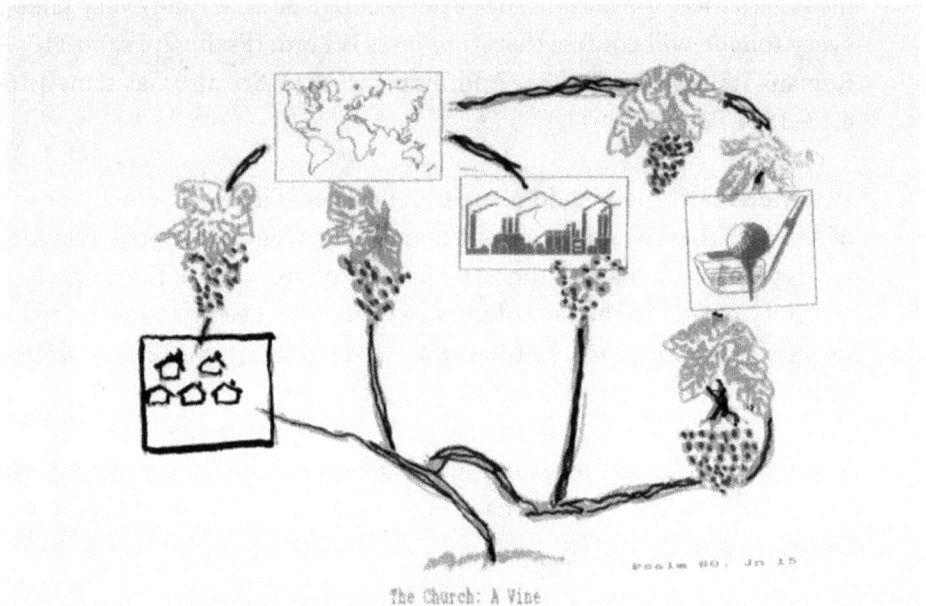

The Church: A Vine

The vine and vineyard theme in the Old Testament

"In days to come Jacob shall take root, Israel shall blossom and put forth shoots and fill the whole world with fruit." (Isaiah 27:6)

Key Old Testament passages: Isaiah 27:2-6; Isaiah 5:1-7; Jeremiah 2:21; Isaiah 3:13-15; Jeremiah 5:6-13; Ezekiel 5:6-13; Ezekiel 15:1-8; Jeremiah 6:9; Joel 1:5-7; Psalm 80:7-19

The vine and vineyard in the New Testament

Key New Testament passages: Matthew 21:33-46; Mark 12:1-12; Luke 20:9-19; Matthew 20:1-16; Matthew 21:28-32; John 15:1-17

As Jesus and the Eleven left the the upper room where they had shared the Passover meal and the "first communion" to walk to the garden of Gethsemane, Jesus made a statement that, in effect, said, "Everything has changed."

"I am the true vine, and my Father is the vinedresser." (John 15:1)

416

The seed and the vine

A seed, although not actually a "living" thing, when germinated produces a living plant. Or, in the case of a human being, the seed from a man joined with egg in a woman produces a new human being. The seed, as we saw, speaks about the way sons (and daughters) are multiplied in the kingdom of God. The sons of the kingdom multiply when, because of God's love working in us, we follow Jesus in, "laying down our lives" to announce the good news of the kingdom in the way we live and also in the message we speak.

A vine develops from a seed. A vine is a living thing, an organism. As the vine grows and branches come off the trunk, leaves grow on the branches. On a grapevine, among the leaves, grapes grow in clusters. Inside the grapes are seeds.

Jesus is the "Seed" of God, the seed of the woman, the seed of Abraham, the seed of David. From that seed, the true vine grows. People who are born of the Spirit are the branches. Like grapevine branches, we are destined to bear fruit—fruit with seeds that will multiply the growth.

The key to growth in the true vine and to bearing fruit is love because God is love! [John 3:14-17; Romans 5:6-11; Ephesians 2:1-7; 1 John 4:9-10]

The great commands: Matthew 22:35-39; Mark 12:28-34; Luke 10:25-28; John 13:34-35; John 15:10, 12-14; 1 Thessalonians 4:9-12; 1 John 2:7-8; 1 John 2:3-11, 3:11-24, 4:7-5:3; 2 John 4-6; 3 John 3-8.

- Who is my neighbor?
- Who is my "one another"?

One way to discover how to live in God's kingdom is to find and obey all the Biblical instructions concerning how God's people are to behave toward one another because we love God.

Beware: we cannot obey these commands simply by our own power. That is the way of law and is futile.

We can only obey them in the power of the Spirit. That is the way of love. (Galatians 5:13-6:10; Romans 12:9-21, 13:8-10, 14:1-15:7; Ephesians 4:1-6:9; Colossians 3:1-4:1)g

Loving one another this way will develop the unity that reveals God's glory (John 17:17-26).

The true vine consists of relationships.

- The reality of the one true God is relationships. Three persons—Father, Son, and Holy Spirit—exist in a communion of love and perfect unity.
- We know that we are abiding in God when we love God with our whole being—heart, mind, soul, and strength.
- We know that we love God when we love our neighbor as ourselves, as illustrated by the story of the Samaritan, and as modeled by God's love for us when we still ungodly, and seen in Jesus laying down his life that we could be alive in him.
- The world will know that we are followers of Jesus when they see God's love in action, revealed in our relationships. They will know God loves them when we live together in unity with the Father and the Son.
- God's primary purpose is not buildings, organizations, and meetings. God wants *a people*, a family, united with him and with one another. God, through Jesus is creating a living organism—the people of God who are the body of Christ.

Four "Pictures" of God's People on the Earth
The Spiritual Family

The Church: A Household of households
Ac 2.42-47; Ps 68.6; Ep 3.14-18;
Ep 2.19; 1 Tim 3,15; Ro 16.5;
1 Cor 16.19; Col 4.15; Phm 1

Serving: God's family of families, the servants of all

"For this reason I bow my knees before the Father, from whom every family in heaven and on earth is named..." (Ephesians 3:14-15)

The very mention of "family" can be sensitive to many people, at least in the USA where many people have been hurt because of births outside marriage and because of broken homes. In many American churches, single and divorced people can feel like outsiders.

God himself is "family"—Father, Son, and Holy Spirit who are one.

God has made provision among his people for those who are alone:

- "Father of the fatherless and protector of widows is God in his holy habitation. God settles the solitary in a home…" (Psalm 68:5-6a)
- "So then you are no longer strangers and aliens, but you are fellow citizens with the saints and members of the household of God…" (Ephesians 2:19)

God the Father, source of all fatherhood, trains his children to obey him, to love one another, and to work together. He works to establish good order in his family so that it fulfills its purpose. "May the God of endurance and encouragement grant you to live in such harmony with one another, in accord with Christ Jesus, that together you may with one voice glorify the God and Father of our Lord Jesus Christ." (Romans 15:5-6)

The first church in Jerusalem lived like a large family from its beginning and Paul expected the churches to have the same attitude also. (Acts 2:4–47; Acts 4:32–35; 2 Corinthians 8)

These first converts' love and care for one another was not organized by a political or economic system. It was not a response to demands or pressure from the apostles. These disciples were motivated by God's love which the Holy Spirit had poured out on them. The Holy Spirit was leading them to fulfill the new commandment Jesus had given.

[Acts 5:3–4; Romans 5:5; John 14:26, John 13:34–35; John 3:16–18; Galatians 5:13, 6:10]

Love is expressed in serving (Galatians 5:13–14).

We are created in God's image; therefore, we know that God serves too. God rules with a servant's heart.

Jesus did not come among us as a ruler, according to the ways of the world, even though he created all things. He came as a servant because human beings are created servants. (Philippians 2:5–8, Matthew 20:25–28; Mark 10:42–45; Luke 22:25–27; Matthew 23:8–12)

God's children, the sons of the kingdom, must also become motivated by a heart to serve like our Father and our Lord Jesus. Then we will *serve* in whatever ministry and calling he's given.

When he had washed their feet and put on his outer garments and resumed his place, he said to them, "Do you understand what I have done to you? You call me Teacher and Lord, and you are right, for so I am. If I then, your Lord and Teacher, have washed your feet, you also ought to wash one another's feet. For I have given you an example, that you also should do just as I have done to you. Truly, truly, I say to you, a servant is not greater than his master, nor is a messenger greater than the one who sent him. If you know these things, blessed are you if you do them. (John 13:12–17)

God's children are called to live together as his family, loving and serving one another.

Our love and service does not end with the family of God.

God our Father calls us to follow the way of our elder brother, Jesus the Messiah, in the power of the Holy Spirit. Like Jesus, the sons of the kingdom are called to reveal what God is like to those around us who are still outside God's family.

"You are the light of the world. A city set on a hill cannot be hidden. Nor do people light a lamp and put it under a basket, but on a stand, and it gives light to all in the house. In the same way, let your light shine before others, so that they may see your good works and give glory to your Father who is in heaven." (Matthew 5:14–16) (John 9:5 & 12:35–36; Colossians 5:1–2, 8–10; Philippians 2:12–16; Galatians 6:10)

Four "Pictures" of God's People on the Earth
The Royal Priesthood

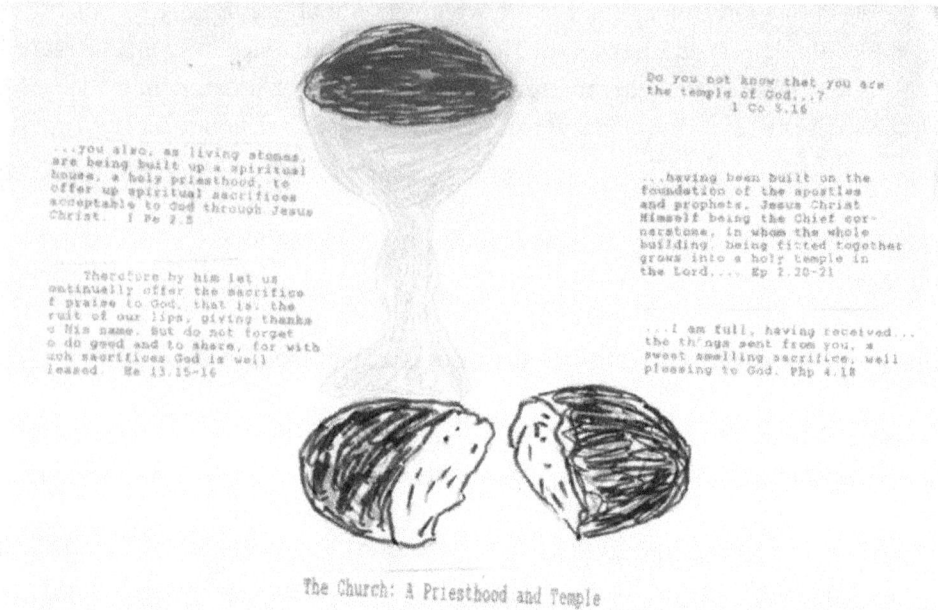

...you also, as living stones, are being built up a spiritual house, a holy priesthood, to offer up spiritual sacrifices acceptable to God through Jesus Christ. I Pe 2.5

Do you not know that you are the temple of God...? 1 Co 3.16

...having been built on the foundation of the apostles and prophets, Jesus Christ Himself being the Chief cornerstone, in whom the whole building, being fitted together grows into a holy temple in the Lord.... Ep 2.20-21

Therefore by him let us continually offer the sacrifice of praise to God, that is, the fruit of our lips, giving thanks to His name. But do not forget to do good and to share, for with such sacrifices God is well pleased. He 13.15-16

...I am full, having received... the things sent from you, a sweet smelling sacrifice, well pleasing to God. Php 4.18

The Church: A Priesthood and Temple

A Royal Priesthood — representing God to the earth and representing a fallen world before God

"...you yourselves like living stones are being built up as a spiritual house, to be a holy priesthood, to offer spiritual sacrifices acceptable to God through Jesus Christ... you are a chosen race, a royal priesthood, a holy nation, a people for his own possession, that you may proclaim the excellencies of him who called you out of darkness into his marvelous light. (1 Peter 2:5, 9)

1. God created and redeemed humans to be a "royal priesthood."
God's purpose for humans from the beginning has been that human beings represent him on the earth to the rest of creation (Genesis 1:26–28).

Humans were created in God's image and likeness in order to be a "picture" on earth of what God is like.

- We were created to reveal his glory—his character which he described to Moses in Exodus 33:12–34:8 (Note especially 33:18 and 34:5–8)

We were created to be "royal," the representatives of God's authority on the earth.

- We were created to have dominion—to be servant-rulers like God is, using the authority he has given us for the good of others, and of the rest of creation, without abusing it by making others dependent on us (Luke 22:25–27).

Human beings were created with a body from the dust of earth but made alive by God's own breath—his Spirit (Genesis 2:7). We alone of all creation are both of "earth" and of "heaven."

- Humans represent the physical creation before God.
- Humans represent God to the physical creation.
- Humans were created to be a priestly "bridge" between God and the earth.

God redeemed his Old Covenant people from Egypt and called them back to his original purpose, but because of fear they drew back. (Exodus 19:3–6; 20:18–21; Hebrews 10:18–21)

God's redeemed New Covenant people working with Jesus the great high priest are called to fulfill the God's priestly calling for human beings. (1 Peter 2:4–10; Revelation 1:4–6 5:5–10)

2. As the "royal priesthood" we are called to offer up "spiritual sacrifices."
(1 Peter 2:5; Hebrews 13:15–16; Philippians 4:14–18; see also Psalm 116:12–14)

- "I appeal to you therefore, brothers, by the mercies of God, to present your bodies [plural] as a living sacrifice [singular], holy and acceptable to God, which is your spiritual worship." (Romans 12:1)
  - We are called "to lay our lives down" for the purposes of God. We are called to serve him—to do his will—and not to serve ourselves.
  - That means that we are called "to lay our lives down" for our brothers and sisters also.

3. God is building us together into a temple to be his dwelling place on earth.
(1 Peter 2:5; Ephesians 2:19–22; 2 Corinthians 6:16, 1 Corinthians 3:16–17)

4. The Lord's Supper, the Thanksgiving: worshipping God, edifying one another, proclaiming Jesus' victory, and renewing our covenant in Christ. (1 Corinthians 11:18a, 23–26; 1 Corinthians 14:26)

5. Breaking bread—of special significance in the New Testament.

- Distinctive use of the Greek word κλαω "to break" in the New Testament (Luke 28:28–31; Acts 2:42, 46; Acts 20:7, 11)

6. "For as often as you eat this bread and drink the cup, you proclaim the Lord's death until he comes." (1 Corinthians 11:26)

- In the Spirit we proclaim Jesus' victory over the powers of darkness in his death (Colossians 2:15).
- As the assembly of God, through our proclamation, we loose on earth, what has been loosed in heaven (Matthew 16:19, 18:18).

"With the bread the unity among the brethren is symbolized. Where there are many small kernels of grain to be combined into one loaf there is need first to grind them and to make them into one flour... which can be achieved only through suffering. Just as Christ, our dear Lord, went before us, so too we want to follow him in like manner. And the bread symbolizes the unity of the brotherhood. Likewise with the wine: many small grapes come together to make the one wine. That happens by means of the press, understood here as suffering. Hence, whoever wants to be in brotherly union, has to drink from the cup of the Lord, for this cup symbolizes suffering." (Hans Nadler, Anabaptist martyr, trial deposition,1529)

About the Author

Steve Humble is a husband, a father, and a grandfather. He has sought to faithfully follow Jesus for more than fifty years. He was born and raised in Central Ohio. As an adult, Steve lived in the upper Midwest for thirteen years and now has resided in central Kentucky for thirty-four years. He is an avid reader and enjoys collecting and listening to a wide range of music.

Connect with Steve online:

Email: steve.g.humble@gmail.com

www.ingramcontent.com/pod-product-compliance
Lightning Source LLC
Chambersburg PA
CBHW080050120426
42742CB00051B/3277